HARTMUT M. VOLZ

ADRENALINE

Udo Müller –
The exceptional story
of a passionate entrepreneur

HARTMUT M. VOLZ

ADRENALINE

Udo Müller –
The exceptional story
of a passionate entrepreneur

ECON

MIX
Paper from
responsible sources
FSC® C014496

Econ is a publishing affiliate
of the Ullstein Buchverlage GmbH

ISBN 978-3-430-21098-0

Translated from German by Annette Charpentier

Typeset using Slimbach LT
Typeset by Büro Beck, Kempten
Printed and bound by GGP Media GmbH, Pößneck
Printed in Germany

Content

SHOWTIME

THE TIMES ARE CHANGING

THE BIG TEST

THE FUTURE

EPILOGUE

PREAMBLE

How do you create a business empire of more than 150 companies in numerous countries and with more than 10,000 employees – from nothing?

- *by having the courage to risk everything time and again,*
- *by constantly curbing your own vanity and instead looking for the best ideas, no matter where they have come from,*
- *by acknowledging that the greatest obstacle to success is success*

You can presumably guess that all three character traits are necessary. And a few more elements that will be mentioned in this book.

This is the story of a boy who had promised his mother at the tender age of 5 that he would one day build a factory for stockings and socks for her. Of a teenager who was fascinated by the teachings of the Indian guru Bhagwan Shree Rajneesh and at 19 founded his first company. And the story of a man who has reinvented himself and his companies time and time again – from the classic buy/sell model, which had made him the top company in post-unification eastern Germany, to a leveraged buyout financed by an American hedge fund, which made him market leader in the united Germany.

What then followed was a worldwide expansion, abruptly halted only by the global financial crisis. Shortly afterward, the next venture: A spectacular stock market entry after successfully conquering markets in Turkey, Poland and Germany. Followed by another crisis, this time because of the global debt situation which brought everything down again.

Then came another new start, utilizing very early digitalisation, which baffled the industry and increased shares value tenfold.

And then came the attack of all attacks: a spectacular short-selling movement from the U.S., and the ultimate crisis for outdoor advertising: a pandemic during which no one was allowed out of their house. All of a sudden no one needed outdoor advertising anymore …

This is the story of Udo Müller. Initially not an outstanding student, rather middling, but ultimately someone who achieved the third-best exam grades in the history of his school. A handball professional on the national team. A physician who, despite high grades, dropped out shortly before finishing his doctorate. But most of all: a thoroughbred entrepreneur!

Within three decades he turned the small, local Cologne-based advertising company Ströer into a uniquely diversified media empire. Time and again he failed, and high-flying plans came to nothing. But Müller openly talks about those failures.

Müller's story is also the story of German economics over the past four decades: from the years before the Berlin Wall came down to the pioneer times when Western economics took over the East. When after the Millennium, American turbo-capitalism arrived in Germany and people clamoured to become stock market millionaires. It encompasses the global financial crisis of 2008-2009, which had a dramatic effect on every company. And finally the biggest change of all time: digitisation, forcing practically every company to reinvent itself if it wanted to survive.

Through Udo Müller, we see a prime example of the transition from the Old Economy to the New Economy, as well as the personal and financial risks of an entrepreneur who more than once put everything on one horse, but whose courage and perseverance was always rewarded in the end – sometimes apparently by pure luck alone.

This is a book about extraordinary passion and unconditional engagement, neck-breaking risk-taking, economic failure and, ultimately, economic breakthrough and success.

Berlin, Border Crossing Friedrichstrasse

It is a cold night in January 1988 when Udo Müller leaves his Charlottenburg office carrying two parcels. A few years previously, the Godesberg man and two associates had founded the Berlin advertising agency *Lunenburg & Partner*.

Müller, who is only 25 years old at this point, has nevertheless already had a remarkable career as a sportsman and serial entrepreneur. Two years after he started to play handball, he featured on the under-18 national team. As a professional, he played in the Bundesliga for Reinickendorfer Füchse, a well-known Berlin club. At the same time and together with his friend Dieter Nerlich, he founded the company Füchse-Werbung, which published the Foxes' official program for every game. He was only 19 then. In the company's first year, the partners made a six-figure profit. Then he did the same for the professional soccer club *Blau-Weiss 90*. And together with a photographer friend he sold art posters worldwide with the company *Artlight Poster Production*.

For the two years prior to this cold night, Müller and Nerlich had been partners in their *Lunenburg & Partner* company. And he knows that if he is successful tonight, he will be heading for even more success. Much more.

It's nearly midnight when Müller gets into his Mercedes and drives to Kochstrasse, close to the Wall. There he changes to the underground line C. This line goes underground through the territory of East Berlin for several kilometres before it carries on towards Tegel in the West. The next stop is Bahnhof Friedrichstrasse, or Friedrich Street station, in the East, directly on the demarcation line. Passengers can get straight back to the West after a few meters as soon as the train doors are closed. This has been an everyday occurrence ever since the city was divided.

The train has only a few passengers on board as it slowly rolls toward the dark East and passes without stopping at the disused stations Stadtmitte and Französische Strasse, to stop a few minutes later than planned in Friedrichstrasse station. Müller gets off, and his eyes follow the departing train. Now he gets slightly nervous. He is alone in the bright light of the platform, far below the surface in the no-man's-land between East and West.

Bahnhof Friedrichstrasse – Berlin's notorious underground station. Since the Wall was built in August 1961 it became the most important transport link in the divided capital. It's here where the S-Bahn (regional trains), the underground system and long-distance trains from East and West cross. The "antifascist protection wall", as the GDR calls the Wall, winds its way about a kilometre from here. Every day, tens of thousands of Berliners cross the Iron Curtain to the "other side" and back again to the free part of the city.

A labyrinth of corridors, barricades and walls ensures that people from the East don't even catch sight of the West. Travellers must pass controls by deliberately unfriendly GDR-border police and officers of the Stasi. Dozens of surveillance cameras cover every square inch. This night, too.

Müller looks at his watch. It's a quarter past midnight. The next train arrives, stops briefly, and moves on. It's the last one tonight. Passengers hurry to the stairs to catch their train to the West. Then Müller is alone again on the platform and waits. The meeting point and the time have been set by his business partners.

Müller has a rendezvous with the class enemy. He wants to get into business with East Germany. He doesn't only want to organise advertising in GDR sport venues, something he and Lunenburg have been doing for a few years in the West. He also wants to do something new, something that has never happened before.

It is something that will gain the attention of the whole industry. And if it works out, many new business opportunities will open for our Müller.

It has been three months since the first contact with the people of the East German agency *Interwerbung*. One of the top officials had asked Horst Lunenburg for a meeting. Horst, however, thought it was simply a routine visit and let the guest know that he didn't have much time.

The man from East Berlin wasn't too happy about this treatment, but the reason for his visit was too important, and time was at a premium. He quickly came to the point. This time he wasn't talking about the regular advertisements in socialist sports stadiums, but something quite delicate: Western adverts on GDR territory.

Lunenburg didn't grasp the significance and didn't feel inclined to ask any questions. "I'm really in a hurry," he said finally again and grabbed his coat. "You should talk to Udo Müller," he added. "He's our man for special cases."

Half an hour later Müller and the man from the East were sitting in the Grunewald restaurant La Cascina. The conversation was awkward. The guest seemed disappointed because he hadn't been able to talk to Lunenburg himself. He carefully studied the menu and eventually ordered a "large grilled fillet steak" and a glass of "good French red wine". Müller ordered the same.

They chatted about the similarities between their businesses. *Interwerbung* handled foreign sports adverts mainly via the worldwide Swiss marketing agency Lüthi. For a few years now, Horst Lunenburg had been the local partner for the politically neutral Swiss company, particularly for advertising in the GDR. Müller knew what they were talking about. But generally, this part of the business was dealt with by Lunenburg.

Interwerbung was managed by the GDR Ministry for Foreign Trade. There was also a company called DEWAG, which in the GDR had a monopoly over advertising. It was an official branch of the state party SED, the one and only ruling party.

Finally, the meal arrived. Müller looked at the man opposite him, how with the greatest attention he cut his meat and ate it, piece by piece, with obvious pleasure. Maybe he was in his 30s, Müller thought, about 10 years older than him.

"I envy you," Müller said, unexpectedly.

The man opposite raised his head, half puzzled, half suspicious. "Envy me? But why?"

"Because you seem to enjoy this simple piece of meat so much."

"Well, we don't get this kind of food every day."

"And here, if you want it, you get it every day – but we have forgotten to really appreciate a good meal." In the next few minutes, they began a conversation about happiness, how important it was for society and individuals. They quickly agreed that it was a personal feeling, but in the centrally managed state of workers and farmers, it would feel different than in the Federal Republic, with its emphasis on consumerism.

"The less you have," said the guest, "the easier it is to feel happiness." Then he added with a smile and pointing to his wine glass: "And I'm a good example."

Eventually the man from the East came to the point of his visit. "It's a delicate matter," he began. *Interwerbung* had been given a new brief from the Ministry for Foreign Trade. He explained the details.

Müller became more and more curious and asked a few questions. "Did I get this right? You want us to erect large advertising panels, billboards, practically in front of the Wall and the death strip, as well as along the transit lines and in front of the Intershops – advertising Western consumer goods which cannot be bought in the GDR at all?"

"I would describe it differently," came the answer, "but that's it in principle. The advertising is not meant to address our citizens but should be visible only to West Berliners and train passengers from Berlin-West."

Then he asked whether Müller could imagine tackling such a brief.

And, of course, Müller said yes. He saw immediately that this wasn't only big business and a possibility to get in touch with big national clients such as the tobacco industry. Just imagine: the brightest and largest advertisements would be on GDR territory where official propaganda demonised the consumer society! At the very least, this would be an ironic footnote in the history of German-German idiosyncrasies. But Müller also clearly saw something else: The GDR had to be in serious economic difficulties if it was ready to abandon its socialist principles for some foreign currency. The communist state of workers and farmers was obviously in a deep crisis, worse than anybody had suspected.

And that was exactly the case. The GDR economy was flatlining and being propped up artificially. By 1986, two years before the meeting between Müller and the man from the East, the GDR was nearly bankrupt. But officially the state still ranked 10th on the list of world economies.

Hardly anybody knew the truth. In top offices, there was a secret and strictly confidential file listing the true, utterly dire economic situation. It explained word by word that the GDR would, by 1990 at the latest, be too deeply in debt to be governable. If the "continuous borrowing of necessary hard currencies from non-socialist economic areas wasn't stopped".

So, the GDR had to find new ways of getting foreign currency to avoid Western credit. And in their desperation, socialist rulers were looking even for small fry.

Interwerbung, too, had been briefed by the Politburo to find creative solutions. It was fortunate that a few years ago a small Wuppertal-based billboard advertising company had come up with an idea to display large product advertising, by Western companies, in busy border crossing areas – on GDR territory. The idea was at first discarded as non-socialist, but opinions had now changed.

The advertiser from Wuppertal hadn't convinced the state entrepreneurs that it would be a good business partner. Therefore, *Interwerbung* had contacted three advertising agencies in West Berlin. In addition to *Lunenburg & Partner*, it also asked for project tenders from a subsidiary of the Berliner Verkehrsbetriebe, VVR, and the Berliner S-Bahnwerbung (BSW).

VVR and BSW didn't take the confidential invitation seriously and sent *Interwerbung* the usual standard project offers.

That's how *Lunenburg & Partner* came into the picture. And with it, Udo Müller. And he tackled the situation strategically.

Müller suggested that the panels for the large billboards would be produced in the East, rather than by the usual companies in the West. To cut a long story short, Lunenburg got the order, and the historic business could take off.

As a test run, 10 large billboards were to be installed in Friedrichstrasse underground station, on the platforms used by the Wessies. The next step was planned for the Wollankstrasse S-Bahn station, entirely on Eastern territory but used by West Berlin Transport. Here, for technical reasons, the Wall had been unable to mark the GDR territory.

But this was only the beginning. Several other places were also earmarked for Western advertising, both in Berlin and along transit roads.

Looking for firms who might be interested in placing adverts was easier than expected. It was mainly tobacco companies, such as Reemtsma, Philip Morris and British American Tobacco, who were very keen on the new advertising possibilities in the East for their popular products.

If the billboards were sufficiently successful, Müller calculated that the GDR would get an annual income of several hundred thousand Dollars. That was clearly more than the rivals had been offering. East Berlin seemed happy and pressed for the contracts to be signed.

But the planning hit an unexpected obstacle. If Müller ever got through by phone to *Interwerbung*, the East Berlin partners were either not around or he was told they would get back to him in a few days. At the same time, the tobacco companies were pushing him to start the new advertising.

After three long months, a partner at *Interwerbung* finally got in touch. It was very embarrassing, he conceded, but the state joinery who had been tasked with the construction of the large panels, nearly 10 square meters, couldn't meet the demands in time. At last, the reason was clear, and Müller couldn't help grinning: They couldn't find suitable dowels in the whole of the GDR. And if they were confessing to this, Müller reasoned, it would probably be a good idea if he could source not only the wall plugs, but perhaps a decent electric drill as well.

Müller quickly bought the required equipment in the nearest hardware store and a few days later took it, as arranged, by the last underground train to the meeting point in East Berlin. He also brought a few bottles of Schnaps, to keep the workers happy. Now the first posters could be mounted – shortly after midnight, after the last trains had departed and the platforms of Line C at *Bahnhof Friedrichstrasse* were empty.

This is a historic moment. Müller looks at his watch again. Finally, an inconspicuous door behind the line towards Alt-Tegel opens. A group of workers comes out carrying all their work gear – ladders, glue, and brushes – to the platform. From the other side Müller's contact moves nearer, accompanied by an officer of the GDR Border Force and a few more soldiers. They guard the scene. For the workers it would be all too easy to flee to West Berlin from this point.

They greet each other briefly, then Müller organises the arrangement of the panels. The posters can be mounted. One large advertisement after another brightens up the now dimly lit platforms. It's the first consumer message from the West – in high-quality colours.

"Well ..." Müller says with a smile. "Everything looks more cheerful now, doesn't it."

But the officer from the border police suddenly shouts: "No, no, Herr Müller, that won't work. That's not possible!"

Shocked, Müller turns around, his eyes following the pointed finger of the officer to the posters. In the bottom right corner, he sees some familiar words: "*The Federal Minister for Health warns: Smoking can be dangerous.*"

"But that's the law," Müller shrugs. "It's on every cigarette advert and packet."

"It doesn't matter. It's not possible."

"What's the problem? It's not political. It's about health."

"Not political? It says: The Federal Minister warns ... and then he repeats loud and slowly: "The F-e-d-e-r-a-l M-i-n-i-s-t-e-r ..." Running out of breath he continues: "A Minister of the Federal Republic is not allowed to say anything on GDR territory. And definitely not on large posters. It must be removed."

Now the colleague from *Interwerbung* intervenes and remarks that it's meant for the wellbeing of the GDR. He makes a short phone call, resulting in a compromise: "Okay. Stick something on the Federal Minister. Then the posters can stay."

And so it happens. The warnings by the Health Ministry disappear under three layers of brown paper. Müller is grinning. He is sure that the tobacco industry clients, paying for all this, would not object to it.

In the following weeks GDR border police notice a motorbike frequently driving along the western side of the Wall. Sometimes slowly, sometimes fast. Sometimes the mysterious biker stops to look at an empty plot, sometimes he takes photos of the Wall. Is he a spy? Organising refugees? Or a harmless idiot?

The mysterious biker on his blue Suzuki Endura is Udo Müller. He has studied the old street maps in the West Berlin planning bureaus where the exact division of the city can be traced, determined by the Americans, British, French and Soviets in 1945 when the city was split up.

The representatives of the victorious powers must have had a lot of vodka, whisky, and cognac during the weeks when they determined the demarcation lines. From the city's boundaries in the north and the south, Berlin is divided by a line of 43.1 kilometres, but often randomly, straight through streets, buildings, and houses. It was now a paradise for Müller's advertising ideas.

West Berlin is divided from Brandenburg by another 122 kilometres of so-called "death strip", with more than 300 watch towers and border posts, where guards are ordered to shoot. This wouldn't work for large billboards. Not enough people pass by.

But it was different with the demarcation line that snaked its way through the city along the Wall. The border did not always align perfectly with the actual line. Administrators in Berlin repeatedly had to correct it in places. And some Western streets went straight over Eastern territory.

It was for such places that Müller was looking when he ran his bike along the Wall. And he found a lot of them. He detailed them on his large-scale road maps and suggested to *Interwerbung* to place more large panels there, plastered with adverts for consumer goods, facing the West but not visible for comrades in the GDR. Thus, they were even acceptable to hardliner SED functionaries.

He calculates the whole deal to be worth 700 mill Dollar. The comrades are delighted.

Interwerbung hurriedly presents Müller's plan to the appropriate officials in GDR Berlin. And they very quickly come to an agreement. Currency is the magic word. A lot of currency for the empty coffers. Pecunia non olet, the Romans would have said. Money doesn't stink.

By the spring of 1988, Müller sees clearly that the communist state is in its final days.

LIFE STORIES

The beginning

Sometimes it's just the magic of a particular moment that determines the rest of one's life – and sometimes it even goes unnoticed. Udo Müller was 10 years old on that day. It hadn't started particularly promisingly. Udo had had a bad night, again troubled by the wild dreams he had been experiencing frequently over the past few weeks. He was tired and listless, had his breakfast in the kitchen and then went off to school. Once there, he deliberately took his time, ambling slowly toward the classroom on the third floor. It was going to be an art lesson. Boring.

All things considered, the entire first year at the Bad Godesberg Adenauer-Gymnasium, a grammar school, had been bad. Only yesterday his mother had had an unpleasant meeting with his form teacher. Udo's performance wasn't good enough.

Weeks ago, Elisabeth Müller had hired a private tutor because of Udo's bad grades in mathematics. And even in German, the most important subject, he was only just able to get the grades – and only then thanks to some good will from the teachers. Udo was hardly doing better in other subjects. His only good grade, a "Sehr gut" in sports, didn't make up for it.

Slowly, young Müller ambled up the stairs towards the art room. The material for today's lesson – everyday items like empty toilet paper rolls, cigarette packets with silvery paper, the caps of beer bottles – he didn't have any of it. He had simply forgotten all about it. The lesson didn't really interest him.

Oh, Udo! Even before he moved to the grammar school, his then form tutor had warned his mother: "Your son is a dreamer. He won't succeed. He either doesn't want to concentrate, or he is unable to do so. Sometimes your son appears completely absent, as if he is not really there."

Oh, the dreaming. His mother knew all about it. When Udo found real life too much or too awkward, he fled into his own world and dreamt, with his eyes wide open. It was not a good habit, if you wanted to stand out as a good student.

But then, at the end of Year 6, when he was just about to start secondary education, Udo suddenly flourished. To everyone's surprise he gained the grades for moving up to grammar school. Just like that. How he managed to do it remains his secret.

Regardless, he was accepted at the chosen school. And Udo learnt the lesson that, if he wanted something badly, he could do it. A few years later he achieved excellent results in other exams. Just like that. He only had to want it. At least that's what Udo thought.

This newly found ambition quickly vanished at his new school. Day to day school life was boring, and Udo fell into his old habit: daydreaming.

So, today it was art. Awful. The students were to create small sculptures from the materials they had brought along. The work was supposed to stimulate their creativity.

Udo found the task boring. He hadn't brought any materials. Good job that his friend Martin Diederichs gave him an empty cigarette packet.

Then, suddenly, Udo became curious. A cigarette packet. He could make something out of that. It consists of two parts, the outer package of printed cardboard, and the inner part, the shiny aluminium foil. Udo had his own concept of creativity. To create added value. Turn one into two, or something like that …

He pulled the aluminium foil from the cardboard and, after some persuading, swapped it for three bottle caps with the classmate behind him. Udo swapped those with other students, gaining four or five more objects.

Every time he was able to find the right words and convincing arguments, sometimes coaxing his classmates. He was good at persuading others. If in those days there had been a school psychologist, he would have considered this "a certain manipulative tendency".

Udo's busy trade was infectious. The art lesson turned into an exchange platform. Everybody offered their objects, negotiated, and Udo was always right in the centre of it.

By the time the lesson ended, most items had changed hands several times. Some students had more than before, others clearly less. Udo had the largest treasure trove. When he left the classroom and walked down the stairs, he experienced a completely new feeling: The wonderful sense of success.

That moment, he thought then, would be the beginning of his career as an entrepreneur. He wanted to become a tycoon, a person who always has the right ideas and can convince others.

This episode in the art room, he thought even then, would later be the start of an autobiography that charted his ascent to an extraordinarily successful entrepreneur.

Back at home, he was still feeling euphoric. His mother was amused listening to Udo's story and remembered the day when her boy, at only 5, was already brimming with ideas. Back then, he had announced that one day he would become a producer of lady's stockings. At the time, those were a little luxury for his mother.

His mother had smiled and stroked his head. She would be happy if her little daydreamer got any decent job at all. And if he should turn into an honest, god-fearing man.

Hidden Talents

Since the mid-1960s, the Müllers had been living in one of those quarters in Bad Godesberg that had been built for civil servants of the Federal Government. In August 1969, the small town merged with the then capital Bonn. It was reasonably comfortable, with lots of green spaces, and a short commuting distance from the Federal ministries. One was mainly among fellow conservatives and Catholics, and it was good for bringing up children.

It was towards the end of the sixties and the world-renowned German economic miracle was beginning to show its first cracks. A social democrat from West Berlin, Willy Brandt, was at the helm of his party, planning to become Chancellor. He pleaded for more democracy and a new relationship with the Eastern bloc. Brandt was the right person for the young, post-war generation, hungry for more freedom.

It was a time of awakening and changes. The Cold War between East and West frightened people everywhere. The border between the hostile blocs divided Europe into a good and an evil part. From the Western point of view, the East was evil. The Iron Curtain ran through the middle of

Germany, from north to south. In the East there was the socialist GDR, the self-styled "state of workers and farmers". In the West was the Federal Republic, which, with the help of American capital, had grown into an economic world power. Right in the middle was sleepy Bonn as the provisional capital of the Federal Republic of Germany.

In nearby Godesberg, Udo grew up well cared for in a civil servant household. After the war, his father had managed, thanks to his diligence, ambition, and energy, to rise from an apprentice at a regional council to become a Senior Councillor in the Bonn ministerial bureaucracy. His wife, Elli, short for Elisabeth, looked after the house and the two children – Udo and his 6-year older sister, Jutta. It was a typical German family.

From the outside, everything looked well-ordered and with no problems. Udo loved his mother and respected his stern father. But Dad wasn't at home a lot and was devoted to his work. That's how it seemed, anyway. There was little time left for the family.

Gradually the children noticed that their parents' mutual affection had vanished. There were constant arguments about money. Their mother had to scrimp; their father saved money whenever he could. The son felt for his mother and comforted her with the promise: "When I'm rich, I'll buy you everything you want." He meant it seriously, in a childlike way.

Elisabeth invested all her energy and love into her two children. She was worried about her son, but she looked at the handsome boy with pride when on Sundays he went to church, obediently did his job as an altar boy and tried hard to be a good son. All in all, it was a happy childhood.

The only demand his mother could not satisfy was his unlimited desire for knowledge. Elisabeth Müller remembers Udo pondering existential questions from a very early age. Why am I on this planet? What will happen to me when I am not here anymore? The fundamental questions of life often kept him awake at night. And they remained, for him, without a satisfactory answer.

Udo only felt real acknowledgement when playing sports. He flourished. He had a passion for athletics because in that discipline it was down to him alone whether he won or lost: faster, higher, stronger was his motto.

Ever since he was 9, he had strived to become a top high-jumper. Higher and higher. At 15, Udo was among the 30 best athletes of his age, even though his growing body wasn't particularly suited to the discipline. His coach already planned to turn the ambitious boy into a dynamic decathlon athlete. "The boy has the necessary ambition and the talent."

His difficult early years also seemed to have been left behind. Udo was on board now. His results still alternated between "very good" and "barely good enough", but none of his teachers doubted anymore that Udo Müller had the talent for an academic career.

His maths teacher in particular thought that Udo had a clear talent. His ability to think analytically, according to the teacher, was far above average.

Two years after Udo needed intense tutoring to scrape the necessary grades, he started tutoring students on the same subject himself. For money, of course.

Udo developed his own rules. He was annoyed that he only got paid for an hour, when he actually spent 90 minutes including small talk with a student's mother and travelling to their house.

He changed the pattern and only offered double lessons of 45 minutes each. With the small talk this stretched to two hours, but it was only a third more time spent while he doubled his fee.

His talent for maximising profit became obvious, time and again, as it had in the art class all those years ago. For example, when the kids met up to play pinball in a cinema in Godesberg in the afternoons, he sold all the free games he had won thanks to his abilities. The money wasn't the sole appeal. It was more the thought that he had successfully realised a plan.

Even his mother wasn't exempt from Udo's profit-oriented thinking. One day, he asked if his 100 D-Mark monthly allowance could be paid weekly instead. He would be able to manage his money better, he argued. Which was sensible. But it was not the whole truth. Udo had calculated that 52 weeks at 25 D-Marks over the year gave him 1,300 D-Marks, and the monthly payment totalled only 1,200. Without any effort he increased his pocket money by 8 %.

And so the boy who had conquered persistent uncertainties as a youngster became a confident teenager – but only gradually, because many doubts remained.

They particularly concerned his Christian beliefs and God's almightiness. This was an important subject for his mother. Even as an altar boy, Udo had had problems with the Catholic dogma. What was good, what was evil? Heaven or hell? Rich or poor? Why can't poverty be eradicated?

And then there was the priest with his constant threats of hellfire. Maybe he only told those stories to enforce obedience? Suspicion seemed appropriate in this world of sin and graceful absolution.

Udo was 15 when his father's double life was unearthed. He had secretly established a second family and shuttled between the two. This explained his extreme parsimony. To maintain two families with his civil servant salary was not easy. Maybe it also explained the cool distance Udo had always felt between him and his father.

His father made a decision. He moved in with the other woman, while the children stayed with their mother. It was a hard blow, Udo's first life crisis. His mother was suffering, and the son tried to fill the gap as well as a teenage boy can.

But there was nobody he could talk to about his anxieties, his doubts. Not with his older sister who had her own interests. Not with his mother, who he was trying to help and support. And neither with his friends in school and at the sports club.

Frauke and the meaning of life

At this point, well on his way to becoming a grown-up, Frauke entered Müller's life. She was tall, slim, beautiful and four years his senior. She was Udo's first tender love. He was just 15. She was much more experienced than him and didn't seem to keep many rules. His friends admired Udo for his conquest. And Udo admired Frauke.

Frauke already had her own flat, was in charge of her life and not superficial like many others. She regarded life in general with a lightness unknown to Udo. There was no trace of a conservative German civil servant family in her.

Frauke was fascinated by a kind of esoteric philosophy. It was a trend then, the Far Eastern way of life. Lightness with the aura of a deeper meaning. Udo was fascinated.

It was a charismatic Indian man, who called himself Bhagwan Shree Rajneesh, who first attracted many young people in the Western world. The media was full of stories about the guru and his disciples – world-weary people hoping to find enlightenment in religious centres like the faraway Indian city of Pune.

Bhagwan questioned nearly all religions and philosophies and pleaded for an unconditional freedom of the individuum, above all moral doctrines. His promise to the constantly growing group of disciples he called Sannyasin was the enhancement of the consciousness towards a spiritual feeling of oneness with the cosmos.

This psycho-religious group was considered the most defined and influential on the broad spectrum of such movements. It was mainly students, particularly young women, who were attracted to it. Many made the pilgrimage to Pune, where Bhagwan had founded a meditation centre, an ashram, for people searching for another meaning of life.

The disciples seemed to freely donate their earthly belongings to the eccentric guru and willing to give up their normal lives and careers for a life in the ashram.

Udo was never tempted to go to Pune. Young Müller felt too closely associated with this world to immerse himself in the guru's vision. He looked at things pragmatically and didn't want to change the whole world. He only tried to understand himself better. His conflicting feelings, his personality, dominated his dreams. That was hard stuff for a teenage boy well on his way to becoming an adult.

Bhagwan's teachings gave Udo comfort and answers to his fundamental questions, but most of all it was Frauke who gave him support and new strength.

He had the most wonderful years with Frauke in sleepy Godesberg. He could talk to her, about his fears and everything under the sun. Together they searched for a direction and answers. For Udo, it was the beginning of the adventure to find himself. The long way towards his authentic self.

In one of the long conversations with Frauke, Udo remembered an event from his childhood. He was 6 or 7 years old and had received a gift of a small model aeroplane, which could be catapulted into the air with a rubber band. Outside, on a large field, he repeatedly sent it shooting into the sky and watched it circling through the air until it landed in the long grass. But then suddenly he couldn't find his beloved toy anymore. Anger began to bubble up. The thing must be nearby! But it seemed to have disappeared into thin air. Days later, back at home, he was still shouting with frustration, tears, and anger.

It was only a small, unimportant episode he now told his girlfriend. But the story had contained a lesson for him that became a rule for life: You shouldn't waste too much time on things you cannot change. Bhagwan had shown him how to tolerate disappointments and inevitabilities in a relaxed way. He would never again fight or waste energy on things he couldn't change.

It was the late 1970s, a time of conflicts and uncertainty, and not only for young people. The first global oil crisis marked the end of seemingly infinite economic growth. On German streets, thousands demonstrated against nuclear energy. The left-wing extremist group RAF was spreading fear and terror. For the conservatives, the liberal zeitgeist of hash, hippies and miniskirts were the signs of declining morals.

Frauke had fallen for the allures of Far Eastern spirituality, a sense between self-determination and abandonment. Udo, too, felt attracted by it, at least a little bit.

Sometimes the young couple talked endlessly until late at night. How can I change my life? Why are there so many conflicts in this world, so many opposites? How do I find the right direction?

To explore this further, Udo wanted to write a book. The title was to be: "About the Nature of Personality". The 15-year-old observed sharply how TV was changing society. He thought that the new media made people more and more dissatisfied. The flood of colourful images suggested that there was always someone who was even better, more successful, happier. The constant comparisons were terrible for the human soul, the teenager concluded. If you made your happiness dependent on what other people have, you had lost already.

Müller's ideas would be confirmed four decades later by scientists from all over the world. The victory of the internet and social media and the global comparison of the individual they enable, don't only fill many books, they fill whole libraries.

Hermann Hesse's novels "Steppenwolf" and "The Glass Bead Game", his novella "Narcissus and Goldmund", Erich Fromm's "The Art of Loving" and "To Have or To Be" with the promising subtitle "The psychological basics of a new society" were considered the moral leitmotif and offered hope for the young post-war generation looking for meaning.

Udo was fascinated by Hesse and Fromm. Their books illuminated the problems he was dealing with. But he was missing the answers he somehow thought to have found with Bhagwan.

There were enough problems and conflicts around him. And there was his parents' broken marriage. Udo was trying to deal with it, but knew he simply had to live with it. He now always tried to accept issues that couldn't be changed. The Far Eastern philosophy had taught him that it wasn't worth the fight.

As often as possible, he spent his time between school, sport, and domestic obligations with Frauke. With her, he felt understood. But passions also have a tendency not to last. The bliss, or what the teenager in love thought was bliss, fizzled out. Udo was increasingly annoyed by Frauke's uncompromising attitude, but he didn't talk to her about it and withdrew into a defiant silence. It seemed wiser not to voice all his thoughts. He had read that on the advice page of a women's magazine, and it fitted his state of emotions.

"What's the matter?" his girlfriend often asked when Udo was staring vacantly into space. The answer was always the same: "Nothing." Udo kept his feelings close to his chest. And then followed silence, tense silence. The atmosphere between them chilled.

Eventually Frauke exploded. Udo had come back to her flat after training and dropped wordlessly onto the sofa. They started to argue. Then they sat side by side, silently, and couldn't really tell what they had been arguing about. "What's the matter?" Frauke wanted to know. Udo hesitated. He really wanted to open up but wasn't ready. "Ask me later, and then I might tell you."

Frauke had had enough. "I'm sick and tired of this, acting offended and keeping shtum," she shouted angrily. "You either talk to me, or you get your things and leave – for good."

To cut things short, Udo stayed and learned a lesson for life. He realised that although he claimed that he needed more time to make decisions than other people, this argument was only a pretext. A pretext for not to have to decide anything at all.

He had reached the conclusion that one had to make decisions actively, so that things really would change. And all one's problems must see the light of day instead of growing bigger and bigger in the dark. Only that would create real freedom.

Frauke expressed it with one of her guru's wise sayings: "People build walls to protect themselves. Bhagwan says the opposite is true. Tear the walls down, say goodbye to your secrets, and only then will you be strong and inviolable."

Udo later explained his feelings: "The Indian guru's demands that I open up unconditionally felt like a sudden enlightenment. My vulnerability suddenly became my strength. Because when you are not hiding any secrets that other people could find out, you are truly inviolable."

From then on, the young couple had more open discussions, and Udo had another insight: Arguments and reconciliation are the driving forces of a good relationship. One is the foil for the other. It is the polarity of Yin and Yang, sine and cosine, confrontation and harmony.

Frauke was a good sparring partner.

Ego versus team spirit

It was merely a coincidence that one afternoon after school, Udo walked past the training ground of the *TV Bad Godesberg* handball team. That was a few months before he met Frauke. Udo was obsessed by sports, but high-jumping had lost its appeal, maybe because he now realised he didn't have the right physique to be among the best in that discipline. He simply wasn't a lanky guy with very long legs.

He stopped at the playing field and watched the young players, more curiously than interested. "Don't hang around there, come and join us," the trainer shouted. So, Udo joined the team, and he enjoyed playing the game with the other youngsters. The ball in his hands felt like a friend.

By the following Saturday, he was already named for the team. His energy had been noted, and he scored two goals. A week later, he played again and managed to score 12 times – half of all the goals by his team. The jumping skills he had developed as an athlete were an advantage. And left-handers like Udo were always in demand in games like handball.

But something had changed. As a high-jumper, Udo had been an individualist, a solo fighter. Now he had to surrender his ego to the spirit of the team. But it was a good fit, and soon Udo played in the regional team. Two years after his first match in Godesberg, Udo was called up to the national team for under 18s.

At school, his performance improved too, to his mother's delight. Frauke and the Far East were still spiritually present, but his thoughts focused more and more on his worldly future. Particularly on his future handball career.

He examined his options critically. Dreams from his childhood, like the one where he opened a stocking factory, were no longer considered. Generally, his dream to become an entrepreneur seemed to have faded into the background. After he left school, he planned to study history and journalism.

Udo was fascinated by the turmoil of recent German history. The end of the German Empire, the 1920s, the Weimar Republic, Hitler, the Nazis' rule of terror. How did the German society end up with fascism? What lessons could be learned? What did an open society actually mean? He wanted to find out.

The young student planned to write a comprehensive biography of Gustav Stresemann, the nationalist-liberal chancellor of the Weimar Republic. When his teacher asked Udo for his reasons, he answered: "There is only one book about Stresemann, by Felix Hirsch. And that doesn't do him justice." He would do better.

For Udo, Stresemann was ahead of his time and the first German politician thinking in European terms. Maybe, the young Müller thought, as he looked to the future, it would be a good topic for his doctoral thesis.

The final exams were not a problem for Udo. Again, he surprised everyone. His high average grade placed him third in his graduating year. But even though he requested a retest to improve his math grade and get a place at medical school, his attempt failed.

He intended to start university straight away, but this plan hit a snag. He was called up for compulsory military service in the Bundeswehr. On October 1st, 1980, Recruit Udo Müller was to present at the air force barracks in Essen.

Frauke would have liked it if Udo had claimed to be a conscientious objector, but Müller didn't want to do that. He considered himself a dutiful citizen. But maybe he was only curious – again. Or maybe it was because, as a member of the handball national team, he would be entitled to certain privileges in a sports division of the army, after completing his short basic training.

After a few days in barracks, Udo was convinced that the military was not for him. He decided to serve as short a time as possible.

It was the time of the Cold War, and military service was a serious issue. The Bundeswehr was considered by many to be a kind of "school of the nation" for young men. But soldier Müller didn't want to use his service time for military purposes. He wanted to work on his own future. It meant he had to get out as quickly as possible.

Because of his flat feet, he could only wear his bright red Adidas trainers, even when in uniform. Those trainers had the necessary insoles, which were missing from regular combat boots. He made an application for the insoles but was told that they would not be available for a while. What else could he do but wear the red trainers with the insoles when in uniform? His superiors took this as a repeated and outrageous provocation – particularly because the uncomfortable combat boots were often used as a means of discipline.

And then recruit Müller reported "back pains" and a strange strain in his knee. The baffled medic referred him to a nearby military hospital, but no plausible diagnosis could be made. The medics described the athlete as "physically not very resilient".

After six weeks of limping around with a grimace on his face, interrupted only by medical tests, the diagnosis came: Recruit Müller suffered from a slipped disc and was considered unfit. The future handball professional was discharged from his service for the Fatherland.

In the meantime, Frauke had started training as a naturopath in Munich. Maybe Müller was still influenced by her when he reconsidered his future possibilities. The desire to be an entrepreneur had been forgotten in Frauke's arms anyway. Udo now wanted to study medicine instead of history and journalism.

"If you do economics, you turn into a money monster," Müller said now. "If you become a doctor, you stay human." He preferred to be a human.

Medicine then. In the early 1980s, many young people had the same idea. Far too many. It was the most sought-after course. There was hardly a profession better respected than that of a doctor. In the autumn of 1980, there were 40,000 applicants for 6,500 places at medical school. And Müller was one of them. His preferred place of study was the renowned university of Munich. Where Frauke lived already.

But who studied what and where was not decided by individuals, rather by a central office in Dortmund, the ZVS. What with the number of applicants, it was very likely that Müller would miss out.

The passionate handball player now focused his energy

on his future as an athlete. In a way, a career as a pro in handball was more important, because he already had a firm offer. The busy chairman of Hönningen, a club in the Third Division, based near Bonn, had ambitions to move up to the Second Division with the young left-hander as its star. That was tempting.

For the first time, Müller negotiated a contract. And he rediscovered something he had seemingly forgotten: how much pleasure there was in negotiating. To be his own employer. He also took the chance to test out his market value.

The result was not at all bad. He got a car plus petrol money for the journeys to training as well as about 1,000 Dollar for expenses for the first season. There would also be win bonuses and a potential promotion bonus to be decided separately. Müller was a dealmaker.

But it didn't go any further. Müller had just completed his first few days of training in Hönningen, when the ZVS got in touch and offered him a place to study medicine at the *Freie Universität Berlin* (the Free University of Berlin). The offer had come much quicker than expected, but Müller went for it – even though it was far away from Frauke.

At the beginning of October 1980, without having played a single match for Hönningen, he got into the club's car with a packed suitcase and set off for Berlin.

Frauke came up from Munich to accompany her boyfriend on his way to a new life. It was one of their last trips together. The distance between Berlin and Munich was simply too much for the couple. That and their differing life expectations.

Berlin is calling

Udo Müller's life journey didn't begin with the desire to become an entrepreneur. Sure, as a little boy he wanted to own a stocking factory, but that was long forgotten. The plan to study history and journalism had also vanished a while ago. Now it was medicine.

When, on September 28th, he took off for Berlin in a car sponsored by Hönningen handball team, he had two goals. Firstly, he wanted to get his medical course completed as quickly as possible, to gain his doctorate with the highest grade possible, and, if all went well, to be one of the youngest professors of medicine in Germany.

His second goal was to be on the national handball team.

Müller was highly motivated when he started the course. He eagerly went to all the lectures and seminars and at the same time planned his future as a handball pro. He thought his best chances for that lay with the leading Berlin club Reinickendorfer Füchse, the *Foxes*, and it seemed to be a good time to get on the team.

The *Foxes* had just moved up to the Bundesliga, the top division, and their sponsor, Willi Bendzko, a wealthy but controversial property tycoon, planned to build the team with a selection of experienced young players who could go on to succeed internationally. Someone like the 19-year-old talent from Godesberg was very welcome. Left-handers, especially those recruited already for the Under-18 national team, were very sought after in handball and not easy to find.

And Müller, of course, wanted to sell himself as expensively as possible. His first experience with Hönningen came in handy. He pretended he was also in negotiations with the *Foxes'* Berlin competitor Blau-Weiss 90. That was only partly true, but it helped. Müller got a decent contract of more than 8,000 Dollar per season plus a rent free flat in the famous Corbusier House.

The Corbusier House. This world-renowned block of flats in the swanky district of Charlottenburg belonged to Bendzko, whose real business was to buy blocks of flats, turn them into condominiums and sell them on at an inflated price. Special Berlin tax advantages helped. It was a business model that didn't make Bendzko particularly popular.

As a sponsor of the *Foxes*, the businessman, hated by left wing students, was trying to improve his image. The student Müller rented his first elegant home from a property shark.

So, Berlin it was now. His career with the *Foxes* didn't start with as much success as he had hoped. Head coach Peter Frank was less impressed by Müller's career so far than Müller himself was. Playing in the Under-18 team? So what? The experienced handball trainer had many more renowned players on his books. The *Foxes* boasted well established German and Yugoslavian national players, including the World Championship player Zvonimier Serdarusitsch, national goalkeeper Klaus Wöller and Roberto Pries. These were big names in handball, and young Udo from Godesberg could learn a lot from them.

Pries, in particular, stood between Udo and the main team. He was not only a left-hander who played in the newcomer's preferred position, but Pries was also a friend of sponsor Bendzko, as the two of them owned a small company together. And, of course, Pries had a special position with head coach Frank, who made the new boy train a lot, but let Pries play the matches. Müller became impatient, desperate for his chance.

Within the squad, the confident and slightly arrogant

new player wasn't exactly given a warm welcome either. Handball is a tough team sport. Each player has to fit in for the benefit of the team's success but at the same time be a confident solo star. Ego *and* team spirit. For the first time in his young life, Udo felt really challenged. He had to balance the tough training regime of a pro athlete with the demands of his medical course.

One evening he came home from the cinema to another shock. Thick smoke was billowing from the seventh floor where his flat was. Dozens of firemen and police swarmed the area. A terrorist attack couldn't be ruled out. The Corbusier House was also known for frequent suicides. People often jumped from the roof.

Müller stopped and looked up at the billowing smoke, overcome by a completely new feeling: homesickness. He wanted to get back to the familiar surroundings of Godesberg, to his friends and his caring mother. That night he slept at a friend's house.

But the next morning, things looked up again. His flat had not been damaged, the initial shock had passed, and training was on. He didn't have to think about anything, he just had to function.

Udo again felt that he was on the right path towards securing place in the top team. And soon it was back, his sense of superiority.

Off the pitch, the new player also tried to separate himself from his team-mates and make himself stand out. When they went to a bar after a match, he drank water while his colleagues drank beer. And while the others ordered juicy steaks, Udo insisted on being a vegetarian.

One of the well-established players, Dieter Nerlich, noticed Udo's aloofness. He was six years older, a trainee teacher, born in Berlin. Like Müller, he lived in the Corbusier House and had been briefed by the coach to look after the idiosyncratic guy from the Rhineland. They trained together, sometimes went to the cinema together and had long conversations about life in general. Nerlich even found some of Müller's words of Far Eastern wisdom worth a thought.

For example, the thing about inner conflicts. Nerlich initially couldn't understand the Bhagwan story. After all, the guru preached material abstinence yet surrounded himself with pretentious wealth.

Müller explained this obvious contradiction: "Bhagwan says, 'I don't want people following me because they see me as a kind of redeemer. And they imagine a redeemer as someone who is half-starved sitting in front of a hut. I want Sannyasin, disciples who follow me with conviction. That's why I have dozens of Rolls-Royces, to frighten away the former type.'"

That sounded ingenious. You either accepted Bhagwan's explanation and followed him because of his wisdom, or you considered the whole thing a fraud. Both opinions can be true but cannot be reconciled. You simply have two positions that cannot be combined. Udo lectured, Dieter listened. "Just as I think it's possible to be reborn, I can accept it that Bhagwan could be a redeemer or a fraudster. One must tolerate such uncertainties. And one can learn from them."

Nerlich was impressed by the wisdom and by how relaxed Udo was. They discussed all sorts of things, and it was the beginning of a lifelong friendship between the two men.

Before Müller's second season with the *Foxes*, there was an opportunity to produce a program booklet for the home games containing club news, team formations and information about the team's opponent.

Müller immediately saw this as a business chance and discussed the idea with his friend Dieter. He was not so much interested in the information part than in the potential for selling advertisements to Berlin companies.

Müller and Nerlich were not the only applicants. So, the pair talked the national goalkeeper Wöller into joining them. Wöller was generally much liked and could be used by the would-be publishers to gain trust within the club.

The plan worked. The three got the job and started straight away. Wöller quickly found the project too time-consuming and left. More precisely, Müller and Nerlich talked Wöller into leaving because "as a much-needed national goalkeeper" he didn't have much time for the publishing work.

Müller, however, had great fun with the project. He took satisfaction from both the success and the challenges. It was a special feeling that he hadn't yet experienced from either playing sports or in his university studies.

So, Udo Müller was again on his childhood path to becoming an entrepreneur. Together with Nerlich, he founded "Füchse-Werbung" as a properly registered company. They stayed up late at night writing short articles about the team's next game and organised the printing and distribution of the programs. But, more importantly, they got Berlin companies on board as paying customers for the adverts.

The programs, which were quite substantial because of the adverts, were titled "Aktuelles aus dem Fuchsbau" ("News from the Foxes' Den") and were distributed free among the fans at home games. Müller, the organiser, presented himself with a photo on page three ("Dear Handball Friends ... Yours, Udo Müller").

Selling the adverts was a doddle. Some clients may have believed they were supporting the club and didn't realise that Udo and Dieter, entirely legally, were claiming all the profits. In the first year, the pair made a decent return of nearly 125,000 Dollar. Just like that.

Medicine isn't the answer either

And how did it go with Udo Müller's most important project, his course in medicine? It was going well. The student passed all the necessary seminars and lectures for the first exam, the *Physikum*. He learned all the functions of the human body, at least theoretically.

But Müller also had the chance of making use of his entrepreneurial genes. When the professor asked in one of the lectures whether a student would pe prepared to photocopy 150 pages for all the others, Udo volunteered.

First, he checked the prices in the local print and copy shops around the university. Then he toured the city to find cheaper solutions. After visiting about a dozen, he asked one of them to copy the lot. There were 400 students attending the lecture, so it was a decent business.

But the price he asked his fellow students to pay was the one quoted by the university's copy shop. "I had to tour around a bit, but the margin of 20 % wasn't bad," he remembers years later.

As for the practical parts of the course, the future professor found them a bit more difficult. He gained his first impression of medical reality during a two-week internship at a clinic in Grunewald.

It was an unpleasant stint. Work started at 6 o'clock in the morning, much too early for Müller, but he turned up on time, nevertheless. He donned the white coat and reported to the duty nurse.

Every day was the same. During the first hour there was nothing to do, then he was allowed to help take lunch to the patients, and eventually he could watch while the patients received some treatment. He was only allowed to look, not to touch. Sometime in the afternoon, he could go home, exhausted but without any noticeable increase in knowledge.

After a week of drudgery, Müller went to the head nurse and asked whether he could come an hour later in the morning, because in the evenings he had to go to his demanding handball training. "There isn't much to do in the mornings anyway, and I'm just wasting time." The stern head nurse rejected the request.

The hospital routine, and the medical role in general, were not what the student had expected. Mostly, he saw emergency cases. People who had swallowed pills in failed suicide attempts. Drunks who had been injured by a fall or in a fight. Müller, inspired by humanist ideas and eastern philosophy, found the quick and routine treatment of these people living on the margins of society to be undignified. And he was quick to let those around him know his opinions.

Two days before the end of the internship, the head nurse asked the perennial complainant Müller to her office. "I am suspending you. You can go." Müller: "I wouldn't dream of it. I'm finishing here as agreed." A discussion followed, and the nurse concluded: "Okay, but never again ask for a job in this hospital. There is no room for you here." Müller shared her opinion.

He hadn't really got a foothold in the world of medicine. But give up? No, Müller wouldn't dream of it. He would carry on, get his doctorate, and then see. Even without the former passion, he went to the seminars and passed the necessary tests and exams.

He took his next step towards becoming a doctor in 1983. Suddenly his ambition returned. He prepared for his exams weeks in advance, and, after passing, the practical part started.

Müller was convinced that his ability to control his nerves in extreme situations made all the difference. The more pressure he was under, the more concentrated he became. It was the same when he played for the *Foxes*, when the team ran into the stadium towards a cheering crowd.

When preparing for the first state exam in 1984, a year later, he developed a specific strategy. Müller looked for fellow students as sparring partners. "I learn better when I have to explain things, rather than to just listen."

He took on a kind of teacher's role and deepened his slightly shaky knowledge in diagnostics, therapy, prevention, and rehabilitation, as well as learning the basics of medical behaviour. He was always focused on the game of questions and answers in an exam.

Then the day came. There were more than 200 multiple-choice questions. Müller had gone through all possible topics, right up until exam day, supported by doses of glucose as his favourite "doping" method. His adrenaline level was up, just like before an important Bundesliga match. Alert and highly concentrated, he started the exam.

Quickly, and without much thinking, Udo went through the questions. If he knew the answer, he took only seconds to place the tick in the right place, ignoring most of the other questions for the time being. After about 60 minutes, he had answered nearly half the questions. When Müller took a short break, the other students looked annoyed.

Then came the second round. Now he took a bit more time over each question and assessed the plausibility of each answer. That could take 20 to 30 seconds per question. Five minutes before the end, nearly all the questions had been answered. Sometimes he had had to guess.

But some questions remained unanswered. They were about the principles of modern care and the legendary British nurse Florence Nightingale. Müller didn't know the right answers but knew where to find them. He asked for a toilet break, got a book about the history of medicine from his pocket and found the answers. Done.

The second big medical exam was over. And it turned out, Müller's results were among the 10 bests in the whole country.

Everything seemed to go well. But Müller still didn't feel at home in the world of medicine, quite the opposite. Cutting up bodies, microscopic anatomy, hospital routine. Nothing quite met the expectations he had about life as a doctor. He found it all too technical and geared towards efficiency. He thought hospitals were simply repair shops that did not seek a holistic view of the patient.

As time went by, Müller realised that medicine was not the challenge he had expected. He also disliked the strict hierarchy in hospitals. "It was all about following orders without discussion or initiative."

But there were other things that Udo was fascinated by. Handball, of course. He still wanted to be in the national team and play for the Federal Republic. Udo woke up in the morning thinking about his sport and went to sleep thinking about it too. That was his ambition. He wanted to be among the best.

But Müller was also successful as a budding entrepreneur. He learned a lot about business from the world of medicine as well as from handball – and vice versa. The team sponsor offered each player a 500 Dollar bonus if they won the semi-final of the German cup competition. Udo Müller and his friend Dieter Nerlich were very keen to be called up, but the coach only wanted them for short periods. On May 19th, 1984, the *Foxes* beat Essen in the semi-final by 22:15, one of the best results in the club's history.

They were now in the German Cup final, where they would play Grosswallstadt, a team that had already won this year's championship. But the *Foxes* had now also qualified to play in a European competition, which meant two more home games: the German Cup final and at least the first round of the European competition. Müller and Nerlich could therefore produce two more programs. Each would earn them 6,500 Dollar, and as far as they were concerned, it compensated for not being called up to play the match.

Even many years later Müller will often ponder whether fate somehow intervened in his life at that point. Sometimes, skills are not enough, and one needs a bit of luck to achieve something. There's another example from his handball years. The team had travelled to Zaporizhzhia, in what is now Ukraine, for the semi-final of the 1982/83 IHF Cup. It was part of the Soviet Union at the time. Müller knew that Soviet people were particularly keen on Adidas sports gear, so he took everything with him that he could find, and then successfully sold the gear from his hotel room.

That alone wouldn't have been particularly interesting. Most people who travelled to the Soviet Union did it. Tourists often sold their extra pair of jeans or five bars of Western chocolate. With athletes, it was more about training gear.

Müller knew that he had to exchange the roubles he had earned before he left the country. When the group arrived at the airport for their return flight, Müller was among the first who headed to the bureau de change. After he had changed his roubles into D-Mark, the office ran out of foreign currency. All the others had to leave their roubles behind.

Back in Berlin he carried on with his medical course. One particular operation he observed and assisted with stayed with him forever. The episode showed him that one should never give up and how important it was to stick with something. Never lose sight of the goal. This kind of perseverance is always rewarded. There is always a way out. But one has to find it.

The operation was on a young boy who had a brain tumour. The surgeon opened the boy's skull and began to prepare the site of the operation, the actual removal of the tumour.

It was an extremely critical phase – and the surgeon had to try numerous times before he could find the best point for the incision. He moved his hand in exactly the same way about 50 times, without showing the slightest sign of frustration or annoyance. It was a stoic performance, but with only one aim: to complete a successful operation.

To this day, nearly 40 years later, Udo Müller talks of this surgeon with utter admiration. The man operated for six hours after the skull had been opened. And all the time his concentration and determination remained the same. "As a handball pro I was super fit," Müller remembers, "but after that operation I was so exhausted that I had to go home and sleep for two hours before I went to training. However, the surgeon performed another operation that day. This left a deep impression on me."

The *Foxes* in the meantime were firmly established at the top of the Bundesliga, and Udo Müller had become a regular member of a team brimming with world class players. His dream of being called up to the national team was within reach. Simon Schobel, the new national coach, had taken him aside after a Bundesliga game and indicated that. “Top performance. You’ll get an invite for the next training camp of the national team.”

But then, in September 1985, came a shock. It was during another one of the *Foxes’* sold out Bundesliga matches. Müller was on the pitch from the start, he was in good form and enjoying the cheers of the fans. All was going well for the *Foxes*, and it was going well for him.

But then, still in the first half, he tried a jump-throw and collided with another player. Pain shot through his right leg. He slumped to the ground. Müller knew immediately that something bad had happened. The team medic only diagnosed a muscle injury. After a week off he recommended Müller could run again, but his knee dislocated in front of his very eyes.

Müller was certain that something was not right. But he was finally a member of the core team and desperately wanted to be a handball pro, so he stabilised his knee with tape and continued playing through the pain.

But weeks later he went to hospital, and his worst fears were confirmed. He had suffered a cruciate ligament tear. Even worse, a cartilage plate in his ankle joint had collapsed. The operation took five hours. The ankle was sawn off, the bone plate taken out and then wired together again. The knee was cut open and the cruciate ligament isolated from the patella.

Any time before that, Udo wouldn’t have given a thought to whether that was the end of his athletic career. He would have had the operation and eagerly started training as soon as possible afterwards. He really believed he was on the way to the peak of his athletic career. But after a few days of agonizing considerations, he made another one of his lonely decisions. Still in hospital, Udo Müller ended his career as a handball pro.

His medical career didn't quite go to plan either. He had never felt completely comfortable with this choice of career, but still, in the fourth year of his course, he started his dissertation about a new method of operating on the meniscus after a cruciate ligament tear. Before, the whole knee joint would have been cut open to operate on the meniscus, but with the new less invasive method it was done with the help of two small tubes. A small camera was threaded through the left tube, the scalpel on the right. Maybe Udo chose the topic because of its personal resonance. Müller increasingly had knee problems because of the high physical demands of handball.

Müller was highly motivated to write this dissertation. The new method of operation would be assessed on the first 100 patients. Fifty patients were supposed to fill in a questionnaire; Müller would examine the other 50. The results were sorted according to a grading system. But when he showed the results to the lead doctor, he was not happy with them. The figures weren't good enough.

"What do you mean, not good enough?" Müller asked.

"The results are not good enough. They have to be better," the doctor replied.

Müller was baffled. "I thought I was supposed to work scientifically. Thesis, antithesis, synthesis."

The medic replied: "No, you are to *pretend* you could work in an academic, scientific way."

It was a shock for Müller. He was keen on working scientifically. The dissertation was to be his ticket to the world of academia. Instead, they wanted him to confirm methods with manipulated research results if necessary. That was not his thing.

As mentioned before, he had never really arrived in the world of medicine. The first two years had been mainly about the science, pure learning without any patient contact. An exam phase had followed that, and only in the fourth year were the students introduced to the world of hospitals and patients. He had had repeated doubts whether it was the right thing for him to do.

The critical point came after a lecture on histology, one of the core subjects of classical medicine. It had been a normal day, everything was going as usual, but when Udo left the lecture hall and slowly went down the stairs, he suddenly knew that medicine wasn't for him. The disappointment with his dissertation, the way medicine was practiced in hospitals. For quite a while he hadn't felt comfortable with any of it. But it was at that moment that it became crystal clear to him. In his last semester, a few months before his second state exam and shortly before he was going to start his internship at the university hospital – that's when the disappointed student finally threw in the towel.

The decision had been a long time coming. For quite a while, he had convinced himself he was one of those ambitious people who never give up, never lose sight of their chosen goal. He would overcome all obstacles. He had sworn it to himself. But this time, his decision was different.

He had invested five years of his life in medicine. But the passion had disappeared – if there ever was any passion. And so he made the decision and turned against a career as a doctor, against medicine, and against an academic title. No Dr. med. Udo Müller. No Prof. Dr. med. Udo Müller either.

He left the university without looking back. The world of medicine was behind him. For good. He never started the internship he had arranged.

Müller was now 24 years old, so young that he could have become one of the youngest medical professors in the country. At least that had been his goal over the past few years. But now he gave up this career as well as becoming a handball pro, and all the fame and prestige that would have come with it.

His new aim – and one that contributed considerably to his decision – was to become a publisher. It was definitely less socially prestigious, and definitely riskier. "For the first time in my life, I put all my eggs in one basket," Müller remembers years later.

But the years of studying medicine had not been wasted. Udo had learned a lot. To some degree, he needed to convince himself that these past few years had been useful, but it wasn't too difficult. Now was the time to think of the future and to realise a bigger dream.

A publisher now

The small publishing project for the *Foxes* had been a good exercise for Müller and a good introduction to this new world. Soon Udo and Dieter extended their activities to another successful sports club and, in 1984, they founded the company Blau-Weiss 90 Werbung OHG, to publish programs for the club that had recently been promoted to the Bundesliga.

They also started an agency called *Bandenwerbung* OHG, as well as *Artlight Poster Production* OHG, a small company producing artistically reproduced photos which Udo ran with a photographer friend. They distributed beautiful photographic images via a network that stretched as far as Japan. It was Müller's first project beyond Berlin's boundaries.

But soon a problem appeared for the two young entrepreneurs: the taxman. Müller thought he had found an effective strategy to avoid paying much tax. He figured out that the annual tax-free turnover limit for small companies was 25,000 Dollar and carefully made sure that each of his numerous companies remained below the limit.

He founded one company after another, among them *Müller Werbung* and *Nerlich Werbung*, and the increasing turnover was shared between them.

When Udo, on Dieter's insistence, finally got an accountant, it was nearly too late. The tax office had been watching the chain of not so small "small companies" with suspicion. Hastily, the accountant organised the network of firms into some kind of a system.

Now free of the demands of his medical course and of handball training, it was time for Udo Müller to start bigger projects anyway. He wanted something that everyone in Berlin would talk about. He wanted to publish a sports magazine.

On March 25th, 1986, the following message from the newswire *dpa* landed on all newspaper editor's desks: "The *Berliner Sportmagazin*, coming out this Wednesday, will be the first illustrated sports publication for the city. The monthly will cost 3.50 D-Mark and have 64 pages. The initial circulation will be 6,000 copies. According to the publishers, the aim of the magazine is to announce and report on sports events in the city in an unbiased and critical way."

"The producers and publishers of the sports magazine", *dpa* goes on, "are Dieter Nerlich and Udo Müller, two former *Foxes* handball pros, and Frank Schlageter, former goalkeeper of the five-time German champions Frankenthal hockey team, currently the coach of the Brandenburg women's hockey team."

It went on: "The first edition will focus on players from Blau-Weiss and Eishockey Preussen. But more niche sports such as trampolining, table tennis and nine-pin bowling will also be covered. There will be 25 pages listing sports events, including smaller company and disabled clubs. All clubs will be listed with their location and phone numbers for easy contact."

The next day Müller and Nerlich, with great pride, read about their venture in all the dailies. The popular radio station RIAS got in touch to arrange an interview with the "courageous young publishers".

"Do you think your magazine will be a success?"

"Of course!"

"Is the new publishing house planning further magazines?"

"That's quite possible."

"Who is financing the project?"

"We are!"

The last statement was met with disbelief. They were investing their own money? That was hardly possible. Rumours circulated in the publishing industry that the property shark Bendzko was behind it and that the two young entrepreneurs were only his puppets.

Müller and Nerlich had the magazine produced and printed with Stiftung Synanon, a company involved in fighting drug use while also running a printing shop. For the first edition, Müller and Nerlich went to help with the setting, which at the time wasn't fully computerised. They brought several helpers but underestimated the amount of work: they all laboured right through from Friday afternoon until Sunday afternoon to get it done. "I was in a kind of trance and hadn't known that you can work through two nights without a break, without sleep," Müller remembers.

But it turned out to be worthwhile. The first edition was

a huge success, not least because of the media coverage. The distribution was taken on by the small publishing house of the city magazine *Tip*. Mega publisher Axel Springer, whose papers *Bild*, *BZ*, *Die Welt* and *Berliner Morgenpost* dominated the market, had refused to take on the new magazine. Müller thought it rather a compliment.

A few days later, the first run of more than 4,000 copies was sold out. It was a success no one in the business had expected. Now the managers in the Springer building were on high alert. Reporting on sports had so far been the monopoly of the large press empire.

Müller and his small team worked non-stop on the second edition and were planning topics for the third. Udo Müller already saw himself at the start of a successful career as a publisher.

But the high of the early success didn't last long. Müller and Nerlich were preparing the delivery of the third edition when couriers arrived in the yard of *Tip* magazine carrying the returns of the second edition. (This is a specialty of the publishing business. Unsold books, papers and magazines can be sent back by bookshops and small outlets as returns, and they are reimbursed.)

"We were on a real high, having finished the third edition," Müller remembers, "and then one courier after another came back with unsold copies of No. 2."

Müller soon realised that the second edition of the magazine had been a flop. "The couriers showed us their paperwork, and it was awful." Almost half the copies they sent out were being returned unsold.

For the young publisher, it was the greatest shock since his mother had told him that her marriage had failed. "I was so convinced that the project would be a success," Müller says years later. "I was simply devastated when so many copies of my magazine came back."

The second edition barely sold 2,000 copies. The third was practically a non-starter. The two men even personally took to the streets and went to sport venues to try and flog the *Berliner Sportmagazin* for only 3.50 D-Mark – like market traders. But it didn't help. Stacks of unsold copies piled up in Müller's flat in the Corbusier House.

The plan to cover the whole spectrum of sport in Berlin every month had failed. Even sports fans really only wanted to know about their own club. They couldn't care less what the others were doing. And the big clubs, like Hertha Berlin, were covered by the city dailies like *Bild*, *Morgenpost*, etc. The fans didn't need monthly updates.

After three months, they had used up 40,000 Dollar of their capital. Müller's dream of a fabulous career as a publisher had collapsed before it had even properly started.

So, there he was: no academic laurels, no cheers from the handball fans, no success as a publisher. It meant going back to the start.

But where was the start? Udo hadn't felt so alone and depressed since he was 15, when his parents got divorced. But what had he learned from the guru of his youth? Let go, look ahead. That was easier said than done.

At some point while playing sport, studying, and juggling his many commercial activities, Udo and Dieter had met the advertising professional Horst Lunenburg. More than 20 years older than Müller, he was the successful owner of a medium-sized Berlin advertising agency. Lunenburg liked the two unconventional youngsters, and Müller and Nerlich planned to find a new base for their business. Together and on equal terms they founded a new company: *Lunenburg & Partner Werbeagentur* GmbH.

It was a good fit. The young men had the enthusiasm, the older man good connections. The trio established two agencies under one roof – one for the marketing of sports events, and a classic agency with copywriters, graphic designers, and consultants. Müller and Nerlich didn't care much that their names were not part of the company's name. Lunenburg found new clients, the other two saw to the rest.

In less than a week they renovated an old flower shop in Grunewald and turned it into an office. The furniture that Müller brought over from his home came from Ikea. It was their first proper office. So far, Müller and Nerlich had run their businesses practically from their flats. But now Udo Müller had a specific wish: "I want to have so much work that I don't know what to do first."

But he was still a newcomer in the world of beautiful images. So, once again he had a lot of learning to do. He grabbed the folders with the agency's correspondence and documents and began to read. It gave him an idea of the marketing terminology. Then he got hold of specific books, particularly one by New York advertising guru David Ogilvy: *Confessions of an Advertising Man*. It was an eye-opener for Müller. He also found a book by the Frenchman Jacques Séguéla to be helpful. The book's title was *Don't tell my mother that I'm in advertising – she thinks I'm a piano player in a brothel.*

At 24, the former medical student, ex-handball pro and failed publisher had arrived in the world of advertising. He was an entrepreneur after all.

Adverts for Checkpoint Charlie

Nearly everyone who visits Berlin goes to Checkpoint Charlie, the famous border crossing in *Friedrichstrasse*. Here, during the Cold War, armed soldiers from the U.S.A. and the Soviet Union faced each other eye to eye.

Ever since the construction of the Wall, there had been a kind of historical museum about the German division on the West side. To get tourists to visit the museum it needed advertising – not a lot, just a few brochures.

For Udo Müller, it becomes the first contract for his new agency – and such a historically important one! That compensated for the meagre 1,000 Dollar fee.

But soon there are more lucrative customers on the books, such as the department store giant Hertie and the pharmaceutical company Schöning. The agency employs copywriters and graphic designers, and soon two dozen creatives work in the office of *Lunenburg & Partner* on campaigns for sales promotion. They're soon the fastest growing agency in Berlin.

On his way to work each morning, Müller passes the famous Deutschlandhalle which had been built for the 1936 summer Olympics. It had been destroyed in the war, but the government of West Berlin restored it in the 50s. Now it is the largest venue in West Berlin, and has hosted, among others, concerts by the likes of Jimi Hendrix and the Rolling Stones, who played to tens of thousands of people.

In short, the Deutschlandhalle was an iconic site in West Berlin. For about 35 years, Manfred Bertuch, a legend in the Berlin advertising scene, had done the marketing for this prestigious venue. But he was retiring, and the Berlin senate had put the contract for advertising out to tender.

It was clear that Udo Müller should compete for it. And, of course, he had to win. It would be his breakthrough in the Berlin advertising scene.

Müller was still fuming about an incident when he had presented an advertising campaign to the top delicatessen company Lindner. The family company had been a customer of his agency for a while, and the copywriters of

Lunenburg & Partner had designed an advert, as requested, about fresh eggs. But one of the young Lindners didn't like it, saying some of the information was wrong. Müller objected, because quite obviously young Lindner didn't know his own products. He insisted they kept the text for "purely factual reasons".

Young Lindner looked coolly at the advertising guy. Müller later remembers his words: "When I say it's green, then it's green. No matter what colour it is. And if you don't like it, you can go." Müller went. "I had become an entrepreneur because I wanted to be myself, not dance to somebody else's tune."

But something very important became clear to him then. He was only a small guy who had to jump when the client clicked his fingers. It was a depressing thought.

He was utterly replaceable, dependent on his clients. But that wasn't at all what Udo had wanted. He wanted to realise his own ideas and identify with his work.

And he was dead sure that he would achieve this. Whenever he had really wanted something so far, he had always got it: he thought of his swapping of cigarette packets as a 10-year-old in the art class, his high exam grades, the call-up to the national handball team and results that ranked him as the 10th best of all medical students in Germany.

To want something unconditionally also meant that Müller would work for it unconditionally. "You have to want it more than anybody else in the room, that's the most important aspect," he says. "Failing is not an option. I *must* succeed. And I will succeed."

So, each day when he drove past the Deutschlandhalle, he said to himself: "I'm going to win the tender and get the contract. Or I'll die." The last sentence was only a metaphor, of course, but it really felt like a matter of life and death to him. "Nobody wanted that contract more than I did."

And he got it.

Unusually, the creative proposal and the marketing concept were tendered together, so Müller had to apply his tactical skills as he pitched against his rivals. At first, he convinced the creative staff of the rival agency GKM to cooperate with him. His argument was that Lunenburg was a partner of the Switzerland-based International Sport Agency Lüthi. But Müller needed GKM because of their good contacts to the Berlin senate, owner of the Deutschlandhalle.

After they won the contract thanks to GKM's good connections, the partners met for a strategy meeting. Now Müller suggested separating the various aspects of the job. "You are better creatively," he said, "so you should take on the design." Lunenburg would see to the marketing of the perimeter advertising.

And that's how it happened. It's not known whether the GKM people realised straightaway that their agency had the less lucrative part of the deal. Müller, however, estimated the income from marketing the perimeter and billboards for his agency to be about 650,000 Dollar per annum. No amount of copywriting and pretty formatting can ever earn such a sum.

Everything in its own time

Despite his success, Udo Müller often felt that he had been born at the wrong time. He would have loved to have been busy in the immediate post-war years, in the 50s and 60s, when the German economic miracle was admired all over the world.

It had been the companies' new freedoms and ideas then, their passion and willpower, that had contributed to the rapid economic development: creative people who saw their chances and secured their slice of the pie. The Grundigs, the Neckermanns and so many other medium-sized companies. They were at the right place at the right time.

But by the 1980s, the economy seemed to have become rigid, there was hardly any space for innovation. The pie had been distributed, and Udo envied the generation of founders in "Stunde Null".

But with his spectacular success in winning the advertising contract for the Deutschlandhalle, he had shown what was still possible – if only he wanted it badly enough. And he wanted it, no question. A few years later came the next big chance, advertising to the West near the Eastern border and on the transit routes within the GDR.

Since that night in January 1988 on Friedrichstrasse station, the economic difficulties of the GDR had become more and more obvious. Within a few months, Müller had identified dozens of possible billboard sites for advertising to the West near the border – on GDR territory, along the Wall.

How would things develop with the GDR? Was a new important breakthrough on the cards? Again, Müller turned up at Friedrichstrasse station in the middle of the night. A few minutes later the last train towards the district of Wedding would leave. When the West Berliners passed through in the morning, they would see newly erected advertising posters.

His role as a conduit between communism and consumerism was developing very nicely. He felt something like a sense of history when shuttling between the political systems of the Cold War.

An incident in Gartenstrasse

For quite a while now, Udo Müller had had a permanent visa for the GDR, so he could come and go whenever he liked. But in the West Berlin senate, no one knew about the private deal between *Lunenburg & Partner*, with Udo Müller as their representative, and the German Democratic Republic, represented by *Interwerbung*.

Udo Müller was quite well-known by the soldiers at the border crossing. When one Monday morning he stopped at the checkpoint, the officer briefly looked into Müller's Mercedes and said: "Müller, you disappoint me. Who can we trust if not the people who do this all the time?"

"What do you mean?"

"What's that on the passenger seat?"

"Oh, the *Spiegel*." Müller had forgotten the Hamburg news magazine, despised by the GDR government.

"You don't want to take it with you?"

"No, of course not. Can I leave it with you?"

"Are you mad? I'm not touching that crap. Follow me."

Müller had to get out of the car and put the copy of the *Spiegel* (No 33/1988) through a slit into a box. Then he was told never to bring such a polemical magazine again and not to read it either. And then he was allowed to carry on.

But the problems with the West Berlin police were even worse. Müller had found several perfect sites for his billboards at the border between the districts of Wedding and Mitte – a wall of yellow bricks, more than two meters high and 600 meters long. It enclosed the raised area of the disused Stettin Station on Gartenstrasse.

The Berlin Wall now ran along the former railway tracks. In front of it was the Death Strip, which couldn't be seen from the road. The actual border was in the middle of about three meters of pavement, between two granite slabs, typical for Berlin's old paving. One half of the pavement was on GDR territory, the other was in the Wedding district. But nobody really knew.

In Berlin's everyday life some strange border arrangements didn't matter much. It was normal for West Berlin traffic to use the busy Gartenstrasse towards Bernauer Strasse. And the divided, unkempt pavement wasn't used much anyway. Now Udo Müller came with his billboards, and all hell broke loose.

On one Thursday afternoon in June 1988, a *Lunenburg & Partner* van stopped in Gartenstrasse in front of the yellow brick wall. Without any haste, a gang of workers started to fix large wooden panels to the wall, which legally was the property of the GDR.

The workers had been busy for more than half an hour when two West German police cars arrived with blaring lights and sirens. Several policemen got out quickly and shouted at the workers to stop immediately.

"No can do," one of the workers replied defiantly. "We have orders." The relationship between citizens and police in the West was decidedly more relaxed than in the socialist East, so Müller's people didn't obey orders immediately.

But the policemen meant it. "Whether you know it or not, you are on GDR territory. This will have consequences. Please leave the GDR immediately!"

The state and Müller's workers were facing off against one another on an invisible borderline between socialism and capitalism on the pavement of Gartenstrasse. The officers couldn't act, because the workers and the material were right at the wall, on the territory of the "other Germany".

The police had clear orders to prevent such violations of

the border. The Senate and its Western allies didn't want to provide an excuse for the GDR to interpret such incidents as provocations. But the workers felt they were in the right because they too had clear orders, and they didn't care about the political intricacies.

The scene on the border had the characteristics of a satire, mixed with panic, and with a global political backdrop. It lasted a few minutes, then the workers gave in. They figured they would leave the problem to the advertising guys at *Lunenburg*. They had to submit their names and addresses and that of the company and could then go home. The wooden panels and advertising material was confiscated.

A short time later the phone rang at *Lunenburg & Partner*. It was the police. As Udo Müller wasn't in the office, the call went to Dieter Nerlich. The caller sounded stern. He asked whether they could be quite right in the head to fix advertising material on GDR property? They could be charged with border violation and state security would be involved.

Nerlich tried to explain the situation. The policeman at the other end couldn't believe it. There was a private contract between a company licensed by the GDR foreign trade ministry and a West Berlin advertising agency to install billboards on the border? Nerlich was asked to present the relevant contracts.

The next day the work on Müller's advertising wall continued without any issue. The officers and civil servants in the Berlin senate were shaking their heads. What in all the world was happening in the GDR?

AWAKENING

A cool encounter

Late summer 1988. Heinz "Heiner" Ströer takes a Lufthansa plane from Cologne to Berlin. He is not expecting a chummy meeting. He isn't underestimating the situation. However, with an open conversation among men the issue should be off the table in no time. That's what he thinks, anyway.

When the plane lands at Tegel airport, slightly delayed, Karl-Heinz Wiesner is already waiting impatiently for his boss. Wiesner runs the Munich company *Superposter*, which belongs to one of Ströer's subsidiaries. He keeps having problems with some clients. A few weeks ago, out of the blue, several property companies cancelled their advertising contracts with Ströer. Some asked to immediately end their contract; others demanded much more rent if Ströer's advertisements were still to be mounted on their walls. Of course, it happened occasionally that a business complained about the conditions of a contract. But this seemed to be a veritable rebellion.

Wiesner found the source of the unrest. Evidence led to a small advertising agency in the upmarket Berlin district of Grunewald named *Lunenburg* & *Partner*. Further research didn't yield much more information. Before now, Lunenburg was not a major player in billboard advertising.

At first, Wiesner tried to sort out the problem on his own. A few days previously he had gone to Berlin for clear-the-air talks. The co-owner of the agency, Horst Lunenburg, had greeted the man from Munich in a friendly manner. But when the visitor came to the point with the words: "Mr. Lunenburg, you are poaching our business," Lunenburg called in his young partner Udo Müller, and the atmosphere became more unpleasant. Müller was less friendly than expected.

Half an hour later, Wiesner left the agency and called his boss Heiner Ströer with a warning. "That man can be very dangerous for us." What Wiesner had found so upsetting was Müller's arrogant manner and the coolness with which he was being treated.

Ströer found the whole episode less unsettling, but he took the warning. Someone had dared to meddle with what he called his pitch. In his hometown of Cologne, Ströer was called the "King of Advertising", and he now became curious. He secretly fished for more information about the outsider.

Udo Müller? In the West German advertising scene nobody knew Udo Müller, this young buck from Berlin.

The only information they could find was that he was in his mid-20s, had abandoned studies in medicine and was an ex-handball player. With his friend Dieter Nerlich and the considerably older Horst Lunenburg they were partners in an advertising agency. They had a few local clients. Classic advertising, yes, partly outdoor advertising, but really small fry.

And those guys were supposed to be a danger? That's how Ströer saw it. The Lunenburg agency and this Müller were nothing more than a few incompetent novices. The experienced master of the advertising trade was sure to clear up the problem in no time, using his own rules. He hails a taxi, confident and relaxed, and drives to Grunewald, with Wiesner beside him.

Horst Lunenburg is waiting for them and greets Ströer with perfect manners. The gentlemen are still engaged in polite small talk when Udo Müller enters the small meeting room and instead of a friendly "hello", mumbles: "Sorry, had to make a few calls."

Ah, so this is him. Ströer curiously studies the young man who, totally relaxed, takes a seat at the table. He is tall, slim, wearing a black designer suit, white shirt, open collar, his dark hair slicked back with gel. He's not even 30, Ströer estimates.

And then the eyes. They meet only briefly. Ströer isn't sure whether Müller looks at him in a friendly but detached manner, or whether he is coolly sizing him up.

Udo Müller is not one of those genial fellows who meet and greet people with a smile. He seems relaxed, appears slightly bored and waits, leaving the talk to Lunenburg and the visitor. The senior partner likes to present himself as the soul of the agency, in words and gestures. Udo lets him be.

The calendar on the wall says September 23rd, 1988. It also shows a "Saying of the day": "You can do infinitely good things without words, without preaching, without a fuss." No one around the table takes any notice of this.

Lunenburg blathers on about his two successful decades in the Berlin advertising scene. But Ströer is not interested, nor does he care when Lunenburg proudly mentions a partnership with the Swiss sport marketing guru Caesar W. Lüthi. When Lunenburg mentions that Günther Netzer is a client of Lüthi, Ströer smiles. He is a fan of the football legend.

Müller just listens. Lunenburg could be his father. So could Ströer. Müller estimates that the equally silent

Wiesner is in his 30s. At 26, he is definitely the youngster in this group of experienced advertisers. But it doesn't feel that way.

Müller has now been living in West Berlin for eight years. Cosy Godesberg and beautiful Frauke – all that seems to be a long time ago. Müller now feels like a grown-up.

When Lunenburg finishes his eloquent presentation of himself, Ströer comes to the point. "I think," he begins in his sonorous voice, "that we have to communicate about a few fundamental issues."

He says he is disappointed by the aggressiveness of *Lunenburg & Partner* when acquiring new sites for advertising. It's not the done thing in the world of outdoor advertisers who, despite the competition getting tougher, would remain on friendly terms. It is not acceptable to poach existing sites by offering higher rents. To offer up to 1,400 Dollar annually for a site that currently costs only 300, would be uncooperative and not in line with accepted fairness practices in the business. He also doubts very much whether it could be economically feasible.

Time and again, Ströer tries to get eye contact with Müller, who of course knows why the man has come over from Cologne. And of course, Müller also knows what he wants. But no one can deter Müller from his strategy, not even the almighty Ströer. Müller is not a modest man, and he doesn't see any reason to be overly respectful.

Ströer's business model is simple. Property owners let walls and building facades to him. He applies for a wooden panel to be fixed to the wall, and as soon as the permit is given, he rents it out as advertising space to brands like Mercedes or Marlboro, Ariel or Aldi, Budweiser or Bollinger.

In the 1980s, about 130 outdoor advertisers share the market without any problems. There is obviously room for everyone. The rough annual calculation for a single large billboard is approximately: 300 Dollar rent to the owner of the wall or building, about 300 for maintenance of the board and fixing the adverts in place every 10 days. Income is 900 Dollar, meaning 300 Dollar profit for each and every site. Not a bad margin.

Since Heiner Ströer started his advertising company in the 1950s, he had earned a fortune with his wooden billboards. He now owns more than 15,000 of them between Munich and Hamburg. And he wouldn't dream of parting with even a single site.

The Ströer company is one of the big fish in the small pond of outdoor advertising. It is a growing market, but only covers 3 % of all advertising in Germany.

For quite a while, Müller had been investigating this obviously lucrative market. But to simply do the same as all the others is not his thing. Müller wants more than just to stick posters on wooden boards. He knows that it would take years to get as far as the established companies, because many of the profitable sites are already reserved. With new sites, one would have to find out about the owner, apply for permission, draw up contracts. No, to get established in outdoor advertising properly, it would take innovation and new products.

One of them is "Prisma vision", a new technology from Sweden. The size of the advert stays the same as on traditional wooden boards, roughly nine square meters. But three different images rotate, changing every 10 seconds. Müller has calculated that an electric "Prisma vision" billboard could yield 10 times the profit for each site. Additionally, the rotating images would attract more attention.

But that is only one of Müller's ideas. He considers "Prisma vision" as only a first step toward getting some fresh ideas into the rather staid advertising business. To market the new medium successfully, Müller needs first-class sites on private ground in big cities. He is not willing to consider the needs of established companies like Ströer's.

The solution is obvious. Müller is in West Berlin, the desired sites to get the business started properly are in the Federal Republic. But they have to be found.

Müller places small adverts in the "situations vacant" section of regional German newspapers with the heading: "Wanted: Bike riders for well-paid, easy jobs". Soon he has hired a team of bicycle and motorbike riders to make their way through selected cities on the lookout for promising sites for Müller's "Prisma vision".

He assesses the material he collects from the riders. The owners of possible sites are offered contracts which pay considerably more than for conventional billboards. Müller wants to make sure that existing scouts for advertising sites never learn about his activities so that they can never pass on the information to established advertisers such as Ströer.

It's precisely because Müller is often most interested in the exact sites already reserved by Ströer or other outdoor advertisers. Either that, or sites that Ströer is eyeing up for his new product: "super posters". He plans billboards that will be more than twice the usual size, roughly 20 square meters. That means that sites further away from the customer and the street, like on high building walls, are now also considered for poster advertising. Conflict seems unavoidable.

Heiner Ströer soon realises that the problem cannot be solved by a chat among men. The key to the conflict is not the older Lunenburg, but young Müller. He decides to find out more about the man and his strategy.

"I'm hungry," the man from Cologne suddenly says with a broad smile. "Is there a good restaurant nearby?"

Wiesner watches his boss and is relieved. Heiner Ströer surely has a plan and will sort out this young man quickly. With money, if necessary. It wouldn't be the first time that his boss has solved a problem that way.

It's gonna be a long evening ...

So, the small group leaves for an Italian restaurant. After ordering, it's only Ströer and Müller who do the talking. It's a lively conversation about their life experiences, the business world, the times they're living in. Karl-Heinz Wiesner and Horst Lunenburg do more of the listening.

At about half past nine Lunenburg leaves. Wiesner stays a bit longer, then he says goodbye as well. He is a touch disappointed. Why does his boss listen to this Müller so intensely? He never delivered the clear message Wiesner had hoped for, the one that would tell the other party what is what.

For Heiner and Udo – they are on first name terms by now – the evening is not even close to being over. They talk like two friends who haven't seen each other for a long time and have a lot to catch up on. The young advertising pro now behaves totally differently than in the office, when he appeared more distanced and slightly arrogant.

At some point before midnight the restaurant closes, but Ströer and Müller want to carry on. The two Rhinelanders, two very different characters, move on to a pub at the corner and eventually end up in the rowdy piano bar "Chez Alex" on Ku'damm.

It was one of those encounters when two people meet and instantly develop a total trust in each other, but still have to find their boundaries. That night Müller, unusually for him, talks a lot about himself. Ströer too discloses a few episodes from his life. But they keep some secrets to maintain a mutual curiosity.

The next day begins early for Ströer with a lot of strong coffee and a couple of aspirins. What a night! Later Müller's girlfriend had joined them. The sun was coming up when they left the nightclub in high spirits, and Udo lifted his girlfriend high in the air, pirouetting like an ice dancer. A remarkable guy, this Udo, Heiner thinks.

Ströer is in a hurry. He has another important appointment at 7 o'clock. In the GDR, people start work much earlier than in the West. But they can also go home earlier.

Ströer's meeting with *Lunenburg & Partner* wasn't the only reason for his Berlin trip. For quite a while now, Heiner Ströer has been watching the situation in the GDR with growing interest. A while ago he had heard a rumor that the socialist regime was allowing advertising by Western capitalist companies on socialist territory in areas near the border – but only visible for passing Wessies, of course, and in exchange for hard currency. Heiner Ströer didn't want to miss out on this new version of inter-German business. A communist company called *Interwerbung* seemed to be in charge of it. So he had asked for a meeting.

During the second half of the 1980s, it was obvious that the East was changing rapidly behind the Iron Curtain. The calls for more freedom and democracy were getting louder and louder.

In Poland, people had openly asked for more freedom. The Hungarian government now allowed its citizens to travel abroad without many restrictions. Only a few weeks ago, the Soviet president Mikhail Gorbachev had announced that socialist states were free to choose their political system.

But in the capital of the German Democratic Republic, the SED leaders don't expect or plan any changes. Here, the rulers believe themselves to be in total control, even of the people who regularly demonstrate in Leipzig, Dresden and other cities every Monday. But how long will the security police, the much feared Stasi, be able to suppress the calls for more freedom?

One of Ströer's basic beliefs is that freedom would always be economic freedom as well. That is the main reason for his Berlin visit. On his flight over, he had read about the "expected end of socialist planned economies like in the GDR".

Heiner Ströer doesn't want to miss out on a good opportunity. When the sun of the free markets rises in the East, he wants to be warmed by its first rays. On this 24th of September 1988, at 7 o'clock precisely, he has an appointment in East Berlin.

The controls at Checkpoint Charlie in Friedrichstrasse take much longer than expected, similarly the drive to the drab district of Karlshorst. Ströer is annoyed, he will be late. Punctuality is one of his most important values.

Interwerbung is in Hermann Duncker-Strasse and is a subsidiary of the state advertising department, directly reporting to the Ministry for Foreign Trade.

Among its briefs is the live broadcast of GDR sports events to the West. The adverts are organised by *Interwerbung*. So far, the state organisation has earned a few hundred thousand D-Mark or U.S. Dollars for allowing class enemies such as Coca Cola or Volkswagen to appear on the perimeter advertising.

This business is now set for careful expansion – at least

that's what Ströer has heard, and he wants to explore it. His plan is to erect billboards along the transit routes between West Berlin and West Germany and to manage them.

The offices of *Interwerbung* in Hermann Duncker Strasse have nothing of the chic and glamour of advertising agencies in the West. Behind grey walls the rooms are identical to other drab offices in the East. Here, the business is not about beauty and illusions, it's only about getting hard currency.

Despite the long night and his headache, Ströer feels positive. For about half an hour he, as usual, sells the advantages of working with his agency and makes some suggestions as to how the two entities can work together.

At the end, one of the functionaries praises his "fantastic presentation", but then expresses his regret that the tender unfortunately had been closed and the contract gone to someone else.

Ströer is surprised and disappointed. "May I ask who has got it?"

"Yes, of course, we don't have any secrets. It's the West Berlin agency *Lunenburg & Partner.*"

"*Lunenburg & Partner*?" Suddenly he feels it again, the effects of his late night, hammering behind his forehead.

"Yes. Lunenburg. Why?"

"I am a tad disappointed. Is there anything that can be done?"

"Well, maybe you can contact Mr. Müller from the agency. Udo Müller. Wait, I can give you his phone number."

Müller, Müller, again this Müller. Heiner Ströer's thoughts shuttle between annoyance and admiration. Now he wants to see him again soon, this Udo. He doesn't need the phone number; he's got it already.

The future partners

Müller too doesn't go straight to bed after the memorable night with Heiner Ströer. Instead, he heads straight to his favourite café near the Ku'damm for breakfast and from there to the agency.

He has a pounding headache. The ambitious young entrepreneur doesn't often indulge in nights like that. Later that morning he finally rings *Interwerbung* and asks them about Ströer's recent visit. The news is to his liking. Herr Ströer has been rejected. They referred him to a Mr. Müller at the Lunenburg agency in West Berlin.

Just before lunchtime, the phone rings. It's Heiner Ströer. "Hello Udo, how are you?" Without waiting for an answer, he adds with a laugh. "What a nice evening we had!" He was on the way to the airport and just wanted to say hello. Then he tells Udo about his visit to the East but doesn't reveal his disappointment with the comrades of *Interwerbung*. They exchange a few more polite phrases and promise to meet up again soon.

Müller is happy about the call. He likes Heiner Ströer and will treat him with respect.

"We have to see each other again," Heiner said on the phone. "I need to talk to you about something. Can we meet up soon? It's about the special size boards for adverts by tobacco companies."

A few days later Müller flies to Frankfurt. The meeting is in a restaurant near the airport, where Ströer is seeing some of his top managers. At 10 o'clock, as arranged, Müller arrives at the hotel, asks at the reception for the Ströer meeting, walks past a small group of employees towards to the conference room.

"Can I help you?" asks one of the employees.

"I want to see Mr. Ströer."

"He is still in his room."

"Then call him please."

"Concerning what?"

"We had arranged to meet."

"I can't disturb the boss just like that, maybe he is still asleep. We had a late night yester … working."

That very moment the boss turns up. "Udo, my boy," he greets Müller. "Let's have a coffee. Have you had breakfast?" He tells his employees to start the meeting without him.

Once alone, Ströer asks a strange question: "What is it you want to achieve in life, Udo?"

Müller only thinks about it briefly. "To sit in front of a hut somewhere in the Himalayas and not own anything." Ströer is not sure whether it's meant ironically. Possibly one of those esoteric sayings.

Without thinking about it further, Ströer comes to the point. He had asked Müller to come to Frankfurt to talk about a joint project.

"There are interesting developments in the East," the entrepreneur begins. Without pussyfooting around, and with a smile, he adds: "But you know that." Then he talks about his idea.

The economies of the Eastern bloc countries were in a state of flux, and Hungary was the most liberal of all the socialist states. They were only waiting for ideas and investment from the West. Ströer had contacts for developing outdoor advertising in Budapest and other Hungarian cities. He talks for about a quarter of an hour. Finally, he says: "So, Udo, wouldn't that be something for you? You take that on for me, and we take it from there."

Müller hadn't said a word. Of course, he could imagine cooperating with the older man, but not like that. It should be on equal terms. "You take that on for me." That sentence had annoyed him. It didn't sound like a real partnership. And under no circumstances is he prepared to be outsmarted.

"I don't think that's for me," he says after a short pause.

Ströer is surprised. "Think about it," he says. "Let's go to Budapest together, and then you can decide." Then he mentions his second issue, which is obviously more important to him than Hungary. The special size board project.

He wants to cooperate with Müller on the oversized billboards. The tobacco industry in particular likes the larger sized panels, because they would remind people of the shape of cigarette packets. Ströer had already secured more than 500 sites all over Germany, but that would not be enough for his clients to create and print the extra-large posters. Reynolds, owners of the Camel brand, was finding things much too slow.

"You know, Schubert from Reynolds advised me to look for a partner, look for this Müller for example, from Lunenburg & Partner, he said." After a short pause Ströer adds: "What do you think?"

Later Müller cannot remember exactly why he spontaneously agreed. It was not his usual style. Maybe he felt flattered, but maybe it was because he found the idea genuinely good.

HISTORY LESSONS

The Wall comes down, the path is free

From the corner of his eye, with the sound turned down, and while he is on the phone, Udo Müller watches the 7 o'clock news on TV. He is about to leave for an event celebrating Berlin's first private radio station's 10th anniversary. Maybe he could do with letting off some steam. The past few weeks had been quite stressful.

November 9th, 1989, is one of those drab autumn days in Berlin. For the whole day, a cold and damp airstream had been blowing in from the Atlantic. The atmosphere is tense.

Everywhere in the East – the "state of workers and farmers" – socialist rule had been slowly collapsing. The Monday demonstrations in Leipzig are now attended by tens of thousands of people. They demonstrate fearlessly for more freedom. In East Berlin, too, demonstrations have become a weekly event. The mood of the people is getting more and more threatening for the SED leadership. But in West Berlin, life seems to be quite normal.

This Thursday, the Central Committee of the SED, the only party in the country, is meeting in the House of Ministries on the corner of Wilhelm and Leipziger Strasse, the former ministry building of the Nazis' air force. Nothing much has changed here since the end of the war. It is the second round of a non-public meeting scheduled to last three days. On the agenda is the high debt level to the West. The atmosphere is tense. The GDR has lived beyond its means for years, and now even the highest ranked ministers are complaining. They demand solutions.

Müller's concept for advertising billboards is not on the agenda. It would be just a drop in the ocean. Today they are asking for widespread, major solutions, not just small actions. The mass protests that have been going on for weeks are putting pressure on the people in power. Additionally, citizens are leaving the country in droves via Hungary and Prague.

In October, Erich Honecker was forced out of office, toppled by his own comrades. Representatives of the Home Office and Security in East Berlin are working on new regulations for travel, directed by Egon Krenz, the new number one. The pressure needs a release valve.

On this November 9th Müller too is busy with an inter-German issue. In the afternoon, he is attending a meeting at *Interwerbung* about more permits for billboards on GDR territory along the Wall. The comrades agree to all his suggestions. At about 6 p.m., he returns to his office, crossing the border at Heinestrasse, as usual.

At the same time, a televised press conference is about to start in the East Berlin House of Ministries. The new government spokesperson Günther Schabowski has only been in his post for a few weeks. He is a jovial comrade in his early 50s and now informs the foreign media correspondents about the meeting of the Central Committee. Journalists from West Berlin and the Federal Republic have to be registered as foreign correspondents too.

Just under an hour passes without any particular news, but then Schabowski reads out a resolution by the Council of Ministries which has been handed to him by party leader Krenz just before the press conference.

Schabowski himself reads the text about "Travel relief for GDR citizens" for the first time. His voice is somewhat muffled: "... private travel abroad can be applied for without conditions (such as special occasions or family connections). Permits will be granted at short notice."

When a journalist asks when the new regulations will be introduced, Schabowski again looks down at his paper, slightly unsure, but can't find any reference to the timing. Attempting to appear at least half informed, he says: "To my mind, with immediate effect. Now ..."

A West German news channel is reporting live from the Schabowski press conference. That is the program Müller is following in the background. But gradually he grasps the meaning of all this. What did that spokesman say? The GDR is opening its borders? Müller quickly turns the volume up and immediately wonders what it means for himself and his business.

Lost in thoughts of other things, Müller drives to the radio station's party. There are more than 400 guests, from politics, economics, and culture, but there is only one topic of discussion, which is spreading like wildfire. No travel restrictions for GDR citizens! However, nobody yet believes that the border could fall altogether.

Around 9 o'clock, one of the guests jumps on stage and shouts: "The border is open, the Trabis are coming!" Now Müller can't hold back any longer. He has to leave the event, run to his car, and drive to Checkpoint Charlie.

The checkpoint, the most important border crossing between East and West since the start of the Cold War, is only a few kilometres away. During the Cuban Missile Crisis of 1962, the year Müller was born, American and Soviet tanks were facing each other here, ready to attack. World War Three could have started here. A single stray shot fired at a tank could have triggered a disaster. But the

Soviet and American soldiers held their nerve. There was a positive outcome. That day, when the world held its breath, was consigned to history.

Checkpoint Charlie was a symbol of the Cold War. As we have seen, the museum of modern history on the West side became Müller's first client at *Lunenburg & Partner*. He often stood on the first floor of the museum and looked over to the East, thinking what would have happened if back then even a single shot had been fired.

Now he wants to get to Checkpoint Charlie as quickly as possible. As if in a trance, he drives his Mercedes towards Friedrichstrasse, parks his car near the Springer publishing house and walks to the border. Who knows what to expect. But one thing he can see very clearly: What is happening at this moment is history, real history that will be remembered for a long time. And he is a witness.

Even from afar, Müller can already hear the shouts: "Wir wollen rüber! – We want to come over!" It's coming from the crowd on the other side of the border.

Müller can see the GDR soldiers at the border crossing linking arms, trying to form a human chain across the road. But there is not enough of them, half the road is still open. The American soldiers on the other side stay in their cabins and silently watch the scene.

The growing crowd slowly comes closer to the barriers, driven by an atmosphere of provocation and jubilation. More and more people join them. Traffic ceased more than an hour ago, no car can get through, neither to the East nor the West.

The commanding officer at the check point sends a fax to his superiors: "Violation of the GDR state border from Berlin territory (East). In front of the crossing up to the border about 3,000 people, behind, several hundred citizens on foot and in cars." He waits. No reply.

In desperation, the commanding officer now tries to contact someone in the Ministry for State Security. Nobody answers the phone. No orders are being given. Eventually the officer orders the iron gates to be closed. A few boisterous people rip the caps off the soldiers' heads. What if someone shoots, Müller thinks.

Then a young man simply walks across the border. He moves directly towards Udo Müller, waving his blue GDR passport. He has obviously got past the border control and says: "Over there, they are shouting: 'We want to get out!' It's totally crazy!"

Of course, Müller has observed developments in the GDR over the past few weeks and months. The growing Monday demonstrations in Leipzig, the nervousness of the SED elite. Thanks to his permanent visa, he has been over there often enough. He has sensed the low mood of his business partners, their fear of the future, but also their hope for change.

Müller watches the absurd scene, surrounded by a crowd. The atmosphere is like a street carnival: people are shouting, singing, laughing, dancing. It's ever more apparent that history is being made, and he is right in the middle of it. But how will it all end? What happens if things get out of control and turn violent?

Müller is not the only one having thoughts like that. The night before, the commander at the border crossing had ordered soldiers to hand in their automatic pistols, but they still had their revolvers in their holsters.

Müller can feel the boisterous atmosphere everywhere. Suddenly a fleet of Trabis, horns blaring, rattle past. The border must be open! Somewhere there must already be an open road, maybe several.

He hastily runs back to his car, drives to Brandenburg Gate, and parks up nearby. It's well after midnight. Hundreds of cheering people have climbed on to the Wall, which at this point is nearly two meters wide. Müller is helped up by strangers and enjoys every second of it. Nothing will be the same again. Only yesterday they would have been shot here.

The Brandenburg Gate, symbol of the German divide, is in front of him, illuminated only by dim border lights. Müller has dreamt for a long time of touching the Brandenburg Gate. Now he jumps down from the Wall, three meters and 60 centimeters high, and lands painfully on his hip. He makes it to one of the columns of the Gate, with the damaged sculpture of the Quadriga at the top. The pain will only set in later.

Müller often had conversations with his partners at *Interwerbung* about the critical situation in the GDR and once joked: "When I can touch the Brandenburg Gate, the GDR will be a free country." Now he remembers how they answered: "You will have to wait a long, long time for that." It was just meant to be a harmless joke, nothing more.

But now he is standing at the symbol of the German divide, and his hands reverently touch the rough sandstone, the faded paint and the bullet holes from the final battles of the Second World War.

What a night! Müller doesn't feel the cold and dampness anymore. At some point between 1 and 2 o'clock, he walks along the former elegant boulevard *Unter den Linden* towards the East Berlin TV tower, the landmark of the GDR capital, visible for miles around. Since the 1960s, the slender tower has been the proud symbol of socialist power, 200 meters high. The massive globe of glass and steel on the top was to remind people of the glorious success of the Soviet Sputnik satellite. But now the symbolism is empty. Müller throws his arms around the tower as if he wants to embrace it.

He is still not tired. It's 3 o'clock in the morning. Müller runs to his car and drives towards the border crossing Invalidenstrasse. He parks the car. Here, too, there are cheering crowds. It's a historic moment.

He then thinks he can see Stefan Heym in the crowd, the famous writer, well-known in the West as well as in the East. Müller has just read Heym's latest novel, *Five Days in June*, a reckoning with the Stalinist past of the GDR. This and other works have caused many problems for the awkward writer in the GDR. He was considered an "undesired" citizen. But Heym had stayed in his homeland, in his heart still a socialist.

Müller had loved the writer since his school days and had referenced him in his final history essay. Now the man is standing right next to him. But Udo is reluctant to address the old man in the beret and with his long white hair. After a few moments he disappears in the crowd. It was Heym, or was it …? Yes, it was, Udo Müller is sure of it, and now he is mad at himself for not having spoken to the writer.

Historical events only rarely reveal their lasting meaning at the moment they occur. But the night of November 9th in East and West Berlin is different. Disbelief about the sudden fall of the Wall is short-lived. The people's emotions soon break through. They are drunk with happiness.

It's a completely different picture among those who have defended the GDR for many years. In desperation, the old SED functionaries now try to save what is not savable anymore. Like a brood of nervous chickens, the directors of state-owned factories and manufacturing plants, the top guns of the socialist economy, now hurriedly offer their services to the advance parties of capitalists travelling the country on the lookout for things they can use.

Müller's business partners at *Interwerbung* are uncertain. Some of them hope to start a new career in a reformed GDR. Others are already adjusting to the market economy in the West. They are sure that the system will be reorganised in the style of the capitalists. One must adapt quickly .

Companies in the West are also looking for new horizons. There are 16 million people who have been shielded from consumerism but who can now be supplied with all the lovely things that only yesterday seemed unattainable. Cars, cars mostly. And television sets, video recorders. Cigarettes. Western brands, of course, not the GDR stuff, which burns the tongue. There is a lot of scope for a lot of business. The people hope for better times and a bright future. Goodbye to "making do"!

At the same time, civil rights campaigners are trying to create order amid the rapid democratic changes in socialist communities. Nobody had been able to prepare for the Wall coming down, and definitely not for its consequences. There are changes everywhere, and a fear of an uncertain future.

On November 10th, about half a million people respond to a call for a demonstration on East Berlin's Alexanderplatz. The SPD leader Willy Brandt tells the crowd: "Now what belongs together will grow together!" Another sentence for the history books.

That day, Udo Müller also starts adapting to a GDR that is now modelling itself on the West. Friedrichstrasse was yesterday. Today the new Federal States are all open to him. Very soon the rules of competition will replace the old system of a centrally planned economy. The race to find the best starting block has begun. The agile young entrepreneur knows this. And he wants to be a part of it when the failed socialist state begins its long walk towards capitalism. He wants to be a part of it from the very beginning. Müller has his own vision of the future. His billboards, his advertising columns and bus shelter panels will cover the country from the sea to the mountains. Finally, his vision can become reality.

Everything is happening at breathtaking speed. The GDR is still alive, but the socialism of the SED kind is dead. Müller can expand his dealings with *Interwerbung* without a hitch. He can now erect billboards in the East Berlin districts of Marzahn and Mitte, Friedrichshain and Pankow. Before that, he had been confined to sites near the border. The German Democratic Republic is still a sovereign state with border crossings and controls. But it won't stay like that for long, Müller is quite sure. He is aware of the psychological climate in East Germany.

He puts up posters around Friedrichstrasse station, just as he did before the Wall came down, mostly adverts for cigarettes and washing powder. New boards also turn up, measuring nine square meters.

The day after the Wall comes down, Udo has a long conversation with his new friend Heiner Ströer in Cologne. Very quickly the young entrepreneur and the experienced businessman agree: They will cooperate closely in the future and soon establish a joint company focusing on outdoor advertising in the new Federal States. The future was taking shape.

Müller and Ströer now meet up regularly. The Cologne advertiser is also determined to go into business in the East, in partnership with Udo. They are a strong double act, that's for sure. But, as usual, he is cautious. His young friend, however, sees his chances and pushes for speed. The experienced entrepreneur and the young buck – can it end well?

Udo Müller uses a metaphor to describe the situation: "These weeks and months are like a wide open gate to incredible possibilities and opportunities. But each day that gate closes a tiny bit, and so speed is vital."

He wants to take over the best sites for outdoor advertising, from north to south, straight away. But that won't work without problems. At the Sonnenallee border crossing, for example, which is still controlled by GDR soldiers, there is a noisy incident at the end of November.

Müller's workers are erecting new advertising panels right next to the now obsolete Wall. A small digger works into late afternoon, digging holes for posts. Then there is a sudden loud bang, and the whole of the brightly lit crossing is cloaked in darkness. Armed soldiers are nervously running around. Commands can be heard. Handheld flares light up.

After several minutes of confusion, they track down the source of the bang. The digger cut the main electricity cable. The border soldiers are still not sure whether it was an accident. But luckily a top employee of *Interwerbung* is around. He explains the incident to his comrades and convinces the commanding officer that this was a mishap, and not an attack on the GDR. Quickly they find a bottle of Scotch, and the atmosphere is calm. Cheers to the new times!

The bang at Sonnenallee was probably the last incident at the inter-German border. And Müller likes the idea that he played a part in it.

Germany's journey toward a unified fatherland goes on. As do Müller's plans.

Winning after the "Wende"

Friday, December 8th, 1989, nearly a month after the fall of the Berlin Wall. It is late morning and Heiner Ströer's

Lufthansa plane lands on time at Tegel airport. Müller is waiting for him. They are planning to go to Dresden together for an appointment with the city's administrators, arranged by Udo. Ströer's greeting isn't as friendly as usual. He's got a toothache and suggests they first go to the Ku'damm for a coffee, but Müller is in a hurry. "We've got an appointment to keep, Heiner."

Never waste any time. Shortly after the fall of the Wall, Müller had started to look for contacts in the town halls of the larger cities in the East, like Dresden, Leipzig, Jena and Rostock. He always asked for the deputy mayor, and for good reason. During socialist times, the second-in-command was responsible for finances. That is still true. But during these weeks of change, decisions are more and more taken, or at least prepared, at a "round table" of various institutions.

Heiner Ströer is not as euphoric as Müller, but of course he has his own thoughts. What does the new situation mean for him and his company? Are there really that many opportunities in the East, or will the changed GDR pursue a path he should, at least initially, steer clear of? The situation is very unpredictable.

The process of change is in full swing. A few months before the fall of the Wall, the aging president Erich Honecker had been toppled by his own comrades. Now his successor, Egon Krenz, who is already floundering, has to meet the demands of the people. Just like the new president, Dresden's longtime mayor Hans Modrow, who is trying to protect the last strongholds of the SED, the only party.

But in an equally dramatic way, the power of the SED is vanishing on all levels – even in small towns and villages the socialist functionaries are losing power. Only the remnants of a failed system remain. The SED officials, rulers at Moscow's behest, have lost everywhere.

The winner is the West. Heiner Ströer wants to exploit this unique opportunity. And his new friend Udo seems to be the right partner for it. But Heiner is reluctant to take part in an adventure he is slightly unsure about.

Leading functionaries try to remain in power by making their own plans for reform. A quick unification with the Federal Republic is not yet on the agenda.

Heiner Ströer is not very enthusiastic as he gets into Udo Müller's Mercedes and immediately begins to articulate his doubts. On the plane, he had read a *Spiegel* article on "people in panic" about the collapsing GDR economy. The situation was uncertain, and he thinks it would be best to wait a bit. Only yesterday, he received some information from his professional association warning of legal problems when doing business with the GDR.

But there is another reason why Heiner Ströer is reluctant. In the West, he had concentrated on partnerships with private property owners. But in the GDR, there are hardly any private properties. Land and buildings usually belong to the state, as do factories, companies, and institutions. In the West, public advertising space is considered a separate business section, overseen by *Deutsche Städte Reklame* (DSR) and their community officials. Ströer knows that the DSR will expand its business to the GDR. Should he really go into battle against the DSR when he could never compete with it at home? These are the thoughts that go through his head on the journey to Dresden. The weather is grey, the landscape is even greyer, the towns and villages are in a deplorable state. And he's got a toothache!

Ströer's mood doesn't get any better after they leave the autobahn and drive towards the city of Dresden. It's not an enchanting view. All the houses need renovation, the roads are littered with potholes. Heiner Ströer is not easily depressed, but all this makes him feel very low.

The Dresden town hall is in a complex of massive, grey buildings at the Alter Markt (old market) in the city center. Müller parks his Mercedes next to two or three similar vehicles with Western number plates. They walk the last few meters, past a larger-than-life statue titled "Trümmerfrau". The bronze monument from the 1950s is to remind people how Dresden was rebuilt after the war. Now again, one has to turn ruins into new life. Socialism is on its knees.

Ströer looks up to the blackened stone figures on the side of the bleak building, dating from Prussia's glorious times. There is an inscription under each of them: "Strength and Sacrifice"; "Faith and Belief"; "Wisdom and Goodness". These are symbols of the old Reich, but now severely dated. They are surpassed by the massive 100-meter-high tower of the council building.

It is nearly 4 o'clock in the afternoon, bang on time, when Müller and Ströer enter the building. A guard in a dark uniform asks for their identification. So they still do those controls here. They are sent up to the first floor and asked to wait.

"Like at the dentist," Ströer hisses morosely. Then Müller is called. Three men meet them in a small office. They are to deal with the first flurry of managers and entrepreneurs from the West.

The atmosphere is friendly as Heiner and Udo present their plans. Ströer offers to set up 180 billboards around Dresden for the elections on March 10th, which can be used by the various political parties. Free of charge. In return, Ströer wants to use them commercially after the elections.

The three men have a short discussion among themselves, then pronounce: "Sounds good. Please telex us your offer. You will get a decision immediately."

Müller interrupts: "We don't have a telex. Can we fax it?"

"Fax? We don't have a fax."

There it is again, those small differences in terms of technical progress. The telex is a remnant of the 1930s, when the Deutsche Reichspost, the old German postal company, offered this public service. The gadget, lovingly called the "ticker" because of its sound, was the main means of communication until the 1970s. Faxes took over during the 1980s, and the typewriter-like devices with punched tape streaming out of them were consigned to museums. Well, in the West, that is.

In the East, the old machines are still in use. There are even different networks for the public, the army, and the Stasi, but they have one thing in common: technically they are completely obsolete.

Müller looks quizzically at Ströer. The older man offers a compromise. "We have an old Telex in the basement, and we'll get it going again. It should work."

It does work. And now the decision is due.

Sports unite the world

A few days later, the tender is on its way to the Office for Media and the Economy in Dresden. Like everywhere else in the GDR before the elections of a communal parliament, representatives of all parties and groups are to make political decisions, including rights and obligations, as representatives of the "people". It is a democratic transition.

The representatives of often opposite groups meet for so called "round table" talks. From the central round table in Berlin down to those in smaller communities, first decisions are being made that may lead to a new and better future, hopefully with more freedom and democracy.

January 9th, 1990, is a Tuesday. The city's Round Table is meeting again in Dresden town hall. This is the appointment our two advertising experts had been looking forward to desperately. The steps toward the new future will have to be carved out as quickly as possible. But today the building is more crowded than they had expected. In the corridor numerous smartly dressed gentlemen are waiting. There's not a single woman in sight. The takeover of the GDR seems to be a predominantly masculine affair.

Then the door to the discussion room opens and a tall man comes out. Müller and Ströer recognise his face. They know him, but he doesn't know them. Hanischfeger is one of the top managers of the media giant Bertelsmann. A short time later our two are called into the room.

"That's something," Ströer whispers. "First they ask a global company, and then us." Udo smiles. Together they enter the dimly lit conference room. The pair had agreed on their proposal. The older man offers his experience and the necessary starting capital. The younger doesn't have any money but is hellishly ambitious. Müller can see the run-down GDR already covered with advertising posters.

A middle-aged man greets them in a friendly manner and introduces the other business partners. Ströer studies the people in the room with curiosity. At first glance, it is a somewhat peculiar group. Beards, long hair, grey jackets, hand-knitted jumpers. But he senses a spirit of adventure, sees optimism and zest for action in their faces, and he feels quite moved.

Immediately, the successful entrepreneur is transported back to the 1950s when he broke out of his close-knit home town to conquer the world. The people here probably have the same feeling, he thinks. Great!

The chair turns to the guests from the West. "Gentlemen, please present your proposals." Ströer's sonorous voice fills the room. His is more than a business proposition. He talks in moving words about the historic dimension of these weeks, congratulates the Dresden people for their peaceful revolution and the journey to freedom and democracy which had been suppressed by a dictatorial power for such a long time.

He then starts telling his own story. The freedom offered after the fall of the Nazi dictatorship was his chance to choose a completely new path and embrace new opportunities. "I wish you the same freedom," he concludes. "You have every chance to create democratic communities, with a space for everyone. The doors to individual success are wide open." These are the words of an experienced entrepreneur who is used to taking on responsibility, a responsibility the socialist state had suppressed, and which had to be learned anew.

The others listen to him in silence. Müller has never heard his fatherly friend talk like this. Later he confesses that he nearly shed a tear, and the same was true for many others in the room.

Then the two explain their offer to put up 180 billboards for the March elections, which can be used for free by the parties. In return, Ströer wants to use those boards for commercial advertising afterwards. The city would get a percentage of the turnover.

It sounds fair. Ströer gets the provisional go-ahead from the Round Table. The contract with the executive branch, the city's administration, is to be drawn up later.

Then Müller asks to speak. There isn't much time until the first free elections in March 1990, and definitely not for the campaign beforehand. He says he has prepared a contract with the same conditions as in the West, which he advises would best be signed immediately so work can start straight away.

That makes sense. After a short phone call, Ströer and Müller are taken upstairs to the office of the city's administration director Rudi Hladitsch. Hladitsch mentions that he originally comes from the Baltic coast, from Rostock.

"I once played handball in Rostock with the *Foxes*," Müller recalls. And now it all comes back, his past as a handball pro. He will never forget January 9th, 1983, as it was his most spectacular game. The *Foxes* were in third place in the European Cup competition.

Hladitsch smiles. "I remember the match. I did the announcements that evening." And suddenly the two strangers, in a nearly reunited Germany, immediately delve into fond common memories. "Do you remember ...?"

That January, eight years ago, the *Foxes* were fighting for a place in the semi-finals. Their opponents were *Empor* Rostock. It wasn't only a difficult match in a sporting sense. SED officials often presented meetings like this as a battle between the two political systems.

Müller remembers it very clearly. The *Foxes*, with a few hundred fans from West Berlin, went to the Baltic coast as the clear outsiders. *Empor* were considered an internationally renowned team, and their superstar Frank-Michael Wahl was the best player at the time.

The first half turned out as expected. After 10 minutes of the second half, Rostock were ahead by five goals, 14:9. But then the chase began. The Berlin men scored one goal after another, their opponents hardly at all. Shortly before the end, the *Foxes* led by one goal, 17:16.

The *Foxes* fans cheered and shouted and made a hell of a racket with their shrill little whistles. On the GDR channel, the speaker Hladitsch said: "What you hear in the background is not the sirens of the boats in Rostock harbor, but the mechanical emotions of our guests from West Berlin."

Müller's memories now come thick and fast. There were two minutes left in the game. Now came his most significant moment: The Rostock goalkeeper could only knock away a throw by the *Foxes* after a fast counterattack. Müller dived into the circle and pushed the ball with his fingertips, and the ball rolled into the goal. 18:16! Then came another attack from the home team that Wöller saved magnificently. Then the final whistle. The *Foxes* had beaten one of the world's best handball teams. It was a sensation.

Müller's goal was particularly celebrated. The TV sport programs repeatedly showed his dive into the circle, slowing it down and enlarging it. The Berlin papers carried a drawing of it.

The home game in Berlin, in front of 10,000 people in the Deutschlandhalle, was no less dramatic. This time Rostock won 14:12.

The aggregate score from both games was 32:32 – a draw. But the larger number of away goals scored by the *Foxes* determined the outcome. The *Foxes* were in the semi-final. It was the best result in the history of the club at that point.

Serious contract negotiations are paused for even longer as Müller remembers another episode from the post-match banquet, held in the clubhouse of the West Berliners. Sponsor and *Foxes* owner Willi Bendzko took Rostock's star Frank-Michael Wahl aside and tried secretly to persuade him to stay in the West using flattery and the promise of heaps of money. Bendzko tried to make Wahl the icing on the cake of his star-studded team.

There was already a car waiting outside with a running engine to take the defector to safety from the Stasi officers in the main room. But Wahl rejected the offer because of his family who lived in Rostock. What Müller didn't know was that at the exact time he and Hladitsch were reminiscing about the past, Wahl was negotiating a lucrative contract with another West German club. A year later he played in the Bundesliga and in the unified German national team.

After the Rostock game, the *Foxes* didn't get any further in the European Cup. They lost both times against the top Soviet team Zaporizhia.

After the recollections, negotiations continue in a relaxed and friendly atmosphere. The partners sign a contract regarding the 180 billboards. For strategic reasons, the men from the West avoid going for as much profit as possible and agree on the same conditions as they have with West German communities.

"Our aim is a long-term reliable partnership," Müller says and means it. For him January 9th, 1990, will be the start of a successful future.

Good Wessie, bad Wessie

Over the subsequent days and weeks, Udo Müller travels from town to town in the former GDR, negotiating at Round Tables, meeting newly installed mayors and, if need be, old functionaries. He has no time for a social life. His priority is to cover the budding new Federal States with billboards and adverts, and he must always get there faster than his competitors.

Müller knows that these weeks present a unique opportunity. He thinks of the post-war era, the 1950s and the 1960s. During those decades, German businesses created an economic miracle in a newly founded democracy. He still wishes to have been part of it, as Heiner had. But Müller started in the 1980s, when all the claims had been staked out and the cards had been dealt.

But now history seems to repeat itself. Only, everything will be faster. Days, weeks, months go by like a whirlwind. Whoever is too late now only has himself to blame. Famous words by Mikhail Gorbachev spoken to the recalcitrate GDR leadership. But they didn't listen.

As quickly as possible, Müller sets up a team, finds office space, rents storage. He ignores the warning of the West German advertising association to be careful drawing up contracts because of the unsettled legal situation. He wants to exploit all possibilities before the window of opportunity closes again.

In this pioneering spirit of a new Germany growing together again, there are opportunities everywhere. You only had to grab them. Courageous innovators are at the forefront. The legal situation is vague, and risks cannot be calculated easily, but the first few months seem to be important to pave the way for the coming years. What a stroke of luck, the 27-year-old Müller thinks. Things like this only happen once in a lifetime.

Heiner Ströer had made approximately 1,4 million Dollar available for investment. In 1990, even for the German advertising king, it was not easy to put up such a large sum. But it seems worth the risk. Heiner trusts his young partner. Maybe there is a bit of vanity at play: the new company with Udo is registered as *Ströer City Marketing*. Heiner insists on his name in the company's logo, Müller doesn't care what it is called. He is content to run it according to his ideas. Heiner carries on with his business in the old Federal Republic. Udo is allowed to whizz around in the East, with all the risks involved. The older man only insists on solid bookkeeping and regular reports.

A lot of the agreements with the municipalities and Round Tables might be questioned again after the elections for the East German Parliament on March 18th and particularly after the local elections on May 6th. There is a risk that all contracts and agreements with the old administration will need to be checked and potentially renegotiated.

There's a hint of it in Potsdam, even before the elections. In the new capital of the Federal State of Brandenburg, Müller had presented his concept regarding the setting up of billboards on public land to the provisionary councils and administrations. They had signed a contract.

The core of the agreement between the cities and the Ströer company is the usual standard contract, the same as the company agrees with communities in West Germany. "There must be no difference in the contracts between East and West," Müller has repeatedly said. "Everything has to be transparent and open." His partner agreed. It was important to stick to the principles of honorable business.

Transparency is also crucial. More and more GDR citizens, who were suspicious of the old structures, are now just as mistrustful of the new characters from the other Germany who are combing through the East in droves, looking for cheap opportunities. They fear the country is being sold off.

And, indeed, some of the remaining old functionaries try to settle business quickly in their favor. From the West, the fortune hunters have set off in droves to exploit the capitalist vacuum in the East. Müller wants to avoid even the slightest suspicion that he is doing the same.

But it doesn't always work. In Potsdam the young entrepreneur experiences his first setback.

On the evening of January 16th, 1990, only a few days after the Potsdam deal, he happens to get news about a press conference focusing on the business of the West German company Ströer.

A group calling itself "Argus for the environment and town planning" ("Arbeitsgemeinschaft für Umweltschutz und Stadtgestaltung") is inviting journalists to the former Stasi building at 11 o'clock the next day.

Müller attends, more out of curiosity then concern, and without an invite. He is shocked to hear what *Ströer Marketing* is accused of. They talk of a secret contract with former communists in the council. They read passages from the contract, punctuated by highly critical comments. The atmosphere is tetchy.

Müller is annoyed and takes the microphone. It was a "peculiar interpretation of democracy" that he, as a person concerned, hadn't even been invited to explain his plans. A big man walks towards Müller and shouts: "You only want to destroy our jobs, you liar!" For the journalists present, the roles too have been divided up – here are the cheated Ossies, there the greedy Wessies.

Müller isn't given a chance to explain his plans. To calm the atmosphere, he agrees to have clear-the-air talks with the leader of the Argus group. She invites him to her flat in the afternoon. Müller tries to explain the economic principles of his company and the rules for outdoor advertising as well as the financial advantages for the city of Potsdam.

He feels that the conversation is going well and concludes in an optimistic tone: "We have talked a lot. I always put my cards on the table and would be grateful if you could present my position to your group in a more balanced way."

"We haven't talked about anything," comes the sharp answer. "You have only tried for two hours to influence me. I don't believe a single word you said." Müller is shocked and disappointed and walks back to his car. He hadn't expected such a suspicious attitude.

The next day the headline in a Potsdam newspaper states: "Secret deal with Western company." The other papers don't present it much differently. Müller is suddenly the archetype of a greedy Wessie who does business with former communists.

The whole Potsdam project is now at stake. There is more and more pressure on the council. People who had voted for the contract before are suddenly unavailable. What should he do?

After several phone conversations with his Cologne-based partner, Müller gives up Potsdam. He is very disappointed. But he quickly realises what had really been behind this rebellion. A short time later, a competitor from the West takes on the outdoor advertising for the city, and not on better conditions. There must have been other powers at work. Well, other Wessies.

Obviously, life not only punishes those who come too late, the opposite can also be true. Müller was too early and got caught between political frontlines and differing economic interests. Tough luck. Forget it. Move on.

Hard but fair

In order to secure as many sites as possible as quickly as possible, Müller organises his own sales force for acquiring new customers, modelled on the system run by insurance companies. He divides the country into districts, roughly matching the new Federal States. Each district is appointed a leader, who divides his/her territory into smaller parts and employs his/her own people searching for new sites.

It is the first time such an organisation has been set up in the East, but it follows the same principle Müller had employed when looking for sites in the West. That was two years ago, when he bumped into Heiner Ströer, also looking for sites. Sometimes history does repeat itself.

Müller now also spots a chance to get a foothold in the market for so-called street furnishing on public sites. This concerns advertising on bus shelters, clock towers, information boards, high-tech public toilets or kiosks. This kind of outdoor advertising had been invented by the French advertising company JCDecaux. In the Federal Republic, it is mainly run by *Deutsche Städte Reklame* (DSR).

The young entrepreneur and his employees are regularly visiting large publicly owned manufacturing plants and factories, which often occupy a lot of land in town centers. They also seek out the owners of private properties. In the larger cities, local scouts search the streets for suitable buildings and sites. Müller's people are highly motivated. They are always the first to look for advertising space in their own neighborhoods. And for each signed contract they earn hard cash.

Compared with this part of the business, the production of the wooden, nine square meter advertising panels is very slow. Müller has given the contracts to build them to local companies. They are all excellent craftsmen, but the sudden rush of orders and time pressure is obviously too much for many of them. The production of the boards often holds up the whole process.

There is, for example, a company that specialises in building work for exhibitions and trade fairs. They need nearly half a day to produce one of the standardised panels. Müller is horrified. One of Ströer's companies in the West would take about half an hour. But they lack modern tools – there are no electric drills, no nail guns – and instead they offer solid craftsmanship with plane and chisel, tools straight from a museum.

Müller takes the boss of the workshop to Berlin, where a subcontractor has been manufacturing Ströer panels for the past few weeks using modern equipment. "Look, that's how quickly it can be done with the right equipment," Müller says and promises to obtain the suitable tools. But the head of the company remains skeptical. "No, Mr. Müller, we simply can't work that fast."

It doesn't take long to show them that they can work that fast after all. Mr. Müller sees to it. More and more sites and spaces are becoming available. Everything develops so quickly that the generous starting capital is nearly gone.

Müller then gets an offer for a further 200 sites. Will things have to slow down because of a lack of money? In a meek fax sent one grey Sunday, Udo admits that his starting capital is nearly gone and asks his partner for advice. "What shall I do?"

Early Monday morning, Heiner calls him back. "Udo, carry on. We are buying."

"I thought we were running out of money."

"It will be possible. But you have to promise me one thing. Slow down a bit and don't open up another office for a while."

After this short conversation, Müller understood a couple of things about how their further cooperation would pan out. For one thing, Ströer's economic plans are clearly flexible, and there is more money available for investment than he lets on. Furthermore, Heiner still trusts him. The show goes on!

The potential clients for advertising in the East are crazy about the new opportunities. The agencies are practically queuing up at *Ströer City Marketing*. Between the sea and the mountains in the East, 16 million new consumers are to be wooed as soon as possible, to experience the leap from an impoverished economy to the world of consumerism.

Müller's agency reports one success after another. By spring 1991, 7,500 sites have been rented out all over the East for the coming autumn. But only 2,500 billboards have been erected so far – only one third.

Heiner Ströer is impressed. It had taken him more than 20 years to get his current 15,000 advertising sites. The post-war era of reconstruction seems to be repeating itself, but at breakneck speed.

The crucial part of the process is still the production of the wooden panels. Clients have booked their adverts for sites that don't yet exist.

Müller's aim had been to become the leader in East Germany's outdoor advertising market, but because he didn't have enough money at the start, he had altered his usual process.

Before this rapid expansion, the first step was to identify a good site for an advert and contact the owner. Then they would draw up a contract about the site's use. After waiting for official permission, he would start building the panel, and only when the panel was up would he start offering it to clients. It could be another two or three months until the actual poster was fixed to the board.

Following this process, Ströer had to shell out money months in advance – and the speed at which Udo Müller was working in East Germany meant the advance sums had been rising astronomically to several million Dollar.

So, Müller changed his strategy and offered the advertising sites in advance. The income started flowing much sooner. The expenses for rent and production of the billboards could be refinanced much quicker.

But what if the panels for the posters were not ready for the first bookings?

That is exactly the problem he faced in Berlin in August 1991. At the beginning of September, about 400 more sites had been let than there were panels to place on them – prepaid, as usual. It would be an expensive scandal if it couldn't be resolved. Müller, in a panic, calls all available gangs of workers to the capital to catch up. They work in two shifts and get all the panels done.

The posters are hung where they should be, just in time. Heiner Ströer is quietly pleased that his young partner is also able to manage a crisis.

Like in a trance

Now Germany is a united country again. Müller and Ströer also made their partnership official on March 20th, 1990. That's the day they signed the company contract for *Ströer City Marketing GmbH,* based in Cologne. Heiner Ströer continues to lead his group of companies in the West and remains the overall manager. The new venture, however, belongs to both of them equally and is designed to open up the market in East Germany. It is run by Müller alone.

The elections of March 18th, 1990, make the political situation clear. The CDU is the strongest party, mainly because Helmut Kohl promises sunny uplands to the brothers and sisters of East Germany, while the Social Democrat candidate prophesies hard times. Who wouldn't choose the sunny uplands?

The GDR districts become Federal States and are reorganised along pre-war borders.

But for Udo Müller one problem remains. What will happen to *Lunenburg & Partner,* of which he still owns one third? Lunenburg and Dieter Nerlich are annoyed because they hardly ever see Udo now. But the partners eventually agree: Müller sells his share in the agency at the symbolic price of 25,000 Dollar. He remains a silent partner in future *L + P Medienservice GmbH*, and Lunenburg and Nerlich carry on their business without him.

During this time of rapid development, our young entrepreneur feels as if he is in a trance. "It's the Wild East here," he says when he reports to Cologne. "It's quite incredible what is happening." Müller is in his element: working alone, applying his own strategies.

But the greatest danger to him is himself. He travels around the new Federal States for seven days a week. Sometimes, when he is overcome by tiredness, he pulls over, has a short nap, and then convinces himself he has the strength for the next few hours. He senses his physical limits but ignores them.

At the end of 1990, he moves to Dresden – above the "Blue Wonder", the internationally-renowned cantilever bridge across the Elbe, once considered a masterpiece of Saxon engineering. At the end of the 19th century, Dresden was a flourishing royal residency, and the hills above the Elbe were the most desirable neighborhoods.

This didn't change despite four decades of socialism. The Ministry for State Security kept a remarkable guest house in the area with stunning views across the city. The building, surrounded by a large park, was built in the 1830s by a wealthy company owner. This exclusive address, occupied by the Stasi during the GDR era, was so secret that it wasn't registered anywhere. Number 6 Hermann Proll-Strasse didn't officially exist, not even to the justice department.

It was here, protected from outside eyes, that Russian secret service officers met with their colleagues from the Stasi. It was also here, reports say, that the young and ambitious. KGB officer Vladimir Vladimirovich Putin spent many a night drinking vodka and perhaps dreaming of a glorious future.

This was where Erich Honecker and his comrades relaxed. Cuba's Castro and North Korea's Kim-il Sung stayed the night. Bayern's First Minister Franz Josef Strauss slept here on one of his secret visits to the GDR – in a room bugged all over. He negotiated millions of loans to, among other people, Alexander Schalck Golodkowski, head of the department of commercial coordination.

And now Udo Müller. He has found a place to stay in this villa, renting one of the apartments in the mostly empty building, but which still exudes the old socialist glamour. He is looked after lovingly by a couple of caretakers.

But Müller doesn't always stay in such lush surroundings. Quite the opposite: most hotels are booked up when he finds himself looking for a place to stay at the end of a day. He often sleeps in one of the many privately owned B&Bs across the country. He can do without much comfort, as long as he finds a bed somewhere.

At the end of one long day in the autumn of 1991, Udo goes back to his place in the Saxony town of Chemnitz. The room is in a small building adjacent to the main house. His hosts apologise that they can't offer him anything better, but Müller doesn't care. He is exhausted, lies down on the straw mattress and drops off immediately.

At some point in the night he wakes up abruptly. He is itching. He scratches his arm. But it gets worse. Now the itching is everywhere. He jumps up and finds the reason: Bedbugs, everywhere, mean little bedbugs. They are small insects, hardly visible, but particularly unpleasant parasites. Müller even remembers the Latin name for the tiny bloodsuckers: *cimex lectularius*. His medical course hadn't been completely in vain. But it doesn't make the situation more tolerable.

He spends the final hours of that night in his car, scratching and itching until the morning. He sometimes drops off, but proper sleep is impossible. In the morning, his hosts are inconsolable about this attack on their guest and don't want to accept the agreed payment for the room. It turns out that the old straw mattress had been on the bed since the Second World War.

The next night, Udo is determined, he will be back in his Dresden place or home in his Berlin flat.

The rivals wake up

The Dresden office of the Müller-Ströer company is also near the Blue Wonder bridge over the Elbe. It comprises two rooms in a kind of shed, with only rudimentary furnishings: two desks, a few chairs, a phone. In the adjacent shed are the materials for sticking up advertising posters: buckets of glue, brushes, ladders.

And of course the adverts themselves. They consist of A1 format sheets which combine to make the larger posters, nine square meters in size. That means 18 single sheets. In the early days, they are glued to panels of treated birch wood. Later, it's aluminum, which is easier to handle.

Late one afternoon, Müller arrives at the Dresden office and his district manager meets him, looking worried, handing him a letter from Dresden council. "Our contract with the council is under question," he says, his voice trembling slightly. "They want you to appear before an enquiry committee. For corruption, abuse of office and bribery."

Maybe Müller is too exhausted to get upset. "Rubbish," he mumbles and promises the worried man that he will see to it in the morning. "I need some sleep first."

It has been a year since the local elections. Many of the companies once owned by the state are now close to collapse. Everywhere in the former GDR, suspicions are growing against companies from the West and their owners, who are breezing through the former socialist economy attempting to replace it with free market principles. Many.

Many people feel that they are considered collateral damage and arecheated by the businessmen. Entrepreneurs from the West are generally distrusted. It's why all the contracts agreed so far are being reexamined. Müller can understand the anger but knows that he has always acted correctly and fairly. He doesn't panic.

The contract under scrutiny concerns about a hundred advertising sites and columns, which was signed shortly before the elections and after the first agreement about political party advertising. As was the case in Potsdam, it seems Müller is trapped between various interested parties. It might be that he was simply too quick to act here as well.

But this time the young entrepreneur doesn't want to give in so easily and asks Heiner Ströer to come to the meeting with him. His friend always appears an honorable man and may make a better impression on the committee than his own rather breezy manners.

That proves to be exactly the case. After four weeks of detailed investigations all critical questions are answered, and doubts removed. The contract between the City of Dresden and the Ströer company remains valid.

At the same time, the contract is subject to a meeting of the council to be formally confirmed by the deputies. This leads to a memorable scene. Müller is warned anonymously that the committee does not only feature friendly faces. He is told that there may be an unpleasant debate.

Then he receives an offer that might be tempting to many people in his situation. There could be ways and means to reassure his opponents. Did this sound like bribery? Müller rejects the offer but remains a tad unsure. You never know who is pulling the strings in the background.

Furthermore, competing companies are also now fighting for lucrative contracts with the city and for favorable sites. Again, the competition includes Deutsche Städte Reklame, with its brilliant contacts, the Düsseldorf-based Moplak agency and a Koblenz entrepreneur Günter Freund. Not to forget the German subsidiary of the French JCDecaux and the old-school Berlin outdoor advertiser Hans Wall.

Finally, a date is confirmed for the crucial meeting of the city parliament. Müller turns up on time and, unnoticed, takes a seat in the audience. "Contracts for outdoor advertising" is on the agenda. There is only a short debate, followed by a vote, which, to Müller's joy, is unanimously in favour of Ströer.

But there is a surprise. The Berlin advertiser Wall had applied for the advertising rights on Dresden bus shelters and got the contract, which also had to be confirmed by the council.

But when this comes up on the agenda, someone else makes a proposal for a counter initiative. Instead of Wall, they say JCDecaux should get the contract. There is an application to simply replace the name of Wall with that of the French company, and, to Müller's great surprise, it is voted through. Apparently, the French advertiser managed at the very last minute to push its Berlin-based competitor out of the way.

How this happened is not under investigation. Hans Wall, who will later sell his company to JCDecaux, didn't have a chance. Müller is amazed, but at least this didn't concern him directly.

Don't fight with Müller

Trust is a special thing. Trust cannot be bought, it can only be gained. After the first year of German unity, the belief that the West is a force for good is becoming less fervent. Fortune hunters are combing through the East. On the lookout for anything useful, they suck the last breath out of the former state-owned companies. They always promise a lot but end up only exploiting everything that can be exploited.

Since the fall of the Wall in 1989, what was once the wilds of the East have become an Eldorado for financial criminals, fortune hunters, fraudsters, and rip-off merchants. As has always been the case, control mechanisms in the East do not work. There are not enough officials pursuing the crooked businessmen hoping to profiteer from unification.

All business people from the rich West are considered mean Wessies, people to be wary of. You recognise Wessies by their dark, expensive suits and posh ties. The younger ones often use a lot of hair gel.

Of course, there are also good ones, quite a few in fact. But they can't break into the public perception. Bad news always sells better than good news, just as in the media industry. Bad news forms people's opinions.

Müller wants to be one of the good guys, both in person and in the media. Ever since he first started, he has tried very hard to be absolutely fair and clear about his ideas when meeting potential business partners. He is not merely planning to make a quick buck. He wants to build a base for a sustainable business, with an eye to the future.

It's what he does in Halle, where the members of the council have become very suspicious. They want an official tender for the advertising panels. And why not? The best offer should win, after all.

Müller's offer for the community is, as usual, the same as he uses in his standard contracts in the Federal Republic – even though it doesn't really pay enough because of the high initial investment and lower turnover. But for the young Ströer executive, it is a question of transparency and building trust. However, it's not pure altruism. Quite the opposite: he expects the conditions in the East and West to balance out very soon. And when they do, these investments will be profitable for both sides, and the partners in the East won't feel cheated.

So, there is an open tender in Halle. But the department head for planning doesn't know how to organise it. He asks Müller for help because he trusts him. Now Müller is also an adviser. He gives tips, helps with the proposal, explains how it works. He suggests dividing the tender into two parts. One company should get the panels, the other the street furnishings, the shelters at bus stops and similar buildings.

Together with another half dozen advertisers, Müller submits his offer. He wants the panels, and for the street furnishings, he suggests the Düsseldorf company Moplak. Müller is optimistic, not only because of his good connections. He also knows that the conditions he is proposing are good. He knows that he is the favorite of the planning department.

What Müller doesn't know is what goes on behind the scenes. The planning department is responsible for fact-finding, but the final decision is the mayor's. And Müller's competitors sense a chance for intense lobbying. These competitors now work hard behind the scenes. Müller cannot be sure of the outcome.

A few weeks later the item appears on the agenda of a council meeting. But Müller has got appointments in Berlin on this important Thursday and misses it. As soon as he can, he calls the head of planning.

"How did it go?"

"I'm terribly sorry. It went to Deutsche Städte Reklame."

Müller has been outdone.

"Impossible!" Müller is completely surprised. "What happened?"

"There was an instruction from Mr. Bettels ..." then the line breaks down.

Bettels has recently been appointed office manager for the mayor. A young man from northern Germany, only 27 years old. Much too inexperienced, really. But the chaotic times make lightning fast careers like his possible. In the East, what is lacking most are administrative workers with experience in the market economy. Applicants from the West can often snag jobs. Bettels is one of them.

Müller goes to his car, angry. He drives, no, he races from Berlin to Halle and parks in front of the town hall.

In the planning department he is told the following: "Shortly before the meeting, the office manager took away our proposal, which favored Ströer."

"Without any discussion?"

"I'm not getting into a fight with them. If I get dismissed, I'm on the street. Mr. Bettel sits on the lap of the top dog."

Müller tries to remain calm. "I want to talk to Mr. Bettels. Now."

"I can try, but you won't get an appointment quickly," the head of planning says. He picks up the phone but is unable to arrange a meeting.

That doesn't wash with Müller. He races up the stairs, ignores a surprised secretary and stops dead in front of the office manager's desk.

Bettels is a charismatic young man, maybe a bit too chubby for his age. Müller introduces himself and says what he wants, takes a seat without being asked and starts, as calmly as possible, his complaint. "Please explain your reasoning ..."

Bettels responds coolly. "Disregarding the fact that you have no appointment with me, the case is closed."

But he nevertheless tries to explain his decision. He says that it wasn't about the conditions, the money, but says that DSR would be a better partner for the city because its shareholders would be the communities. Ströer is purely a private enterprise without much experience in outdoor advertising on public land.

It's a good response. It can't be dismissed out of hand. But then again, why would the business of outdoor advertising be in better hands with communities rather than private companies? No, the office manager's argument is thin. There has to be something else. Müller assumes that Bettels might have his eyes on a post on the supervisory board once Halle becomes a member of DSR.

He has another try on that basis. And then he decides to bluff. The only thing he can think of is something to do with business rates. "But I don't understand why Halle wants to do without the business tax, which I would have to pay for my new central office in Halle. DSR has its central office in Leipzig. Halle doesn't get anything."

"How do you mean?"

"Business tax is always due at the site of a company's central office."

Bettels looks at his visitor for a long time, then promises to check the decision again. After that he sees his unwelcome visitor out. Is there any hope?

A few days later Müller can't stand the uncertainty anymore. He rings Halle. The line is bad, then stops altogether. But he thinks he has understood the following: "Ströer … has … got it." Big cheers in his Berlin office. Müller pops open the champagne. What a victory! It's always worth fighting a bit.

About half an hour later, the head of planning rings again. "We were just interrupted, Mr. Müller. DSR has got the contract." Müller is angry and deeply disappointed. The almighty competitor has won after all. Obviously Bettels hadn't taken long to get to the bottom of Müller's bluff regarding business tax.

A few months later, the newspapers report a scandal in Halle, featuring Bettels in a leading role. It says: "The Chairman of the communal building society wangles millions of D-Marks to family and friends by not tendering contracts."

The Chair of the society is the office manager of the mayor, i.e., Bettels. Among the people favored is his uncle, a builder from Lower Saxony, who had moved to Halle.

Trust is a fleeting thing after all.

A counterattack in Magdeburg

It is a quiet Saturday afternoon in Cologne. The Ströer headquarters are deserted, as they are on most weekends. The caretaker, Karl-Ludwig Scheel, is sitting in his living room waiting for his favorite sports program to start. He never misses it. He has been working for Heiner Ströer since the beginning of the 1960s and was his first employee.

The telephone rings. On weekends calls are diverted to the caretaker's flat. The caller introduces himself as a lawyer from Heidelberg and asks to talk to Mr. Ströer.

"He isn't in," Scheel says and points out that it's the weekend. But it is urgent, the lawyer tells him, and asks to be called back as soon as possible.

"What is it about?" Scheel asks with a mixture of curiosity and duty.

"It's about something in the former GDR," the man answers vaguely. Then he adds that it is really important.

Mr. Ströer is on Majorca this weekend, his favorite place. But he can always be contacted in an emergency.

"Müller can see to it, please contact him straight away." Ströer is doubtful whether the Heidelberg call is really that important. But it's about the East, and that is Müller's thing.

Müller finally dials the number around midday Sunday. The lawyer answers immediately and tells him what the call is about. He has been directed to write a report for the city of Magdeburg about the legal allocation of outdoor advertising rights and wants to talk to Ströer about it.

So, it is about rights, specifically the Magdeburg subsidiary of DEWAG and its employees. DEWAG, the advertising arm of the state SED party, with a monopoly over advertising rights in the GDR, was founded after the war in the Soviet occupied zone. Of course, advertising was also happening in the GDR: Large billboards featured socialist propaganda or showed rules controlling socialist consumer behavior. The panels were everywhere in strategically suitable sites, bearing slogans such as "Fight fascism" or "Support friendly states". But also: "The customer is king in the co-op." The propaganda has now disappeared, but the advertising panels are still around. Meanwhile companies affiliated with DEWAG are either being scaled down or sold off.

This process of privatisation and scaling down is being handled by the Berlin-based Treuhand agency. Müller knows the organisation well. In Halle, DSR, who recently defeated him so painfully, had practically taken over all local advertising boards. Until now, Müller had assumed that DSR already owned the DEWAG subsidiary there and had also secured the local rights for advertising. But he had still applied for the rights, of course.

But what could the lawyer's report be about?

The lawyer says he is a consultant to the council and wants to talk with Müller about outdoor advertising in the new Federal States. He asks if they could meet.

Müller agrees. Maybe there is still a chance to get into business with Magdeburg? Why else would this consultant want to talk to him?

Two days later, the lawyer and the young businessman meet up in Cologne. Müller's ears prick up when he hears that DSR is indeed managing the business in Magdeburg but without any legal contract. Some local politicians would regard that as a hostile takeover. The lawyer says that he'ss a passionate market economist and doesn't approve of councils dealing with a business they didn't know anything about. Müller agrees and talks a bit about his experience on the subject.

The lawyer hears what he wants to hear and begins to write the report the next day.

Shortly afterwards, the Magdeburg round table comes to a decision on outdoor advertising. Müller's tender is on the table, as are tenders from some competitors. Müller has already presented a contract which only needs signing, but he fears that a lobbying campaign from local politicians will mean DSR will win the contract.

However, to his surprise, the round table decides on Müller. The mayor, eager to escape more lobbying, signs the contract immediately after the meeting. But when the DSR people hear about it they are beside themselves, not only because Magdeburg had been their territory before Germany divided, but also because Müller had acted so quickly that no one in DSR had even realised what was happening.

Law and justice

The battle over the best sites goes on. In autumn 1990, Müller takes over the DEWAG branch in Dresden from the Treuhand agency for approximately 500,000 Dollar, including buildings. On the final balance sheet there are also undefined liabilities of 750 million Dollar. The official reason is that this represents only a technical item, and there are no legal obligations for the buyer. Müller's accountant makes an enquiry but eventually agrees. So, Müller signs the contract in good faith. A bit too much good faith, as it turns out.

A few months later the Treuhand company sends a reminder for the debt of 750 million Dollar, previously described as a mere formality. Müller thinks it's a mistake and rejects the invoice. But the federal agency insists on payment and threatens an enforcement order.

In panic, Ströer's accountants and lawyers check the legal situation and come to an unexpected verdict – unexpected for Müller, at least. If the case went to court, the experts say, they would probably lose. The lawyers suggest coming to an out-of-court settlement or paying the debt in instalments.

But Müller is not going to give in. He knows he acted in good faith. So, they meet again in court. On the day of the trial Müller is flanked by two lawyers. The judge suggests an out-of-court settlement. If they pay part of the sum, the case would be dropped.

But Müller rejects it angrily. If the state is going to outsmart him, he needs to see it in a definitive verdict. Müller does not actually use the word "outsmart" for what he thinks the state is doing. He is more profane.

"Calm down, Mr. Müller," the judge warns him. "If you are not able to follow the procedures calmly, I will send you out." Ströer is ordered to pay 750,000 Dollar and the legal costs.

But Müller won't pay. He carries on fighting. The verdict simply doesn't conform to his sense of justice. Regardless, a payment of that size would be very bad for the books, which are in the red already.

So begins a bitter legal fight that lasts for years, with the small company Ströer City Marketing, represented by Udo Müller, taking on the Federal Republic of Germany, represented by the Treuhand agency. For Udo Müller, it's all about justice and the rule of law. (And maybe a bit about his ego as well.)

Exactly 10 years after the first verdict, a Dresden court rejects Treuhand's demands for good. The legal costs are to be paid by the state. Müller's initial adversaries have long moved to other positions or retired. The monstrous. Berlin privatisation agency Treuhand has long ceased to be.

Müller is happy. He simply did not want to accept the principle that the law is above justice. It was obviously worthwhile.

The birthday bash

It's July 1992, Udo Müller's 30th birthday. He wants to celebrate it alongside his business success in the East.

Money is no object. His bank account is about 30,000 Dollar in credit. That should be enough for a good party. Didn't Bhagwan say that money was like water in the sink? If you don't pull the plug every now and then, no fresh water can flow in. The old money needs to be spent so that new money can flow in. A natural circle. It's quite logical – or is it?

Müller also has a good idea what this party should be like: Unusual! All he needs now is to find the right venue, somewhere symbolic of his Berlin years and the fall of the Wall. He has looked along the border – it's three years already since it came down – but finds nothing suitable. An old GDR watchtower would be much too small for his grand event.

When Müller first walked past the former Grand Hotel Esplanade in 1992, he saw a wreck. The bleak building on Berlin's Bellevue Street near Potsdamer Platz had certainly seen better times. Bullet holes from Russian artillery bear witness to the battle of Berlin in the final days of the war.

During the times of the last Kaiser, the rich and the beautiful met here for tea. Princes, counts, and barons made polite conversation in the Kaisersaal (the emperor's hall), and the monarch himself sometimes dined here. After the First World War, during Berlin's roaring 20s, the hotel became a favourite meeting point for couples. On Sundays, people of all walks of life gathered for a tea dance on the terrace.

(Many years later, another historical moment occurred here. In April 1948, 1,700 students chose the location to protest for the freedom of science, in what became the first origins of the Freie Universität – where a 19-year-old Udo Müller from Godesberg began his medical course.)

But time moves on and the hotel's pomp is long past. Another lost war later, and the former impressive building is now badly damaged and stuck between East and West.

But Müller is interested in the old Grand Hotel. Yes, this will be the place to celebrate his 30th birthday. As he wanders past, he notices the entrance is wide open. Müller steps in and takes in the surroundings. There is the old bar, but without any bottles and cocktail shakers. The Kaisersaal still boasts some of the charm of its golden years. (Müller always had a penchant for imperial, grand bourgeois architecture.)

In the vast entrance hall, a few young people are running around. They're actors from a Shakespearean company rehearsing *As You Like It*. Shakespeare's words echo through the big hall. Udo Müller is delighted. This is the right place for his party!

Since Udo has been living in Berlin, he hasn't celebrated any of his birthdays properly. He has never actually invited anybody to a party. It somehow never worked out what with his work, with all that stress. Ever since he joined *Lunenburg & Partner*, he had worked non-stop – five years without any holidays.

And now he plans to catch up on all that he has missed in one go. Modelled on F. Scott Fitzgerald's *The Great Gatsby*, there shall be a fabulous party!

Müller quickly comes to an agreement with the actors. He offers free advertising for their next Shakespeare play for the use of the Grand Hotel Esplanade for one evening. Both parties benefit from the deal.

Planning for the night actually began a long time ago in the mind of the nearly 30-year-old. He comes up with the idea of celebrating "the 12th anniversary of my 18th birthday". And the guest list? That's easy: Friends, acquaintances, business partners, the usual gang from the Berlin advertising scene.

Finally, the momentous day arrives. It's a Saturday. The old Esplanade is ablaze in a mixture of run-down charm and modern flair. For tonight, the old hotel belongs to Udo Müller and, of course, his guests.

Around 10 o'clock, about 250 partygoers are crowding around the bar and in the old Kaisersaal. Heiner Ströer has come with his son Dirk and his girlfriend. It is only the second time that Udo has met Dirk, who is seven years his junior. The first time was only a fleeting encounter, and they barely talked.

But this time they greet each other warmly. "You really look like your dad," Müller says to the younger man. "And I'm really proud of it," the son answers.

Udo is a relaxed and confident host, and Ströer is impressed. "You've learned a lot from me," the older man says with a laugh. "And not only about business."

The "12th anniversary of my 18th birthday" turns into a fabulous. party. The last guests only say their goodbyes at 7 in the morning.

On his way home, Udo hears a report on the car radio about an event in the old Esplanade, where figures from Berlin's advertising scene are said to have had a brilliant party. Udo doesn't get his head around it immediately, that *his* birthday party is being reported on the radio!

But it was not only his 30th birthday that Müller celebrated in great style. It was also the young businessman's success. His ambition and readiness to take risks will, against all the odds, make him one of the most successful entrepreneurs of his generation. The end of the GDR was also the start of a new world, the world of advertising. And that was worth celebrating.

Udo Müller is young, and he is hungry for more.

CHANGES

A new wind is blowing

The businessman's drug is success. Heiner Ströer had a lot of it. His advertising panels were up and down the country: more than 15,000 large billboards were scattered through West Germany before unification, every single one on private ground with a little sign at the bottom saying STRÖER, in capital letters, 40 centimetres wide, 10 centimetres high. That's his brand.

So, the entrepreneur always also advertised himself, and the Ströer name, like none other, stood for quality. Thanks to his contributions in this field, and to his diligence, the company had grown to be one of the leading private advertisers, but it was still also a so-called *Mittelstand* company, a way of describing a stable and honest mid-sized business in Germany.

At the top of the outdoor advertising industry stood *Deutsche Städte Reklame*, DSR, comprising 27 municipal subsidiaries. Their advertising panels were primarily on public, council-owned ground.

From the word go, there had been a clear difference between Ströer and DSR. Ströer's company still belongs entirely to the man who shares the company name. Even his partner, Udo Müller, is not a co-owner, nor does he have any other function. And the not insignificant profit is also entirely Ströer's.

But they both have equal share in the company known as Ströer City Marketing GmbH, which they had founded in 1990. Here, Müller is in charge. Ströer is just an active board member, financier, and paternal friend in the background.

The marketing for the company, which now has 25,000 advertising panels, is run from Cologne. So far, there are no profits because of the high investment costs in the new Federal States.

"You are still young," Ströer says to Udo. "You don't need any money yet. That'll come later." So, Udo has to be content with his salary as the general manager. But he doesn't mind, quite the opposite.

Ströer knows that his young business partner has lots of ideas and plans. Udo plans to consolidate the fragmented German outdoor advertising market, he wants to expand abroad, introduce new forms of advertising, buy out competitors – he wants to grow, and the sky is the limit.

He repeatedly talks about the changes to come for outdoor advertising: large, lit glass boxes showing rotating adverts, and the immense possibilities of the embryonic digital age. Müller knows that soon the wooden panels with glued-on posters will be a thing of the past.

Heiner Ströer sees many things differently. He too wants to expand abroad, preferably to the east. But he doesn't yet want to abandon the good old, tried and tested wooden panels he has worked with for more than four decades.

These panels are called 18/1, because large advertising posters come in A1 size, and you need 18 of them for the large walls. The old-fashioned Heidelberg printing machines could never print in a larger format than 59.4 × 84.1 cm. So, 18 posters in A1 makes 18/1.

These good old posters are up in their tens of thousands, on wooden panels and facades, showing cars, cigarettes, washing powder and nappies. It's a German success story hanging everywhere, and Heiner Ströer doesn't want to part with the concept.

But the good old days are over, no matter how much the old advertising giants are romanticising them. Now, toward the end of the century, the climate has become rougher. Udo Müller is convinced that the current changes will only be a transition. The world of outdoor advertising is about to enter the digital age.

The end of tranquil times

Rather like at the end of a competitive boxing match, the world of advertising was getting scrappy. The rival fighters were seeking the knockout blow.

Maybe it's because of Müller's influence, pushing aggressively in the East, that the atmosphere in the West is changing too. Until now, it had been quite relaxed in the old Federal Republic. Now it's getting tougher. Every site has become a battlefield.

Müller and Ströer have been working together for four years. Four years during which a lot has changed in outdoor advertising. What was once a friendly marketplace has turned prickly. Udo Müller is right in the middle of the fight.

Heiner Ströer is sitting in his office in the company's Cologne headquarters, lost in thought. He looks again at the headline in the local paper of January 29th, 1994: "The war of the advertising kings". Below is the portrait of a friendly looking gentleman-entrepreneur, Heiner Ströer. He likes that image of himself. The grand old man of the advertising scene hates conflict. And now he is right in the middle of a public confrontation.

Ströer is still well liked in this world. They all admire the "old man", but don't fear him. With Udo Müller it is exactly the other way. He is not liked, but he is feared.

Ströer remembers his first meeting with Müller in that Frankfurt restaurant. It was in 1988, and he had asked Udo what he wanted most from life. "I want to be in the Himalayas, sit in front of a hut, and not own anything," he had said, and the naivety of the young man had made Ströer smile. But even then, he had sensed that young Udo had promise.

But there was no reason to smile about what Müller had said after the fall of the Wall, when they were setting up their shared company. Now big plans were his life's ambition, his visions. He had passionately talked about the unique chances after unification and what he wanted to get out of it. He had mapped the future of the company in three phases, a kind of strategic master plan.

Phase One was ambitious but obvious: To be better and faster than the competitors in expanding into the new Federal States. He wanted to be number one. Then he wanted to enter the market for "street furnishing". Done.

Now Phase Two was due. Müller also wanted to get contracts with communities in the West for advertising on public ground. At the end of this phase, Ströer City Marketing was to be the number one in outdoor advertising in the whole of Germany. It wouldn't be easy.

There were many bigger fish in the same waters, bigger financially and more powerful. Above all it was the mighty DSR. Then the French company JCDecaux, which was a major global advertiser.

Heiner Ströer lets his young companion dream. It can't

be wrong to have ambitious plans. It doesn't matter if they are not particularly realistic.

But Müller wants much, much more. And that's Phase Three: turning the company global, fighting for the big European and Asian markets and God knows what else. "Think big," is his latest mantra. At some point he wants to be one of the three largest advertisers in the world. Udo has a specific, concrete strategy. He thinks differently from others, from his rivals. He also thinks differently from Heiner. Maybe his former goal in life of the hut in the Himalayas and his vision to be a successful entrepreneur were not really a contradiction. Who knows what happens between wish and reality.

But back to reality, or, more precisely, to Udo's Phase One. The advertising world is riven by insecurity. In the East, Müller can celebrate successes such as in Dresden and Magdeburg, as well as with his aggressive search for privately owned sites.

The number of billboards owned by the old Ströer company and the new Ströer Marketing has risen to 40,000 and is growing daily. The two companies are feared by their competitors. And some of the advertisers are getting more and more nervous.

At a conference of German advertisers, the boss of the Düsseldorf company Moplak, which is also active in the East, angrily confronts Udo Müller. "Before you turned up, everything was more peaceful," he says. And Hans Wall, the Berlin poster man, refuses to shake hands with Müller. To hell with that guy.

Other rivals, such as Günther Freund and his successful Koblenz company awk Außenwerbung suspiciously eye their Cologne-based competitors and their young rocket man. Müller is a clear obstruction.

The industry is still clearly divided. On the one hand,

there is the rather cumbersome business with private sites shared by numerous external advertisers. On the other hand, there is the much larger public business, dominated by the DSR companies, or managed locally, as in Cologne.

But one thing is clear: The outdoor advertising industry is facing changes, and there are new challenges for a world that has previously been safe and cosy. Many of the old guard do not like it.

But there are also moments when Heiner Ströer feels uncomfortable. He finds his dynamic young partner far too hasty, too forceful. In moments like this, he feels as though he has created a monster, as if he is Frankenstein, or the magician whose apprentice is about to outdo his master.

But now, in 1994, he needs Müller's clout. The enemy is at the gate. It is about Cologne and the Cologne advertising company Kölner Außenwerbung GmbH (KAW), a subsidiary of the municipal utilities company. The city's plan is to privatise KAW and turn it into a public-private partnership (PPP). The question for Ströer is how much he wants to be involved in a battle to gain some control of the company. He doesn't like that kind of skirmish. It goes against his desire for balance and harmony.

But his rivals are out there, eager to land the big trophy, and it isn't only strictly business. Vanity, envy, and mistrust play an even bigger role. And Udo Müller, the troublemaker, is right by Ströer's side.

The Cologne public company isn't really a good fit among Ströer's other businesses. He specialises more in private outdoor advertising. But this is entirely concerned with billboard advertising on public land. Only a few years ago he wouldn't have bothered at all. But now he will have to, and by his side is a partner who is well versed in public outdoor advertising. So, why not?

Ströer pushes the newspaper to one side. He doesn't like the choice of words. "The war of the advertising kings". He, who has always strived for harmony, for whom friendly competition was vital for his well-being!

Of course, Heiner Ströer is interested in the business, but he also values his honour and good reputation. Cologne is his city. His advertising panels are all around the cathedral. And they can't be allowed to go to his rivals. If there are advertising kings, as the newspaper suggests, then there can only be one in Cologne, and that is Heiner Ströer.

But there will be an unpleasant battle. Günther Freund, the bullish owner of awk Außenwerbung from Koblenz, has sent a confidential offer to the Cologne magistrate.

Freund wants to acquire the company at all costs and lets the politicians know that he would be willing to pay more than the highest bid of his rivals. He even mentions a concrete sum: he is willing to pay 350,000 Dollar more than any other bid. The letter ends with a clear offer: "We also ask you to tell us what we can do in the future to benefit the city of Cologne." It is a declaration of war, mainly aimed at Heiner Ströer and his junior partner Udo Müller.

Ever since the expansion in the East, Freund has been bothered by the newcomer's strategy. And obviously the businessman, accustomed to success, wants to take revenge. Hans Wall, the Berlin advertiser, also wants to prevent Ströer from acquiring the Cologne outdoor advertising company.

But it is JCDecaux who probably has the best chance. Nobody is financially so powerful as the French company. Decaux does not see any reason to be cautious. and has a solid knowledge of contracts with municipalities. His father was the "inventor" of town or street furnishing, a brilliant idea that shook up the advertising scene.

In big cities such as Hamburg and Munich, JCDecaux pioneered the use of bus and tram shelters and information panels for advertising posters. But the French company doesn't only want a share in the PPP of the Cologne business. It wants everything – and it offers a good price too.

JCDecaux already has the required permission to advertise on bus shelters. If the company can buy KAW in its entirety, it could prevent a different owner possibly cancelling the contracts for those bus and tram stops.

The negotiations are complicated further by the sheer number of factors at play. KAW is a subsidiary of the city utilities company. The granting of advertising rights are in the hands of the city parliament – and without at least a 10-year contract, KAW is not worth much. So, in addition to deciding about the sale of the company itself, the city parliament needs to rule on the extension of advertising rights and, finally, what to do with the smaller agreement with JCDecaux about the bus and tram shelters. As usual with municipal companies, many local politicians of various. parties are on the committees, boards and panels. Potential buyers need to negotiate with every single one of them. It is a complex jigsaw puzzle, with every piece in some way connected to every other one.

After numerous meetings and negotiations, the main players finally reach a reasonable compromise, to the satisfaction of everyone involved. The Cologne transport department will partner with JCDecaux regarding the advertising contracts for bus shelters. The city parliament extends the advertising rights for them as well as for the advertisers of KAW, which will be sold to Ströer.

So, Ströer and Müller have got what they wanted. With KAW, they now own their first company for public-space advertising in the former West Germany. Even better, it's in their hometown, the city of Cologne. It's an important milestone.

The sale of KAW is representative of the massive changes in the industry. Many cities are now privatising previously state-owned companies, including those that deal with advertising in outdoor spaces. A pattern is developing in many areas: First the big fish swallow the little fish, then the big fish are devoured by the even bigger ones. Once, there were more than 100 national and regional companies concerned with outdoor advertising in Germany, but only the strongest will survive. That's a fact.

The question is whether Ströer will be among the winners. The financial scope of the company is limited, partly due to Müller's expensive activities in the East. He is now in charge of the overall company strategy: a modern businessman, embracing new opportunities in a rapidly changing field.

Ströer is sitting alone in his office, lost in memories. Back in 1965, when he first branched out by himself with 20 advertising panels, his old colleagues had mocked him with the name "Poster Heini". Now, nearly three decades since those humble beginnings, the turnover of his group of companies is 750,000 Dollar. They call him the "advertising king", at least in Cologne.

But the king is only too aware that the crown prince, Udo Müller, is preparing to conquer the throne. It's Friday. Udo called him a short time ago telling him he is flying over from Berlin this evening. It's going to be a long night, that's for sure. But Ströer is looking forward to it.

A grand old man and entrepreneur

Heiner Ströer has come a long way in the advertising business. He started right at the bottom, in the 1950s. It was the post-war era, with new horizons opening up, at the start of a new free and democratic society. People were moving towards the economic miracle – truly a miracle after the terrible years of Nazi dictatorship and war.

Success could literally be found on the streets and Heinz Ströer wanted to go it alone, to be his own boss.

Heinz Ströer was born on August 8th, 1938, in the Lower Saxony town of Nordhorn, near the Dutch border. His family was on the breadline, and that didn't change even after the war as the new dawn was breaking.

At home, with his parents, he had learned to accept a life of poverty. They told him to be modest; it was not possible to make grand plans. The little boy was reminded constantly that only a few paths were open to him; it was a world of the "haves" and the "have-nots". Heiner wanted to go to grammar school like his earliest best friend, but his father turned down the request. "It's not for people like us."

However, Heiner was allowed to go to middle school and did well without much effort. At some point he read in the local paper that things were looking up everywhere in the country. He learned that the country's economic turnaround was admired all over the world. But at home, it seemed that none of the Ströers noticed it. They were content if father had a job and if they had one warm meal per day.

Heiner wished for more. He wanted a small slice of what life out there had to offer. He wanted to get beyond the limits of his home. It was mainly his mother who didn't want to let him go. "We are simple people," she used to say. “We have no room for big dreams.” But eventually his father relented: “Find your own way, my boy. You are good at maths, make use of it. We cannot help you any longer.”

Heiner found more help in the sports club. Ever since he was a boy, he had played football for the local club. His coach noted his talent and asked a friend from a more successful Düsseldorf club to have a look at the boy.

Aged 16, Heiner set off to the big city. It wasn’t just the football that motivated him. He wanted to take whatever chances were on offer. He was offered a position with the Düsseldorf football club Fortuna, and it came with an apprenticeship at a Düsseldorf publishing house.

Soon, the apprenticeship became more of a priority than the football. “Don’t worry about me,” he wrote to his parents. “They are very happy with me.”

After the successful apprenticeship, the young publishing assistant transferred to the Düsseldorf advertising agency Gramm, which was soon taken over by the New York advertising company Grey. Gramm & Grey, as the new company was known, became one of the biggest advertising agencies in the world.

Young Ströer wasn’t so much attracted by the world of beautiful images, positive slogans and the scent of the big wide world. He was more fascinated by the business connected with it: The contact with the clients, the commercial interests.

Shortly after his 20th birthday, the rapidly growing agency promoted him to head of outdoor advertising. It was only a small niche in the vast advertising universe, but Heiner felt he was on his way up.

Barely a year later, the small advertising agency Jörger head-hunted him for the post of director in a small town further north. For Ströer, it was another step forward, and the prospect of a provincial life didn't put him off. But he soon got into an argument with his boss about the direction the agency should take. The new director wanted to expand and saw his chances in billboard advertising. But the founder of the agency thought his young employee was moving too fast and tried to reign him in.

Ströer was annoyed. He thought for the first time about owning his own company. Even if it was only a small firm, he wanted to be the one in charge.

That same evening, Heiner Ströer met up with the metal worker Karl-Ludwig Scheel. They didn't know each other well, but Scheel sometimes took on small jobs putting up posters for Jörger. Over a beer, Ströer told him about his plan to establish a company for outdoor advertising. He proposed that Scheel could be his first employee, responsible for the operational side of the business.

Scheel liked the idea and discussed it with his wife. She said no. "You don't know the man. He wants to be the boss but wants you to do all the work. Don't do it." But Karl-Ludwig was intrigued by the challenge.

Three weeks later the business was up and running. In a garage-turned-workshop, Scheel knocked together the first large wooden panels, fixed a frame to them and drove the billboards from one site to another in his own little Renault 4. He glued advertising posters for cigarette brands to them. Ströer found more sites on private land and more companies who wanted to advertise.

The cooperation worked well. The initial 20 billboards quickly became 100. Ströer was happy and told his companion: "Once we have 200 panels, it's enough. We can both live on that quite well."

That's what it was like in the 1960s, when everyone was happy simply to live in freedom and peace. The economic miracle had become the everyday norm.

But by the 1980s, the company had 15,000 billboards , and what was once a modest business was now a small empire of several companies and subsidiaries of Heinz W. Ströer GmbH & Co KG. The boss was a successful businessman with a villa in Cologne and a holiday house on Majorca.

Brothers in arms – or rivals?

It's hard to tell when Heiner Ströer first took a shine to the young Udo Müller. It began during the merry summer night in 1988 when they met for the first time in West Berlin. Since then, their feelings for each other have developed and they share a connection that extends further than just a working relationship.

But whenever Ströer began thinking about his young partner and his role in the future, he also began thinking of his real son Dirk. There were times when Ströer junior felt jealous of Udo. Had a stranger taken his place in his father's affections?

For a long time, Dirk only knew Udo Müller from the photos in which he stood beside his father, and from what his father said about him. They were happy pictures, like family photos. And they left a lot of room for imagination.

Dirk was 23 when he finally met Udo, at the latter's 30th birthday party in the ruin of Berlin's old Hotel Esplanade. (Prior to that, they had only glimpsed one another from a distance.) For Udo and Dirk, that evening marked the beginning of a special relationship. "Emotionally, Udo is the big brother I never had," Dirk still says to this day.

Soon, both were referring to each other as "brother" in public. It happened naturally. And, just as naturally, the old Ströer called them "my boys".

But was there still a rivalry? Was Dirk happy with his role as the "little brother"? And what about Udo? Did he only play the older brother to strengthen his position?

Regardless, Heiner Ströer enjoyed the closeness. The boys often spent weekends together, went clubbing or flew out to Ströer's house on Majorca. There was always a decent crowd: Heiner's partner Katharina Wittich and her son Timo were part of it, as was Dirk's friend Johannes Erlemann, the son of a Cologne industrialist. Udo's mother was also a welcome guest in the Ströer household. Sometimes Dirk and Udo brought their girlfriends. Father Ströer enjoyed his role as the benevolent head of the family.

But there were also moments when worries took over – about Udo, who wanted too much too quickly, and who seemed to actually seek out risk; about Dirk, because he didn't seem very ambitious and rather spent his days focusing purely on leisure.

But there was also another side to Udo – a self-deprecating, happy person enjoying his life. It wasn't that long ago that he jumped on a chair at a company party in Cologne and belted out a popular song by a local band. "I am a robber!" he sang at full volume in Cologne dialect. "I never worry!"

During the loud cheers and applause, Heiner has his own thoughts. No, Udo isn't a robber, but sometimes he is a bit too careless, naïve, and ambitious. He rushes ahead without thinking. But he can fight if he has to, and when he does, he fights as if his very life was at stake.

For a while now, Udo's childhood dreams have become concrete visions and plans. That thing with DSR, for example. Compared with them, the industry leaders, Ströer is not much more than a medium-sized family business.

Dirk likes to mention something that routinely happens

with Udo when they are jogging in the morning. Both their flats are close be dotted to Cologne city centre, so they meet up for a run quite often.

The start and finish line is a small transformer box on the pavement between their flats. When they have completed their circuit Udo, out of breath and dripping with sweat, stops in front of that box, beats it like a drum and shouts: "DSR – buy it out. DSR – buy it out."

It is Udo's dream to one day takeover the leading advertiser DSR. And every time this happens, Dirk shakes his head and says: "You're crazy!"

A concerned Dirk recently asked his father whether Udo meant it seriously, this take-over of their giant rival. "I'm afraid so," the old man says. "But it's completely absurd, of course." Sometimes, when they eat out at their favourite Italian restaurant and Udo is in high spirits among familiar people, he similarly ends his stories with the sentence: "... and then we buy DSR." Everybody laughs. That would be the same as a mouse eating a cat.

Lost in thought, Ströer looks at a picture on the bar in the headquarters' basement. It shows a particular advertising tool, a large glass and metal case on a slim column. The caption reads "Megalight", followed by technical data. Udo brought it over a few weeks ago. Tonight, *Megalight* is on the agenda.

The telephone interrupts the boss's contemplations. It's Müller. He might be half an hour late, he says. "Take it easy," Ströer answers. "I'm spending some time down memory lane."

"Enjoy it," Udo says. "Because soon we'll be talking only about the future." Udo seems in a good mood, but somehow his words also sound like a hidden threat. An hour later, they are at the Italian restaurant discussing their next steps concerning Megalights. At some point, they will be dotted along streets and other sites, equipped with advertising. Again, it's going to be a long night.

Gut feelings decide

Every investment starts with a gut feeling. It's the same whether you're building a house or managing a large company. Some people don't trust their inner compass and hide behind an expert's opinion. But for those who dare, a good gut feeling can be the start of a new adventure. Udo Müller is one of those daredevils.

He has a gut feeling about the Megalights. No more glue, wood, or paper. Instead, an electrified, illuminated glass case, as big as the largest billboards but also visible in the dark.

But modern technology does not come cheap. This is an expensive investment, and Udo Müller wants to go for it. A Megalight can cost up to 26,000 Dollar, a large wooden panel only 1,000. No wonder Heiner Ströer and his experts are skeptical.

Inside the Megalights (the name is Udo's invention), large, bright adverts rotate every few seconds in metal and glass cases. They are on a high column, set at a right angle to the roadside. They are four meters wide and three meters high. This sophisticated construction doesn't only grab the attention of pedestrians, it can also increase the company's turnover – if it works and the customers are sold on the idea.

Müller has been watching new developments in advertising for a while. JCDecaux had started using so-called Citylights – large advertising panels, measuring two meters square, backlit behind glass – as a new "premium advertising medium". The company was smart in the way that it positioned them against the more traditional posters. It annoyed Müller so much that he invented the Megalights, which were even bigger.

But there was a problem. Ströer's billboards in the old Federal States stand or hang on private sites. But the size and shape of Megalights are better suited to public sites. However, they tend to be owned by communities. DSR owns most of them in the old Federal States.

In the East, over in the new Federal States, Müller had managed to break DSR's near monopoly and arrange contracts with some councils. But it's nowhere near enough to establish a lucrative business for Megalights in the whole country. If he wants to get the big advertisers on board, he needs a national network.

It's a problem that needs to be resolved quickly. Also, the simple wooden billboards are still very popular with Heiner Ströer's clients. So why, Ströer asks, should we take on this additional risk without any real need? The Megalights cost so much money and to make them an attractive marketing concept, Ströer would have to set up several thousand of them.

The calculation is simple: it would cost millions to carry out Müller's plans for the Megalights. He wants an initial 250 in the East, before beginning an equally expensive and uncertain search for suitable sites in the rest of Germany. Then there's the cost of setting them up, maintenance, and rental contracts. It would require a lot of money and work for an uncertain outcome.

Ströer asks his directors for an internal assessment of the Megalight plan. The most important question is whether there are enough private city sites on busy roads. The verdict of the sales crew is unanimous: No. All the good sites are in municipal ownership, where DSR has priority. But Müller won't take no for an answer.

Heiner Ströer is still unsure. It's Udo's gut feeling versus the advice of his experts. Müller had already indicated that he will not accept a negative decision. He wants the Megalights.

Heiner Ströer makes a far-reaching business decision. He wants to avoid exposing the company to too much risk, while also giving in to Müller's strategy. His 15,000 traditional billboards in the old Federal States will remain in the hands of the existing Ströer company and will continue to be owned by Heiner alone. All new activities of the business group, including the Megalights, future digital media and street furnishing are to be dealt with by the mutual Ströer City Marketing. Young Udo is a grown-up businessman now, Heiner Ströer thinks. Time to cut him loose. He will have to learn to assess risks on his own.

Maybe his gut feeling is good?

NEW GROUND

Temptations in Ankara

It's the summer of 1996 and Udo Müller is planning the next step towards his ultimate dream, on the Cote d'Azur. He wants to dominate the outdoor advertising industry around the world. Udo Müller has never had a problem with thinking big.

He has arrived at a small workshop on the shores of the Mediterranean, where a young man named Olivier Michel produces bus shelters and modern advertising frames. In his search for a place to produce his Megalights, Müller had heard about Michel.

Müller began this quest a year ago, when he started a joint venture in Warsaw, Poland, with the Vienna businessman Heinrich Schuster, an old acquaintance of Ströer. They went on to establish another Ströer company in the Czech Republic, but the two ventures in Eastern Europe didn't bring them much joy. Ströer had relied on Schuster's business experience in the East and Müller on the instincts of his senior. But the only thing they produced was reliable losses, both in Warsaw and Prague.

At one point Müller went to Prague and queried why it was taking the company so long to set up new billboards. It was taking even longer than it did during the communist times. The director had responded sharply: "You don't expect me to spoil our beautiful city with your billboards?" she said. Hmmm ...

But now it's the sunny South of France. The Frenchman and the German meet up on a beautiful June day. The manufacture of the new frames is already set for France, but Michel suggests positioning a large number of the glass showcases in the country as well.

And why not? It's a bold idea to launch an attack like this in the homeland of their rival JCDecaux. So, Udo Müller and Olivier Michel set up a company for outdoor advertising in France.

Müller can rely immediately on a solid base for the deal thanks to Olivier's connections in France. He comes from the same family as Baron Marcel Bich – a billionaire well known as an international sailor, but even more famous as the founder of BiC, the world's largest producer of plastic pens, cigarette lighters, and razors. Michel is part of the clan. What could possibly go wrong?

Michel, too, is convinced he has found the right partner. He thinks the first Megalights can easily be placed in Lyon and along the C te d'Azur. It will then be a case of expanding across the vast country of France, drawing on the power of BiC.

But the Decaux family is also influential in France – as Müller soon finds out. Potential advertising clients continue to favour the established company over the German invader. The first Megalights are quickly set up, but there are no clients. No clients, no posters, no income.

After more than a year and a lot of effort, debts are approaching nearly $ 20 million. There are still few adverts when Müller sells the expensive project to a private investor, who again passes it on, with profit, to a U.S.-based company. It was a setback, and not a small one, for young Müller and for Ströer.

It is the same with businesses all over the world. One company always must lose – and in this case, it's the one from Germany. But is that a reason to give up? No. Olivier Michel will continue to produce glass cases for the German market, at least.

At some point during this period, Michel introduces Müller to a Turkish contact named Mustafa Ilbak. Mustafa is one of the biggest outdoor advertisers in Turkey. Bingo!

Although the Istanbul agency is, by German standards, medium-sized, Müller's ears prick up when he hears that Ilbak is putting together a tender in Ankara for bus shelters, financed by advertising, and is looking for an experienced partner.

Udo Müller and Heiner Ströer fly out to Ankara in the early autumn of 1997. Ströer is only slightly curious. He is not convinced that gaining a foothold in the relatively unremarkable Turkish capital would be worthwhile but agrees that they can investigate it. Maybe he will be surprised.

The Turkish capital is completely different to what the visitors expected. Ilbak shows his German guests modern streets, a clean new underground system, elegant shopping centres – and nowhere even a hint of advertising. There are hardly any billboards, no giant posters, and no street furnishing financed by adverts. It's a paradise for advertisers. Müller feels like a painter in front of a blank canvas, bursting with inspiration. He already sees the finished painting: Posters, posters, posters.

Old Ströer is also quite taken. He only sees one problem: Who is going to pay for it? Before a business can take hold, there is usually a very difficult and maybe impossible financing process.

Ströer reminds his young partner of their first attempts abroad, which were not what you could call successful.

They have given up in Prague. The Polish business limps on only because Schuster has promised that better times are imminent. He is on remand, so to speak. And then there was the disaster in France. Should they really attempt another adventure in Turkey? In Ankara there is a chance to be one of very few businesses in the outdoor advertising market. They will start with a 10-year contract for "street furnishing".

Müller wants to do it. Ankara is a modern capital: Lively, dynamic, fascinating – and without any advertising. It's a dream for any agency. He doesn't want to miss this opportunity; he can't allow it to be missed.

Soon the decision for the exclusive contract on street furnishing is due. Müller is in Ankara and waits in his hotel, while his business partner Ilbak takes the sealed envelope to the committee. That's how it works in Turkey: The interested parties deliver their offer in a sealed envelope. The envelopes are opened in front of the committee, and the one containing the highest bid is the winner.

Ilbak and Müller get the contract. They can now furnish Ankara exclusively with their advertising media: the backlit glass advertising panels at bus shelters plus the Megalights. Müller is euphoric. The first capital outside Germany is completely in Ströer's hands. The defeat in Prague, the problems in Poland and the disaster in France are quickly forgotten.

But Heiner Ströer remains skeptical. He considers Turkey an immense risk. But Müller's ambition is unstoppable. Heiner Ströer senses that Ankara is only the beginning of the Turkish adventure.

Juggling too many balls

One thing is clear to Müller: If the company is to grow, it's not enough just to find more and more sites for more and more advertising media. The company must also develop new kinds of advertising and integrate it into the business. New markets must be found and conquered. Rivals have to be taken over.

They need both of what economists call organic growth and inorganic growth. With the former, an existing business is expanded, for example, by finding new sites for an existing product like the Megalights. The latter means that more companies need to be bought up.

A new deal with a company called blowUP fits the bill. Their slogan is: "We build big brands." The posters are big, so big that they cover whole buildings.

"We need something like that," Müller says. He is still eyeing international expansion. And, coincidentally, the blowUp franchiser in Vienna has trouble with its partners in Germany and wants to get rid of the company as soon as possible. They come to a quick and financially reasonable deal.

In the summer of 1997, before the Turkish adventure, Müller took over 100 % of the Austrian company. It wasn't a huge deal. He only had to pay a few million dollars for blowUP. But theirs is a special kind of outdoor advertising that Müller believes he needs in his growing range.

What is not so good is that the German licensees had not been informed of the sale. They would have liked to take over the Austrian branch themselves instead of having this Udo Müller telling them what to do.

The ink is barely dry on the deal when Müller invites the dozen or so independent licensees to the Ströer headquarters in Cologne. He proposes that he also takes a share of their companies so that together they can increase growth in the market. To gain their trust, he also later visits the licensees at their respective sites. He comes to an agreement with one of them to buy the majority of the shares.

Soon, Müller also secures a share of the other licensees. The size of his share is always different, depending on the seller, but the principle is the same: The seller parts with shares in the business but carries on running it. Müller provides the finances but stays in the background.

After two years, the blowUP business is consolidated, and Udo has learned an important lesson: If you get into business with a partner running it, you need to make sure that each participant has an equal interest, that they are "aligned" as Müller puts it. Otherwise, there might be the temptation to spend more attention and energy on one's own share.

That was the case here. Even though all parties were concerned with marketing the blowUP, profits tended to vary depending on the size of the share each partner owned. The bigger a partner's share, the higher the profit. And vice versa. Müller decided that interests in a future business with a partner would always have to be "aligned".

The giant posters are a real innovation. Only new digital printing techniques make it possible to produce large posters to be printed on vinyl. Giant plastic sheets the size of a football pitch can be printed on and fused together. Soon the giant posters will advertise the brands of international clients too – in Great Britain, Spain, the Benelux states. The blowUps are not competing with the traditional advertising media – and that is a great advantage.

The marketing of the innovative blowUPs in Europe also gives Müller the opportunity to get to know the markets abroad. It also makes it easier to establish contacts and find suitable targets for Ströer's "inorganic" growth strategy. The integration of blowUP is also an important strategic building block in their expansion plans.

Whether in Leipzig or London, Madrid or Munich, Berlin or Barcelona, Müller's giant posters soon become an established part of the cityscape like no other medium. Müller's production company even finds itself in the *Guinness Book of Records*, when the company produces the longest and biggest love letter in the world. This special project was the idea of the marketing director of a British company, which hired Ströer for the job. Ströer is soon the leading company for large poster advertising in Europe.

But the debts are still increasing. After a lot of effort, they have found 250 sites for Megalights in the new Federal States, but still they have not erected even one example of the new and expensive media. Müller, impatient as ever, is behind with his plans.

But still, presentations about future Ströer developments manage to convince the company's creditors – at least alongside Müller's visionary descriptions of the beautiful new advertising landscape in Germany and the rest of the world.

But reality doesn't always match Müller's lofty plans. After striking the Ankara deal, glass shelters and Megalights are running off Olivier Michel's production line in the South of France at high speed. But then the Turkish economy tanks, the inflation rate rises steeply, the orders fall away. Turkey turns out to be a financial high wire act without a net. And it becomes clear how expensive the Anatolian dream really is.

Dreadful figures

It's a rainy day in the summer of 1998. Heiner Ströer, again, is struggling with the balance sheets of Ströer City Marketing. Suddenly, a dull feeling of panic hits him. It is one of those days when the fear of the future is muscling in on Ströer's otherwise relaxed spirits.

The figures are dreadful! The old companies are doing well, as usual, but those managed by Udo aren't looking good at all. Particularly the international businesses. Expensive dreams, that's what they are. Nothing but expensive dreams.

Ströer jumps up and runs over to Udo's office. "You are driving us to bankruptcy!" he shouts, exasperated, and shows him a letter from their bank in Cologne. "Loans, loans, loans ... How can we ever pay back all those loans?"

Müller leans back in his cushioned office chair and stretches his legs. In a deliberately calm manner he says: "Pay them back? No, that'll never happen." Ströer stares at the man in disbelief. Debts are a no-no for an old-school businessman like him.

Again, two different business theories clash. On the one side is the modest, financially conservative senior. On the other is the junior who smoothly adapts to global possibilities, to a so-called "two-speed economy".

Rapid growth, courage, risk-taking, hard competition. That's how it goes. But can this principle also be applied to the limited area of outdoor advertising? That's the question that Heiner Ströer asks himself time and again.

"Let's remain a boutique business," he suggests repeatedly. He means that they should not pursue big, risky dreams.

Ströer and Müller quarrel for more than an hour that

day about the right way of looking at things. Eventually the older man concludes: "Just like you, I am an entrepreneur with all my heart. But your world is different from mine. It's much more dangerous."

For quite a while now, Heiner Ströer has been watching the activities of his partner with increasing nervousness. First, the bankruptcies in France and the Czech Republic, then the new products like the blowUPs and the expensive Megalights, and now another adventure in Turkey. For the careful older businessman, they are juggling too many balls. And it is not always clear where they will come down.

It's possible that Udo is always one step ahead of his rivals. But perhaps he is also going too far. Heiner Ströer endures sleepless nights while his partner dreams of success. But he also realises that if Müller stops his pursuit of these wild dreams now, everything might indeed come crashing down. He must carry on.

The evening ends, like so often, at their favourite Italian restaurant, with pasta and good red wine.

But one sentence lingers in Ströer's mind: "I'm not interested in paying off debts," Müller had said, as if it was the most normal thing in the world. "It's like when you build a house and get a mortgage. Taking credit is like writing a cheque for the future. You only have to make sure that it doesn't bounce." The most important thing is the value you create in the meantime. In other words: Even a billion Dollars of debt is not a problem if the company is profitable enough to yield the interest, taxes, write-offs and other expenses. Müller is not afraid of high debt, as long as the relationship between debt and profit is right.

Of course, Heiner Ströer knows that each new investment carries a risk. That's the basis for all business. But the future remains a vision: Müller dreams of one day buying the advertising giant DSR. But he is just about the only one who has that idea.

Dirk Ströer, who knows about this father's worries, thinks that his "big brother" is a nutcase when he drums on the old transformer box after their morning run, shouting "D-S-R – buy it out, D-S-R – buy it out."

Izmir – a necessary risk

Not long after Heiner Ströer's panic about the company's financial situation, another one of those incalculable risks turns up. Again, it is expensive, again risky, again in Turkey.

The city of Izmir, home to more than 3 million people, is planning to build new bus shelters with integrated advertising space. Müller has the chance to put in an offer. But Turkey is on the brink of an unpredictable economic crisis.

What should Müller do? So far, Turkey has cost them more capital than planned, and they have hardly seen a flood of Turkish Lira into the Cologne coffers.

Izmir seems to be a riskier place to do business even than Ankara. But for Müller there is no alternative if he wants to set up a national network in Turkey. This is his chance to strike a strategically important deal in Turkey's third largest city, and he has to grab it.

Things are not much different for an ambitious businessman than for a poker player. Müller realises that this is another one of those moments.

But a new player has now also turned up. A shrewd businessman from Izmir travels to Cologne to convince Müller. Together, the Turkish man says, they could win the tender for the bus shelters in his hometown. "It's worth a million," he insists. "But we have to do it together." It does indeed look very tempting.

But there is more to it than just that. The man says: "In Ankara you have the wrong partner. Mustafa Ilbak is nothing but an Islamic right winger." Maybe Müller should heed the warning. But it's only a vague accusation and he isn't sure if it's enough for him to pass up the opportunity to gain a business foothold in a city like Izmir.

It later turns out that the two Turkish businessmen have been rivals for a long time. Both court Müller's favour in their own way. Müller might end up crushed between the two, but he continues to play the dangerous game – and ends up with two partners in Turkey.

But it seems to work out. The combination of Müller's product, know-how and capital, and his partners' negotiation skills, seem to work. They get the contract for the bus shelters in Izmir and start building them immediately, exclusively with money from Germany.

So, the dream goes on. It must go on. Without Izmir and further growth, it wouldn't be possible to set up a national Turkish marketing network. Ankara alone is too small. There is no alternative to this risky enterprise. If Müller stops his courageous investments, it could all end in tears. If he continues, Ströer could soon be the undisputed number one in Turkey. That's Müller's vision, anyway.

Izmir means a lot of stress for the finance officers at home. They have to present the new investment proposal to the banks and to create a transparent legal structure for the German-Turkish connection.

During the negotiations in Izmir, the Cologne representatives feel as though they are in a different world. But this is the 1990s, Turkey is now booming and seems to be on a path toward integration in Europe, both economically and socially. It seems a good place for investment. And the bankers agree.

But maybe it is going a bit too well. On a quiet Thursday

evening, just as Müller is planning for a private weekend in Berlin, his secretary puts through an urgent phone call from Turkey. Müller needs to go there immediately. There are a few problems that could jeopardise the whole business.

"You have to come to Izmir tomorrow," his partner says. "Otherwise, your money is gone." He doesn't say "the" money. He says "your" money. And that means several million. Millions for which Müller is the guarantor. The Berlin weekend is cancelled.

Müller lands in Izmir late on Friday afternoon. His Turkish lawyer meets him at the airport and briefly explains the situation. "There are a few points in the contract regarding your partnership that are unclear."

The events of the next few hours will be forever etched in Müller's memory. His Turkish partner claims that Müller hasn't honoured some agreements and wants to sue him for breach of contract. It means he wants to push Müller out of the contract but keep the money.

Müller has a short conversation with his lawyer who considers the situation "pretty dangerous." His old business partner in Ankara had kind of warned him. Too late.

The meeting cannot, by any standard, be called a pleasant talk between partners or even a negotiation. Müller and the Turkish man shout at each other at full volume. The interpreters struggle to translate the tirades from one language to the other.

This goes on for hour after hour all through the night. There is no solution, and Müller leaves the next morning for Cologne without any sleep. Nothing is cleared up. There is no agreement.

More than € 10 million are at stake. That could kill Ströer City Marketing, not just in Izmir. Müller feels like a roulette player. "Rien ne va plus" – no more bets. The ball is rolling.

During the next few days, Ströer's lawyers check the contracts again. They are not optimistic. There might be a good chance of winning in a German court, but the venue would not be Cologne but Izmir.

There's a sense of alarm in head office. But Müller seems amazingly calm, at least outwardly. This is a character trait even he had been unaware of before now: He can keep his head, even when under severe stress. He can always remain cooler than his opponent. Müller thinks he has sussed out the game his Turkish adversary is playing.

The conflict goes on: Phone calls, lawyer's letters, shouting. If it has to go to court, Müller will run the risk of losing the €10 million that Ströer has already invested. Another option is to buy the shares of his Izmir partner for another 10 million. But that would double the risk in Izmir – and leave him without a local partner.

It's a very tricky situation. It would be hard for the German company to lose €10 million. And if Müller invested another €10 million, only for the Turkish business to then flop, even the parent company in Germany would be in danger.

Udo Müller decides to take the risk. Again, he puts everything on one horse. He buys out his Turkish partner investing €10 million in the Izmir business, which now belongs entirely to Ströer.

Heiner Ströer apparently takes a back seat as this dangerous affair plays out. But nobody knows yet that the older partner has other worries.

Two generations, two different philosophies

This is a normal week in Udo Müller's life: From Monday to Friday at some hotspot in the Ströer world, up to

18 hours daily of work and stress. On a plane nearly every day, about 200 flights per year.

During his first years in Cologne, Müller lived in a suite in the Cologne Centre Holiday Inn. He got himself an additional clothes rack for his smart suits plus a stereo with loudspeakers. That was enough at the time.

By now he has a lovely flat in the city with an attractive roof terrace and a bit more privacy and style. He still spends the weekends in Berlin, his favourite city. Or he meets up with Dirk and friends in Heiner Ströer's refuge on Majorca. Ideas, plans and projects constantly swirl around in his head, wherever he is.

Heiner Ströer himself is now running his business at a slightly slower pace, particularly the companies in the old Federal States. He finds that sticking to a routine is the best path to success. The regional heads mostly work independently and professionally.

The marketing of the advertising media is run centrally by a service company founded by Udo and Ströer together. But in contrast to the mutually owned Ströer City Marketing, Heiner Ströer Außenwerbung – outdoor advertising –, which focuses still on traditional billboards and posters, yields a nice profit.

It seems that Heiner's conservative business strategy is much more successful than Udo's risky tactics. There are two different generations at the wheel.

And Dirk, the son and heir? Encouraged by Udo, he has tried twice to find a place in his father's business. But it's not for him. He wants to find his own way – but he does want to be an entrepreneur, most of all, his own boss. It's just that he doesn't want to hang posters on walls.

It's the late 1990s and the digital wave is about to roll in. Dirk is intrigued. The digital era could be his thing, and he concentrates on this new world.

He finds a suitable moment and asks his father for a loan of more than 50,000 Dollar. In partnership with a friend, he wants to invest in an internet start-up – an online advertising agency named Orange Media. His father doesn't really expect to get his money back, but he is happy to learn about his son's ambitions.

Dirk and Udo don't spend so much time with each other anymore. They both have their own projects. Müller is relentless in driving his employees, both at head office and elsewhere, to their top performance.

Müller works on the future of the Ströer-Group. His strategy is clear. On one side, he is pushing for organic growth with the new glass media in outdoor advertising – the Citylights and Megalights, the elegant advertising columns and modern bus shelters. On the other side, he is also pursuing takeovers of businesses at home and abroad. Without further acquisitions, the company hasn't got much chance against its rivals in the long term. They wouldn't be able to become one of the big players. Ströer agrees.

So, they need to buy and finance success. It's a risky strategy, but there is no alternative for Udo. Heiner Ströer is still anxious about large investments and running up debt, but he agrees with the plans.

Ströer City Marketing, previously a rather small company, undergoes drastic changes. Its turnover continues to grow year-on-year and at the end of the 1990s is about 100 million Dollar. Müller is optimistic. In the coming years the turnover will be more than doubled again. The future is bright.

Rising debts but a new head office

The head office in Cologne is bursting at its seams. They need more space for the growing number of employees.

In the summer of 2000 – Udo and Heiner have been working together for more than 10 years now – the idea comes up to build new headquarters for the group of companies in Cologne. Müller imagines a big, imposing building symbolizing the dynamic, expanding group. And even the usually skeptical Heiner likes the idea.

There is, as usual, only one problem: A building like that would cost millions. And Ströer City Marketing doesn't have the money. But the solid old company, owned by the senior partner, does. So, Heiner Ströer suggests financing the building alone. And the planning begins.

At the time, there are not that many companies in Germany following such an aggressive course of growth. The rivals, such as DSR in Frankfurt, awk in Koblenz and Wall in Berlin, watch from afar, harbouring quiet reservations about their powerful competitor in Cologne.

Their skepticism is not misplaced. Parts of Ströer City Marketing continue to go downhill. The Turkey business, for example, has turned out to be a complete disaster. Müller managed to buy out his dubious business partner, and the company is now completely owned by the Ströer group, but he has invested 20 million in Izmir alone – and the situation is getting more and more critical as the economic crisis in Turkey continues to worsen.

The Cologne bank is alarmed. The Turkish investment now amounts to nearly 30 mill Dollar, and the income hardly covers the costs of the office.

The bank urges Udo and Heiner to sell the whole Turkish business as the inflation rate over there climbs toward 20 %. Müller takes the demands of the banks seriously and desperately looks for a buyer. He enters negotiations with New Outdoor, a subsidiary of the News Corporation, owned by the media tycoon Rupert Murdoch. But the negotiations fail. Müller's asking price is too high. He contacts two other interested parties, but nobody wants to proceed.

The banks are getting nervous. They wonder whether Müller is bluffing and not really looking for a buyer.

But that is not the case. Müller is looking hard but he also doesn't want to sell for less than the company is worth. In the world of advertising, people begin to wonder at what point the banks will turn off the tap and force Ströer City Marketing itself to be put up for sale.

But just as the situation seems to be getting even more desperate, all of a sudden and to everyone's surprise, the economic situation in Turkey changes. Udo Müller, again, had put everything on one horse and at the last decisive moment had the necessary stroke of luck. The Turkish economy begins to grow at such a pace that the Ströer companies manage to turn a financial burden into an engine for growth.

Megalights – the secret project

Udo Müller is constantly pondering how to turn his Megalights into a major success. They are strategically very important for the company. In contrast to the traditional billboards, they can be marketed as prime advertising media and can generate much higher revenue.

In the new Federal States, Müller has managed to set up about 250 Megalights on private land and, for the first time, also on public land. He is now number one in this field. But to market them in the whole of Germany, he needs a nationwide network in the West. Apart from Dresden, Leipzig and what was once East Berlin, all cities with more than half a million inhabitants are in the former West Germany.

Those cities, though, usually let their sites for classic billboards on long term contracts, nearly always to DSR, which is owned by councils. Long-term agreements are also in place for street furnishings, typically JCDecaux's Citylights, the two-meter-square backlit advertising spaces. The French market them very successfully as prime advertising spaces.

Ströer can't muscle into this market. All suitable sites have been rented out long-term. But the massive Megalights are the first new, major product to be launched in the outdoor advertising market for two decades – and this is where Müller sees his chance. He wants to conquer the market for high-quality advertising and to become number one in the whole of Germany. But he needs more sites in the large Western cities – and as he can't get hold of public spaces, he will have to find privately owned sites.

So far, this market has been managed by freelance agencies who offer the sites, together with private contracts, in bundles of 30 or 50. Müller doesn't like the system. Often half the sites are not particularly good but have to be taken on anyway. Moreover, he is bothered by the fact that the agencies are in the know about the sites and not he himself. He doesn't know, for example, whether he could persuade the owners of some sites to sign a contract if he only offered a little bit more money.

He decides to disrupt the system, to organise it differently, make it more professional. He knows from his time in Berlin that it isn't that difficult to identify promising sites. Back then, he had just driven along the old border on his motorbike and found several interesting sites on every trip.

Now he is on the lookout for someone he can trust, who doesn't have any contact with the rest of the advertising world. Someone who is passionate, a quick learner, diligent and secretive.

Müller already has an idea whom he can ask to solve his problem. During his last skiing holiday, he met a young man, in his mid-20s, named Alexander Stotz. He studies business management, is the son of a Düsseldorf ice hockey pro, and is a nice, lively guy, quite unconventional.

On the last day of the holiday, Stotz had jokily said he could always do with a few more Euros. And if Ströer ever needed a student intern, he would be available. So, Müller calls the young man. It is the start of a long friendship.

Guided by Müller, Alexander begins to train small groups of people to secretly search for possible sites. Following a pattern Müller sets up, Stotz and his helpers search along busy roads in most German cities, following a well-prepared map.

Eventually they find more than 1,000 possible sites. Stotz delivers the data to contractors in the respective cities to set up rental contracts with the owners of the sites and houses. If the offer is rejected, they make a note. Six months later they will try again, in the hope of eventually convincing the landlords.

As soon as they have signed a new contract, they apply for permission from the council. To deceive their rivals, the Megalights are described as "billboards on columns". Who knows what contacts the rivals might have inside the respective planning departments. Müller knows that his plan can only work if he keeps it top secret.

Often the planning departments reject the applications.

When that happens, the lawyers step in and take them to court. "Such a trial can take a few years," Müller says. Once the application is granted, the foundations are placed – and immediately covered up. Without his rivals having noticed anything, the concrete foundations for the new advertising media, weighing up to a ton, are ready. Everywhere.

It's clever but also expensive. Ströer not only pays for the building work for the future Megalight sites, but the company doesn't yet know whether they will ever market this kind of outdoor advertising in a profitable way. Added to it comes the cost for acquisition, planning applications and legal advice. And of course the rent for hundreds of Megalight sites, even though there is only a slab of concrete in place.

In the summer of 1998, an interesting possibility comes up that might help the company to get a foothold in council land in a large city in West Germany. Düsseldorf puts out a tender request for "advertising panels on a single column". That describes Müller's Megalights perfectly. They want 50. That will not be enough to meet Müller's plan for a complete network, but, thanks to Stotz and his team, he has already secured a good number of private sites his rivals have no idea about.

Düsseldorf is one of the few cities with more than 500,000 inhabitants that has not previously asked DSR to manage its outdoor advertising. Despite DSR's absence, there is no other company that has secured access to a complete package.

Düsseldorf is also interesting for Müller for other reasons. Alongside Hamburg and Frankfurt, Düsseldorf is one of the three main bases for many of the major advertising agencies. If Müller can manage to set up his Megalights as a new premium product all over town, the employees of the agencies would see this innovative outdoor advertising medium each day on their way to work.

Apart from Ströer, DSR is bidding, of course, as well as the Düsseldorf-based company Moplak, and familiar rivals awk and JCDecaux. During the tender process, the applicants are driven through Düsseldorf, looking at the planned advertising sites, with the councilors responsible for the decision-making. It's an established routine, but for Müller it is particularly enjoyable. He knows that wherever they might go, Ströer has already put foundations down on private ground and has the area covered.

This means that Müller can attempt to win the tender by offering the city a particularly high rent, accepting that his margin will be smaller. He knows that he will have the 50 additional Megalights on private sites. He can combine public and private revenue.

Müller's strategy works. Not only does Ströer win the Düsseldorf contract, but the company also takes a decisive step towards a nationwide network of Megalights.

The competitors soon begin looking for private sites and notice that Ströer has been everywhere already. Even if they can identify the occasional promising site, it isn't enough to create a lucrative network in the city.

One after another, the rivals give up. First Moplak, then Wall and eventually DSR, which has just been renamed DSM: Deutsche Städte Medien. "Medien" sounds more modern and supposedly more dynamic. But that is just the name. It's only Ströer that is truly a dynamic, modern company.

For all that, the bankers remain worried about Müller's strategy. After all, it's their loans that are financing the whole show. The new, technically demanding Megalights need millions to set up during the early installation phase, without a single Euro of profit. Staffing costs, rents and building work mean the investment costs are high.

It's a slow process. The company has permits for more than 1,000 sites, but after two years only half are working. Müller cannot yet guarantee his advertising clients a nationwide network. Not yet.

But, of course, he continues to exude pure optimism. "Our goal is growth," he tells *Handelsbatt*, a Düsseldorf business magazine, when asked about his strategy. "Simply growth." At what cost, Müller doesn't say. And he also remains silent regarding his long-term goals.

The former follower of Bhagwan might also have said that "the path is the goal". But the question remains whether everything is slowly moving uphill, or whether it is plunging towards the abyss.

It doesn't matter to Müller. He steps on the gas pedal again.

Another Warsaw Pact

Some people are just lucky in choosing their profession. Oscar Silber is one of them. He is a man in his 70s who loves to travel, has numerous connections and a single client. The man with a French passport and a Polish background has been looking after the worldwide poster advertising for Renault lorries for a long time. It's a lucrative business, and Silber does a lot of travelling. It's a lot of fun as well.

There is even time for the odd additional little business, for example this thing in Poland. When the Iron Curtain came down, Silber quickly founded a company in Warsaw for large panels in the so-called Austrian format. That meant advertising space of about 12 square meters which was also successful in the Czech Republic, Slovakia, and Hungary. It came as no surprise, because German companies were busy focusing on their eastern regions, leaving the path free for others to pursue business plans in the countries of Central Europe.

Heiner Ströer and Oscar Silber have known each other for a long time. The old man from Paris also likes Udo Müller. He enjoys the way Müller manages to disrupt the scene. They meet up every now and then, also because Ströer City Marketing is active in Poland. It's a relaxed relationship, without much rivalry.

It's a quiet Wednesday in May 1999. Müller gets the news from a confidential source that Silber is selling his Polish company. He is immediately on high alert. He dials Silber's Paris number.

Müller comes to the point without small talk. "Oscar, you want to sell Poland?" He can sense Silber's surprise.

"No, I don't *want* to," he says. He adds after a short pause: "I have sold it already."

"To DSM?" Müller knows that DSM, which is already active in Poland, is looking for companies to take over to offer their clients a more comprehensive deal.

"Yes, to DSM. They made me a particularly good offer, and I have agreed."

"Have you signed?"

"We are signing next week, Monday morning."

"Let's meet up before that."

Müller takes several minutes to convince Silber, but he eventually agrees. "Okay," he says. "I'll come to Cologne tomorrow." Then he adds: "I'd like to see Heiner again."

There is no time to lose. Müller urgently calls in some colleagues and they quickly develop a plan for how they can usurp Silber's deal with DSM. Any plans for a relaxed weekend go out the window.

Poland is not a new prospect for Heiner Ströer and Udo Müller. With their partner Heinrich Schuster, the men from Cologne own a shared business for bus shelter advertising in Warsaw. Schuster also has his own independent company for billboards. But both companies are run by the same Polish man, a Mr. Kaczan.

They have had an agreement over finances for the past three years. Any profits are supposed to be distributed depending on whether they come from the billboards, in which case they go to Schuster, or the bus shelters, which will be split among members the joint venture. But the Cologne headquarters has not seen a single Euro of profit so far.

Only a week ago, Müller called Warsaw to ask how things were going. He couldn't get hold of Schuster, so he had a chat with the Polish manager Kaczan.

"How is business with our bus shelters, Mr. Kaczan?"

"Bad, as usual, *szanowny* Pan Müller."

Then "nice" Mr. Müller asks after the billboards. As expected, the situation is completely different. "Oh, they are more and more in demand," Kaczan says. "I've just sent off a report to Mr. Schuster. In the past year alone, coverage rose by 10 %, and profits ..."

This confirms Müller's suspicions. He is sure that his Austrian partner Schuster manages the marketing professionally – but focuses mainly on his own company. Müller is annoyed. As was the case with blowUPs, the interests of the partners are not aligned. It needs to change.

This is how things stand when Müller gets the insider tip about Silber's intention to sell. But why does he want to sell?

On Thursday afternoon Oscar Silber flies in from Paris. Udo meets him at Cologne airport. In the old head office, Heiner is waiting for his old acquaintance, but Ströer declares immediately that he will keep out of the Polish business. That would be Udo's thing.

Then the negotiations begin. As a reason for selling, Silber cites the increasing expansion of the outdoor advertising world. "There's too much competition. The market needs to be consolidated. But I'm too old for that," he says.

Silber's Polish portfolio would be a starting point from which Ströer could restructure its business in Poland. Warsaw's wide city streets, often with four or six lanes, are ideal for the larger advertising formats – far better than the two-metre-square frames on bus shelters.

The evening goes well, and the three men end up in a good mood, exchanging old stories and new insights at their favourite Italian restaurant.

On Friday, the morning after, Udo Müller and Oscar Silber negotiate the Poland deal. Silber doesn't want to take anything less than the price offered by DSM but isn't intent on driving it up either.

All the while, Ströer's department of mergers and acquisitions, which is responsible for such transactions, calculates the financing of the deal. Lawyers draft a contract. It's a lot of work in very little time. Müller always asks a lot of his staff. The weekend, which should have been free, is instead spent preparing a detailed contract.

On Monday morning Silber, Müller and his team fly to Warsaw to complete the last-minute deal. They sit in the lawyer's office from 9 in the morning until 9 at night. It takes hours to finalise the deal. Silber needs to convince his Polish partner why the sudden change of buyer makes sense.

In the Frankfurt headquarters of DSM, they know by now that Silber has gone to Cologne. The boss, Egon Böttcher, doesn't officially know the reason, but Cologne …? He guesses that Müller might be muscling in.

Böttcher tries again and again to get through to Silber on his mobile while the old man is sitting with Müller in the lawyer's office. Eventually Silber answers the call.

Böttcher comes to the point straightaway and asks whether there are any problems. Silber answers with a single word: "Why?" He then reassures him that they need not worry in Frankfurt. Everything is going as planned. With a wry smile Silber turns to Müller. "I don't have to say *which* plan is going well."

The truth about the deal only reaches Frankfurt the next day. DSM has been outsmarted right at the finishing line. DSM's boss is furious; Müller is delighted.

He now has his own business in Poland.

The future is suddenly bright

Udo Müller would love to be always everywhere at the same time, just as he was during the early days in Berlin. But that doesn't work. He is now learning to play the role of chairman of a major company: thinking strategically, motivating others, giving sensible guidance without losing sight of the small details. However, without good circumstances, without luck, even the best investment is doomed to failure.

It is particularly true for fragile, foreign businesses such as in Turkey. But gradually the tense situations in Ankara and Izmir are relaxing. At the end of the 1990s, the Turkish economy is improving. In the battle for the attention of the growing number of consumers, there is now more and more advertising.

In the rapidly growing megacity Istanbul, with its population of 10 million, Mustafa Ilbak is rebuilding a billboard business that had lain dormant for a while.

Müller has learned from past mistakes. Instead of having different shares and different interests in co-owned companies, he suggests to Ilbak that they bundle the various companies together and run them all as a joint venture. The proposal includes 100 % of the subsidiary in Izmir, their 50:50 joint venture in Ankara and Ilbak's billboard company in Istanbul.

Ilbak agrees, and the result is the outdoor advertising company Ströer Kentvizyion, based in Istanbul. It is a strange partnership between the Turkish man who doesn't speak any German or English, and the German who doesn't speak any Turkish. But it works – sometimes based on gestures alone, sometimes using an interpreter, but always with lawyers.

Ilbak is a family-oriented man and insists on having his younger brother Murat on the board. Murat is just 20 years old and doesn't have that much experience. Müller has a few reservations but agrees.

As they celebrate the new partnership that evening, in one of the best restaurants in Istanbul, Murat turns up for the first time. He is a good-looking man, in a dark suit, open shirt, hair slightly gelled back. He behaves well and remains quiet when his big brother praises the cooperation with Udo. Udo returns the compliments in good spirits, but suddenly the young man chimes in, uninvited. "It's all very nice," he says loudly, turning to his brother. "But I don't know why we need the Germans for the business." He speaks in English, so Müller can understand. Mustafa admonishes his brother, telling him to hold back.

"It's okay," Müller says. He understands the young man and addresses him directly. He explains the parameters of their cooperation and Murat's role in the organisation during the initial phase. But Murat doesn't look too impressed. He arrogantly shrugs his shoulders.

For Müller, there is some déjà vu. "The boy is all right," he says later. "That's what I must have been like when I met Heiner Ströer for the first time."

Over the following months, Murat indeed turns out to be a real asset for the company. Firstly, Müller can speak English with him. He also turns around the difficult situation in Izmir. Suddenly the money starts coming in and bills get paid. Is it because he has some Turkish connection? It remains Murat's secret how he managed to pull it off. All Müller knows is that the Cologne bankers are settling down.

The economic climate, too, goes through a very positive period. Long may it continue. A certain Recep Tayyip Erdogan, elected as president in 2004, is thought to be behind the upturn. He supports the idea of his country applying for membership of the European Union. Müller's business in Turkey can only benefit from things, whatever happens.

And what about Poland at the beginning of the new millennium? Only a few years ago, the Polish economy was considered a prime example of laziness and sloppiness, for being backward and wasteful. But here, too, they are looking to new horizons. At the turn of the century, the country west of the river Oder has become much favoured among economists and financial institutions. It is considered one of the best examples of a country transforming into a market economy. Experts such as the U.S. economist Jeffrey Sachs praise the "most successful reform of modern times". Michel Camdessus, director of the International Monetary Fund, says that Poland has the "biggest growth in Europe".

In the outdoor advertising sector, now commonly also called "Out of Home" (OoH) advertising, the changes mean three things: High demand for investment, solid growth, but also the incalculable risk of going under amid aggressive competition.

Oscar Silber, the French investor, preferred peace and quiet and sold his Polish poster business. DSM tries to sell off its small Polish subsidiary after a failed expansion in the country. The new Poland is a shark pool, and DSM considers the risks too high. DSM's board wants to concentrate on the internal German market. Egon Böttcher doesn't see any more opportunities in Poland after Müller had outfoxed him over the Silber deal.

There are several interested parties for the Polish subsidiary, most significantly the Warsaw media company Agora. Agora publishes leading daily newspapers such as the liberal *Gazeta Wyborcza* and the advert-heavy free paper *Metro*, whose circulation is one million copies. The company also has radio stations and, together with its subsidiary AMS, is considered one of the biggest players in outdoor advertising.

Ströer City Marketing is also interested, but DSM doesn't want to sell to the Cologne company. The hijacking of the Silber deal still hurts.

However, Müller simply has to wait. He watches the long negotiations between Agora and DSM with excitement. Then there are some rumours that Agora might have problems financing the deal.

Again, Müller calls Böttcher and offers a quick solution. Maybe he knows how much pressure the DSM boss is under. Böttcher fails in his last attempt to push Agora to complete the deal. Müller exploits the short time window and makes a concrete offer. Grudgingly the DSM board agrees. Müller's offer is accepted.

There is disappointment on the Polish side. The Agora manager calls Müller and angrily warns him: "You had better not come to Poland in the foreseeable future!"

But having won the Silber trophy, the DSM treasure, and some smaller acquisitions, Ströer Polska becomes one of the biggest outdoor advertisers in the country. Moje gratulacje, Mr. Müller. Herzlichen Glückwunsch. Congratulations.

But it's another matter whether the Polish economy will grow as quickly as the Turkish.

FIRST IN CLASS

DSM – the old lady of advertising

The headquarters of DSM – where Egon Böttcher, the company's head, and his boardroom colleagues Theo Merkel and Wolfgang Niederwipper work – is in an elegant villa in the upmarket Westend of Frankfurt, formerly occupied by one of the city's bankers. But for a while now, the bourgeois interiors have been replaced by the bland style of a business office.

Among the many small companies in the German poster advertising business, DSM, (formerly known as Deutsche Städte Reklame), is a giant. Anyone wishing to advertise in public spaces in Germany will need to get past DSM first. Most of the company's regional offices in German cities are more luxurious than the headquarters of their rivals.

The market leader has some unbeatable advantages in the industry. For one thing, every municipality has more than enough public spaces for poster advertising. Furthermore, the cities themselves are shareholders in DSM, so DSM is always one step ahead when councils tender for outdoor advertising. But it often doesn't even get that far. In some cities, there are existing advertising contracts that have been in place for several decades, all in favour of DSM.

It sometimes seems as if three central facets of Out of Home advertising in Germany are written in stone:

Firstly, there are the various private enterprises. Hanging posters here, or setting up more modern media such as Megalights, first requires negotiating a deal. There needs to be a contract for every single site with a private owner.

Then there are the advertising spaces in trains, along railway tracks and on stations, which are controlled by a railway advertising organisation.

But unassailably ahead of everyone else, with access to public and communal sites as well as the regional train system, is DSM.

In a memorandum from 1921, the Frankfurt Economic Department said about the growing market in outdoor advertising: "Advertising in tram carriages is also on the increase as the tram company works to decrease its deficit."

The report concluded that "extraordinary revenue" could be generated by a "municipal organisation for advertising". However, it cast doubt that the salary structure within the Chamber of Commerce would be sufficient to support a director of public advertising, even if a new department was created.

Therefore, it recommended the foundation of a private limited company, to be run by someone suitable for this new task. The memorandum stated: "The soul of an enterprise is its manager. In the area of advertising, the business can grow and flourish, new ideas can be generated, and new attractive propaganda be found and tested, even accepting some failures."

And so it happened. On May 23rd, 1924, the Frankfurt magistrate founded Reklamestelle Frankfurt, which soon became Städte Reklame GmbH and eventually Deutsche Städte Reklame. The aim was to expand the new business and to include more cities and towns as shareholders.

Reklamestelle Frankfurt developed quickly into a company active in the whole of the country. Several large German cities became shareholders.

The business continued to prosper after the end of the Second World War. The loss of member cities in the east of the country was quickly overcome by West Germany's "economic miracle" of the 50s and 60s. The East became less important to the communities in the new Federal Republic. By the beginning of the 1990s, when Heiner Ströer and Udo Müller became business partners, DSM was the industry leader with a turnover of 240 million Dollar, 20 times as much as Ströer.

But the once almighty DSM does not impress anyone anymore. It has lost its dynamism and creativity. The far-reaching network of companies is not very flexible. The communal shareholders have become complacent thanks to the guaranteed flow of income. The advertising panels by the side of the road are not very attractive, and only the name has changed: Deutsche Städte Medien.

This advertising giant has featured in Udo Müller's dreams for many years. By now he has conquered everything except DSM. He is number one in the former GDR, has entered the street furnishing sector, has placed Megalights in the West, has taken over the Cologne outdoor advertising market and acquired blowUP. Müller has taken over the premium Out of Home market as far as he possibly can. Nothing more is feasible ... unless DSM was up for sale.

More than ever, he contemplates how and under what circumstances Ströer could take over DSM. The chances are slim, and maybe only theoretical. For one thing, the company is so much bigger than Ströer, and all 26 of its stakeholders would need to consent to the sale. Finally, there is the question of financing. How could the much smaller Cologne company get the money to buy DSM? All things considered, the whole idea is more unrealistic than ever.

But still ... A company's size in this sector earns many more advantages concerning costs as well as turnover. And the more often Müller games the possible scenarios, one thing becomes more and more clear: any deal between Ströer and DSM would be unbeatable in every respect. The combination of the two companies would guarantee an enormous. increase in value.

Ströer and DSM sell the same product to the same clients. If they work together, or if one takes over the other, they will only need one sales force instead of two. Even the network of regional offices is practically identical. "We could calculate the savings precisely," Müller says, "because we know how much it costs us to put up a poster and what it costs DSM." It is equally clear how many offices and employees are required per 1,000 advertising sites. The advantages of cooperation – also called synergy – can be clearly determined. And the savings would be considerable.

It might be more difficult to calculate the expected combined turnover. If the leading two companies merged, the new company would enjoy a huge gap over whichever company would then become the second in line. "We would be a considerably stronger operator in the advertising market than ever before," Müller says. "It would be very difficult to put us under any pressure.

The advantages of being big

Bigger is not always better. In the Out of Home advertising sector, at the beginning of the new millennium, size promised considerable advantages. The market was fragmented with many different actors. Some, like DSM, had mostly public sites to offer its customers. Others, like the railway advertising organisation, only trains and stations. The private outdoor advertisers are strong in some regions, but not at all present in others.

None of them can offer a large advertiser, such as Coca Cola or McDonalds, the necessary sites for a national campaign. For that reason, too, it is extremely difficult for Out of Home advertisers to make direct contact with these companies.

Everything has to go through middlemen, the media agencies. And they too fight among themselves, particularly over budget allocations. If they get a deal, they might suggest to their client how the adverts should be distributed – over print, TV, radio and outdoor. (At this point, online advertising is not yet a factor.)

Large consumer brands are nearly always interested in national campaigns. During the years of the economic miracle after the Second World War, newspapers got the lion's share of the large advertising budgets. Television was not widespread yet, and at the time only one channel broadcast advertising. But the time and slots were limited.

That changed fundamentally with the introduction of privately-owned TV channels. On January 1st, 1984, what later became SAT1 broadcast an opening speech by its then manager Jürgen Doetz, followed by Händel's *Fireworks*. RTL+ launched a day later, broadcasting from a basement studio in a suburb of Ludwigshafen.

The media agencies began to allocate large portions of their advertising budgets to the new TV stations. The more popular with the public these privately-owned TV channels became, the more attractive it was to advertise there.

Soon the private stations were able to dictate the conditions, even to the mighty media agencies. Contracts became more and more complicated and less transparent. If you booked a large amount of advertising minutes, you were often rewarded with a kickback and free slots. The agencies could pass them on as they try to secure new customers.

Additionally, the contracts were structured in a way that the largest media marketing organisations got the largest portion of their clients' advertising budgets. Udo Müller learns how significant this can be one day when talking to the so-called "Sun King" of the German agency scene, Aleksander Ruzicka.

Ruzicka is a dazzling figure: a trophy hunter, a party king, an innovator and the highest of high-flyers. He started his career at 25 with Kai Hiemstra, a legend of the German advertising scene. After Hiemstra's agency was taken over by the French Carat group, the man described by *Handelsblatt* as the "aesthetic Bohemian" becomes general manager and successfully expands his role. In 1989, Carat changes its name to Aegis Media Group, and, at the age of 39, Ruzicka becomes the head of the company's German operations. He manages about € 1 million per year in advertising money.

Knowing all about these figures, Müller wants to learn from Ruzicka how he can secure a little slice of that cake.

"Aleksander, if you have a 500 million Euro turnover with the TV stations, can't you hand over 1 % to me for outdoor advertising?" he asks him. Five million would be peanuts for Ruzicka, but for Müller at the time it is a lot of money.

Ruzicka explains things in detail. The deals with the TV stations were structured in a way that by far the largest part of the fee paid to the agencies comes from the final tenth of the contracted sum. That way the stations set up triggers for the agencies to place as much advertising as possible with them.

"Let's assume the agency and the TV station have agreed an annual budget of 500 million. Of up to a volume of 450 mill, for 90 % of the deal the agency only gets 20 %. For the last 50 mill they get 80 % of the agreed sum. Or, for the final ten percent of the deal the agency earns four times as much as for the first 90 %."

Ruzicka smiles and explains, with a hint of pity in his voice: "Udo, if I give you 5 million from the TV deal for outdoor advertising, I lose money, even if you give back the 5 million as a kickback. You can't pay me anything back that would make sense for me."

Müller is baffled. More than ever, he is convinced that he badly needs to acquire DSM to grow. He needs a national network before he can even approach the major clients. He needs a critical mass to continue to be a player in the media world.

Another encounter shortly afterwards is equally unpleasant. Müller can still remember it clearly. In this instance, the agency was a bit smaller than Aegis, but the main buyer was equally confident.

"I have about €1 billion to spend on advertising," he told Müller. "Eighty percent is for TV and print. The remaining 20 % I can spend on radio, or even your outdoor advertising."

"And what do I have to do to get it?" Udo asks.

"Depends on what you pay," the chief buyer says. "If you kickback 20 % we have a deal."

The usual margin at the time was 10 %, maybe 15 %.

"No can do," Udo says. "That's too much."

"Okay, end of conversation," his adversary says with a shrug.

Müller is annoyed now. This kind of business practice drive him nuts.

"That's blackmail!" he shouts at the agency boss.

The man doesn't bat an eyelid. "No, Mr. Müller, you got that wrong. It has nothing to do with blackmail. It's an entrance fee."

Müller can only stare at him.

"If you want to go to a nightclub, you don't say that you're being blackmailed when they ask for money at the door. You simply have to pay to get in. And here, we are the bouncers. If you won't pay us, you don't get in. You can't go to the party. And if you try to get in through the back door, we will throw you out. Repeatedly. Until you understand."

Müller doesn't want to bribe a bouncer.

"That's completely unacceptable," he says. "What do your clients say about this kind of business practice?"

He goes home outraged. For several days, he wonders whether he should go to the press with this knowledge. Obviously, the agencies do lucrative deals with their clients' money. And it's also obvious that the agencies make money with kickbacks, free minutes and free placements on their clients' backs too. Times are wild.

So wild, in fact, that the worst offenders are being sued. In 2006, Alexander Ruzicka, "advertising's bird of paradise" (*Handelsblatt*) is convicted of fraud and sentenced to 11 years and three months in prison. He is accused of defrauding his customers by at least € 10 million.

For Udo Müller, these experiences underline the importance of being big in business. If Ströer wants to be successful, the company must grow. Grow quickly, grow substantially. Normal, organic growth, in line with the increase in the country's GDP, will never be enough. He needs growth fuelled by takeovers or mergers.

And because of that, there is only really one option – even it is only theoretical. Ströer needs to take over DSM.

But even within his own company, Müller's high-flying plans are not taken seriously. With a gentle smile, one of his closest colleagues says: "Dear Udo, we are much too small to swallow such a big lump."

But why must it always be the big entities that swallow the little ones? Müller wants to turn it around. Sometimes the quickest creatures can eat the slower ones. And that's his challenge. He trains his focus on the project, his victim.

In the meantime, Müller tries to get into business with DSM in other ways. If the mouse can't catch the cat, maybe it can nibble a bit at its tail? DSM shouldn't have any reason to object to closer cooperation if it is advantageous for both sides. Quite the opposite. The bigger company could benefit from the smaller one's fresh approach and flexibility.

Müller details an idea for a mutual marketing organisation. He asks DSM's senior management for a confidential conversation. "I've got something in mind that might benefit us both," Müller says. Böttcher is reluctant at first, but eventually agrees.

They meet in Castle Lerbach, near Cologne. It is a high-end hotel with a highly respected restaurant, and Müller wants to project the fact that he is serious. They greet each other in a friendly manner but there is not that much respect toward Müller and Ströer City Marketing.

All three of DSM's most senior executives have come to the meeting, which suggests to Müller that his plans have a chance. His main aim is to get a foot in the door of his principal rivals. That's what he told his own colleagues, back in the office.

At first glance, his proposition doesn't look spectacular.

He is suggesting the foundation of a mutual marketing company, a cooperation that would increase both sides' power in negotiations with agencies and clients. That's the extent of the proposal.

It's not a bad idea. At present, DSM's advertising spaces are not fully booked. And Ströer too is continually having to fight for clients now. It's the first decade of the new millennium, and the dot-com bubble has burst, sending many ambitious start-ups into bankruptcy and the shaken stock market into steep decline. The economy is in crisis mode, with clients forced to slash their advertising budgets to save money.

The three DSM executives listen to the proposition in silence. Then Egon Böttcher responds. Ströer isn't the right partner for a mutual enterprise, he says. These are the words of a giant talking to a dwarf.

To bring the talks to a close diplomatically, Böttcher mentions possible complications regarding competition law. "The Cartel Office [Germany's national competition regulatory agency] would not allow this kind of partnership," he says. The reason is that DSM would end up dominating the market.

So, his first attempts to get a foot in the door end with it slammed in his face. But did Udo really believe it would be so easy? "If you want to sell up one day, just let me know," he tells Böttcher on the way out, only half-joking.

The cat laughs with malice. Was that a little mouse squeaking? Müller might be a whiz kid, but the DSM goliaths don't take him very seriously. And that's their mistake.

But Müller knows more clearly than ever that he needs DSM. His plans don't have much of a future without the industry leader from Frankfurt. Possibly he doesn't either.

Pride and Fate

It's this dull feeling of helplessness. Dirk Ströer spots his father in the crowd at the Cologne IT-Fair *demexco*, slowly ambling along the aisle towards him. His elegant cashmere coat is open; his hands are folded behind his back. He is looking good, Dirk thinks.

But that is only on the outside. Three hours earlier, Dirk rang his father asking whether he would come to the fair. Dirk wants to show him the exhibition stand of his company Orange Media. It's his first public presentation to the world, and he is very proud of it.

Heiner Ströer held the receiver close to his ear but was hardly listening.

"Are you still there?" Dirk said.

"I'm not feeling well," his father answered quietly, then, after a short pause, added: "Okay. I'll come. I need to talk to you anyway."

Heiner rang Udo a few minutes later but did not have to say much. Müller understood immediately. They had talked a few days ago about an imminent medical procedure. Udo stood by the window of his office, looking out to the wintery garden and the bare trees.

After a few seconds, he said: "Bowel cancer is curable, Heiner."

"I hope so. But it's pretty advanced."

Heiner had now received the results of a coloscopy. He should have had it done a while ago, he knew that. But he repeatedly found an excuse to delay the unpleasant investigation.

Bowel cancer is one of those vicious diseases that often only announces itself when it is too late for a cure. But maybe it will all end well. He is having an operation next week, followed by chemotherapy, and then he can only hope, hope, hope. But he is preoccupied with thoughts of the possible consequences as he sets off to the fair and to see his son.

Heiner makes his way through the throngs towards Dirk's stand and tries to smile at his son in appreciation. Dirk now knows about his father's condition. He hugs him. "It's going to be okay," he whispers. It's the first time that Dirk feels stronger than his father.

The bad news came at the worst possible time for the business. Ströer City Marketing is in the process of becoming a stock corporation, something that requires the full concentration of everyone involved.

Heiner and Udo had been discussing for a while the pros and cons of turning the company into an *Aktiengesellschaft* (AG) – i.e., a stock corporation – rather than keeping it as a limited liability company – (a *Gesellschaft mit beschränkter Haftung* (GmbH)). They eventually came to a decision. It wouldn't alter their positions. The two founders would continue to own 50 % of the company each, with Udo Müller becoming CEO, while Heiner Ströer would join the Advisory Board..

The advantages are obvious for such a quickly growing company as Ströer City Marketing. A stock crporation is the best legal construct for a large company that must satisfy its high financing demands in the capital market and invest its own shares in further acquisitions. And Müller needs more and more capital for his high-flying plans. They don't want to go to the stock market yet, but their path to the capital market is clearly marked out.

By the end of the first quarter of 2001, at the latest, the new company will be registered as *Ströer Out-of-Home Media AG,* based in Cologne. Heiner and Udo want to delay any floatation as long as possible. They don't intend to share their company, and definitely not with greedy shareholders. At this point in time there is no great need for additional capital from the stock market.

But this health news presents a complication. Ströer's diagnosis doesn't change his attitude, but Müller doesn't want to simply carry on as before. He is close to his paternal friend, and the news has hit him hard. They intend to keep the information a secret. "If people ask, I have a disc problem," Ströer says. "Cancer always sounds terminal and has a negative impact on outsiders. However, everybody has back problems."

Ströer doesn't want to sit on the board of directors anymore and suggests that his son Dirk replaces him. "My boy will take my seat," he says. "That's a positive step to the future."

His plan is to retire to the Majorca house after the operation, with his partner Katharina, at least for a few months.

The company returns to business as usual. They have started looking for suitable candidates to fill the board. Ströer and Müller want a strong and independent committee. They choose a chairman: the president of the Federal Agency of Accountants. Ströer has known Wolfgang Bornheim since he was at university. While he was a student, Bornheim designed the logo for the aspiring outdoor advertiser which remains in place to this day.

Müller also likes Bornheim. He is a decade younger than Heiner and a decade older than Udo. He is not only a reliable friend, but also has some impressive talents beyond the law and taxes. For example, he has a pilot's license for jets, and is a very good cook. But it is mainly his excellent business expertise that makes him the ideal candidate for the Chair.

Another important hire is Prof. Dr. Dieter Stolte, a renowned former director of the ZDF television network, who was the editor of the daily newspapers *Die Welt* and

Berliner Morgenpost. He is known as a forthright voice in the media, dating from his role on the board of Deutsche Telekom. Stolte has experience not only of the media industry but also in controlling large companies.

As it once was for Heiner, his son Dirk can learn a lot from these two high-flyers on the board. It also won't be bad for Udo to have someone watching over him closely.

The one thing Heiner Ströer will not abandon despite his illness is the building of the new headquarters. He is closely involved in all the planning.

The vacant plot is only a short distance from the old central office in a Cologne suburb. But an impressive building is growing there. The size and style of the new HQ, with its many offices and conference rooms and a sumptuous entrance hall, are a source of great pride for Heiner Ströer.

In his hometown Cologne, the company's expansion is a source of excitement. When the Lord Mayor comes to lay the foundation stone, he brings an unusual present: A document. The access road to the new head office, financed by the company, will be officially named Ströer Allee, i.e., Ströer Boulevard.

It is almost unprecedented. Very few streets are ever named after a living person.

There is a hint of melancholy too – memories of the company's beginnings with 200 billboards and a single employee. Then the meeting with Udo in Berlin. Those were the exciting years when everything started. But they seem a long time ago.

SHOWTIME

The Americans are coming

New York, New York. Money is more prominent here than anywhere else in the world: amid the hurly-burly of Manhattan, at the mouth of the Hudson River, in the office blocks of Third Avenue and Wall Street. It's the capital of capital, the centre of the financial world.

This is the beating heart of the global economy. It's where the bulls and the bears fight on the stock market. The big finance beasts deal with big money. From here, the hedge funds cast out their billions like fishing rods, luring them with their bait. They are the godfathers of money. Their dangerous offers are hard to reject.

Around the turn of the millennium, an atmosphere of boundless growth is spreading, driven by the new possibilities of the internet. In September 1998, Larry Page and Sergey Brin founded Google in California. Three years later, Apple founder Steve Jobs introduced the iPod. Mark Zuckerberg is still a teenager at high school, but in 2004 launches what becomes Facebook, while still a student.

It is a time of "anything goes", of infinite possibilities and infinite hope. Global stock markets rise to astronomical highs, driven by the hope that this new growth will never end.

Only size matters. More is always better. According to current philosophy, only the company with the biggest turnover can survive. Until now, the accepted wisdom was that DSM was not for sale because of its complicated shareholder structure. That had kept the Americans from stalking their prey in Germany. But things are starting to change.

Udo Müller is not the only person with DSM in his sights. He is, however, the only one who has been dreaming of Germany's biggest fish for a long time. Years later, when everything is over, he will know that ignorance sometimes is bliss. As he comes to learn in the decades after he begins his pursuit of DSM, he would never have given himself a chance of buying the much bigger company.

But he did it, of course. He was an entrepreneur, after all.

During the final years of the last century, the world economy changed dramatically. The digital age dawned, and traditional industry no longer drove the economy. The old limitations on capital were no longer in place; money is no longer an object. A new and expensive game has started. It's dog eat dog.

Around the globe there is a wave of company takeovers. No one has ever seen anything like it before. The big players are going on a special kind of shopping trip. They're foraging, hunting, and the hungriest party wins. The business pages are covered in reports about the trade in companies. There are friendly takeovers and hostile takeovers. No industry is exempt.

On every executive floor, the only question seems to be, "To buy or not to buy?" Sheer size seems to be the all-deciding factor for future success. Some seek the chance to sell their company and make real money, others believe they can only secure their future if they are doing the buying.

3M National is a good example of how the big buy-and-sell feast works. In the middle of the 1990s, the American outdoor advertiser operated in 19 U.S. states putting up large posters for consumer goods. Then the company was swallowed by the bigger Gannett Outdoor, which in turn was bought by Outdoor Systems, which was bought out by Infinity Outdoor, only one year later.

At the turn of the century, Infinity is taken over by the media empire Viacom. A company best known for its radio and TV stations has established a subsidiary by buying poster advertisers, and it is preparing to take Viacom Outdoor International to the stock market. But even that isn't the end of the chain.

There are rumours that the media giant CBS will take over Viacom Outdoor International. The new company will be called CBS Outdoor and attack the current global leader in outdoor advertising Clear Channel Outdoor. It's a dizzying process.

At the same time, Clear Channel Outdoor is going on a shopping trip in Europe. It already has 700,000 large advertising billboards in more than 20 countries, mostly either in the Americas or Asia. Now the company is coming across the Atlantic. The destination is good old Europe.

In Germany, outdoor advertisers enjoy something of a niche existence. Print media, plus TV and radio, still dominate the world of advertising. At the beginning of the new millennium, only 2.7 % of advertising budgets in Germany go to outdoor advertising. In France, where JCDecaux has already consolidated the market and is the absolute number one, it is about four times as much. In the whole of Europe out of home advertising comprises 7 % of the total advertising spend.

A consolidation of the German outdoor advertising market – or, to give it its more modern name "out-of-home" advertising – should help promote conditions for the kind of national networks that larger clients demand. This should increase the share of advertising spending, at least in theory.

There is a lot of money at stake. Companies spend €18.166 billion annually on advertising. If the share of poster adverts could match the French model, it would equal €1.816 billion. As it stands, it is a mere €169 million.

There is a second reason why Europe is so attractive for the American company: the difference in how European businesses are assessed, compared with those in the U.S.

Clear Channel International has established its headquarters in London, in Golden Square near Piccadilly Circus. From here, a certain Roger Parry is managing the European shopping list of advertising companies.

When he looks at potentially attractive companies, he ignores the turnover. Often it doesn't say much about the profitability of a company. Instead, it's the EBITDA that is important: the Earnings before Tax, Depreciation, and Amortization.

Why is EBITDA so important? Here's a short lesson in business studies:

EBITDA is a company's annual financial results before interest, taxes, depreciation on fixed assets and immaterial assets such as the value of a brand or patents.

EBITDA is sometimes also described as "sustainable operative cashflow before taxes". *Sustainable* because the financial flow is not distorted by exceptional items. That is important for assessing the value of a company by EBITDA.

But a company's real worth is sometimes still relative. Objectively, the formula for calculating it is "EBITDA times factor X minus debts". X is the multiplier the buyer is willing to pay.

In the last century, an eight to 10-fold EBITDA was a basis for takeover negotiations. According to this calculation, Ströer City Marketing, for example, with an annual turnover of € 10 mill and a multiplier of eight to 10, without considering its debts, would be worth some € 10 to € 100 million.

But it's not the same during these crazy times. Now Clear Channel offers 14 times the EBITDA. Ströer City Marketing is immediately worth 50 % more, thanks to just one signature. That's how it was during this limitless spending spree. Some of the European OoH advertisers simply didn't know what had hit them when they first received this kind of offer.

For Clear Channel, the European OoH advertisers were still a bargain despite these price hikes. In the United States, companies were being valued at 20 times their annual results, or even more.

There is one more reason why takeovers in Europe were still very interesting for American companies.

A brief experiment: Let's assume *Clear Channel* takes over a European company with an EBITDA of € 100 million at factor 14 and assumes its value at € 1.4 billion. If the deal succeeds, the value of *Clear Channel* at the American stock market increases – with a factor 20, to then for example € 1 billion.

Clear Channel benefits in several ways from this miraculous increase in value on the stock market, and the potential credit volume increases in line to make further buyouts possible.

It's no surprise that hungry investors believe the party has only just started.

Roger Parry's scouts propose one candidate after another to London. The state-owned train advertising concession in France is added to Clear Channel's portfolio with minimum fuss. In Spain and Italy, they find prey as well. Who can possibly say no to Clear Channel International's blank cheques?

The wealthy businesses of Germany represent a potential jackpot. Roger Parry is particularly keen on DSM and Ströer. He would love to buy out both and then fuse them together.

But there is someone else dreaming the same big dream. It's a relatively unknown entrepreneur in Cologne name Udo Müller. He is not thinking of *selling* his company. He wants to prove that a German company can become a powerful player in international media. He himself wants to take the plunge once DSM is up for sale. But how? There isn't that much luck around to make *that* happen.

Mr. Parry's plan

Every success relies on a bit of luck. Ever since his teenage years, Müller has admired the works of the Nobel prize winner Hermann Hesse. Hesse's novel *Der Kurgast* (The Spa Visitor) is about a passionate gambler who always banks on his luck and his instincts. He either has all or nothing: The moment of winning is wonderful, it says there, one had implored fate and subdued oneself to it. One believes to have access to the great secret, have an inkling to be friends with it and it turns out to be true, it gets confirmed, one's secret quiet imagination, one's little wish is suddenly shining. A miracle is happening, the inkling becomes reality, one's number is being chosen by the almighty lucky ball. The man at the top of the table calls it, and the other man at the table throws one a handful of shiny silver coins. It is very pretty, this pure happiness, and it has nothing to do with the money. It goes on: One can experience this kind of happiness on higher planes, in the lighting up of a deep insight into life, a moment of an inner victory, and, mostly, in the creative moment of finding something, the flash of an idea, the triumphing touch of the artist. All this is in higher regions, like the experience of winning, like object and image.

As an entrepreneur, Udo Müller would refuse the comparison with a gambler. But he wouldn't deny that a bit of fortune is part of the business. Since 1990 at the latest, the economy has become his biggest gamble. It's like a giant game of roulette, where capital and ideas are the rolling ball. Risk-taking is part of it. And luck.

He sets the ball quietly rolling again in August 2000, in the parking lot of Castle Lerbach. Udo Müller likes to use this hotel near Cologne for important meetings. A while ago, he met here with DSM's top executives. His suggestion that the companies cooperate had been rejected quite brusquely. Today, however, he's discussing internal issues with Ströer's senior managers.

As they stroll through the parking lot, a mobile starts ringing. It belongs to Alfried Bührdel, Müller's finance chief. It is a call from the private bank, Sal. Oppenheim. A few days ago, Bührdel had asked the bank about refinancing a few loans. It's a purely routine request.

Müller walks ahead while his finance manager takes the call, but soon he turns around. "Udo, there is a problem," Bührdel says. "Oppenheim has rejected the request." The reason is that the bank "would be conflicted" – i.e., that they have a conflict of interest.

In this case, Sal. Oppenheim is working already for another company in the advertising industry. But it must be particularly delicate, otherwise the rejection would not make sense. This other business must somehow also affect

Ströer. Who could it be? Suddenly DSM comes to Udo's mind again. Does it have something to do with their major rival?

The next morning, just as Müller sits down at his desk, he receives a return call from an investment banker friend. Müller had tried and failed to contact the friend yesterday but sent an email asking after Sal. Oppenheim's possible deal.

Yes, he had heard some rumours, the friend says. DSM might be for sale, and negotiations might already have started. But he cannot confirm or deny it. Something was up, though.

Müller dials a Frankfurt number and gets Egon Böttcher on the line.

"Egon, I just heard that you want to sell."

They talk for about two minutes. There doesn't seem to be much to say. Lost in thought, Udo walks over to Heiner's office. "Egon says there's nothing to it. He says he would contact us first." Then he adds: "The denial is ridiculous. I'm sure there is something going on."

Müller is alarmed. In moments like these he feels like he did years ago, as a handball pro before a big match. The adrenaline level is rising. And at this moment it's rising dramatically.

But he needs more facts. He asks the Bonn agency Pleon to do some research. The agency has excellent contacts to the right communities and Udo asks them to discreetly enquire of the DSM shareholders whether the poster company is to be sold. The shareholders should know what is going on, after all.

A short time later the phone rings at HQ. A certain Mr. Roger Parry from London wishes to speak to Mr. Müller.

After a short, polite exchange, the manager of Clear Channel comes to the point.

"I guess you know about the DSM sale," he asks Müller. Before this moment, the two men had never spoken.

Müller's pulse is racing.

Bang! The rumours are true. DSM is indeed on the market. And this British guy talks about it in such a casual way, as if he's putting together a shopping list for a barbecue.

Müller tries not to show his excitement. He needs only a fraction of a second to answer equally casually: "Yes, yes, I heard about it."

Talks like this between potential buyers are essentially illegal. The specific details are bound by a non-disclosure agreement. All interested parties must sign it before they can look at the sales papers of the company involved. Penalty for breaking the terms can be high.

But Parry doesn't seem to mind. He wants to talk it over in detail as soon as possible, he says.

Hardly three days have passed since Sal. Oppenheim rejected the mandate for refinancing loans. Now the reason is clear. DSM is really and truly for sale. Sal. Oppenheim is managing the sale and has already contacted potential buyers such as Clear Channel.

But what are Parry's real plans? The surprising phone call was a lucky opportunity, but now there's going to need to be action. Müller wants to go to London the next day anyway. He has an invite from the Bankers Trust International to go to a conference, on, of all topics, company takeovers. Sellers and potential buyers will meet, hunters and their prey. Müller is probably seen as prey.

While the conference is still going on, Müller meets up with Parry. They greet each other in a friendly manner. The British man doesn't come across as a tough guy intent on the kill.

Parry seems to assume that Müller is fully informed. On

the table is a so called factbook bearing the number 17 and a "strictly confidential" stamp. In very small print, Müller can make out the sender: Sal. Oppenheim.

Müller tries to appear as casual as possible and picks up the folder. He can't believe what is happening. For such a long time, he has dreamt about buying DSM, but everybody has always maintained that the company would never be for sale. The municipal owners would never all agree to it.

But now the factbook is on the table in front of him. It's 68 pages of all of DSM's important business data. Only the most sensitive figures are redacted.

Parry's plan is as follows: he wants Clear Channel to take over Ströer at a good price. Then they buy Deutsche Städte Medien together. Müller can be the top manager of the new Clear Channel Ströer Germany, a fusion of both companies.

Parry talks like a godfather making an offer that nobody would reject. He ends with the words: "Doesn't that sound good?"

Müller nods, smiling. Only now is he sure that DSM really is for sale. And he also knows that the long-winded process us.t have started months ago. Müller says goodbye after an hour, but they agree to keep talking.

He has hardly taken a step outside before he first rings Heiner Ströer on Majorca, then Wolfgang Bornheim, the chairman of the board, in Cologne. They have no time to lose. Müller wants a meeting of all the relevant Ströer committees. He wants DSM more than ever.

While still in London, Müller arranges to meet the European Head of the U.S. investor Springwater Capital. Müller knows him through a mutual acquaintance. If he is to have any chance of joining the game to win DSM, he will definitely need more capital. A lot of capital. And the meeting with Springwater will help him get it.

However, the answer comes promptly and is absolutely clear: No. The Springwater representative says that a small enterprise like Ströer couldn't hope to take over a giant like DSM.

Should he accept Parry's offer after all? No! He has envisioned buying DSM for so long. And it still dominates his thoughts. On his flight back from London, Müller gives the project a code name: "Mission Thunder".

Mission Impossible would have been better. He knows as well as anybody that it's practically impossible for a significantly smaller, less profitable company like Ströer, which already has high debts, to buy a giant like DSM.

The insiders keep silent

Of course, Egon Böttcher had lied when he denied that DSM was for sale. And he knows he did the right thing. It would have been awkward to tell Müller the truth. Ströer could never be a potential buyer. Why give him hope?

At the time, the multiples factor was extremely high, maybe even higher for a strategically important asset like DSM. With a then EBITDA of € 10 million, the sale could make more than € 100 million, at least according to Sal. Oppenheim's estimate. They have set the price high to convince the shareholders of the sale. The market, after all, is going crazy. So, if you want to make hay, why not now? This Ströer, the little number from Cologne, would only get in the way.

But this kind of deal is not done within days or weeks. Six months passed between Böttcher suggesting it in the working committee of the board, asking for strict confidentiality. The working committee, with six members, is the strategic board of DSM. It's the company's government. The supervisory board is the parliament of council shareholders, represented by one or two members depending on the size of the community. The working committee wants to get some facts together that will inform an attractive offer, the kind that would make a deal irresistible.

In such a large committee, a sensitive issue like a sale would be talked about to death and be all over the newspapers the next morning. That's the reason why Böttcher has committed the members of the working group to strict confidentiality. Of course, in the end, all committees must consent to the sale. After that, the potential contract would go to the parliaments of each of the 26 municipalities, who are the shareholders of DSM.

It is a gigantic project. The proposed sales contract needs to be irresistible. With a good deal, every shareholder will get at least € 10 million, and probably much more. Nobody says no to that. For large shareholders, such as Frankfurt or Munich, it would probably mean up to € 100 million.

Three weeks later, Ströer gets a mysterious letter. The sender is a local politician from a north-western city. He asks Mr. Müller for an expert opinion "as arranged on the phone". Included are the strictly confidential copies of the sales plan for the DSM working committee.

Also included is a list of interested parties. There are only seven candidates. Except for JCDecaux, none has experience in outdoor advertising. That enrages Müller even more. This is not a fair sales process!

Another strange aspect is that the only OoH advertiser in the pool of candidates already has a joint venture in Munich called DSM-JCDecaux and as such has close contact with DSM. Also, one of Sal. Oppenheim's lawyers involved in the sale, had, in his previous. position, advised

JCDecaux on entering the German market. Why is there no public, open tender, which would raise the price? Maybe because this way, there's the highest chance for the existing DSM management to remain in their positions after the sale? Maybe with better conditions?

There are many improbabilities. Too many.

Udo Müller addresses them whenever he can. He also directly addresses DSM's board, which means the cities involved. Frankfurt and Munich are the most important shareholders, so Müller calls the Frankfurt town hall and is connected to the city treasurer, a certain Dr. Constantin Alsheimer. "Alsheimer with an s, not with a z. He is not ill," says the receptionist. Haha!

Alsheimer is the office manager in the Frankfurt treasury but hasn't been in the job long. It's only his second role after graduating, having previously worked for Commerzbank.

Müller comes to the point straightaway and asks about the DSM sale. "What sale? I don't know anything about it," Alsheimer says, promising to seek out more information.

Only an hour later he rings back. "No one here knows anything about a DSM sale," he says.

"Well, in that case I have a surprise for you," Müller replies.

He sends a copy of the sales document via courier to Frankfurt. They are greatly upset. Are people secretly trying to sell their valuable heirlooms?

But it soon turns out that Frankfurt had actually been informed. Their representative on the board was Hans-Jürgen Moog, an ex-mayor who had been allowed to keep his position on the DSM board. As an old-school lawyer and civil servant, Moog had felt obliged to keep the confidentiality requested by DSM.

DSM's managers had had a clever plan. Of course, they knew that the deal would only have a chance of being signed off if all 26 municipalities agreed. There had to be such a fat sum at stake that the politicians in the community parliaments wouldn't have a choice but to agree to it. The sales contract therefore had to be negotiated and ready for signing, with a very good price attached.

But the Frankfurt council is now upset. Böttcher is called in and he tries to limit the damage with the argument that no sensitive information had been shared, and that nothing had been finalised yet. He says the council should understand the need for confidentiality.

But Müller has set a fuse burning. He assumes that there have been secret negotiations with JCDecaux already. Within his inner circle, Böttcher had sounded quite sure of himself for a while now. "There will be a big bang," he had boasted confidently. He thinks he can ignore Müller for a while.

But in fact, the atmosphere on the executive floor of DSM, as well as with the shareholders in the communities, is more turbulent than expected. It gets worse when the information leaks that the DSM management team is trying to extend their highly lucrative contracts for another five years.

At the same time, Ströer's chairman Bornheim contacts his equivalent on DSM's committee. He seems to be informed about everything but does not know that Ströer has been excluded from the list of bidders. The controller promises he will investigate it.

After a few days of tense silence, a remorseful Mr. Schlaberg of Sal. Oppenheim contacts Müller. It's good news. Ströer is invited to enter the bidding process.

There is a loud cheer in Ströer Allee 1. Müller's work

has been worthwhile. Now even the cautious senior partner is convinced. "When a big jumbo jet is flying past, we will jump as high as we can," he says.

The Ströer supervisory board also agrees. It's hard to tell if every member really believes that success is possible – "Müller will need to work hard to convince them," Bornheim's deputy admits – but they hurriedly put together a taskforce for Operation Thunder.

How do you buy a company?

Question: How do you buy a company?

Answer: With a lot of money and the right consultants.

Next question: How do you buy a company without any money?

Answer: "You don't."

Defying conventional wisdom, a confident Udo Müller begs to differ. He knows what he wants. He knows how capable he is. And he hopes that time is on his side.

He wants DSM. He has done ever since he went jogging with Dirk Ströer, a very long time ago. Now he has taken the most important hurdle: Ströer has been included in the bidding process. And at the time, there's money to be found abroad, and various possible strategies to help with company takeovers.

The most interesting approach for Müller is the so-called Leveraged Buyout (LBO). In an LBO, the takeover itself generates great synergy in a very short space of time, and the shared EBITDA rapidly improves. For that reason, everybody involved accepts a significantly higher level of short-term debt.

Example: Company A, with an EBITDA of € 10 million, wants to buy out the much bigger Company B, whose

EBITDA is € 10 million. Their shared EBITDA is € 10 million, and the possible debt level, with a normal leverage, is about five. The total credit limit would then be five × € 10 million, or € 150 million.

Now Company A argues that the takeover will result in the EBITDA doubling to € 10 million over a short period of time, 18 to 24 months at most. The claim is validated and confirmed by an independent third party, usually a renowned consultancy firm.

The creditor then accepts, for this time span, to double the leverage to 10 – and the company's creditworthiness climbs to 10 × € 10 million, or € 100 million. It is twice the original sum.

That way, company A, with an EBITDA of a mere € 10 million, could indeed get credit of € 100 million. The creditor in such a high-risk scenario will always insist on a tight audit and that the promised increase of the EBITDA will be realised in the promised time.

This is done by so called "covenant testing". Every three months, the business figures are compared retrospectively. If Company A really manages to increase the EBITDA to € 10 million, the leverage drops accordingly to a somewhat normal – for those times – debt ratio of five, with a total debt of 5 × € 10 million, or € 100 million.

Müller is sure that after a takeover, he can reduce costs significantly while increasing turnover and margins. That's his plan.

But what makes total sense on paper is not necessarily the same in reality. Udo Müller has never managed an LBO. And he is not the only one who wants to own DSM, and who is ready to pounce. The others are total pros with brimming coffers. There is the familiar French rival JCDecaux, as well as big American poster advertisers such as Clear Channel Outdoor and Viacom. There is also the large investor Apax Partners from London. Müller's chances are small if not completely hopeless.

But maybe not? One thing is clear: If he wants to pull it off, he needs all the good advice that is available. In this industry there is such a thing, but it's very expensive. Müller gets the absolute top advisers on board. He knows that he must impress potential investors but mostly the sellers – and knows also that his name and his company alone are not good enough.

The consultants are to bring structure and a strategy to the deal and show how they can raise the capital. Projects like this are highly desirable for the top firms, who charge up to € 100,000 for their consultancy – per month! The investment banks alone usually ask for a minimum of € 1 million per mandate. With negotiations usually taking between one and two years, any failure can quickly become a money pit.

Worldwide leading investment banks include Morgan Stanley, Rothschild, J.P. Morgan, Merrill Lynch, and Deutsche Bank. Sal. Oppenheim, too. But their experts already work for the other side and are therefore unavailable.

Müller also discusses the potential takeover with some of his good friends who are well-versed in the jungle of capital. Eventually Morgan Stanley in Frankfurt get the gig. One of Müller's friends knows a German manager there, Lutz Rettig, and he promises to do all he can. It's all a matter of trust.

Morgan Stanley. After they accept the Ströer job, a team of six analysts under Herman Dambach begins to prepare for the next phase. They look for possible investors and the right strategy for the mergers and acquisitions (M&A) process, and they begin "due diligence" work.

"Due diligence" in a company takeover is the promise to act conscientiously. It also means a fine-toothed audit of the company, examining the business, finances, tax and the legal side of the business. A different specialist is responsible for each aspect.

For the commercial due diligence, Müller goes to Boston Consulting Group, known worldwide as BCG. Taxes and finances, the financial due diligence, are investigated by specialists from Ernst & Young. For the legal due diligence, it is Freshfields Bruckhaus Deringer, better known simply as Freshfields.

All four consultancies are the absolute top of the range. Their assistance is expensive, but it's still a very good move by Udo Müller. Compared with the other bidders, Ströer is much, much smaller, and doesn't have as much capital for swallowing such a big fish as DSM. But by signing with the top consultants, they send a clear signal that they are serious – a seriousness visible to both DSM and Ströer's potential creditors.

These top consultancy names ensure that leading international creditors don't immediately throw Ströer's proposal in the bin. Udo Müller's name alone does not command such respect.

In the end, the consultancy services will cost about € 100 million. But Udo Müller considers it money well spent. "I wanted to signal to everybody: I've got the money and I mean it seriously," he said. Two decades later he describes the move, jokingly, as his very own Potemkin Village.

They don't have much time. Everybody expects Sal. Oppenheim to ask the bidders, after their expression of interest, to submit a first indicative non-binding offer. One quickly must put the main data together and develop a strategy.

What will the possible price be?

How much is DSM worth for Ströer? What about when the synergy is factored in?

How much is Ströer worth?

What is its credit limit?

How much credit would the banks grant the company, and on what conditions?

Do they need more equity capital? And how much?

They model various. scenarios, often until late at night. It's like working on a story. The aim of the story is to convince investors of their eventual success.

Every coup needs a story

The specialists of Morgan Stanley know one thing for sure: If they stand any chance, then Udo Müller must be at the centre of the story. They need his vision, his dynamism, and his unlimited willpower.

They have to promote Müller's successes when he presents Ströer as the dynamic out-of-home advertising company – with excellent management, numerous product innovations, fast growth, and a clear strategy.

But isn't that true anyway? The company he works for is ranked number two Germany, the largest advertising market in Europe. Ströer is also number one in Poland with its fast growing economy, perfectly positioned in the growing markets of Central and Eastern Europe. The company is also now number one in now prosperous Turkey, the most important of the emerging markets at Europe's fringe, with above average growth potential.

Together with DSM, Ströer would be the dominant power in Germany, could consolidate the fragmented market and build the desired national networks. It would be top in all areas of Out of Home advertising, from the classic posters to the new modern advertising media such Megalights, as well as all other street furnishing.

It would be a match made in heaven. They are a dream couple. Ströer is number one in Eastern Germany, with advertising on private land and with billboards. DSM is number one in Western Germany, with outdoor advertising on public sites, and has a strong position in street furnishing, mostly with bus shelters.

There is no question that the combined companies wouldn't only be very strong locally, but also for the first time able to offer national advertising campaigns. This would make it possible to increase OoH advertising's share of larger advertising budgets, to shift it from the meagre 3 % to the European average of 7 %.

Sure, DSM's people would like that. They would not own a share of the company anymore, but they would retain the public sites on which the advertising media are placed. The lease payments are in proportion to the advertising income. The planned takeover of DSM could double the share of the advertising budgets, meaning the communities would also receive double the lease, in perpetuity.

It has the makings of a good story. It only needs to be bolstered with good figures, facts, and a clear vision to make a convincing presentation.

Udo Müller is 39 now but looks younger. He looks after himself. He appears dynamic and well-groomed, but still serious. He wears a dark, designer suit, open collar, elegant shoes and, of course, has carefully styled and gel-slicked hair. Every single hair is in place.

This appearance, combined with his confident manner, are an advantage in the dance to secure capital. Young managers in the money markets all share the same sartorial style. But the decisive factor is how they tell a story on the route to success. And the strategy behind it.

They work into the small hours crafting a convincing

script in their fundraising efforts. Müller knows that the story needs to be exceptional.

They also need to describe this promise in figures. Müller plans to double the value and profit of the combined companies in less than two years through a combination of synergy, cost cutting and growth. Ströer and DSM combined could raise their EBITDA in 18 months from € 10 million per annum to the proposed € 10 million, thanks to the sum of the synergies. It's an alluring vision.

Now the case is taking on speed. The big wheel in the game named Deutsche Städte Medien begins to turn. Müller sets off, flanked by his closest colleagues and consultants, on the search for other people's money. It is a hard slog. There are appointments scheduled one after the other, back-to-back. When Müller talks to Dirk Ströer by phone, he describes the situation using football metaphors. It they're "in the game", things are going well. And if they're "sitting in the grandstand", the outlook is bad. There is a constant up and down. It's an emotional rollercoaster.

A day that changes the world

The date is etched into our brains. The short sequence of numbers: 9/11. It is a day when 3,000 people lost their lives and the world was plunged into a deep crisis.

Suddenly, without any warning, politics, economies, people all change the world over. Wall Street stocks go down steeply. The party is over. On the Frankfurt stock market, the bubble of the celebrated new economy also bursts.

Ströer too is not immune to the crisis. Morgan Stanley's money managers begin panicking. The team working for

Müller is first reduced from six to three. In the end, only the team leader Dambach is left.

Any market recovery is only gradual. The world of finance does begin to get back on track, but it's slow. Banks and states offer loans, the fuel for under-pressure companies and new business. After a crash, there is always an upturn, the Bull follows the Bear. Everyone gathers their strength to overcome the crisis.

It is February 2002, and the economy is kind of normalising. The sale of DSM is also picking up speed after the enforced break. But Müller, despite all his efforts, is still looking for the necessary capital for the takeover.

He is on the way back to Cologne after delivering another one of his lengthy presentations. "What about the NRW bank?" Müller asks suddenly. The finance manager sitting next to him knows what Müller means. "No idea. Are they ready yet?" (Officially *Landesbank NRW*, this is one of Germany's regional state-owned banks in North Rhine-Westphalia.)

Müller's credit application has been on the desks of the Landesbank for a while, while the institution undergoes restructuring. Under a new name, part of the bank is supposed to concentrate on the support of medium-sized businesses. There is already a snappy advertising slogan: "We support ideas." They plan to get going in August.

But Müller doesn't have that much time. Back in Cologne he uses a few contacts to arrange an urgent appointment in Düsseldorf.

The Landesbank is not officially open yet, but Müller is welcomed as a new customer. His application is buoyed by the fact he's proposing a dynamic new start, as well as by a good deal of regional patriotism. The headquarters of Ströer AG, which would grow dramatically by the possible acquisition of DSM, would be in Cologne, in his home town.

Suddenly Müller sees the possibility of securing € 170 million in loans from the Federal State's subsidy funds, after the Cologne bank facilitates contact between the relevant parties. € 100 million will be so-called mezzanine capital. This kind of loan can be declared as investment capital, which would create a potential for more cheap loans from other banks.

Time is at a premium. The DSM sales process continues. More than 20 bidders are in the game, so they say. Until very recently the market for company takeovers had been drastically overstated, but that changed after the post-9/11 slump. Is the company really still worth € 100 million, as the DSM consultants had repeatedly claimed?

It is a question for Morgan Stanley, where Hermann Dambach, now working alone, is managing the process for Ströer. His team is gone. In any crisis there are also victims among financial professionals.

The hope is now with the Landesbank's super loan. But they still can't provide a definitive answer yet. And there's additional stress concerning the company's imminent move from the old headquarters to the new.

Udo Müller misses discussing things with his paternal friend Heiner, who is unwell. He misses his mentor's admonishments as well as his optimistic encouragements. But Ströer can't be present all the time anymore. He is undergoing chemotherapy, then another operation. He only rarely leaves his residence on Majorca.

Heinz Ströer Außenwerbung is now being run by Dirk and the old manager. Father and son have grown closer in the past few weeks, since Heiner's cancer diagnosis. But Dirk is still in no doubt that out-of-home advertising is not his thing. However, he at least puts all his energy into the new task.

Udo Müller is now running Ströer AG on his own. Anne

Ossenberg, the head of the legal department, is promoted to Müller's general manager. She has to prove herself on all fronts as a crisis manager.

The bidding for DSM is now starting. The first offer will get this game of poker under way. Late one evening, among a small circle of advisers, Müller makes Ströer AG's first offer: €150 million.

It's a high bid and should ensure is Ströer is included in the process. It is courageous because the €150 million don't exist – yet.

And Heiner Ströer, the ailing company founder? He sometimes calls from Mallorca and asks his representatives to be careful. But he is living in a different world now. His illness is sapping his vitality.

Looking for new capital

It's a cool day in March 2002. Udo Müller again hammers his Mercedes on the autobahn towards Frankfurt.

Müller and his finance manager, Alfried Bührdel, are on their way to a possible creditor: A New York investor named Cerberus. is waiting for them. It's one of those notorious hedge funds.

Bührdel is always slightly skeptical. He quickly glances over to Udo Müller, whose hands are resting on the steering wheel. I wish I had Udo's nerves, he thinks. Then he takes a few documents from his briefcase.

So far, there are no loans in sight. None of the money they had hoped for from banks, and definitely not the additional investment capital from private equity funds.

It's been hectic few months. Müller and his experts are constantly on the move between London, Düsseldorf, Frankfurt, and Munich. How often has he done this presentation? Twenty times? Twenty-five? Thirty? Time is running out.

It follows the same pattern every time. Müller presents Ströer AG in the brightest shades. The fast growth of the last few years, the good prognosis for the future. Ströer is more dynamic than any other company. It is the nationwide leader in billboards on private sites, and number one in Eastern Germany. He wants to take over the current number one in outdoor advertising, the company that dominates the publicly owned plots in the West. He then presents his figures backing the proposed leveraged buyout.

By now Müller knows how to present the scenario convincingly, but it doesn't work out as he would like it to. If it gets that far at all, the potential creditors all want to take a majority share in the new company.

But that is not an option for Müller.

Fundamentally not.

He is just about prepared to accept a minority share. But in the long run Müller doesn't want any other owners in his company. After the DSM takeover he wants to buy them out as soon as possible.

And this is Müller's plan. The logic of the deal must be so convincing that he will get maximum credit volume on the combined Ströer/DSM EBITDA. It's not clear yet how much that will be. The credit volume is dependent on how the investors assess the synergy between the companies. Whatever gap remains between the value and the buying price is to be closed by an investor with either sufficient equity capital or the potential to finance it.

As soon as the deal is done, Müller will realise the synergies and raise the EBITDA to a level that will allow the two fusioned companies to get new, additional credit. With that fresh money, he wants to buy out the investor.

That way, Müller would maintain operative control during the whole process.

As we said, that is the plan.

Müller presents it with great enthusiasm and energy. But all his charm, all his talents for convincing people time and again, fail when it comes to the bare figures. The investors are to provide several hundred million Euros but shall have absolutely no say in it. Even if they don't want to engage in the company's operations, they are not even allowed to control their own exit?

Who is this Udo from Germany?

Even during the earliest presentations, Udo realised more and more clearly that his beautiful plan wouldn't work. It couldn't work. But it takes him by surprise that the factor to finally burst the bubble is the Cartel Office, Germany's national competition regulator, or its anti-trust agency.

One of Freshfields' lawyers first plants the bomb.

"What does the Cartel Office have to say about your plans," the Freshfields lawyer asks, almost as an aside.

"What's it got to do with the Cartel Office?" Ströer's amazed lawyers ask. "Even with the combined companies, we are below the critical turnover threshold of € 100 million."

"That might be right," the Freshfields man says. "But if your investor has considerable influence, his annual turnover has to be added to the calculations."

It is a disaster! The private equity funds and hedge funds Müller has met are often worth hundreds of millions, often billions. They have shares in dozens of companies. If the turnover of that portfolio of companies was added to those of Ströer and DSM, according to the Cartel Office rules, a buyout might not be permitted.

But what is a considerable influence? Thirty percent of

the equity? Twenty percent? Or maybe even 10 % of the company?

As the business Müller was planning had never existed in Germany before, the Freshfields expert doesn't have an answer. But after lengthy discussions it becomes clear that this issue could finally destroy Müller's planned deal structure.

Disillusionment is spreading.

Everyone is hugely frustrated. With Müller. With Dambach and his erstwhile Morgan Stanley team. With the other expensive consultants. But the search for a new approach starts straightaway, because that's what good business people do: They find another way. Somehow, somewhere, someway.

That's what happens here. The magic solution now is "mezzanine capital", a new form of credit. The term comes from Italian, from the word *mezzo*, meaning half. Mezzanine financial rules are a mixture of equity and other capital. On the balance sheet they are declared as equity. But often they are not tied to the classic owner's rights, like full voting rights or the right to have an influence in the business.

Essentially, this is exactly what Udo Müller has always wanted.

But these loans are exceptionally expensive and often come with three or four times the normal interest rate. Because of the high risk involved, the only financial companies offering mezzanine capital are British or American hedge funds.

But there are hedge funds and then there are hedge funds. They all are aggressive, but some are so aggressive that they are universally feared. For instance, Cerberus. Capital Management, based near Wall Street in Manhattan. In Greek mythology, Cerberus was the multi-headed guard dog of hell. The founders had chosen the name well. The guardians of invested money and a hellhound could make life extremely difficult for borrowers.

These funds, worth billions, come from American pension funds and rich private investors, all of whom are chasing profits. They believe that the higher the risk, the higher the profit. It's not a business for the weak.

Cerberus has a branch in Frankfurt now, at the heart of the financial district. Müller parks his car directly opposite.

On the 19th floor, David Teitelbaum waits for the two applicants from Cologne. Tall, slim, not even 30 years old, casual, confident. Maybe a bit too young. Careers like his begin early and mostly end early. David has been in the business for four years, working in the large open-plan office of Cerberus Capital Management. His weapon is money, other people's money, that he is supposed to increase. He's one of the Wolves of Wall Street. Greedy. Reckless. Committed only to capital.

Teitelbaum only recently opened this Frankfurt office, but he already has the reputation of a thunder bolt. His behaviour has triggered outrage among some of the old-fashioned German managers. "Unbelievable manners, like a steam roller," is how the chairman of a German car company described the Cerberus man after their first meeting. This harsh verdict made it to the pages of the business magazine *Wirtschaftswoche*.

Now Müller sits opposite him. He feels like he is facing Gordon Gekko, the financial shark played by Michael Douglas in the movie *Wall Street*.

But it doesn't matter. David Teitelbaum also needs to win. The conversation is friendly as a result. The American could be the key to the millions that Müller so far has only been dreaming of.

Teitelbaum checks out his prey. He wants to prove to his New York boss Frank Bruno what a good hunter he is. Bang! Full marks. The duel can begin.

The smart New Yorker says he is flexible and initially offers a lot of money. How much do you need? € 100 million? € 100 million? More? No problem. "We have all the money you need."

Both sign a letter of intent, abbreviated to LoI in business jargon. Then the due diligence process begins: the Cerberus team starts to audit Ströer's figures and business plans.

Müller goes through this due diligence procedure with different partners nearly every week. He and his team have dealt with money lenders such as Providence, Permira, Brockhaus. Private Equity and CVC Capital Partners. Each time the investors are impressed during the presentation and nod approvingly. The plan sounds bold, but convincing. But as an audit continues, an expensive deal can become even more pricey.

They uncover new risks – so called "red flags". Müller knows how this all goes by now.

But, of course, this depends on perspective. What one side sees as a red flag might be a massive opportunity for another. But when Teitelbaum and Cerberus see more and more red flags, and continuously drive up the price, Müller ends the talks.

He wants DSM at all costs. But Müller is not a supplicant. He has a plan, and the plan is damn good. He knows that he can realise it. But he refuses to be treated unfairly.

The young Cerberus manager hadn't expected this. He was sure that the Ströer man was utterly dependent on the Cerberus money. Teitelbaum is dismayed. He has never experienced anything like it. He rings Müller several times afterwards and offers new negotiations.

But for Müller the Cerberus deal is over. He has no idea that what looks like a final setback now, will end up being the seed to his final success, more than a year later.

The end is near

It is May 20th, 2002, early afternoon. Müller is in a bad mood. The out-of-home advertising business is slow, and the chances of winning the battle for DSM are bad. One creditor after another is pulling out, or Müller doesn't accept their conditions. But this is not just the hubris and ambition of an entrepreneur. It is all or nothing. The costs of the preparation work he is putting in are too high. His mountain of debts is also too high. And the takeover of DSM by an aggressive and financially strong investor is dangerously much too close.

Still there is no decision about the loan from the Landesbank. The battle for the desired €170 million seems lost. And Müller is running out of time.

The sales process of DSM will soon enter its next round. The bluffing will soon be over, the cards will need to be on the table. But Müller doesn't have a good hand. And then? Fate will take its course, and Ströer AG itself will become the helpless prey of DSM's new owner. Müller will be considered the loser. You flew too high, Icarus!

But suddenly, it arrives. It's the moment that changes everything. Out of the blue an email lands in Cologne HQ. It's from Sal. Oppenheim bank, which is overseeing the DSM sale.

It says: "The board of Deutsche Städte Marketing informs us that the sales process of the company is being stopped until further notice."

Müller can't believe it. The bold entrepreneur's luck

seems to have returned. DSM's withdrawal shortly before decisive negotiations seems to have come out of nowhere. Stop instead of sale. The battle for a decision has been postponed until further notice.

But what has happened? Some DSM shareholders had felt steamrolled by the board's sales plans. Egon Böttcher can neither convince the shareholders nor force them. The current situation is that the decision to sell DSM might be right, but not without the communities having a say in it. They have to go back to the beginning. The whole procedure must start again.

There seems to be no hurry among the community shareholders. Step by step, they first establish a committee which is to establish an advisory board that will make the sale more transparent and organise an international tender. There will be no more secret deals. That is the good news.

The bad news is the day-to-day business. Ströer's shares in Poland and Turkey are only moderately successful. Globally, the year 2001 was not a good year, and 2002 isn't any better. There is general uncertainty. The aftershocks of the New York stock market crash can be felt as far as Ströer's billboards.

And what does Müller do? He acknowledges the situation but insists on his expansion plans. He acts unconventionally. He rarely follows classic business theories anyway and is driven by his vision, by his gut feeling.

Undaunted, the search for an investor carries on. Time is short, despite the adjournment. At some point the process will start again. And then the finance plan must be at least halfway completed.

The jumbo mezzanine loan he has hoped for from Landesbank has still not materialised. Müller continues to dance through the ballrooms of money. Frankfurt, Munich,

London. Sometimes Canadian investors offer a positive sign. Then a consortium of publicly owned German banks see a good opportunity. The investment professionals of the insurance giant Allianz also show an interest. But still nothing materialises.

Inside the Ströer company itself, the constant stress leaves its marks. Maybe it is because of the difficult economic situation, but there is also uncertainty among the employees. Mid-November, the usual budgeting process for the following year is due, combined with a review of the current year. The figures are worse than expected. "How much do we need?" Müller asks his finance manager.

"€ 10 million. Otherwise, it looks dire."

"€ 10 million?" And after a short pause: "How did it get this bad? Why didn't you stop me?"

The finance manager winces. Stop? My dear Udo, nobody could have ever stopped you. But he doesn't say it aloud. He makes a constructive suggestion: "Maybe the Landesbank will give us an advance on the € 170 million."

"We can only try," Müller whispers. This is the first time that something like fear is rising inside him. Will Ströer run out of money even before the DSM sale starts again?

The power of the banks

The decision is made three weeks later – and it is terse. In a letter, the bank says it regrets that it cannot agree to the request of a part loan for € 10 million.

Can banks treat customers like that when they are on the brink of collapse? Yes, they can. But they shouldn't try it with Udo Müller. Especially not when he is in such a desperate situation.

If he cannot get the € 10 million more or less immediately, it's goodbye to all his dreams. In Müller's case, it would mean the end. The situation is so precarious that in a few weeks the company won't even be able to pay the salaries.

Udo Müller is not only gravely disappointed by the public bank, but also beside himself with anger. "They have to tell me that to my face," he hisses. "I'll go to Düsseldorf."

Again, he is on the autobahn, heading into the city, across the bridge over the Rhine to the headquarters of the bank owned by the Federal State, located in a high rise building of brightly reflecting glass. He told them he was coming in a call on the way. No appointment possible? Not possible? I'm nearly there!

When Müller enters the small conference room, he has calmed down somewhat. Now he needs to be clear minded, not bursting with uncontrolled emotions. He wants to speak to the chairman, but he has to settle for two men from the credit department. It's an open conversation and ends with unexpected insights.

The reluctance to grant the down payment has not so much to do with Ströer, but rather with a conflict within the Landesbank board. As with many public-law institutions, the top jobs are allotted according to political affiliations. And the balance of power in the bank has not yet been well organised. In these circumstances, collateral damage is possible, and the victims will be the clients. But what were the aims again of this new bank? To support local businesses. Yes, but maybe later. In the meantime, the gentlemen need to work out their own positions.

Ernst Gerlach, for example, was a Secretary of State in the Federal Finance Ministry in the 1990s. He is more of a politician than a banker. Now he is on the board of the Landesbank. It seems that it is mainly him who blocks the credit to Ströer, even the down payment of € 10 million.

Are Müller's plans bound to fail because they have become the object of internal power struggles? If so, he must play the game and fight. If necessary, with political means: talk, talk, talk. And he must look for allies. He will not allow them to push him out.

Maybe the bare facts are still enough to convince them. Müller has got the facts: Isn't it the task of the Landesbank to support local businesses?

Of course, it is.

And is Ströer AG, a company on the up, with its HQ in the local city of Cologne, not worth this support?

Of course, it is, but ...

No buts. Not now. Müller is not only capable of presenting his case convincingly, but he can also politely push in the right directions.

A few days later he sits opposite Ulrich Schröder and explains the situation. Schröder is also a board member and is something of an opponent of Gerlach. He consented to the loan application before his colleague vetoed it. He promises again to support Ströer, at least regarding the € 10 million he needs immediately. But he can't and won't take sole responsibility for the sum. Müller must be content with his promise for the time being.

Müller hears nothing more over the next days and weeks. Christmas is approaching, but the mood is low around Ströer. Müller and Dirk fly out to Majorca to see Dirk's sick father. It is not a merry Christmas.

The first weeks of the new year, 2003, are packed with appointments again. But still no confirmation from Düsseldorf. But the day-to-day business must go on.

At the end of January, Müller flies out to Izmir for a meeting with the Turkish partners. Ströer is the industry leader in Turkey now, and the country's surprising economic upturn continues. Müller won't need to get rid of the Turkish share at a loss, as he had feared until only recently. At least there is positive news from somewhere.

It is late afternoon when an employee of Schröder's office at the bank calls the Ströer finance manager Bührdel. The bank reached a decision that morning. The € 10 million mezzanine loan is approved. They will now need talks about how to proceed.

Saved! Again. Everything had been in the balance. The company had exhausted all its possible credit lines, all of them. If the € 10 million loan from Landesbank had not been approved, all the employees' salaries would have been in danger.

DSM: Take two

In the spring of 2003, there is also new movement regarding the sale of DSM. The community shareholders have recruited the international auditor PricewaterhouseCoopers (PwC) to safeguard their interests. The PwC experts will support Sal. Oppenheim – and maybe control them a bit as well.

The company is now being offered internationally and legally watertight. There are now more than 40 bidders. DSM is highly attractive, even overseas.

All the usual suspects line up again. Ströer, of course, plus Clear Channel, Viacom, JCDecaux. Also, on the list now are some much-feared hedge funds and investment groups, including the London-based Apax Partners. The Cologne company remains the underdog in this high stake's poker game.

Again, time is short. The status of the Landesbank mega loan is still uncertain, despite weeks of negotiations. But then the decision is finally made. The bank won't offer any more than the €10 million it has already given the company.

This is already the largest loan Ströer has ever taken out, and the bank's committees could not approve extending it to more than €140 million, even though they positively assessed the concept overall.

And things only get worse. At about the same time the preliminary approval by a public consortium under WestLB, a sister company of the *Landesbank*, is cancelled. The reasoning sounds more like a conspiracy theory. The WestLB a short time later outed itself as a partner of Apax Partners. And Apax itself wants to buy DSM …

Müller hardly has any time to digest this setback when another one arrives. Completely out of the blue, Deutsche Bank cancels existing credits of more than €10 million, with immediate effect.

The reasons are vague. The bank has, so they say, lost confidence in the management. Ströer needs to pay back about €10 million more or less immediately. There is no formal reason to turn off the tap. Interest and instalments have always been paid on time.

Müller assumes that there are other powers at work. What was it again, the advertising slogan of the Deutsche Bank? "Trust is at the root of everything." But who can you trust? Germany's largest bank belongs to a consortium which is accompanying JCDecaux's plans to take over DSM.

There is reason to suspect that the attack comes from that direction. Hermann Dambach, the last remaining Morgan Stanley consultant working for Ströer, thinks it is possible. "We are in a battle," Dambach mumbles. "And in war, nothing is fair." But nothing can be proved, of course.

However, in a dire situation there are also always friends.

Sparkasse Köln, Heiner Ströer's financial partner since the beginning, offers its help. It will take over the loans cancelled by Deutsche Bank.

Sparkasse's company motto is: "You know who you are with." It's only a slogan, but in this case, it fits.

Sparkasse cannot, however, help with the really big loan. Those millions must be sourced elsewhere.

By now the DSM sales committee is asking for a first indicative offer. Can Ströer even take part in this new round of the game? It doesn't have a single cent to play with.

But Müller doesn't ask himself the question.

During this period, there is hardly any time for running the day-to-day business. The company's top managers are all focusing exclusively on the major deal. Müller runs the company more by occasional commands rather than with the usual strict guidance.

On some days, the Ströer management spends up to 18 hours, without a break, producing presentations and attending meetings with new potential investors. They are constantly on the search for money.

There is good news from the home front – the sales department reports better results than expected from the company's many old and new advertising sites – but the management barely has time to acknowledge it. Even the Megalights, which had caused so much controversy within the company two years ago, have become an extraordinary success.

Shares in DSM, on the other hand, are dropping in value. This is partly because of what Ströer is doing. The team run by Müller's confidante Alexander Stotz has planted hundreds of foundations near the best advertising sites in many German cities. Practically overnight, and taking their rivals totally by surprise, Ströer managed to unveil its modern, glazed, and backlit rolling poster displays. By the end of the year, there will be 1,000 Megalights in operation. Clients seeking advertising spaces book whatever is available, and the sales department estimates that income from the Megalights alone will be around € 10 million.

These days the network of Megalights has become a good source of income for Ströer AG. It's helping the company survive. At least the cash flow is bubbling.

Time is running out

Some three years have passed since Udo Müller, in a parking lot near Cologne, received the first hint that DSM might be for sale. That's when the chase began: an adventurous and expensive hunt with dozens, nay hundreds of meetings, presentations, promises, cancellations, hopes and despair – ending with the sellers scrapping it all. But now optimism and hope are rising again. Maybe it will happen after all ...

The financial situation of Deutsche Städte Media has changed fundamentally. The economic crisis has caused a lot of damage. The company's EBITDA has dropped by about a third to roughly € 10 million. But the multipliers have also dropped, and that's good for potential buyers. They are now at eight to 10, rather than the 10-12 level as they were before. But the sale of DSM is also connected to its market-leading position in Germany. How much is that strategic premium worth? And by how much does it increase the multiplier. To 11 points? Maybe 12?

It is clear that DSM is worth less now than it was around the turn of the millennium, before 9/11 and the global economic crisis. The analysts at Sal. Oppenheim now realistically hope for a sales figure of up to € 150 million instead of the € 100 million they had mumbled about before. Still, that would mean a multiplier of 12.5 – a high price, despite a much worse profit margin.

Müller and his team don't know much about this of course. But their calculations also end up in that region and they are ready to bid up to € 140 million. The plans also include a kind of buffer zone, which in this case is € 10 million. Another € 100 million must be found to cover old debts. All in all, they're talking € 160 million. It's a sum far bigger than any potential loan.

But this time luck seems to be on Müller's side. Dresdner Bank and Société Générale, from France, offer € 100 million, working as a consortium. The precondition is a positive assessment of Ströer's business plans and accounts after the due diligence process. The banks' analysts are already hard at work.

"After that, we'll only need another € 160 million in mezzanine capital," Müller announces. "And we're home." He already knows where the € 160 million could come from: Cerberus, the hellhound from New York!

A few days ago, Cerberus checked in again with Ströer's consultant Dambach and asked whether it would be possible, after all, to do business.

"Cerberus? Is that Teitelbaum?" Müller asked skeptically.

Dambach reassured him: "No, no, he is in Japan now."

Moreover, the prior, unsuccessful negotiations took place before the financial crisis. These days, things are different in the global business of company finances.

So there it is: Cerberus again. The fresh negotiations, by phone, are friendly. Frank Bruno, the hedge fund's second in command, says that he will come over himself. Müller interprets this as a positive sign.

The Swedish investor and mezzanine specialist EQT is

also interested. The company, backed by the legendary Swedish industrialist Wallenberg family, is known as exclusive and elitist shareholders.

And there's no sign of luck running out. A Dresdner Bank executive gets in touch and offers to visit Müller personally. Things are obviously getting serious. Dresdner Bank doesn't only offer a loan of €100 million. It offers to shoulder all the financing, including the mezzanine loan.

It is amazing, and even more surprising that it comes from one of those rather conservative German banks.

However, Müller decides it to be too risky to rely on only one source for the loan. He rejects the offer. He considers €100 million from each of Dresdner and Société Générale to be enough.

He wants the €160 million mezzanine to come from Cerberus, or the Swedish EQT.

In two or three weeks, the bidding round for DSM will officially open for a second time, and Ströer will have to announce its first offer. It will be only indicative, legally non-binding, but the necessary capital will have to be in place.

There are still no contracts for the loans from Dresdner and Société. But it is all looking good, they say. Müller is optimistic.

And why not? Dresdner offered to finance the entire transaction with favourable conditions. And there are even two candidates for the expensive mezzanine capital: EQT and Cerberus.

A few days later, the man from the Dresdner is in touch again. This time the message is negative. The accounts have not proved to be so positive as they thought. But it shouldn't be a problem. They just need to change a few clauses in the contract. It's going to be a bit more expensive.

Müller knows all these games. It's always the same old

spiel. They promise the earth at first to lure the client in, and then, little by little, they tie you down to different conditions.

It is hope that dies last

Every day is busy with meetings and talks about how to proceed. Müller wants to contact the municipal shareholders of DSM's sales committee, particularly Constantin Alsheimer from the Frankfurt treasury, who chairs it.

Müller fears that his constant conflict with the DSM management around Chairman Böttcher might have left a sour feeling. He wants to point out again to Alsheimer the advantages that selling to Ströer would have for the communities.

And the advantages are considerable. DSM is number one in West Germany; Ströer number one in the eastern parts. DSM is number one on public sites; Ströer number one on private land. Both compete for the same clients.

Only by selling DSM to Ströer would it be possible to consolidate the German market for out-of-home advertising. And that would provide the basis for offering national advertising campaigns through a single company. It would make outdoor advertising more transparent and attractive for all advertising customers.

That would allow them to charge the highest prices. The market share for out-of-home advertising in Germany would rise to European levels, at least double what it is now. All of this benefits the communities. They continue to own the leases for the sites where advertising media are placed. That lease price depends on turnover: The higher the turnover, the higher the lease.

DSM wouldn't own the advertising media anymore, because they would be part of the sale, but the lease income would rise for good after the consolidation. It is an important argument for every treasurer.

But this only comes to pass if they sell to Ströer. If an American or British finance investor gets the go-ahead, the initial sales profits might be higher, but there wouldn't be any market consolidation, and therefore no chance for higher annual lease payments going into the community coffers.

The DSM sales committee has not agreed yet on a policy. Some communities want to prevent American or British companies dominating the German market, something that only a sale to Ströer can ensure. But most of the communities insist on achieving the highest sum for the sale.

And so it starts again. On August 16th, 2003, Müller sends the first indicative offer to Frankfurt: € 160 million.

Only a year ago, before DSM cancelled the sale because of Müller's secret interference, his first offer had been more than € 100 million. At that time, he had wanted to achieve two things with the high offer. He had wanted to impress the sellers so that they would take Ströer seriously and accept him as a serious bidder.

If the process had continued, Müller would have tried in a new round of due diligence to find the proverbial "fly in the ointment" and then dropped the price. This would have mirrored the way his potential creditors had been dealing with him. They used the due diligence process to find reasons to make the loan dearer.

It never got that far because DSM had cancelled the sales process. But now, a year later, it's not only the financial situation of DSM that has changed, but also the economy in general.

Udo Müller and his consultants decide to change tactics. Now, on their second attempt to buy DSM, they start with the lowest possible bid. They don't have to qualify as serious bidders anymore. The plan is to increase the bid with every round. Everybody knows that the final price for DSM will be significantly higher than the initial € 160 million.

There are several reasons for the change of tactics. One of them is psychological. It is always easier to increase a price than to find reasons to drop it. The other thing – at least as important, if not more so – is the new economic situation and the position of DSM. DSM hasn't managed the crisis very well, like Ströer.

Müller doesn't know the reasons for this yet. Only if Ströer is invited to the second bidding round will the sales data be accessible for him and his team. This is the beginning of the due diligence phase. In all three areas – commercial, financial, and legal – Ströer's experts will analyse DSM's figures. Some of them will be redacted for confidentiality. Still, the due diligence process needs to present a true picture of the object in question. There are also management meetings and direct talks between the various departments of the buyer and seller.

Only after all of that can a possible sales contract be negotiated. It will be included in the "sales data", with input from both sides. It is like a game of table tennis: Müller, his managers and the specialists from Morgan Stanley design a plan, then the DSM consultants and Sal. Oppenheim, PricewaterhouseCoopers and the community sales committee can all comment on it, or not. It is a difficult and always long-winded procedure.

After weeks and months of to-ing and fro-ing, the contract between Ströer and DSM is taking shape. But the financing is still completely up in the air, and only the bluffing Müller and his closest companions know it.

Whenever anyone asked Müller how he was doing during

this period, he would smile and say: "Bullish!" Among stock market sharks, the word carries with it the expectation of rising prices. The image is that of a bull taking the shares by the horns and throwing them up in the air.

At DSM, nobody has an inkling that Ströer AG is far from the land of the bulls. Müller still doesn't have a single cent of the sum he needs. But he keeps on smiling, never looks down – feeling bullish! A good poker player also needs a strong constitution.

When, in the second round of bidding a few weeks later, he must set a price – again indicative and with the option to withdraw without giving a reason – Müller bluffs. He still expects to secure €200 million from Dresdner Bank and Société Générale, as well as €160 million mezzanine capital from either EQT in Stockholm or Cerberus. There are no definite approvals yet, but Müller remains optimistic.

But then another piece of bad news arrives via a phone call from Stockholm. An EQT manager, with characteristic Swedish politeness, cancels the planned financing. "We would have loved to do it, Mr. Müller. EQT admires your courage and your dynamics. But it doesn't make sense to us. The transaction is not serious enough for us."

And it gets worse. The chairman of Dresdner Bank calls. This is the guy previously travelled to the Ströer headquarters, wanting to finance the whole deal.

"Good morning, Mr. Müller. How are you?" Müller gets up and walks to the window, stares outside, slightly nervously, at the autumn leaves of the large trees.

"Good. So far."

"Why? Do you know already?"

Müller will never forget this moment for the rest of his life. Next door, in the conference room, Anne Ossenberg is discussing further details of the sales contract with the lawyers. They continue to assume its success.

Fig. 1: Udo Müller's first project as a publisher: producing programs for the Bundesliga handball team Reinickendorfer Füchse in 1984

ber310 5 sp 169 vvvvl lbn 032

Sportzeitung

Berliner Medienmarkt wird bunter: Neues Sportmagazin =

Berlin (lbn) - Mit dem „Berliner Sport-Magazin" kommt diesen Mittwoch erstmals eine Sportillustrierte auf den Berliner Medienmarkt. Die monatlich zum Preis von 3,50 Mark erscheinende Zeitschrift wird 64 Seiten stark sein und vorerst mit einer Druckauflage von 12 000 Exemplaren erscheinen. Ziel der Illustrierten ist es - so die „Macher" der Zeitung - mit „sachlich und kritischen Reportagen das Sportgeschehen in der Stadt einer breiten Bevölkerungsschicht näherzubringen."

Macher und Verleger des Sport-Magazins sind mit Dieter Nerlich und Udo Müller zwei Handball-Profis der Reinickendorfer Füchse und der ehemalige Hockey-Torhüter der CG Frankenthal (mit der er fünfmal Deutscher Meister wurde) und jetzige Trainer der Hockey-Damen des SC Brandenburg, Frank Schlageter. In der ersten Ausgabe wird die Situation der Fußballer von Blau-Weiß 90 und der Eishockey-Preussen beleuchtet. Aber auch Randsportarten wie Trampolinspringen, Tischtennis oder Kegeln finden Berücksichtigung.

Als ständige Rubriken wird es einen 25seitigen Sportkalender geben, der neben dem Vereins- auch Betriebs-, Freizeit- und Versehrtensport beinhaltet. Außerdem werden sämtliche Vereine mit Telefonnummer sowie alle Sportplätze und Sporthallen aufgelistet.
lbn be az gr
251548 mrz 86 nnnn

Fig. 2: Press agency dpa report about the launch of the *"Berliner Sport-Magazin"* in 1985

Fig. 3: 1986: Further publishing activities: *Berliner Sport Magazin*

Fig. 4: The company founders Udo Müller and Heiner Ströer with their new backlit glass advertising columns at the end of the 90s

Fig. 5: Udo Müller in a tram in Hannover in 2004 in front of one of Ströer's digital public video displays for trains

Fig. 6: A sensation of the out-of-home advertising industry: In 2004, Ströer takes over Deutsche Städte Reklame, which is twice its size, and a year later the advertising company for German railways

Fig. 7: 2006: Star designer John Irving and Udo Müller run the rule over the new design for Ströer's street furniture line

Fig 8: 13. October 2006: Udo Müller checks out the products by Decaux, Wall and Ströer prior to the opening of the public tender exhibition for street furniture in Hamburg

Fig. 9: 2006: A representative of the City of Hamburg congratulates Jean-Francois Decaux and Udo Müller for winning the tender for street furniture in the city

Fig. 10: 2008: Udo Müller in front of the various lines of Ströer's street furniture in the company's own design park

Fig. 11: 2008: Udo Müller in front of Citylight posters in Ströer's design park

Fig. 12: 2007: Udo Müller and the Ströer Malaysia team before the launch event in Kuala Lumpur

Fig. 13: 2005: Market research in Moscow: Udo Müller with the then most important person in the distribution of advertising media, Oliver Michel (right), and other business partners in Red Square

Fig. 14: Udo Müller in front of the Frankfurt Stock Market on the day of the company's IPO July 15th, 2010

Fig. 15: 2012: Udo Müller and Dirk Ströer chairing the Ströer AGM in Cologne

Fig. 16: June 26th, 2017: Udo Müller welcomes a large number of guests at the launch of T-Online Berlin

Fig. 17: June 26th, 2017: Ströer founder Udo Müller and Berlin's then Mayor Michael Müller officially open Ströer's digital newsroom after T-Online's move to the capital

Fig. 18: Chief editor Florian Harms, Berlin's mayor Michael Müller and Udo Müller visit the new digital newsroom with the largest reach in Germany

Fig. 19: June 26th, 2017: Udo Müller being interviewed for television about the launch of T-Online Berlin

Fig. 20: Berlin's memorial church covered by the Ströer subsidiary blowUP in 2019

Fig. 21: 2020: Giant billboard by the Ströer subsidiary blowUP in London

Fig. 22: 2008: Ströer "Megalight" in front of the Petronas Towers [no hyphen] in Kuala Lumpur

Fig. 23: 2012: Ströer "Megalight" in the Turkish capital Ankara

Fig. 24: 2007: Ströer billboard in Warsaw

Fig. 25: 2012: Rembrandtplein, Amsterdam. Super Motion (LED) by the Ströer subsidiary blowUp

But on the phone everything is collapsing. Because Müller didn't know anything.

"To keep it short," the banker continues coolly. "Your loan application has been rejected. I'm so sorry."

Müller feels his heart in his throat. "You are sorry? Is it that simple? You are sorry? Only a few weeks ago you wanted to finance the whole deal!"

"I know, I know. I said I'm sorry. That's all I can say."

"And what about Société Générale?"

It had been agreed that each of the two banks would pay € 100 million into a consortium to cover the necessary sum.

"No idea what the French are doing. As I said, I'm sorry."

With those few words of regret the seemingly ambitious commitment of Dresdner Bank is over. There is no further explanation.

Müller rings the Frankfurt office of Société and asks to be called back urgently. The deal, the French people had repeatedly affirmed, will be their entrance into acquisition financing in the German market. But what now, without Dresdner Bank?

It takes a while until they call Müller back. No, Société Générale doesn't want to pull out, at least not completely. But in the current circumstances, after Dresdner has withdrawn, they can only offer a maximum of € 70 million.

That really hits home. € 70 million rather than the expected € 200 million. What now?

Employees always have a sixth sense for the mood on the executive floor. They don't know the details, but they know when a big coup is in the offing – or is about to fail. In the corridors of Ströer HQ, curiosity is mixed with uncertainty. What happens to us when everything goes down the drain? Rumours reach even as far as the smallest regional office. What is the boss planning? Some believe there is a big, big deal and that their future is safe. Others are worried.

But no one has even the faintest idea what is really happening. And that is a good thing. So it is only members of the closest circle who experience that panic when Udo Müller asks himself again whether he can really tackle the DSM deal.

Königsberg and the Grand Final

It is Friday, December 12th, 2003. Müller has two highly important appointments scheduled in the Frankfurt banking district. One is the final sales contract negotiations at the law firm Gleiss-Lutz. Afterwards, he is meeting with the Cerberus top dog Frank Bruno in the nearby Garden Tower.

They are now only a week away from the final decision. Only another seven days, 168 hours. No more, no less.

What Udo Müller needs now is a veritable miracle. Maybe even two, three or four. He doesn't have the money, nor has he got an oven-ready sales contract.

All he has is a loan of € 10 million from Société Générale. But that won't do. That much is clear.

By Wednesday the following week, according to the seller's timetable, Ströer's offer in the shape of a contract, finalised and negotiated with the sellers, has to be signed by a notary in Switzerland. At the same time, Müller will need the money, an unconditional financing agreement. Only if both conditions have been met will Ströer be admitted to the ultimate showdown, the meeting of the sales advisory committee.

Müller's final rivals are Viacom and Apax Partners. Both

have a lot of money, but no knowledge of the market. Apax is a pure financial investor. JCDecaux has pulled out. The French company found DSM's figures too meagre. That's what they said in public, anyway.

For one thing, JCDecaux worried that it could not profit from the contract in Germany, where it would face competition from existing firms. But it may have also speculated that Ströer would be in serious debt after buying DSM.

Both Viacom and Apax have enough capital to finance the deal. Müller is still looking for money. The uncertainty is nerve wracking. Société Générale has approved the € 10 million loan, but there is no contract yet. Two French savings banks are checking whether they can find the missing € 130 million.

It is 9 o'clock sharp when Müller, his consultant Dambach, finance manager Bührdel and the company lawyers enter the Gleiss-Lutz office in Frankfurt. Bührdel and Müller had set off from Cologne an hour and a half earlier, in pitch darkness.

The final negotiations are to be held as a live drafting. Page after page is projected onto a screen, and the contract is reviewed line by line. There are extensive discussions about details. Each change is noted by assistants and immediately inserted into the document.

It is a demanding process, but still better than sending the contract back and forth between the two sides over and over again. Everything needs to be absolutely correct before the contract is officially confirmed by the Swiss lawyers on Wednesday.

The two negotiating teams sit opposite one other in the conference room. The dozen or so top lawyers each charge up to € 1,000 per working hour.

The work is slow. And even bigger than their salaries

are the lawyer's egos. At times it takes up to an hour to discuss a single page. More and more items end up on the so called "shit list", all of which will be negotiated at the end. It's like in a cattle market: If you give me that, I'll concede that. But no one can afford to be emotional. Even the slightest mistake can cost millions of Euros.

In the late afternoon, Müller and Bührdel go up to the first floor. They have already spent eight hours in the meeting on the ground floor, but they still don't have the finances. They want to ring the French saving banks together. The Morgan Stanley consultants have arranged the timing. The French banks have, of course, had their consultants mull over the documents too. One of them is participating from London. Müller and his finance manager are accompanied by one of their lawyers.

Udo Müller knows that this phone call is kind of superfluous. Even with all the will in the world, the banks won't be able to arrange an "unconditional financing agreement" in the few hours they have before Wednesday.

Even if that miracle did somehow happen, and the French savings banks approved the €130 million loan, they would have to agree with the other creditors of Cerberus and the Société Générale to negotiate a so-called Intercreditor Agreement. That alone usually takes up to two or three months.

It doesn't make sense, this phone call. But Udo Müller is grasping at every straw. He stops thinking about the whole futility of the process. He has stopped thinking altogether. He simply acts.

Maybe there will be a miracle.

Maybe a door will open.

Maybe there will be a way out of the dead-end situation.

Then the British lawyer of the French company says

very quietly: "Tell me, Mr. Müller, I just noticed that the City of Königsberg became shareholder of Städte Reklame in 1928. Has anyone checked whether this city, now called Kaliningrad in Russia, is still a shareholder and whether it can claim any entitlements?"

It brings the ordinarily stoic Müller close to a total breakdown. He slowly gets up. "Sorry, I just have to discuss something with my colleagues."

Outside, he erupts.

"This is the end, Alfried," he says to his finance manager Bührdel. "It doesn't make sense. Kaliningrad! Have they gone totally crazy? Kaliningrad! I don't get it! Let's go home. Nothing is happening here now."

Udo Müller is at the end of his tether. A week earlier, in Munich, he had collapsed with exhaustion. He had been standing at the bottom of the stairs and couldn't manage a single step up. He had run out of charge. The permanent tension month after month had sucked him dry.

And now this question about Königsberg!

Müller's finance manager had always been skeptical of the high-flying plans. He simply answers coolly: "All in all, this project has cost us about € 10 million in consultancy fees alone. That's € 10 million in costs, which we don't really have." He then adds, even more urgently: "If we pull out now, we will probably be bankrupt. That would be the end of the road. For good."

Müller manages a brief smile. Is it possible to imagine a more bizarre situation? He cannot stop now. Simply cannot. He needs to find € 160 million, otherwise it is the end. For him and the company.

He goes back to the conference room and tries, calmly, to find a kind of plausible answer to the Königsberg question.

Half an hour later the meeting is over. Müller and Bührdel go downstairs to the next round with the lawyers. Shortly before 8 p.m., Müller and his consultant Dambach set off for the appointment with Cerberus and Frank Bruno. The finance manager takes over.

The hour of the Cerberus

Off to Cerberus. then. It is their last chance. The very last, final, ultimate chance.

In five days, next Wednesday, the offer Ströer has negotiated for buying DSM is to be certified by a notary. The financing of the deal needs to be in place by then. Either Udo Müller manages to convince the New York hedge fund of his plans, or the game is over. For good.

During the car journey, Müller and his consultant Dambach discuss the only remaining option. Cerberus needs to finance the lot. The two men reckon the chances of that happening are, at best, 50:50.

If they pulled it off, all their problems would be solved. But the possibility has never been mentioned in any negotiations with Cerberus so far. Neither of the men has a clue how Bruno will react to the new proposition.

At precisely 8 p.m., they leave the elevator and are led to the stylish conference room on the 19th floor. Frank Bruno welcomes them: "Hi, I'm Frank. Nice to meet you." It's as if they have known each other for a while.

Bruno is in his mid-40s, of medium height, slim, with dark, straight hair. He settles in his armchair at one end of the oval conference table. Left and right of him are about a dozen experts, highly qualified lawyers and analysts employed by Cerberus.

The pressure of the moment makes Udo Müller's pulse shoot up. His adrenaline level rises. He is wide awake, organising his thoughts. This meeting really and truly is his last chance.

Bruno glances at his expensive watch. His strong, sonorous voice sounds calming. "You have exactly one hour to convince us of your project, Udo." Afterwards he will consult his investment committee in New York and then make a decision.

Müller knows that's it's all or nothing. There's no time for faffing around with pictures, charts, and flowery words. The Cerberus people know all the figures anyhow.

This is Udo Müller, unplugged. He takes the risk. All or nothing.

"There is a small change in the project," he begins. "I don't need €160 million. I need €160 million. I need full financing. And I need binding approval tonight."

If Müller had been facing representatives from a bank, be they from Germany or elsewhere, the talks would be over now. Nobody, whether a savings institute, a high street bank or any other financing institution, would carry on in these circumstances. Even if Müller could do magic. Even if miracles did exist.

But Cerberus is fundamentally different. As a hedge fund, the hellhound lives by taking very big risks and making very fast decisions. Their backers know that, and they expect maximal profit in return. They also know that not every deal will pan out. But the deals that do make so much money that the risk is worthwhile. And if not, then the hellhound would be finished too. This is pure capitalism.

What matters under these conditions are the figures. But what decides the deal are the people.

Will that guy over there deliver what he is promising? Is he totally obsessed with getting what he wants?

That is what Frank Bruno has to figure out. And he

makes his decisions based on his assessment. Bruno is a very experienced hedge fund manager. He is second in command of a company worth billions, the right hand of Stephen Feinberg, who founded the investment company in 1994 in New York. Bruno is one of the deadliest sharks in the ocean of international mega capital. He has the instinct of a hunter, out for fat prey.

A few weeks ago, he oversaw a deal with the German pharma giant Bayer buying its U.S. branch. It was a deal worth billions. No problem.

At the beginning of the coming week, Bruno has an appointment with Mercedes. The Stuttgart car builder wants to get rid of its subsidiary Chrysler. Again, a deal worth billions.

All of this means that the American doesn't wince or hesitate when the German guy starts his all or nothing game. "OK," he replies. "Understood. Explain the deal to me."

Müller inhales deeply. He knows that the next sentence will decide the battle. And that he has this one and only message to give.

"I have to say one thing first," he begins. And then he says it. The sentence that will decide it all.

It is three sentences really, but they go together. And they are exactly the sentences that hedge fund managers and start-up financiers want to hear when they are placing their millions and billions.

But in 2003 nobody knows these exact words. At least not in Germany. Hedge funds are unknown there. Only two years later, in the spring of 2005, the then vice chancellor Franz Müntefering of the SPD talks about "locusts" meaning men like Frank Bruno.

Udo Müller does not have to think for long about what he is going to say. Because what he means is deeply embedded inside him. It is the essence of him.

"Everything I have earned in my life, I am putting into this deal. If it fails, all will be gone. But I know that it will not fail."

He then tells them the story, his and the one of the company, his vision, his grand ambition. His voice is full of emotion. It is about his rising career. The fall of the Berlin Wall, East Germany, his paternal partner Heiner Ströer.

How perfectly Ströer and DSM would fit together: Number one in East and West Germany. Number one on private and public land. Number one with billboards, and number one or two with street furnishing.

He describes what fantastic chances for growth there will be in consolidating the German out-of-home advertising market for the first time. Because then, and only then, will it be possible to launch national advertising campaigns, organised by a single company. The volume of outdoor advertising will double, at least. At the moment, the market share of out-of-home advertising is only 2.7 %, while in the rest of Europe it is 7 %.

But there are also bare facts. Ströer AG is excellently positioned. Its EBITDA has doubled within two years to € 10 million. DSM's, by contrast, has fallen from € 10 million to € 10 million.

And finally, he talks about the targets for the months after the potential takeover goes through. Nothing can go wrong. The savings alone make the deal sound.

"Safe downward" is the jargon in the world of finance. Müller knows what it costs him to put up the posters. And by now he also knows that it costs DSM significantly more.

Those savings alone will raise the EBITDA within two years from € 10 million to € 10 million and thus double the monetary value of the company. The debt level could be significantly reduced at the same time, from eight or nine times the EBITDA to four to five times. Additionally, Müller expects revenue synergies which would improve the EBITDA further to € 100 million.

This is the language that everyone in this hedge fund round understands.

When Müller finishes, the room is quiet. Very quiet.

And then, through the silence, Udo hears Frank Bruno's deep voice: "Okay, Udo, come back to us near midnight. We will now contact the investment committee in New York to discuss a few things.

As he is leaving, Udo Müller turns around once more, as if to emphasise his plea. "To avoid all misunderstanding, we need a full blood transfusion. We need the full financing. € 160 million."

A complete transfusion. Udo Müller will deliver himself and Ströer AG completely to Cerberus. With the Hellhound's money, old debts of € 100 million will also be covered.

What Müller had once rejected when offered by Dresdner Bank, he now is seeking. Ströer AG would only have one creditor. Cerberus. One of the hardest and most aggressive hedge funds in the world.

Frank Bruno smiles. Whether he is impressed or not, one cannot say. Whether he will recommend this deal to his people in New York or not, the same. Only one thing is clear: Bruno knows the risk. He also knows the possible profit. It could be hundreds of millions.

As if guardian angels worked overtime

It is shortly after 10 p.m. when Müller gets back to the Gleiss-Lutz offices. There is a relaxed atmosphere. Champagne is flowing. Finally the contract with DSM is ready for signature. After countless meetings, months of negotiations, it is time to raise a glass.

Müller finds the situation kind of bizarre, particularly as the representatives of the sellers are definitely in high spirits. They think they have nailed it. The first fully negotiated sales contract. Only one more meeting at the notary's office and two signatures, then Ströer can take over the advertising giant DSM.

"What is going on here?" Müller asks.

"We are all very happy," is the answer. "We have negotiated for weeks, and now we have solved all critical points. We have cut the Gordian knot. All critical questions have been answered."

Hardly anyone in the room realises how critical the situation still is. Hardly anyone knows that Müller doesn't have any money.

"At that moment, I felt like the ultimate con man," he remembers. "The highest paid lawyers and accountants on both sides were cheering each other and me. They were relaxed as never before. Everyone was super happy. But we – we still didn't have the money to actually do the deal."

Shame would not be enough to describe what he felt at that moment, Müller says nearly two decades later. "I would have liked to sink into the ground. If it had ever come out that all the time we simply pretended to have the money, while we didn't have a cent …"

But he doesn't betray his true feelings and thoughts. He only pulls aside his finance manager and tells him that there will be another appointment at the end of this long day.

Then he says goodbye to everyone and goes with Bührdel to a nearby restaurant. In the dim light, he tells him about the meeting with Frank Bruno. His finance manager is exhausted. He cannot imagine that Cerberus will approve the deal. An additional € 100 million? Immediately? How could that possibly happen?

Bührdel assumes that Cerberus will supply the mezzanine credit of € 170 million and that € 70 million will come from Société Générale. But even then, they still need another € 130 million.

Bührdel, very tired, glances at his watch. He just wants to go home. He has been out and about since 6 o'clock in the morning. But his boss insists that he comes to the meeting. Shortly before midnight, they enter the lift in the Garden Tower. Again, they have to wait. Bruno and his people are still busy checking the figures of the deal.

Waiting. It's a long 10 minutes. Twenty. Thirty. They are alone with their respective thoughts. They fear, they hope. Then, after an hour, they are invited into the conference room. The decision has been made.

Frank Bruno has turned into the knight in shining armor. He casually conveys the message. Müller will get the money. Udo Müller can hardly grasp his enormous luck.

Bruno jots the figures onto the flipchart: Overall credit volume: € 160 million. Mezzanine: € 160 million. Loans: € 100 million. The whole sum is divided into small and big and even bigger tranches, senior debt, junior debt, interest rates, normal here, with a surcharge there, times four, times seven, times 17 %. Terms, repayment schedule, due dates. The finer details still need to be negotiated. It is a dizzying array.

If the debtor cannot manage the payment of the interest and repayments, Cerberus can market the securities of Ströer. It means that the hellhound will take over the company. With so-called covenant testing every three months it will be checked whether Ströer is meeting the conditions.

And one more thing: the warrant. This is the option for a share in the company. It had been planned before that Cerberus would have a share of 10 % of the company. The symbolic price for this warrant was set at € 1.

Now that Müller has asked for the full € 160 million, instead of € 160 million, it is clear that the warrant will go up as well. But by how much?

"Cerberus had us in a stranglehold," Müller remembers. "We were frightened of this figure."

And Bruno indeed rises the figure, but he is content with 15 %. Müller nods.

His finance manager silently tries to work out how all this can be paid off.

But Müller cannot believe his luck. It is like a bright light shining in a very dark room. He briefly rings the chair of the advisory board, Bornheim, who is on Majorca. It is the middle of the night. But never mind, he has to tell someone about this. The Ströer team withdraws into another conference room.

After talking to their chair, the negotiations really get going. They bargain about every tenth percentage point of interest. It is about different credit forms, different terms, different interest rates.

It is only early evening for the Americans, who have flown in that day, but Müller and Bührdel have been up for 20 hours. Müller in particular is running on pure adrenaline – in the flow of someone who has managed what no one had thought possible. But he can also mess up everything again any minute. Every decision, every question about terms and each of the negotiable sanctions could later be the notorious straw that breaks the camel's back.

It is 7 a.m. when Udo and Frank seal the deal by shaking hands. It is winter, shortly before Christmas. The day breaks as Müller and Bührdel are driving back to Cologne.

Things continue when they're back in Cologne. Müller calls his team together. At 11 o'clock the various. conference calls begin. In the M&A business, Cerberus is what is admiringly called a "deal machine". It specialises in negotiating and finalising highly complex deals within a few hours. The hedge fund has a network of experts around the globe who are always on call.

That's how it happens that Saturday morning. The Cerberus people are in Frankfurt, Los Angeles, and New York. The conference calls last for eight, nine hours. "At some point I thought," Müller remembers, "that Cerberus's legal expert in New York had fallen asleep. But then, after he had been silent for eight hours, he said one sentence, and it was totally on point. It was mad."

By Tuesday, a so-called unconditional financing commitment has to be set up stating that Cerberus commits bindingly to providing the necessary sum – a kind of cashier's cheque. It is not only a lot for Ströer to deal with, but the Cerberus team can also not afford to make any mistakes, never mind the rush.

Guardian angels had been working overtime and influenced fate.

The Landesbank puts the brakes on

It is Tuesday, December 16th, four days after the momentous. meeting in the Frankfurt Garden Tower. Ströer AG's supervisory board has been hastily summoned and is sitting in the conference room facing Müller.

They discuss the opportunities and risks of the DSM transaction and Cerberus's involvement. Müller is in a fantastic mood. Because of DSM's lower profit margin and the changed global economics, the price could drop considerably.

They now focus on strategy for the last round of the sales process. Müller had offered € 160 million as a first indicative price and then raised it to non-committal € 180 million. But all that was only foreplay. He didn't even need the thumbs up from the board for that. Nothing was binding.

But now the cards must be put on the table. Despite Cerberus's involvement, Müller is not allowed to offer more than €160 million. He must not exceed that limit. The rest is meant for paying back existing debts.

The experienced Dieter Stolte, deputising for the chair Bornheim, who is off sick, raises his hand. "I have no objections, particularly as there are no alternatives to Cerberus," he says. "The risk is not on Ströer's side, because in case of failure only the owners would change. The risk is for the shareholders."

Then Stolte addresses Dirk Ströer directly who, as a member of the board, also has his father's interests at heart. "Which means, the risk is entirely with the Ströer family and Mr. Müller. You and Müller, as the only shareholders, could lose everything. The company wins in any scenario."

Dirk briefly glances at Udo, and then says quietly: "I consent." The decision is made unanimously.

Later Stolte will ask Dirk Ströer whether his father would have consented as well, and Dirk will answer: "No, I don't think so."

Heiner Ströer is only informed about the deal in general terms. Udo wants to go easy on his ill partner and spare him any upset.

The next obstacle are the banks, Ströer's current creditors. They too have to consent to the deal. They could block it if they wanted to. Among the creditors are small institutes such as Stadtsparkasse Köln, a savings bank, and more complex institutes such as the regional Landesbank. Müller considers it a mere formality. After all, all creditors will get their money back from Cerberus, and no one will lose a single cent.

Maybe. But apparently the guys from Landesbank see a problem. Around midday, a representative of the Düsseldorf headquarters calls. As things are, the banker says with the usual expression of regret, "No positive decision will be possible."

Of course, a positive decision is possible. They only need to consent. There is no plausible reason to veto the transaction. But block it they do. Some assume that a few of the bankers are also in contact with Apax Partners, the London investor who is also interested in DSM.

Müller is beside himself. It can't be true that one of the most important transactions of the era will fail because of this kind of objection. He calms down again. He schedules a meeting for the next few days with the Landesbank chair Ulrich Schröder to discuss the problem calmly and neutrally. But until then there is uncertainty – except they simply must carry on as if the Landesbank had not intervened.

Late on Tuesday afternoon, further creditors deliver their verdicts in quick succession. The Cologne bank consents, the others too. Phew! OK, next ...

Again to Frankfurt, first to a hotel. They plan to stay overnight and take the train to Basle on Wednesday morning where Ströer's offer for the DSM buyout is to be confirmed by a notary.

But first there are further negotiations with Cerberus on the 19th floor of the Garden Tower. Frank Bruno is waiting for the Ströer delegation. They know it will take hours on end again. Even though the teams have been negotiating throughout the night, from Friday through Sunday, there are still hundreds of details to be dealt with in a complex deal like this. It is now about the unconditional financial agreement – the confirmation for the seller that the buyer has arranged its finances and can pay the required sum.

There is no small talk before the negotiations begin.

Again, everyone must be totally focused. No mistakes are allowed. They could become expensive later. Very expensive.

Müller and Bruno and their teams are sitting opposite one another at the oval conference table. The silence is tense while the structure of the financing deal is explained. Facility agreement, framework agreement, side letter, commitment letter. Technical terms abound.

Cerberus is offering a financing cocktail, a mixture of € 100 million in loans with various interest rates and € 160 million as mezzanine capital. Depending on the tranche, the interest rate is from 4 % to more than 17 %. This is normal with businesses where the interest rate signals the risk involved for the creditor.

Cerberus doesn't have money simply lying around. It needs to obtain it from its own customers: sometimes wealthy private people, as well as pension funds and private investment funds of all kinds. In the U.S. particularly, the latter are very important actors in the financial market. They include, for example, the pension fund of Californian teachers and funds operated by the finance managers of renowned private universities such as Harvard or Stanford.

What is on the table now are the agreements about the exact rules of credit and how Cerberus can exercise the warrant. It is about terms, securities, the targets Ströer must meet.

One of the most important targets is that in the second year after the takeover, Ströer has to raise the EBITDA of the combined companies, the profit before interest and taxes, to € 10 million. That is € 10 million more than both companies together are quoting as their EBITDA at present.

And then the warrant. For € 1, Cerberus gets 15 % of Ströer AG.

Covenant testing will ensure that Ströer sticks to the credit arrangement, as is normal with contracts like this. The word "covenant" derives from the Latin "conventio", meaning contract or agreement. In financial language, it means certain clauses or provisions in a credit arrangement. They are the binding affirmations of the debtor to the creditor.

The covenants will be checked quarterly – covering the past 12 months. What is the EBITDA in the current quarter? What is the "net profit? What is the relationship between debt and profit?

If the conditions are not met in one quarter, there is normally a set time to make good, the "cure period". If in the next quarter everything gets the green light again, the credits go on as agreed.

But if over two or more quarters the covenants are "broken", the creditor can ask for his loans to be paid back immediately. Ströer's situation is such that everything the company owns, down to the last pencil, has been pledged.

"One thing was clear," Udo Müller remembers. "If we didn't manage to push up the EBITDA from € 10 million to € 10 million in 18 months, the whole company would have gone to Cerberus."

But who knew whether Cerberus would really take over Ströer AG?

From the hedge fund's point of view, it was clear: Either Udo Müller managed to do what he stated in the contract, earning Cerberus its agreed part of the profit, or he didn't, and Cerberus would own one half of the German out-of-home advertising market.

Müller would be out then, of course. And Dirk too, as the other major shareholder. Cerberus would end up with full control over the business and could appoint their own managers, who would either carry on with the business or manage the assets of the company in other ways.

Regardless, Cerberus's financial invention is pretty safe. A pro like Frank Bruno would otherwise never have entertained even the idea of the deal.

It's why Bruno accepted a clause that was extremely important for Udo. The German wanted to make sure, at all costs, that Cerberus did not have the power to walk away, forcing him either to sell parts of the company or to go public.

Müller is not ruling out those two avenues as a way of paying his debts to Cerberus. But he wants to be the one who determines the time and the reason for it. He wants to remain the master of his own house.

Bruno consents. His strategy is in line with his gut feeling and is based on his belief that Müller is one of those entrepreneurs who aggressively take their company forward. Sooner or later Müller would have to launch Ströer on the stock market to finance further growth.

"What Bruno suggested made him a good investor," Udo Müller says two decades later. Cerberus too puts everything on one horse. Its name is Udo Müller.

It is 5 a.m. when the last item is finally cleared: the official consent of the chair Bornheim, who took part by phone from Majorca. He faxes it over.

Another night fuelled by adrenaline, but again one step closer to the goal.

Only a few days ago, no one would have believed it. It is now the second night in five days that Müller and Bührdel have spent negotiating. They get the suitcases they had dropped at the hotel in the hope of at least a little sleep, but it's time to move on again. Their train to Basle is due to leave at 6.50 a.m., taking them to the meeting with the notary.

Off, then, to Switzerland.

Müller has heard that the head of the Frankfurt treasury, Constantin Alsheimer, and the DSM lawyer, Heinz Bauer, of the law firm Gleiss-Lutz will be on the same train. Müller and his finance manager go straight to the restaurant car.

A short time later, Alsheimer and Bauer come in too. They are surprised to see the Ströer men, but they discuss the state of play in a relaxed manner and exchange some more ideas. It seems as if Müller has won already.

After an hour, Müller finds himself alone with Alsheimer in the restaurant car and they chat about this and that. The others have returned to their seats and dropped off, exhausted.

Generally, a confirmation by a notary doesn't present any problems. The notary reads things out, the parties listen, then they sign. It can be different, however, when the contract is long, and the notary has had a bad day.

When Alsheimer and Müller enter the office in Basle, they are met by an exasperated representative of the overworked group of Swiss notaries. He can stay for only three hours, he says, and must be careful with his voice, as he had a cold. He says he is unable to read out the complete contract. A colleague takes over the reading as his colleague listens grumpily.

But it is not that easy. There are numerous discrepancies. After three hours, the notary leaves the office and the parties have only got as far as page three of the contract.

So, they carry on negotiating. The notary returns at 8 p.m. Finally, at 10 p.m., the negotiated contract is ready to be signed and confirmed.

It's during these hours that Müller and his team learn

that in a different room of the office another bidder is in the process of having his offer for DSM confirmed. But they don't know who it is.

Finally, late on Wednesday evening, the contract is ready to be signed by Ströer as an official offer. They head back to the station. In Frankfurt, Alsheimer and the DSM delegation get off the train. Müller and his people continue to Cologne, exhausted.

But DSM is still holding back important details in the due diligence process. Over the past few days, the bidders had access to confidential data indicating the true value of the company. But the most important data is redacted from the communal advertising contracts. DSM is reluctant to take the risk that possible buyers go as far as the final stages to get hold of this confidential data, only to pull out of the bidding. The insider knowledge would put them in an optimal position in any new tenders and give them a great advantage over their rivals.

DSM's experts at Sal. Oppenheim and Pricewaterhouse-Coopers have raised the bar high. All the bidders have presented notarised offers by now. But still, the redacted parts from the data sheet will only be made clear when a choice has been made. This is a serious risk for all bidders. It's like buying a cat in a sack.

If the information is correct, there are still three bidders in the race. Viacom Outdoor, from the United States, Apax from London, and Ströer.

Two days later, on Friday, Müller for the first time presents his plans for DSM to the representatives of the company itself. So far, he and his team only had contact with DSM's consultants. Now he talks to the representatives of the communities directly.

What Udo Müller wants is clear: he wants DSM to merge with Ströer. That would be the first and decisive step towards the desired consolidation of the German outdoor advertising market. Together, Ströer and DSM would be big enough to offer the big brand names national out-of-home advertising campaigns all by one company, for the first time.

Ströer's position would be strengthened in the market, and, most of all, outdoor advertising would be made much more attractive. This has been Müller's plan from the beginning – to lift the share of outdoor advertising by consolidating the market to at least European level. The communities would benefit for good as the lease payments for their sites would be linked to the revenue generated.

It's not clear what Apax wants. It is a financial investor without any specialist knowledge of the market. It will presumably break DSM into various parts and sell them separately for a lot of money. Viacom's plans are equally nebulous.

A few hours later, and after an explosive phone call with the American central office, Viacom pulls out. The reason for the sudden withdrawal only becomes clear later: Viacom's owners need money and are in the process of selling their firm to their New York rival CBS. An expensive takeover in Germany would not make sense. Viacom is out.

Only two bidders are left: Apax Partners Private Equity Investment Group from London and the Cologne-based Ströer AG

It all looks like a classic duel.

High Noon.

The final decision is supposed to be made after the DSM sales committee meets. That was the plan, anyway.

But the representatives of the municipalities change the process. At around 8.30 p.m., on the Friday, they inform everyone that there will be another round of bidding, the very last one. On Saturday morning, the sellers will announce the details.

Decision time

Saturday morning. Müller is at home. He gets on the telephone to distract himself. By now, the Landesbank has given its consent, thanks to its chair Schröder.

Approaching 10 o'clock, DSM's representatives get in touch. In the final round of bidding the offers must increase again and the guarantees come down. At least that's what they say.

The latter item concerns the confirmations that DSM must make as the seller. Or, more accurately, the other way around, the demands that the buyers set out in the contract. Ströer, as a buyer, must be sure for example that DSM's advertising sites are indeed legal and that posters are permitted. As DSM has hundreds of thousands of advertising sites, one can include this demand in the contract, but it cannot be bindingly checked before finalisation.

So, the seller must guarantee it – and accept a reduction of the sales price for each site that does not have the correct permissions. The seller wants to reduce this kind of expensive guarantee, and it is the reason for the new demand.

"How long do you need for the new offer?" the seller's representatives ask. They expect a minimum of one or two days.

"An hour," Müller answers.

"An hour? Really?"

"Yes, yes, an hour," Müller says. "We don't need longer."

If the seller's side was puzzled, they didn't show it. OK, they would be in touch.

At around 11 o'clock they call again. They have agreed on a final procedure. There will indeed be a so-called shoot-out, the equivalent of High Noon in the Wild West.

By 1 p.m. at the latest, each bidder must send a fax with their offer price and the guarantees to a phone number at a notary's office in Frankfurt.

There won't be any more negotiations.

The bidder with the highest offer and the fewest guarantee demands will be the winner. If the offer doesn't arrive in time, the other party will win automatically.

Müller calls his team together. They organise a conference call with the Ströer chairman Bornheim and Frank Bruno of Cerberus.

On the table is the notarised offer from Wednesday. It says €145 million.

They start discussing. How much should Ströer bid? €150 Million? €155 Million?

Frank Bruno interrupts. "People, this is a public auction. It's only about money. You have to land a punch."

"A punch?" Müller asks. "What do you mean?"

"Top up substantially. €10 million or so."

It is now 12.50 p.m. One of the team mentions the sum of €170 million for the first time. That would be more than 10 % more than the sum specified in the sales contract. And it would be €10 million more than Müller had set himself as his absolute limit.

Müller asks someone to ring Frankfurt. He wants 10 more minutes. "We won't manage by one o'clock."

The answer is no. Absolutely not. One o'clock is the limit.

By now, it is 12.57 p.m. Either Ströer faxes its offer in the next 180 seconds – or they are out, whatever the offer.

If Ströer indeed wants to offer €270 million, the €10

million above the agreed limit will have to come from Bruno. Only he has the money.

Again, Müller is completely dependent on the hellhound.

Frank Bruno can demand anything he likes in exchange for the missing millions. But the man is a pro. If he pushes it and sets conditions that Ströer cannot meet, he risks Müller pulling out at the last minute. After all, the Ströer man has done that before – when he rejected the conditions of another Cerberus representative, David Teitelbaum, at the last minute.

Bruno clicks in. "Do it," he says. "We'll give you the € 10 million, at a low interest rate."

There are 100 seconds until one o'clock.

Someone pushes a piece of paper to Müller with maybe four lines on it. With trembling fingers Udo Müller puts his signature to it. An offer of € 270 million for DSM.

Someone presses the button on the fax to Frankfurt at 60 seconds before 1 p.m. There is a deadly silence as the hand of the clock jumps to one o'clock.

A minute passes.

Then another one.

Nothing from Frankfurt. Nothing, simply nothing.

"This is torture," Müller says.

After 15 minutes, they get the phone call.

"OK. You've got it."

Udo can't remember much more. The moment is too emotional. He has worked towards this for such a long time. Now he has actually done it. He has made the impossible real. He has swallowed the so-much-bigger number one. Against all the odds. Despite all the obstacles and problems.

Almost as an aside, Frankfurt says that DSM will expect confirmation within an hour that Ströer actually has the additional millions over and above the unconditional financial agreement.

Frank Bruno is on the golf course when he gets the request for confirmation. About 50 minutes later, it is on Müller's desk.

After the Müller team has faxed it to Frankfurt, Constantin Alsheimer suggests signing the new contract in the following week in Switzerland.

Müller rejects the proposal. He doesn't want any more risks and wants to sign the same day in his Cologne office. The DSM people must come to Ströer headquarters.

Half an hour later, Alsheimer calls again. He tries to persuade Müller that it would be much cheaper to go to a notary in Switzerland. He guarantees that nothing will jeopardise the deal. There will be no more bidding rounds.

Müller learns much later that only three million separated the last remaining bids. Apex Partners offered €167 million.

Müller needed half an hour to himself after the momentous phone call from Frankfurt. What an emotional rollercoaster! No one apart from him had believed in this deal. Müller cannot even count how many times everything seemed to be over. When nothing seemed possible anymore.

But now? He is the winner. He has made it!

Notary costs don't matter. "We'll pay for the signing," he tells Alsheimer. "But I want to do it today. Here, at my place."

Alsheimer moans but agrees. The Frankfurt delegation arrives at 4 o'clock and is greeted with cheers in the conference room.

Now the lawyers must pore over the contracts again. Only now are the last secrets unveiled; the redacted passages uncovered.

Towards half seven in the evening, the notary comes to Müller. "We cannot sign today," he says.

"Why not?"

"The powers of attorney of the DSM people are insufficient," he explains.

Müller stops for a second. What the notary is trying to convey to him is that he, as the notary, cannot guarantee this contract and can be made responsible for possible mistakes later.

"Put something together that we can sign," he tells the man.

It is 20:42 when Udo Müller, at his own desk, puts his signature on the contract. Now Ströer and DSM are joined together. Müller wants to be alone and goes into a darkened little office down the corridor. Only very slowly his head clears. And then they all go together to his favourite Italian restaurant. It will be another long night, with pasta and more than one bottle of excellent red.

It is December 20th, 2003. "Operation Thunder" has come to a successful ending. Only days ago, it seemed like Mission Impossible. Now they can say: Mission completed!

THE TIMES ARE CHANGING

The "Poster Pope" is dead

It is another two hours on the flight to Majorca, Saturday, March 7th, 2004. Lost in thoughts, Udo Müller sits by the window of the Air Berlin plane. His eyes look for something substantial in the clouds.

In his mind, he wanders through the images of days gone by. The first meeting with Heiner Ströer in 1989, when they talked through the night about their lives. At first in a restaurant, then in a bar near the Berlin Ku'damm, and then the goodbye at the crack of dawn. The next meeting a few weeks later. The idea to work together. The discussions with Heiner, his advice, his fatherly care, his admonishing words.

Only a few hours ago, he was woken by a phone call. "Father is gone," Dirk said, and Udo quickly had replied that he would be over on the next plane. Then, as if in a trance, he went to the airport and boarded the first flight that would take him to his family on Majorca.

Because the Ströers had been his family for a long time. Years ago, Heiner Ströer had declared Udo Müller, 24 years his junior, his son. Not legally, of course, but emotionally and in every other sense.

Heiner Ströer had proudly celebrated the takeover of DSM three months ago, when the bigger company became part of the Ströer Group. The patriarch hadn't minded that Udo had been the driving force for the deal, nor that the media declared him the smiling winner. He said at the time that it was a good job that he didn't feature in the photos in his current condition. Then he added, drily: "You're not getting any younger either."

It was only a few weeks ago that Heiner had called Müller and asked to come to Majorca as soon as possible. That was at the beginning of February. Not for a second had Udo thought that it could be a final goodbye. He thought it was for maybe one last discussion …

Müller had looked forward to the meeting.

Heiner's body had been ravaged by the illness. He looked at Udo for a long time and then talked about Dirk. With a weak voice, he said: "Always remember that you two are like brothers to me. You are part of my family, as if you were my son. But you are the older one. You have to look after Dirk."

Nothing about the company. No praise, no criticism, no advice. Only Dirk and the family. Yes, he had seen Heiner as his father and Dirk as his brother.

Dirk meets Udo in the arrival hall of the airport in Palma. They face each other in the crowd for a few moments, without uttering a word. What can they say, after all? Express their condolences to each other? They hug briefly and drive to the villa where Heiner Ströer is laid out in his favourite suit, exactly as he had requested.

Katharina greets them at the door. Only last year, Heiner had married his long-time companion in a private ceremony. Timo, Katharina's son from her first marriage, is expected later.

There is a strange atmosphere in the house. For long hours nobody speaks. They are all overwhelmed by the situation. Silence. Maybe that is the most honest way of grieving – together, but each on their own.

The Monday morning papers in Germany will print the first obituaries. "The Poster Pope is dead" reads the headline in the *Cologne Express*. Hundreds of condolences arrive to the headquarters.

Heiner Ströer had been a well-known and popular citizen, highly respected in the advertising industry. Many would like to pay their last respects, but Ströer wanted to be only accompanied by his family on his final journey.

It is a Wednesday. In a Cologne cemetery, a bright blue sky sends its last blessings over the small group of mourners. And now, facing this stark reminder of the finality of life, Udo Müller is hit by a feeling of deep, helpless grief. He cries uncontrollably as the coffin is slowly lowered into the family grave.

Never again will he be able to ask Heiner for advice, never again hear his admonishing words and then the encouraging: "Well, go on then."

Udo feels very lonely.

The year after

During the following weeks, Müller buries himself in his work but thinks constantly of the late patriarch. Heiner Ströer had been able to enjoy being Germany's largest out-of-home advertiser for only a very short space of time. But his company, which he built from very small beginnings, rose to be number one.

"He died at the wrong time," Udo Müller complains. "Heiner could never really enjoy this triumph." But death never happens at a right time, and there is no room for sentiment in day to day business.

DSM now needs to be integrated into the considerably smaller Ströer AG. They must develop a mutual strategy. This won't be possible without sacrifices and minor damage. David has brought Goliath down. But what happens now?

Udo Müller knows exactly what to do. He only has 18 months to realise the cost-cutting agreed with Cerberus. Only 18 months to raise the EBITDA from € 10 million to € 10 million. Only 18 months to turn two companies into one. Udo Müller knows that he doesn't have a minute to spare. And so, on the day of the deal's closing, he and his colleagues are waiting in the car park outside DSM's headquarters.

The so-called "closing" represents the official finalisation of the deal. The lawyers of both sides are connected online or by phone to document the correct transfer of the purchase sum to the seller's account. As soon as the money has been received in the seller's account, the contract is considered done – and the buyer is the legal owner.

As soon as the lawyers give the go-ahead, Müller and his team march towards the DSM building. The imposing entrance door has a very fine brass handle. Udo Müller has used it a few times before, when he had asked the DSM people for a meeting. Every time, they let the Ströer man know that they regarded him as small-fry, and that the honourable DSM wouldn't do business with him.

Now he pushes down the brass doorhandle as the new owner. It feels good. Good and cool. Müller asks one of his team to take a photo. They have time for that.

On the top floor, Egon Böttcher and his colleagues are waiting. They know what to expect. Their contracts will be terminated. And their severance pay won't be too big either. Their plan to extend their own contracts for a few years before the first attempt to sell had failed.

But their departure is accompanied by friendly words, best wishes and face-saving respect. Böttcher and Niederwipper leave DSM a few days later. Both respond with utmost professionalism. Only Theo Merkel will stay. He is the manager who oversees the relationships with the communities, and he will carry on doing it in the new company.

A bit later, there will be another official farewell for the two leaving directors. Müller presents each of them with a double magnum of good red wine from his private cellar.

The fight for DSM had been very intense, and the resistance of its management quite tough, but Müller doesn't want to burn bridges. He knows that you always meet twice in life, as the German saying goes.

The next step is harder. About half of DSM's 1,400 employees will lose their job. Müller and the supervisory board agree that the redundancies should be organised without causing "social hardship". That is easy to say, however, and anyone affected may feel very differently about it.

Again, there are dozens of meetings preparing every step of the integration. How can they achieve the best possible synergy? How can they avoid social hardship, or at least mitigate it? It mainly comes down to the finance department.

The most important question for Müller concerns meeting the business targets in the timeframe agreed with Cerberus. A failure would be terrible news and would give Frank Bruno his foot in the door. Cerberus would become the growling hellhound snapping at Udo Müller's heels.

The operational EBITDA must be increased immediately and significantly for the year 2004. That was the agreement with Frank Bruno, and it is written in the contract. This is a risky target because they must reckon with high transition costs in the first few months. The merger of two companies with very different business cultures – the success-hungry Ströer AG and the world-weary DSM – can hardly be achieved without any problems.

In February, the managers will present the merged companies' strategy at a staff meeting in Frankfurt. From that point onward, the company will be named Ströer Deutsche Städte Medien GmbH. The staff knows that Ströer's concept will mean sacrifices. The mood among them is not good. Integration also means contributions. But it would have been the same if an investor from the U.S. or the French rival JCDecaux had taken over.

In association with the Ministry for Work, they employed a transfer company to retrain any employees deemed surplus to requirements for new jobs in other industries. In the end, no one took the company to a tribunal, something very rare with a takeover.

It is already the end of June when Udo Müller takes first stock. The idea to staff each department equally with employees from both companies was a recipe for conflict. But two decades later, Müller can say, "I was extremely proud of my employees and what they managed during the integration phase. None of them was prepared for such a task. Everything was trial and error. You don't learn how to organise the merger of two big companies anywhere, not at university nor elsewhere."

Müller is well supported by Alexander Stotz, who knows the business by heart. He started as a student intern, searching up and down the country for suitable sites for the new Megalights.

His career took off after that, and after only two years with the company became the head of rights and permissions as well as authorised signatory of the German holding of the Ströer Group. Still, the DSM merger is a big challenge, but it doesn't come as a surprise. And Stotz, who was only in his mid-30s then, made a success of it and today is the CEO of Ströer Media Deutschland, responsible for all out-of-home advertising.

But nobody could do anything about the general economic situation in 2004. Because of lackluster consumer and investment behaviour, companies reduced their advertising budgets. The whole industry was suffering.

During that phase, Frank Bruno proves to be a fair partner. In a critical phase, he goes easy about interest rate payments. The investment strategist isn't overly strict.

By mid-2004, it looks as if the year will be all right after all. The relationship between Udo and his co-owner Dirk also continues without any problems. Dirk just lets his friend and brother get on with it.

In November, all planned targets are met. The difficult year after the merger has been a good one. The subsidiaries in Poland and Turkey are also doing well. In Poland, they have made it to number one in advertising. In Turkey there is a chance to expand. Both companies report positive figures.

At some point during this phase, Müller enters the office of his finance manager Bührdel and asks: "Well, Alfried, what shall we buy next?"

It might have been meant as a joke. But Bührdel doesn't like jokes like that. For him, the everyday business is important, the consolidation of the company. That is difficult enough.

But he guesses that his boss doesn't simply come up with a question like that without some element of seriousness behind it. Every achievement for Müller is always only the first step towards the next move. If there was any chance to get the moon from the night sky, Müller would try it.

"What do you think?" he asks with a suspicious glint in

his eye that Bührdel knows all too well. “What do you think of buying DERG?”

DERG – Deutsche Eisenbahn Reklame, the German Railway Advertiser – is a subsidiary of Deutsche Bahn and owns the monopoly for advertising in German railway stations, alongside tracks and on trains. By turnover, the company is among the top three in outdoor advertising.

Bührdel moans. “Oh, Udo, is that a joke? Let’s sort out DSM first. DERG isn’t for sale anyway.

Müller smiles. “I’m not so sure.”

Advertising on trains

Siegfried Marter is one of those people who finds that little chats at work are part of a good work-life balance. He is the CEO of DERG and would love to call Udo Müller for one of those little chats and tell him a secret. It has been bothering him for a few days.

Marter trusts Müller. He admires him. This mixture of visionary thinking, hard work and a relaxed lifestyle. They have been sort of friends for quite a while and have spent many evenings over a glass of wine talking about life in general. Siegfried has given Udo many a tip on how to live a good life.

But now he must keep a secret that he would love to share with Udo. DERG is up for sale. Hartmut Mehdorn, the CEO of Deutsche Bahn (DB), has decided to boost its balance before floating the company on the stock market. The DERG headquarters are in a plain office district, only a stone’s throw from Kassel’s main railway station. It is not a beautiful building, but practical.

Marter restlessly paces up and down his spacious. office on the third floor. An hour ago, he had returned from Berlin. It was a short meeting with the top boss of the German railway.

The conversation with Mehdorn took place on the 24th floor of the *Bahntower* on Potsdamer Platz and lasted only lasted 15 minutes. By the time Marter is on the way down again, he knows he has a delicate task on his hands. The DERG boss is to prepare the sale of his company. It is a huge challenge. But Marter is committed to confidentiality. It nearly tears him apart, but the plan is still top secret.

For more than a decade, Marter has been at the top of the advertising company owned by the federal railway company, DB. He has always been well respected by the changing chairs of the board. Mehdorn, too, his fourth boss, never had anything to complain about.

In terms of turnover and scope, DERG is number three in German out-of-home advertising. It is also mobile, something none of its rivals can boast. "We advertise where people are" is the company motto. That includes about 6,000 railway stations, 3,600 trains, and 14,700 bU.S.es and trams in the regions. DERG posters are in all the places where big crowds often gather. These are optimal places for advertising!

The company is old and reputable. It was founded in 1866 by royal decree in a southern region. Even then, the owners realised that poster adverts on their own sites as well as on the trains would be a nice little earner. They got the idea from the railway companies in Great Britain.

Over the next few decades, a highly profitable company developed with numerous regional offices. But by 2004, business is not that good. During the last few months, turnover has shrunk to less than € 150 million.

DB's CEO Mehdorn wants to take the state company, worth billions, to the stock market to generate capital for further expansion and modernisation.

The plan is controversial, especially politically. Chancellor Schröder is said to be supportive of Mehdorn's plans, but the government is split.

It would involve separating the train company from the non-train business. Mother Railway has many daughters which really have nothing to do with the transport of people and goods. One of them is the advertising company DERG.

Despite Marter's discretion, Udo Müller has somehow heard these rumours. And he is on fire. What an incredible chance! Coming so soon after the DSM takeover, he could complete the consolidation of the out-of-home advertising market.

DERG would not only perfectly complement Ströer-DSM. The company is also the only big rival that Müller would be allowed to take over without getting in trouble with the Cartel Office and the competition control.

While Udo Müller is "high on adrenaline", as he later puts it, his team is very skeptical. The finance manager Bührdel cannot imagine how the company can manage another takeover so quickly after acquiring DSM. Everyone is already at full capacity working on the integration of the two companies.

And now another months-long, strength-sapping, weekend-losing race for the next company? Only for the debts to be even higher and the screws even tighter?

Müller listens to Bührdel's concerns. But for him, he sees only the positive aspects of the deal, and they are overwhelming. DERG fits perfectly into his strategy of consolidation. He simply must have that company! Also, Müller considers it a gateway to the digitalisation of outdoor advertising. DERG's adverts are mainly in stations and on trains, that is, inside. The company already has several LCD and LED screens where advertising could be presented digitally.

The even more positive news is that thanks to the DSM takeover, he and his team have learned so much about the deal-making process that they could do the M&A and the due diligence aspects themselves. They wouldn't need to hire expensive investment bankers as consultants this time. They would only need the experts for legal issues and the financial and tax aspects of "financial due diligence".

In a very short time, the Ströer boss puts his team together. The process also picks up speed on the other side. The confidentiality Mehdorn wanted didn't last long. "There is interest from all over the world," reports the *Süddeutsche Zeitung* shortly after the conversation between Mehdorn and Marter.

The headline is right. There is considerable international interest in the news. Siegfried Marter has hardly got time to prepare for his role as seller. Soon they count about 40 interested parties.

Viacom, the media company from New York, is back. From London, Clear Channel International. It's what you might call the usual suspects in the battle for the German out-of-home advertising market – as outdoor advertising is now often called.

Affinage Holding from Geneva, the main shareholder in Switzerland's industry-leading Allgemeine Plakatgesellschaft (APG), sees a chance to enter the German market. A few of Müller's old rivals also express their interest, including awg, from Koblenz, and the Berlin advertiser Wall. And, of course, JCDecaux.

"DERG is a goldmine," Hans Wall, the Wall founder, tells the media. He says there would be no better partner for the railway than his company. "We fit perfectly together."

Udo Müller has a different opinion and tells *Die Welt*:

"Ströer-DSM is the only partner who can improve the whole spectrum of DERG." While Ströer's advertising media are mainly by the side of roads, DERG's is focused on waiting areas in railway stations. They would complement each other very well to reach mobile target groups.

That may be true, but the old question remains: Can Ströer AG, with huge loans already, even take part in the bidding? Has the company reached its credit limit in the battle over DSM? Maybe even overstepped it? Only the New York hedge fund Cerberus is a possible creditor. The arrangement with the Americans explicitly excludes the participation of other creditors.

Müller is not an underdog yapping at the heels of the big dogs anymore. He is in that pack. Competitors such as Wall and JCDecaux have only one target. They want to make sure that this time the winner must not be Ströer.

But Udo Müller is already working out a strategy with his team in Cologne. Two questions are important: How can the multiple products of DERG be integrated into the company? And what is DERG really worth?

Experts estimate the real value of DERG to be between €10 and €10 million. But it won't stay within this price range, especially if Ströer is among the bidders.

This time the rivals will try everything to prevent Ströer getting too powerful in the German market. Deutsche Bahn is also optimistic that the price could rise significantly in an auction. With international interest bigger than expected, it might reach even €10 or €100 million. This is what Mehdorn believes.

Cerberus again

Frank Bruno is relaxing with friends after a round of golf in the National Liberty Club when his mobile rings. Frank recognises the German number and answers. "Hi Udo, any problems?"

The German industrialist and his American creditor have been talking every now and then in the months since their previous deal. It seems as if the money mogul has a soft spot for the courageous Cologne businessman. Müller reassures him that there are no problems, but good news. Then he briefly describes his intention to buy DERG.

Frank Bruno likes the idea and doesn't think the € 10 to € 10 million that Müller will need will be a problem. "Sounds beautiful," he says and offers some praise. "As long as I bet on you, I know I'm winning." He says he is coming to Frankfurt in the next few days anyway, and they should meet up.

While European banks make their loans dependent on debt levels, the existing capital of their customers and other economic criteria, the Americans only judge the quality of the management and the cash flow. Every now and then it doesn't work out, but Udo Müller benefits from this money lending philosophy.

For Cerberus, the Ströer-DSM deal had been the perfect entry to the German market – i.e., the strongest economy in Europe, where there are so many extremely interesting and well managed family companies. It is extremely attractive to hedge funds. Everything fits perfectly. The Americans have a lot of money at their disposal, and in Germany there are many opportunities to invest it. Many old patriarchs didn't have the right heirs and either wanted or had to sell. Others wanted to expand, but failed, like Müller, to get backing from the risk-averse European banks. And then there was the new category of start-ups: young, hungry entrepreneurs with good ideas looking for capital.

Cerberus had been exploring the German market for a year already when Udo Müller approached them with the DSM deal. After that, they progressed rapidly: Together with Deutsche Bank, Cerberus took over a property company in the north owning 7,500 rentals. Together with the London Whitehall Street funds of Goldman Sachs, Cerberus swallowed the largest private property company in Berlin.

It did the same to Peguform, a supplier of car products, with 7,800 employees. Cerberus took it over in February 2005, then the 20,000 flats of a trade-union-owned property group.

Cerberus was doing good business in Germany. And Udo Müller had a direct line to its worldwide number two, Frank Bruno.

DERG's boss Siegfried Marter, usually so talkative, goes quiet as things are hotting up. He is flooded with work, more than at any time in his long working life. He is tasked with preparing the sale and making the railway subsidiary look perfect.

The most important instrument during this phase is known as the Mergers & Acquisition database. It is a highly confidential collection of data, listing all relevant facts and information about a company. It means a lot of detailed work. The facts should not be estimates; they must be accurate. But not everything can be made public.

Marter must make sure that only genuinely interested parties get to see the database. During such a process there are always a few people seeking valuable information for their own business. But Marter knows who they are.

He is genial and usually has a good and collegial relationship with all the German interested parties. But now they are all rivals. Marter must not appear to have a favourite. The rivals eye each other with great suspicion.

Müller is very busy these days. He has meetings with board members, worker's councils and managers of the Deutsche Bahn and explores what is so special about train advertising. Sometimes he calls Marter, but their talks are very short and neutral.

All roads lead to *Ströer* (railways too)

So now it is all about railway advertising. Müller's strategy is quite simple. Organic growth, year after year, adds on a few percentage points. But that is not good enough to stay at the top. That's the way of the Old Economy. Success now is a different kettle of fish. It's faster. If Ströer AG wants to remain successful, growth is only possible by taking over other companies. It is a risky but by now pretty common business model.

Experts call it "buy and build". Buying is a large part of inorganic growth. In addition to expansion into new countries, for Ströer this growth also meant the fast and aggressive development of new advertising media, such as the backlit glass cases, and, later, digital media. The company was always at the forefront of technical developments and could exploit possible organic growth in the market.

However, for huge jumps in growth, they had to buy – like now with the railway advertising.

A year ago, when the decision about DSM was imminent, Müller hardly slept some nights. By comparison, the preparations for the deal with DB seem fairly normal.

"Something is missing," he complains jokingly. "Where

is the kick?" The meetings follow a certain routine. Müller presents his future vision to the sellers in a relaxed mood. They are quite taken by Müller's visions. New advertising media in railway stations, for example. Müller doesn't only have a good narrative for them, he can also present it very well.

The Ströer boss bases his predictions on three conditions. One is the assumption of a lot more potential in the German outdoor advertising market that hasn't been exploited yet. As with the DSM deal, he tells the sellers about the higher lease prices they will be able to charge for advertising media in stations and on rolling stock. But that's only possible if they sell to Ströer because he, Müller, can then consolidate the outdoor advertising market.

Also as before, he explains that the share of outdoor advertising in all advertising budgets in Germany is only 2.7 %. In countries like Great Britain, France, Italy or Spain they invest up to twice as much in poster advertising. But Germany could achieve that with a consolidated market. And the increase in turnover means higher lease prices.

The second line of argument is also convincing. Digitalisation increases the attractiveness of advertising spaces. Moving images can supplement one-dimensional paper posters and, at some point, replace them altogether.

Müller can already see attractive videos in all major railway stations. He also has big plans for the Munich company Infoscreen, which came to him as part of DSM's portfolio. DSM had a 25 % share in Infoscreen, with the other 75 % surprisingly held by the steel giant ThyssenKrupp. But Ströer took over the remaining shares with the plan to expand the high-tech company and its digital advertising gadgets. With Infoscreen, he can get his images moving – and they can display information and entertainment, as well as adverts, to people waiting for their trains.

The technology is called "cross track projection". Short videos can be played across the train tracks to passengers standing on the opposite platform, until the next underground or overground train arrives.

Infoscreen also had another digital product to offer, which was already part of the DERG advertising program: 70 infoscreen-towers where images are projected from behind on to a lit screen, which were very popular.

"In addition," Müller continues, "by further consolidating the outdoor advertising market, its competitiveness compared with other kinds of media – such as TV, radio and print – will be significantly improved."

Müller describes a brave new advertising world. The third argument is framed as a question: Who can realise this glorious future best? Udo Müller and his team from Ströer AG, of course. Ströer is the only bidder who can offer national and local marketing, covering the whole of Germany.

A rumor does the rounds after one of Müller's performances that one of the DB executives asks whether it might actually be better to keep the company after all.

By now it is clear that the initially quoted price of € 10 million to € 10 million will have to rise. The U.S. media group CBS-Viacom had decided it belatedly wants a piece of the lucrative advertising cake in the economic stronghold of Germany. The same goes for its rival Clear Channel. These things are not cheap, though. That much is clear. But the money is there, at least with the Americans.

And then there is Hans Wall. The old Berlin outdoor advertiser at last wants to show Udo Müller who is boss in the poster business.

This time it is not only a battle of everyone against everyone else. These days they are all fighting Müller. No one could prevent his rise to the top of German advertising. But now it is important that Ströer doesn't get too powerful.

This competition leaves its marks. The DB people can hardly believe their luck. By the end of October 2005, the price for their advertising agency has risen to € 15 million.

And Müller hasn't even placed a bid yet. He is still negotiating with Cerberus about financing the deal. There seem to be questions. In the hedge fund's headquarters in New York, the analysts discuss how many millions they can send over to Germany.

Frank Bruno and his German client have been in agreement for a while that the DERG takeover would be of great advantage for Cerberus as well.

Bruno feels sure about it for three reasons. With more than half of German outdoor advertising, Ströer would hold a very strong market position. No advertiser could ignore them, and managers of other large media agencies would struggle to put Ströer under any pressure in the future.

Secondly, after a successful DERG takeover, Müller would be in debt to Cerberus for about half a billion euros. It will be practically impossible to pay that back with a normal business. The company will need to float on the stock market sooner or later to rake in the necessary sums.

Bruno was expecting this solution anyway. A guy like Udo, who wants to develop his company by taking over one company after another, will sooner or later have to go public.

The time had not come yet. But as soon as Müller, with sound prospects for growth, floats the company, it would mean a super payday for Cerberus.

The third point of the Cerberus considerations: If Müller, against all expectations, crashes his business, all the assets of Ströer-DSM, plus maybe DERG, would go to the hedge fund. Udo Müller would be out of the game, but another team and another hungry CEO would carry on under Cerberus. Or they would fillet the company and sell the parts. In any case, Cerberus would be the winner.

But there is still the question of how much to bid for DERG to win the auction. Analysts in Cologne and at Cerberus examine all imaginable variables. In the end, they estimate that DERG will cost around € 100 million, 70 % more than the lower end of DB's initial estimate.

The decisive and final bidding round is scheduled for December 16th, 2005. They have been negotiating for a year. Due diligence, a first indicative offer, new negotiations, contract negotiations, renegotiating the user contracts. Müller and his team are at it round the clock. It is only a year ago that they signed the DSM deal. Most of The parties that were initially interested have withdrawn by now. Only three bidders are left: Clear Channel, JCDecaux and Ströer. Again, it is a game of poker for millions.

The DERG sale has a political component too. DB is still owned by the state.

The then DB-boss Mehdorn intends to sell the advertising subsidiary because he wants to present positive figures before he takes the company to the stock market and out of state control. But, at the moment, the state is still the sole owner. And everything in connection with the railway is somehow political – or is interpreted that way by interested parties.

The two other remaining candidates have grasped this as well. One possible criticism of Ströer could be the employment situation. Existing jobs would only be safe if a foreign company took over, because newcomers to the game would urgently need every man and woman with detailed knowledge of the German out-of-home advertising world.

With Ströer it would be different. DERG's employees

would be in the same boat as DSM's. A Ströer takeover would mean major job losses, maybe mitigated by a re-employment company. Costs must be lowered, of course.

Müller is aware that this is his Achilles' heel. It is one of the reasons he holds countless talks during the sales process. He talks to representatives of the railway trade union. He talks to the managers of DB.

The Ströer boss even talks to the Chancellor. Müller manages to get an appointment with Gerhard Schröder, facilitated by one of his contacts. It will only be the two of them, in the Chancellor's office on the seventh floor of the official residence, on Schröder's famous corner sofa, where Müller describes the economic impact if Ströer should take over DERG.

His argument is the market consolidation of outdoor advertising, and the creation of a national champion. Why should global giants always win in the advertising business? With Ströer as a strong number one in all areas, outdoor advertising can develop significantly in Germany and the company can then embrace the massive possibilities of digitalised advertising in the country. That doesn't only secure jobs, it will also create some.

From the Chancellor's office you have a perfect view not only to the Reichstag, but also to the *Bahntower* on Potsdamer Platz. It's there, on December 16th, 2005, just two years after the DSM sale, that another grand finale is beginning.

They are on the 24th floor of the *Bahntower*: The sellers with their consultants, lawyers and analysts. The three rival bidders have set up their base in luxury hotels within view. There is no favourite.

The Clear Channel team is in a suite in the Mandala Hotel. JCDecaux is in the conference room of the Marriott. Udo Müller and his crew are staying in the Grand Hyatt.

One after another, the charismatic DB finance manager Diethelm Sack meets the bidders. "Gentlemen," he says with a little smile to Müller and his team when he arrives in the conference room of the Grand Hyatt. "We want to thank you for spending so much time and effort for nearly a year dealing with DERG. Now you have another hour to consider what the company is really worth to you. There is only one bidding round. Think hard how much you want to bid."

Diethelm Sack is one of the greats among German finance managers. He knows everybody and is respected by everyone. Some also fear him. He is a totally respectable man, but also knows every trick in the book. A real pro.

He explains the rules of the game again. The three bidders only have one chance. They must write down their offer and put it in a sealed envelope. DERG's Siegfried Marter will pick them up and take them to the *Bahntower*. There they will be opened, compared, and the result will be announced.

Around 7 p.m., Marter collects the offers. None of the bidders knows what the others have offered. Again, they must wait. The chair of the supervisory board Dieter Stolte, who lives in Berlin, sits down with the group and as usual is a calming influence. "I have a good feeling," he says in a paternal way when he notices Müller's tense face.

The Ströer boss remembers the situation as extremely nerve wracking. "You pace up and down in that conference room, up and down, and there are all those thoughts," he said. "Is the offer good enough? Have you thought of everything? What have the others offered?" Udo Müller thinks of the last few months. So many talks, so many attempts to convince everyone of your own strategy. Even the Chancellor! But will it be enough?

Shortly before the hour is over, the DB chair Sack rings Müller on his mobile.

"Mr. Müller, something is not quite clear," he says. "Your offer is complex, and we have a few more questions." He gives Müller a few minutes and asks to be called back.

Is it a good sign? Udo Müller doesn't waste time contemplating the question. He explains to Sack concisely what he wants to know.

And waits. After half an hour, Müller's mobile rings. He had expected it, but he winces anyway.

His pulse is racing when he looks at the display. It is Diethelm Sack.

This is the decision. Another adrenaline moment. All or nothing. Everyone in the room is staring at him. There is total silence.

Udo Müller exhales and takes the call.

"Mr. Müller, I want to congratulate you," Sack says. "Your bid is accepted. Congratulations. We are looking forward to working with you."

A great cheer rings out through the Grand Hyatt. In the other hotels, the mood is low. Again nothing. Again, this Müller.

It is a memorable date for the whole industry. The advertising opportunities in 6,000 railway stations, on 3,670 long-distance trains, 14,700 regional trains and 7,000 railway bridges are now managed by the country's number one, DSM-Ströer. The Cologne company now also owns a few more properties, such as the head office in Kassel. DERG is integrated into Ströer DERG Media. Now Ströer AG is in a class of its own in German out-of-home advertising.

When, a few days later, he puts his signature on the contracts in a little ceremony, Udo Müller tries to enjoy the moment. The market share of Ströer AG has, with the acquisition of DERG, risen to more than 50 %.

The consolidation of the German outdoor advertising market is more or less complete. In Müller's view, this is the most important factor to increase the share of outdoor advertising in overall advertising budgets to the European level of 7 %. Is that enough for now? How does it feel to have arrived at a place that only two, three years ago seemed like an impossible dream? To be the undisputed number one in Germany? Nothing more is possible. At least for that moment, Müller feels on top of everything. But only for the moment.

It has been a decade since the outdoor advertiser Hermann Stockem shouted at the puzzled Udo Müller: "Before you turned up, everything was much more peaceful!"

At the time, the boss of Düsseldorf's Moplak only expressed what many of the other outdoor advertisers were thinking. There was this guy with an unfinished medical degree interfering with their businesses while ignoring all the rules. He was definitely not following the unwritten law of peaceful, friendly cooperation.

Today, Stockem smiles when he remembers that fit of anger. "Udo had seen things that we didn't. Maybe we didn't want to see them. And he took the chance, and with his cheek and ideas he changed German outdoor advertising."

This latest success elicits a mixture of resignation and respect in the industry. Again, this Müller! The losers are disappointed. Ströer had simply bid too much.

In the German business and trade press, Müller's latest coup is regarded as a personal victory. The *Handelsblatt* acknowledges that he is always one step ahead.

Ströer's press release about the expensive DERG acquisition sounds comparatively sober. "It was a long and necessary path to consolidate the fragmented German market for out-of-home media," it says. "We have now created a base to make our media competitive in the international fight for advertising budgets."

Regarding competition: The Bonn Cartel Office had taken notice of Müller's fast expansion. Above a combined turnover of € 100 million, a merger has to be registered and checked.

During the sales process, the Cartel Office had asked the bidders to have an informal check done. The foreign bidders complied, even though their turnover was significantly below the upper limit. For them there was no risk involved. Even after a successful takeover of DERG, they would not be in a position of market dominance in Germany.

For Ströer, Müller had it checked, of course. His finance managers had signalled that the combined turnover of both companies would be below the threshold. Still, Ströer complied and explained during the initial check that a merger process would not be necessary as the threshold would not be exceeded.

Still, the Cartel Office sent a faxed and non-official note about the cartel laws after the decision had gone in favour of Ströer – even before Müller and DERG had signed the contract.

At first it came as a shock. For Müller there is no reason why the Cartel Office should ask for a check. He confers with his partners at DB. They, too, are sure that the combined turnover of the two companies in the preceding year had been below the € 100 million threshold, and they sign as planned.

But the authorities don't back off. Only a few days after the completion of the sale in December 2005, the Cartel Office initiates divestiture proceedings.

Three months after Ströer buys DERG, the relevant agencies launch a major operation and drive to various offices one morning and confiscate documents. Seven months later they get the results: The proceedings have been revoked.

Müller is happy about the decision. But he expected it anyway.

With Ströer's acquisition of DERG, just 15 years after starting his career in the industry, Müller has now achieved what he had imagined from very early on. He has now consolidated outdoor advertising in Germany and become number one. After conquering East Germany, Ströer is now also number one in the united Germany. No one can ignore the Cologne group anymore.

After the problems with the Cartel Office, there is no longer the chance to buy more out-of-home advertising companies in Germany. Instead, Müller has got ideas for his next expansion.

"If we compare our path with climbing Mount Everest," he tells the board these days, "then we have only reached base camp." He wants more, much more.

The finance manager growls: "Udo, the higher you climb, the thinner the air."

"But the view gets better," his boss answers with a smile.

The stuff they write in the papers ...

Week after week, the trade magazines print the latest news about Müller and his business. Every now and then, the general media in the country also feature the successful Cologne entrepreneur. The renowned weekly from Hamburg, *Die Zeit*, publishes a respectful full-page portrait of Müller. Then *Die Welt am Sonntag* describes an event with the Ströer boss in July 2005 with the title "Jack-in-the-box".

"It was a dire situation for the 14 journalists in the small conference room one morning in May. Germany's largest outdoor advertising company, Ströer Out-of-Home Media AG, had invited them to a press conference in Cologne concerning the company's latest figures. The person who wasn't there, however, was the boss. Not even his press officer knew where Udo Müller had disappeared to. Instead, he suggested a tour of the building to the waiting guests.

The members of the press pack were outraged. In the end the finance manager Alfried Bührdel had to present last year's figures. But that was more of a croaking than a speech as the slender 43-year-old had a bad cold.

Exactly 20 minutes late, the door opened and a tall man in a pin-stripe suit and expensive shoes entered. Without a single word of apology or apparent feeling of regret, Udo Müller took over. In a monotone voice and with a bland expression, the 43-year-old droned through last year's sales figures.

The son of a civil servant from Godesberg is used to success. When a journalist asked what kind of profession he could never imagine doing, he answered simply: "None." Aged 15, he was among the 30 best high jumpers in the country. Two years later he played in the under-18 national handball team. Aged 19, together with a teammate, he published a program brochure for his handball club. In the first year alone, the teenagers made a profit of 140.000 D-Mark. Aged 21, Müller printed off a few holiday snaps of a friend as arty posters and immediately sold 3,000 of them.

Aged 24, he broke off his medical training and, together with two friends, founded an advertising agency. After a short time, it was among the top three in Berlin, but Müller wanted more. "My business partners didn't have the same drive to expand." So he quit and in 1990 joined up with the late Heinz Ströer. Within 15 years, Ströer Out-of-Home Media grew from a staff of two, himself and Karl-Ludwig Scheel, later the caretaker in the Ströer office, to become the largest German billboard marketing agency. With 1,000 employees in 11 countries and a turnover of € 112 million, Ströer today is the fifth biggest outdoor advertising company in the world.

Müller seems able to sell everything, but not himself. He admits that people consider him arrogant, and it had taken him a long time to understand how others see him. "I can't help it," he says and tries something like a smile. But he really is quite nice, he insists. It is mainly his body language that expresses a lack of interest in everything and everyone. His mother complained when he was young that he would never smile.

But the man whose worst decision, in his own opinion, was the purchase of a pair of pinstripe flared trousers, is not quite so innocent. The athletic entrepreneur likes to present himself as a dandy. His suits are always of a perfect fit, as perfect as his dark gelled hair. Even on a very hot day he looks as if he had just come from make-up.

The ladies seem to like his dry charm. He once dated the actor Esther Schweins, at the moment it is the jewellery designer Laura Reinging. Marina Beutner, marketing boss of the TV station Vox, and a Ströer client for the past seven years, confirms: "Müller only catches your eye on second glance."

Though his body language signals the opposite, Müller is not the type to boast about his success. His passions are art and history, and he talks about it for hours with great enthusiasm. He is considered a tough, unpretentious, extremely professional, and reliable business part-

ner. His talent is undisputed; he has, after all, without any previous experience, turned the whole sector upside down."

Müller, of course, enjoys the media attention, though he doesn't really care too much about the opinions expressed in the press. He wants to fill his billboards, not newspaper columns.

THE BIG TEST

... and now the world!

What is it that drives an industrialist to go beyond the boundaries of reason and economic rules? Is it ambition? Passion? Hubris? It is definitely not calm consideration.

After the enormous. efforts of the past few years, Udo Müller really should allow the company and its employees a period of recuperation. Especially as it takes time to integrate the newly acquired companies into the group.

But Müller wants more. For him, the notion of contentment sounds like stasis, and maybe even going backward. One must go on. When he suggested to Heiner Ströer that they conquer the East German outdoor advertising market, Ströer was a decent, but rather small company. It was ranked fifth in West Germany.

Hardly anybody could have predicted then that Ströer would soon be the strongest out-of-home advertising force in the new federal states. Müller calls that "Phase One". And now, with the acquisition of DSM and DERG he has become the unassailable number one in the whole of Germany. He calls this "Phase Two".

But what is "Phase Three"? It's obvious. After Germany, it must be the whole world. What else? The European and the American markets are mostly consolidated. In the

European Union, JCDecaux is number one nearly everywhere. In the U.S., Clear Channel is top.

But there are still many empty sites in other parts of the globe. There are the emerging markets Brazil, Russia, India, China and South Africa, the so-called BRICS states. In the Middle East, parts of Asia and Eastern and Central Europe. Müller thinks he can still find empty sites for his colourful posters.

He does have an idea for "Phase Three". It is a must, really, particularly if he wants to take Ströer to the stock market at some point. In Germany he is the market leader. He can't acquire more companies because the Cartel Office would probably not allow it. It ties the company's expected growth rate to the economy as a whole; at best only slightly higher.

Furthermore, the much sought after and expected digitalisation of outdoor advertising, offering new and significant opportunities for growth, has still not materialised.

But Germany's mature economy, with the country's aging population and high prosperity, has only been growing a few percentage points per year in the first decade of the 21st century.

It is different in the five global regions Müller is looking at now: Eastern Europe, the Middle East, Southeast Asia, India and, of course, China. Why not repeat there what worked so well in Germany? Ströer has the know-how, interesting products like the Megalights, which are new to those countries, glass shelters and backlit Citylights posters.

Müller plans to cooperate with JCDecaux and Clear Channel to build a global empire. Twice so far, he and his employees have managed large and complicated takeovers after highly competitive auctions and have acquired the necessary know-how. There were also dozens of small deals that he managed in between.

He knows by now how the M&A business is organised. How you can quickly and successfully integrate large acquisitions without major problems.

Müller identifies six locations from where he can launch the new global business: Kiev and Moscow for Ukraine and Russia; Dubai for the Middle East (mainly the United Arab Emirates and Saudi Arabia); Kuala Lumpur for Malaysia and Southeast Asia. In India, he considers the economic centre of Mumbai. And in China, the business hub Shanghai, or the capital Beijing.

Young and hungry employees are instructed to look for interesting and flexible companies that Ströer can take over. Ideally, the companies will be in their country's top three, but they must always be companies where the present owner is happy to remain with the business and provide their know-how. Ströer will take over at least 51 % of the company, thus becoming its majority stakeholder. But the former owner can decide to keep anything between 10-49 %. With anything above 10 %, the shareholders must participate in capital and investments of the company. With the 90/10 model, there is no obligation to take a share in further investment.

Once the core investment has been settled, there is a phase of consolidation, the so-called roll-up. Companies that fit the bill will be acquired and integrated. In many of the target regions, outdoor advertising means just a few billboards here and there. Many cities have not realised yet what a potential source of income out-of-home advertising can be – another reason why Ströer is expecting success with its modern and innovative products. "Buy and build" he calls his strategy.

The aim is that by the end of the process, Ströer will be among the top three in outdoor advertising in as many of the target markets as possible. He knows from his consolidation experience in Germany that only then do the decent profits start coming in.

This is the plan for conquering the world. The only thing that is missing is capital.

Udo Müller wants to get the money from Hermann Dambach. Until the successful DSM deal, Dambach was, as a team boss at Morgan Stanley, Müller's most important consultant. Now he has a new job. In the same year as the DSM deal, the investment banker left Morgan Stanley for the Californian mega investor Oaktree Capital, a hedge fund worth billions. Based in Frankfurt, his role is to stimulate business in Germany and Europe.

Müller asks for an appointment, and soon the two meet in an Italian restaurant in Frankfurt. Over grilled dover sole, the next chapter in the life of entrepreneur Udo Müller begins.

The Ströer boss presents his global strategy. Dambach listens carefully. He knows the industry and understands its prospects. But most of all, he knows Müller and remembers the time when there was no money for buying DSM. Müller then joined up with Cerberus and got the capital. Dambach was there. He knows how it worked.

"Why not do it again?" Müller asks. "Do you think Oaktree will give me the money?"

"How much are you thinking?"

"No idea. € 100 million? € 100 million? Or maybe € 100 million?"

Dambach doesn't seem shocked by the figures. He displays no emotion as he suggests presenting the plan together to the Oaktree bosses in Los Angeles. Such a high-volume deal, even with a super-rich investor like Oaktree, is a matter for the executives.

Things proceed quickly. Back in the hotel, Müller euphorically plans the next steps. He calls Dirk Ströer, wakes him up, and tells him about his plan. Dirk listens, sleepily. Ah, Udo again. First Germany, now the whole world …

The next day Müller is in a meeting with his finance manager and explains his plans. The man who holds the purse strings responds grumpily and doesn't want to talk about it. It's madness. They're still in the process of integrating DSM and DERG into the Ströer system. The debts are sky high and burdensome.

It will be a massive leap. But Müller wants it, and so they must do it. Dirk Ströer is also skeptical but approves the plan in principle. Udo will manage, he thinks.

Müller can convince the Ströer subervisory board chairman Bornheim, his deputy Stolte and the other members of the supervisory board with the argument that for the new project he will establish a new independent company, Ströer Media International. It will be registered in Berlin.

The supervisory board members also demand that there are no financial connections between Ströer Media International and the existing company. If the international expansion should fail, the parent company will not be affected.

Let's embrace the millions

Three weeks later, Müller and Dambach enter a faceless office tower in the centre of Los Angeles. Grand Avenue 333. Right at the top, they find the almighty bosses of Oaktree Capital Group. They are said to be conservative, a contrast with the risk-friendly committees of Cerberus.

Dambach has informed his superiors of the details. The Americans seem to be fond of the smart-looking German and his previous successes. With him they could continue their expansion strategy significantly. But he must be kept on a short leash. They set conditions.

Müller knows that he must accept a deal whereby he will no longer be the only person who makes decisions. It won't only be Udo Müller and Dirk Ströer who are the majority shareholders in Ströer Media International. Oaktree will have a say. The trust that Cerberus boss Frank Bruno instinctively had in him still has to be earned.

The good news, however, is that Oaktree is on board as a financier.

On November 23rd, 2006, Müller signs the contract with Oaktree Capital Group. The Americans hold exactly 66.66 % of the new company, Ströer the other third.

More importantly, Oaktree provides up to half a million Euros. One half will be equity, the other half debt, a loan. Ströer offers a symbolic contribution, in the low two-figure region. It is what the sector calls a "skin in the game", to ensure that the main responsible partner has something to lose if their decision-making is poor – and, of course, something to gain if their decisions are good.

The new company will be registered in Berlin. From there they will conquer the world. That is Müller's vision anyway.

As usual everything must happen very quickly. The contracts with Oaktree are still being negotiated while the company is also finding and renting offices in a building near the Ku'damm. They also assemble a team, with a top manager and about 20 young business graduates with excellent credentials, keen to conquer the world of outdoor advertising for Müller.

In the next few months, the young team will spend more time in Shanghai and New Delhi, Dubai and Kuala Lumpur than in the Berlin office. A lot is going on in the target markets identified by Müller. The rivals JCDecaux and Clear Channel are also around. In Russia, the top publisher Rupert Murdoch, with his News Outdoor group, is knocking on doors.

Oaktree demands that the business consultancy McKinsey will do studies in the chosen markets and identify projects ready for takeover. Müller objects and thinks the millions allocated for that are a waste of money. "We know our business," he says. "We are the best at analysing the market and finding the best partners."

The top companies in the target regions are alarmed. They have seen how JCDecaux and Clear Channel wield their experience and monetary power to attack in their home markets. "Many were pleased that we offered an alternative," Müller remembers. "Especially with family run companies, the chemistry with us often worked very well."

Müller continues to rely on his "buy and build" strategy. With the money from Oaktree, his outdoor advertising know-how and especially Ströer's modern products, the market must be conquered as quickly as possible and then consolidated.

The coffers are well stocked. They have half a billion Euro of firepower from Oaktree. If everything goes according to plan, Oaktree has even offered "unlimited means".

For Müller it is the beginning of a phase of absolute euphoria.

He has made it.

Global business. Now he is really in his element. His great leap forward to the world elite – to adapt Mao Zedong's famous phrase.

He remembers, as if it was yesterday, his first flight around the world to his new territories: From Frankfurt to India, landing in Mumbai, on to Kolkata. Another plane to Malaysia, where in Kuala Lumpur the first Ströer branch in Asia is to be established. Then the vast country of China, stopping first in the mega business metropolis of Shanghai. And onwards, onwards. A short stay in the capital Beijing. And back again.

"I was running purely on adrenaline," Müller remembers. "I was also sure that the market consolidation in Germany had created ideal conditions for a global expansion."

Market consolidation, as fast as possible, is the core of Müller's "buy and build" strategy. As soon as a branch is established in one of the target countries, or a company is taken over, fast growth is the order of the day. It is all about taking over more companies and winning more tenders. In short: Buy and build. And the next step is taking the orders from the advertisers.

In Dubai they can identify a candidate and take it over. After only a short time, the Ströer team, now called Ströer Middle East, manages to win a tender for out-of-home advertising in climate-controlled waiting halls in Abu Dhabi. "It was a crazy success," Udo Müller remembers, still happy about it now. They beat JCDecaux and Clear Channel to the contract as well. A short time later, Dubai decides to build a new super underground and train network. Because of its experience with DB in Germany, Ströer Middle East is perfectly placed to get this order as well.

In a very short space of time, the company gets more contracts in important markets. In Malaysia, Ströer wins a large tender for the Megalights almost immediately. Royalty even turns up at the opening in Kuala Lumpur. Ströer's advertising media stands in front of the world-famous 542-metre-high Petronas Towers, the world's tallest buildings until 2004. Instead of taking over a local business, Ströer establishes a new company here. A poster hangs on the wall of Müller's office bearing the words: "Ströer greets Ströer Malaysia as a new member of the family."

He is courted everywhere. The Indian foreign trade office invites him to a congress in Mumbai. The city has about 20 million inhabitants, in a country of more than 1 billion. Cities are growing ever more prosperous by the minute – and that means advertising too. That, at least, is Udo's hope.

In November 2006, still before the Oaktree deal is finalised, Müller forms his first subsidiary in India – Ströer India – and starts promising talks with his first Chinese business partner in Beijing.

After these initial successes, Müller arranges the first Ströer International management meeting in Barcelona. "It was a milestone," he remembers. "We were very proud. One after the other, the managers of the respective countries, plus our future partner in China, reported on their local situations. What had been achieved, what was being planned. The CEOs of Ströer India, Ströer Malaysia, Ströer Middle East, Ströer Poland, Ströer Turkey, Ströer Germany and the heads of Ströer BlowUP and Ströer Infoscreen, as well as the bosses of the central management departments of Finance, Legal, Human Resources and Product Development.

In Barcelona, one could glimpse the outline of the global Ströer empire.

A dull sense of failure

It is a misconception that a successful entrepreneur is mostly characterised by his, well, successes. Quite the opposite. Failures are part of the business, bankruptcies embedded in the system.

Jeff Bezos for example, founder of Amazon, practically boasts about his failures. For him "burning money" is part of the concept for success. "With Amazon, I have dumped billions of dollars," he once openly admitted on a New York talk show. "But it is my job to encourage people to be daring. And if you act boldly, it leads to experiments. And experiments include failures as well." But a few successes can balance out dozens of experiments that haven't worked out.

That's the nonchalant phrase Bezos uses for his failures: "Failed experiments". As if money doesn't matter.

It is August 11th, 2008. Udo Müller is flying through the night from Frankfurt to Shanghai. Tiredness is taking hold of his body. The last few months have cost him more energy than he is prepared to admit.

His first round-trip to all the new business locations was like a shot of pure adrenaline. Frankfurt – Mumbai – Kolkata – Kuala Lumpur – Shanghai – Beijing – Frankfurt. The second, too, was fascinating. By the third, it was routine. Normality.

On the fourth trip, he notices for the first time the empty expressions of the jet setting managers in the other seats. Without any rest or relaxation, they tour the globe and have long lost their families. They order a second bottle of wine half an hour after take-off – if they don't ask for something stronger straightaway.

The flight takes 11 hours. It is a lot of time for thinking. Udo can't sleep. His mind won't slow down. "What am I doing here?" he asks himself. "Why am I flying to China to fight about an advertising site with a Chinese man and earn money that I can never in my life spend and don't need anyway?"

He feels lost. What happened to his inner desire to find sense in all of this? Why does he feel so driven, here, high above the clouds? Has the time come to stop and think? Maybe even go back?

Does this have something to do with the people he has met recently in Asia who are completely content with what they have got, regardless of how much that is?

He remembers Bhagwan's teachings, which had impressed him so much as a young man. "It is vital to be content and happy with what you have got. It is vital to accept this." He has always agreed with it.

He remembers that even when he was young, he found it strange that everyone was forever chasing new goals – even if they had hardly reached the previous one. There was always another target. When you had barely reached one goal, the next one appeared on the horizon. People were always running after something. Or away from something.

An eternal hamster wheel!

Another thing that bothers him is that the partnership with Oaktree is not going well. It hadn't been right from the beginning, really. The Americans are too cautious for Müller. But for the Americans, the Germans are advancing too rapidly. Mutual accusations are part of their relationship.

In Ukraine, for example, management wanted to expand quickly after investing in a Kiev outdoor advertiser. There was a chance to buy in the east of the country. When the Ströer people wanted to start the due diligence process, the seller refused. He claimed to have another interested party and was nearly at contract stage. If Ströer wanted to stop that sales process so they could check the books and the business, they would have to pay a kind of advance. One million euros. The seller suggested they could deduct it from the sales price later.

The Ströer managers gathered information. It would be

common practice, the local consultant said. So, they accepted the offer.

When the agreement needed to be confirmed later in Los Angeles, a suspicious Oaktree manager asked after the escrow account. The Ukraine expert answered: "There is nothing you need to know."

It was not a good answer. Since then, Oaktree insists on having every credit deal checked and confirmed by a so-called Kroll report. The Kroll Security Group is an important instrument of credit control in the U.S. It has a constantly updated worldwide database listing the business practices of companies and checks it for irregularities.

This procedure is not only expensive but also time-consuming. Oaktree from now on doesn't allow any takeovers without Kroll's consent. Anti-corruption rules in the U.S. are very strict. That includes Oaktree.

They now have a virtual veto on investments. The young Ströer agents are desperate to deliver for a fantastic future. But this time-consuming procedure always interrupts their plans. Back at Ströer HQ in Cologne, two financial experts and three lawyers check the relevant documents. Then they go to Oaktree in Frankfurt, from there to Los Angeles. Only when the check is finalised without any complaints can the money be transferred to the accounts of Ströer International. Müller's strategy is difficult to follow while complying with the careful procedures of Oaktree.

Müller longs for a partner like Frank Bruno, the Cerberus man. There was trust between them. "Oaktree questions every pencil we buy," Müller rages. "It can't work like that."

The global expansion advances much more slowly than Müller had expected. Again and again, there are setbacks.

The huge order for the climatised shelters in Abu Dhabi, for example, doesn't go any further than the prototype stage and the contract.

In China, the market is so fragmented that the local companies are tiny and have hardly any experience. So, despite initial promising talks, it proves to be difficult to take over a local firm for the entry into the market. Ströer now establishes a company in Shanghai, a so-called sourcing and development office, which will buy material, some advertising media, and parts from China cheaply for all the other markets. At the same time, the Research and Development department is relocated in part from Cologne to Shanghai.

In India too it is more difficult than expected to find partners. Müller cancels a possible deal to take a share of a family company in Kolkata during the last stages of negotiations. An India expert warned him that even if Ströer owned the company outright, he would have no say in how it was run in the end. It would always be dealt with by the locals.

Everybody had expected conquering these markets to be different than what they actually found.

And then another shock when Ströer wanted to transfer new funds from Oaktree. "We are not paying," came the cool answer.

"What, you are not paying?" Müller countered. "We have a contract. It is all agreed."

The figures are not good enough, the Oaktree bosses argue. Ströer will only get more money when the business improves. Or if Ströer itself can supply € 10 million. If Müller didn't like it, he could take Oaktree to court.

Müller describes the moment when he realised how dependent he was on the hedge fund as suddenly recognising the locusts.

For the first time, he sees what he has been told about aggressive financial investors: As soon as things don't work out as planned, the money masters become piranhas who can smell blood in the water from miles away.

Müller knows that his company in Germany is maxed out for further loans and that it doesn't have any reserves. But he is also completely convinced that his global expansion will be successful, so he borrows the € 10 million privately.

Now, on the 11-hour flight to Asia, thoughts intrude that he has never experienced before. They are thoughts of failure.

The main reason is something even Müller cannot influence, and the reason Oaktree is tightening the screws so significantly. The global financial crisis.

For some time now, property prices in the U.S. have been falling. This is a consequence of lenders having offered far too lenient credit conditions to private clients, creating a huge bubble.

But the people who set the crazy wheel in motion and drove it faster have benefitted even more: Wall Street banks and hedge funds and other financial institutions. It had always been normal procedure to assess mortgages according to the value of the house, its position and features, as well as taking the credit worthiness of the owners into account and bundling these loans into a large packet.

These credit bundles, often single loans in the tens, or even hundreds of thousands, are being turned into completely new financial products, which then are traded on the stock market.

They are called "asset-backed securities". It could be credits for container ships or airplanes. The main aspect is the value, the asset. That way the creditor banks can spread their risk and create investment potential for others, for example large pension funds or super rich private clients. Rating agencies such as Moody or Standard & Poor's, watch the value of the credit bundles.

The mortgage bundles are also called Collateral Debt Obligations, or CDOs. They too have been on the stock market for years – a standard investment also assessed by the rating agencies. As with LBO credits, there is a senior, mezzanine and equity tranche, with rising interest rates according to risk.

The "Masters of the Universe", as the Wall Street bankers were called during the credit boom, invented more and more methods to issue these credit bundles. They call this area "sub-prime" – either a grotesque euphemism or one of the most unscrupulous banking ideas. "Prime" is the best in the market. And "sub-prime" is rubbish. Simply rubbish.

The U.S. mortgage lenders fuel this madness as well. They require less and less from their potential customers before offering loans. At the height of the boom, people without a secure job, without any deposit and with minimal income were being approved for mortgages. The banks were accepting things like a clapped out, 10-year-old car as security, their customers' only possession.

These worthless credits would then be hidden in the CDO mortgage bundles and sold abroad. German savings banks, and otherwise solid institutions such as the midsize IKB bank, were fascinated by the extremely high interest rates promised by the CDOs – even though they were packed with rubbish properties. Because they had the approval of the rating agencies, the risk seemed manageable. But no one knew what the solid German bankers and some German private investors had actually bought. On Wall Street it was just called "dumb German money".

In hindsight, everyone knew what kind of casino Wall Street had morphed into during those years. When the roulette wheel was turning fastest and most feverishly – from 2006 through the first half of 2008 – very few experts warned of the imminent crash.

And those who did were never listened to. They were dismissed as doom-mongers.

But the signals of the impending crisis were clear to see. In February 2007, a subsidiary of HSBC in New York had to publicly write off $100 million of property loans. In April, New Century Financial, one of the biggest mortgage banks in North America, filed for insolvency. And in Düsseldorf, the aforementioned IKB was also caught out.

Now, in the summer of 2008, bad news are coming thick and fast. There are only a few weeks left until the great crash. In September 2008, the American government lets the U.S. investment bank Lehman Brothers go bust. It had overdone it in a grand style with CDOs and other financial products. This triggers a devastating chain reaction. The global financial system is close to collapse, the world suffers a wealth loss of more than $15 billion.

Udo Müller learned a long time ago that in the world of capital everything is connected to everything. And if what an expert in London had prophesied a few days ago turns out to be true, the emerging markets in South America and Asia will also face a disaster in the next few years. These are exactly the countries where Ströer International wants to create new advertising sites.

What to do?

"As a good manager you have to recognise when it's over, when you have to pull the plug," Müller says years later about his solitary decision above the clouds. The emerging global financial crisis had thrown everything into the air. Advertising orders collapse in many of the new markets where Ströer is now active. Nothing can be planned anymore. Most of all, things are not expected to improve soon. The global financial crisis is only beginning. From now on they are flying blind.

Moreover, Oaktree and Müller's management team in Germany don't believe any more that the global expansion will be a success.

Müller is really the only person who is still dreaming of Ströer International Media. He is on his own. Everyone else is an opponent, plus the global financial crisis.

It is too much, even for Udo Müller.

High above the clouds and on one of his monthly trips to Asia, he decides in August 2008 to end Ströer's global expansion. He faces reality. The bubble is bursting. It is an ending that hurts. It's true, everything is connected to everything.

But it is no good, Müller needs to pull the plug. The adventures of Ströer International are over. There are debts, including some of Müller's private money.

But the company in Germany is not in danger. It proves to have been very sensible to shore it up against the international venture. Müller is glad that his supervisory board had insisted on strict commercial and legal separation.

Phase Three of a vision that had started full of hope, has failed. Nothing can be done when exposed to the ups and downs of the world economy.

Staring down the abyss

And what is the situation like in Germany? In 2007, business was still good for Ströer, partly even better than expected. But a year later, the global economic crisis leaves its mark in Cologne as well. Advertising orders fall. What if even Cerberus needs to adapt? The New York hedge fund has passed on a some of their loans to other financial institutes to minimise the risk.

With a shudder, Müller remembers the debacle in 2003 when Deutsche Bank had nearly brought down Ströer AG. The bank cancelled € 10 million of credit and asked for immediate repayment. They said they had "lost trust in the management".

Müller gets extremely worried when he learns that JCDecaux has apparently approached Cerberus. Ströer and the French advertising giant have a small but friendly joint venture concerning street furnishing in Munich. And JCDecaux is now rumoured to have made Cerberus an offer to take over Ströer's share. It would also be possible to take on some of Ströer's debts.

In Berlin, the French have done something similar to the outdoor advertiser Wall. That was the beginning of the end of this venerable company.

Now JCDecaux is attempting to exploit the deepening global economic crisis for an attack on Ströer. Of course, they have heard that Ströer has ended its international expansion.

Müller won the fight for both DMS and DERG. The French company was the loser. That hurts, especially when you are used to winning, which the French company is. But the battle now seems to continue.

Cerberus rejects the offer. But you never know what might happen.

In general terms, the state of the economy during the second half of 2008 is even worse than feared. The international financial markets collapse after the Lehman bust. Even Ströer's main financier Cerberus is facing considerable losses.

While the German government creates a protective umbrella for its banks, the Americans let several financial institutes go bankrupt. In the motherland of capitalism, they think that those who take large financial risks must face the consequences. Some system-relevant institutions, such as the mortgage lenders Fanny Mae and Freddie Mac, get public support. But a private hedge fund such as Cerberus? No way.

The hellhound knows that, of course, and quickly assesses what it can turn into capital.

One evening, Müller gets a phone call from Cerberus. The hedge fund has passed on several Ströer loans to other investors and syndicated them, as it is called.

Müller is told that this new group of creditors has instructed a lawyer to find out how much the Ströer securities pledged to Cerberus would be worth and how they could be of use if the business continues to worsen.

Müller realises that the piranhas are nearby. He fears that there is really no way to stop them biting.

Bührdel, the finance manager, warned Müller a while ago that in 2009 Ströer might break its covenants, the rules in the contract with Cerberus dictating quarterly targets.

The most significant covenant states that the company's debts can be at most 3.5 times the EBITDA. Bührdel crunches the numbers repeatedly but can't see a way for Ströer to meet the condition in 2009. "I'm not sure whether it will be in the second, third or fourth quarter, but we will break this rule at some point in 2009." They were short by tens of millions and Bührdel said there was no way to meet it.

Breaching the covenant would enable Cerberus to ask for the repayment of loans. There is a so-called cure period, a certain amount of time when the situation can be "healed", but a remedy of this situation would need either new money or a higher EBITDA or a combination of both. And, in the middle of a financial crisis, that is impossible.

The covenant will be broken. And it's clear that Cerberus is preparing for it.

They are staring into the abyss.

Müller is in his Berlin flat when he hears the news. He walks to the window and stares into the growing dusk. He remembers all the stages of his life as an entrepreneur and knows that it will be all over if the company can't meet the terms of the covenant.

Not simply over. Absolutely, totally, the end.

Over.

The abyss. How many more steps until he is in it? One, two, half a step?

The abyss? What abyss?

Udo Müller has repeatedly taken extreme risks to push the company forward. He has always been completely convinced that his plans would work out, even when the rest of the world considered it impossible. He bought DSM without any money of his own. He took over DERG only a year later, and by taking on and beating the bulging wallets of his global rivals. He expanded globally even before those takeovers had been properly integrated. But then came the setback.

And now the abyss. The unavoidable breach of the covenants, as predicted by his finance manager. Followed by the immediate exploitation of the situation by Cerberus and the new group of creditors.

No one will give Ströer new money in this situation. Müller will not be able to change anything about the debts.

The only way to progress is to increase turnover and cut costs. A tried-and-tested method.

The covenants have not been breached yet. There is still time.

But things need to move very quickly. Alexander Stotz, now general manager for the whole advertising media infrastructure in Germany as well as local sales, is asked to check the whole company for unnecessary expenses.

Müller and Stotz enter crisis mode and begin an operation to save the company. They call the windowless space in the basement their "war room", like the crisis center in the White House.

Müller and Stotz give a presentation to employees to clarify the situation and prepare them for the tough months ahead. They use dramatic words and images to demonstrate how serious the situation is. Müller believes in symbols. He projects images on the wall: Ships peacefully floating on a calm sea, but with dark clouds gathering in the background. It is the calm before the storm. That's the company's situation right now.

Expenditure needs to be cut wherever possible. "We all have to pull in the same direction, throw all unnecessary ballast overboard if we want to sail through the storm without damage," Müller tells his employees. "Every cent counts. Literally every Euro. In the end, you always drown in the last millimeter of water."

For the employees in the Cologne headquarters this means the same as for the workers in the field: Save, save, save. Even small and seemingly unimportant sums will help.

Müller asks all departments for a list of subscriptions to magazines, trade journals and newspapers. He then cuts the list to a minimum. Memberships of clubs and associations are checked. Most of them are declared superfluous and cancelled by Müller or Stotz.

Years later some employees still remember a scene in the lobby of the Cologne headquarters. Udo Müller was in the lift when he announced: "Three lightbulbs in one lift? Too many." He told the caretaker to remove two. He enacts similar measures elsewhere, turning the office heating down during winter, as well as the air conditioning during summer.

The effect of such actions is amazing. The whole company gets the message. There is a collective feeling that everyone can contribute – even by switching off the light when leaving the toilet.

Very soon there is a new atmosphere of optimism. In small groups and in many face-to-face conversations with his colleagues, Stotz checks all departments for more efficiency. Soon he presents to his boss a whole catalogue of new and more productive ideas.

The search for a management strongman is also finally successful: Dirk Wiedenmann, 44, a former manager in one of the world's leading media agencies, Düsseldorf's Initiative Media, comes in. He starts at the beginning of 2009 and quickly gains general respect, simply through his robust approach. He is, at heart, a sensitive man but doesn't shy away from tough decisions.

Economists predict a deep recession for Germany in 2009.

This will be the most dramatic contraction since the end of the Second World War. Germany's GDP falls by 5 %. The federal household is not much better off. With a deficit of 3.2 %, Berlin exceeds EU limits.

Soon the sales department notices the first cancellations of poster campaigns and orders. The world of advertising has become more difficult anyway. In the 1990s, clients planned their campaigns a whole year ahead and booked advertising space long-term. Business could be calculated easily. Now, however, companies are more hesitant to make plans for the months ahead. The cycle of bookings gets shorter and shorter and annual planning becomes more and more difficult.

Companies now only make investments where absolutely necessary.

The sales department, the colleagues who market Ströer's advertising sites, make an extra effort. The pressure is reinforced by Müller himself. Nearly daily he asks for information about new orders and, if necessary, exercising a lot of pressure. His employees, more than 1,000 of them, comply.

Müller himself works in sales now. "I randomly called up everyone I somehow knew, or didn't know," he remembers. He once called a neighbor, someone he did not know personally, but who was the boss of the amusement park Fantasialand. "We don't know each other," he said to the man, "but can I come and see you?"

The strategy was sometimes successful. He brought in € 100,000 here, a million there – all better than no orders at all. But it wasn't quite enough to push the company away from the abyss.

Then Müller called the telecoms company E-Plus. In November 2007, Apple introduced the first iPhone to the European market. Despite the economic crisis, people in Germany rushed to buy the new technology with its beautiful large and colourful displays. For the first time a phone offered more than just calls, and it triggered a gigantic boom among mobile companies. More and more new companies and providers turned up, and they all needed advertising.

Before that point, E-Plus had only advertised on TV and in newspapers, but not outdoors. Müller arranges an appointment at short notice and takes his salespeople to the former E-Plus headquarters in Düsseldorf.

As the group gathers in the parking lot, preparing to go inside, he says: "Boys, we are getting € 10 million from this today." His colleagues look at him doubtfully. "You must be crazy, Udo!" Usually, it's a spectacular success if they get anything more than € 1 million from a previously unknown client.

But Müller is in fighting mode. "If we want that more than the others, we will get it. € 10 million is the target. We will get € 10 million."

Out-of-home advertising was a new concept for the Düsseldorf company. Not exactly a good sign.

But Müller's optimism works. € 10 million he wants, and € 10 million he will get. It will be the largest single order in the company's history.

The miracle happens. When the figures are put together for the third quarter of 2009, the relationship of the EBITDA to debts is 3.499, a tiny sliver below the critical marker of 3.5. If Ströer had broken the covenant rules, Cerberus would probably had pulled the plug straightaway.

Only a few thousand Euros saved Ströer in the end. Of course, the E-Plus order saved the company. But every lightbulb that was taken out helped. Every light switch that the employees had flicked. And every poster that they had sold despite the adverse economic climate.

The two lightbulbs from the lift in the headquarters have still not been replaced. Udo Müller will say later: "It was tight. To use a soccer analogy: We were 3–0 down but 4–3 up at the final whistle. What a team!"

STOCK MARKET GAMES

The lure of the parquet floor

Maybe everything had moved too fast over the past few years. It started with the establishment of the company in the former GDR and taking it to the top. Then there were the expensive takeovers of DSM and DERG, fighting international rivals and assuming the top spot in the reunified Germany. And finally the third phase: the failed excursion across the globe with Ströer Media International. Breathless, expensive, not all of it successful. And, of course, investments in modern equipment such as the Megalights and glass shelters.

Even if Ströer survives the crisis without much damage, the debts will still be at a dangerously high level. It is the price of a strategy geared toward unconditional growth.

Udo Müller needs capital, equity, not loans.

An idea for making new money is born during one of the serious conversations with the chair of the supervisory board. "Udo," Wolfgang Bornheim says, "we need money. We have to go public. The banks won't give us another penny."

"We have only just survived by a hair's breadth," Müller replies amazed. "Don't you think it's too early? Will the investors believe in us?"

"Of course. All you need is a good story." Bornheim sounds convinced. "And you have got that."

Müller thinks about it. Wolfgang might be right. The company has proved to be particularly resilient during the crisis, also because of the employees' massive efforts. While many rivals in the media suffered large losses, Ströer's turnover stayed mostly stable. During the biggest financial crisis of all time!

For going public, this is nearly as important as the story of growth. The shareholders want growth, of course, but they also want a company to be secure, to know that a business is stable and won't incur sudden losses.

Ströer can guarantee this. The events of 2008 and 2009 prove it. It is funny, really: The abyss opened as Ströer came close to breaking the Cerberus covenant rules. The reaction was a savings and efficiency program, with an incredible contribution from all employees. And the success was sensational: Not only were the terms of the covenant met, but turnover remained healthy, despite the crisis. And now those factors are precisely what is permitting the company to go public. The Cerberus credit contract had partly helped to take Ströer to the stock market.

There is also the history of growth, of course, which comes with being number one in Germany. But it is also driven by being number one in both Poland and Turkey too. Both those countries are important for investors these days. Poland, with a population of 40 million, is a growing market in Central and Eastern Europe. Turkey, with its 84 million, has the most promising of the emerging economies, where annual growth rates are often in double figures. In a mature market like Germany, it is only ever around 3 % to 5 %.

It is a Monday when Udo Müller enters the office of his

finance manager Alfried Bührdel and says: "Let's talk about new capital."

Bührdel, surprised, finishes his phone call. He knows what Müller wants. He is only surprised by the timing. Why now? They had discussed the subject repeatedly over the past few years: a way to find a better capital basis for the company, maybe by going public. And now Udo simply strolls into his office and wants to talk of going public. But that's the way he is.

During these weeks Müller has many discussions with consultants and lawyers, as well as with his co-CEO Dirk Ströer and friends in the world of finance. Now the decision is due.

The more Müller contemplates the possibilities of going public, the more logical it appears to him. The advantages are obvious. A better financial endowment, increased credit worthiness, higher competitiveness.

The story for the investors sounds good. Ströer is by far number one in Germany, the strongest economy in Europe. But also in Poland, the fastest growing economy in Europe, celebrated in the media as an economic miracle. Even more interesting are the expectations as a market leader in Turkey. They have left behind the economic crisis and were expecting a growth rate of 10 % in 2010 alone.

Who cares that a crisis in Turkey threatened to take down Ströer not so long ago? And that a bank was trying to force Müller to sell his dubious investment. What does the high debt mountain matter when the future is bright, and the company is stable? All that Müller needs to do is tell a good story.

Other insights encourage Müller to take the leap and go to the stock market. He often hears that going public is not only a means to gain capital. The whole culture of the company will change. Everyone will be in a better mood; the company will have a better image; it will be easier to recruit good staff. A stock market flotation brings it all.

And Dirk Ströer also likes the idea.

Udo Müller makes up his mind and begins enthusiastic planning for this next step. It is unusual for him because so far he has been skeptical. But the more he has contemplated it, the more fascinated he has become.

He just needs to articulate this captivating story about the company's success so far and the prospect of more to come. It won't be a walk in the park to take the company to the Frankfurt stock market. Investors and shareholders need to be convinced before they hand over their money. The right words and great plans are necessary. Also, the timing needs to be right to stare the bull down, rather than to face the bear. Müller wants to tickle the bull.

The finance manager suggests that 2011 will be a good time. "The economic crisis should be over, and we will have enough time to prepare carefully."

"No," Müller interrupts. "I want to hear the bell in the middle of next year, 2010 at the latest."

The bell in the Deutsche Börse in Frankfurt is something many a successful entrepreneur wants to hear. On their first day on the parquet floor of the old stock market, each newcomer is allowed to ring the old bell.

Ringing this bell is Müller's latest dream. And he wants to do it as soon as possible. No time to lose.

But going public also means risks. There have been no new launches for nearly two years. A Chinese IT company named Vtion Wireless Technology set foot on the parquet floor in Frankfurt a few weeks ago, but it didn't change the trend. Investors put only €15 million into the Vtion coffers, significantly less than expected.

What makes Müller so optimistic now is the news of

some larger stock market entries planned for the end of 2009. The airplane division of the building company Hochtief, the cable network provider Unitymedia and the Danish energy concern Scan Energy are planning to go public in Frankfurt. Together the three companies are planning to harvest €1.5 billion from larger investors. Müller wants to join the fray.

So here he is, taking his company public. May the bull be friendly to Ströer AG. And again, a game begins whose rules Udo Müller must first learn. Going public is a complicated matter for an entrepreneur. The suitability of a company will have to be checked, an optimal capital concept worked out, a so-called equity story needs to be written, among many more issues.

There is another thing: Many experts also want to earn their share when a company goes to the stock market. But where do you find such specialists discreetly and quickly? On the Internet, through Google. A Frankfurt company named MainFirst is advertising. "The MainFirst Group is a financial services company and offers international brokerage, asset management and corporate advisory services in our offices in Frankfurt, London, Milan, Munich, New York, Paris and Zurich." Those are the right words.

Only a week later a MainFirst expert called Carsten Stecker is part of Müller's small stock market team. Nobody is to know about the planned move, not even in HQ.

Take Off

The thermometer still shows 20 degrees even if the sun has lost its power during the late September days. For more than two hours, a small gang of volunteers has been picking ripe grapes from the vines. A few Ströer employees are among them: top managers Alfried Bührdel and Anne Ossenberg, as well as Stefan Hütwohl, a director in the finance department.

The grape picking excursion is a tradition. People are invited to the Eifel region on the third Saturday in September, where Bührdel's assistant Dorothee Beu-Rudat owns a small vineyard.

Anne Ossenberg loves the annual trip, away from the daily stresses and Müller's eternal presence. They have nearly finished, and a hearty meal with a good Riesling is waiting for the happy pickers.

It is late morning when Bührdel's mobile rings for the first time. Müller calls him often, even at weekends. And sometimes Bührdel ignores it. But not this time, because it will be about the stock market plan.

"Tell me, Alfried, what do you think of 'Take Off'?"

"Nothing at the moment. We're grape picking. I'll ring you back."

Müller has been getting on Bührdel's nerves all week in the search for a name for the stock market venture. But it's the weekend now. Time off.

The harvesters know what this is about. Müller is looking for something snappy, a name that would make the project symbolic and give it something like a soul.

The takeover battle for DSM was called "Thunder"; the DERG operation went by the name "Express". Now they need to find the battle name for taking the company public. It's pure symbolism, but that is what Udo wants.

He seems to have made a decision. Four hours, more phone calls and some glasses of wine later the financial experts and the lawyer are convinced. "Take Off!" Yes, that is it! A take-off is a start, a setting out for distant horizons. Now the project has a name and a soul.

On Monday, back in Cologne, the focus returns to the

rudimentary facts. Stock market experts sketch out the formal steps until the bell rings on the parquet floor of the Frankfurt exchange.

A stock market flotation can be separated into three phases: the preparation phase, launch phase, and secondary market phase. It all costs a lot of money. Up to 10 % of the launch profit can get lost. The company too can go bust if the attempt goes wrong. But Müller can't allow himself to consider this.

During the first step, Ströer has to provide the necessary facts about the company, about the market, the competition in out-of-home advertising, the company's strategy and a general picture of its financial situation. On that basis, selected banks check whether or not the company profile meets the demands of the capital market.

This phase is called "proof of concept" – and the correct choice of bank to oversee the process can play a significant role in its success. So far, so good. The prelude to securing other people's money relies on the choice of other players.

Müller's experts hold talks with specialised money institutions until mid-December. Shortly before Christmas, 10 are invited to apply as consultants for the move to the stock exchange.

Morgan Stanley and Goldman Sachs are among them, as is Deutsche Bank, Commerzbank, the French bank Paribas, Crédit Agricole and the Japanese Nomura group. Also among them is WestLB, for years Ströer's most important creditor.

They plan to make their selection in January, a process they ironically call the "beauty contest". Udo Müller is the juror. Time is at a premium. They need to develop a convincing strategy, quickly, based on the company's figures. They need to write The Stock Market Story.

Christmas is near. When Anne Ossenberg expresses her sympathy to one of the external advisors for having to work over the festive season, he answers with a smile: "No problem. I'll go skiing as planned. We have a lot of colleagues who don't do Christmas. In India for example." The Capital and its unknown helpers never rest.

So, after a year of crises, joy and expectation, Ströer AG's 2009 ends peacefully. Everyone is looking forward to the festive season, including Udo and Dirk who are spending a few days with their loved ones in the mountains. They need to gather strength for the next turbulent year.

When banks are begging

The new year begins with amazing calm in the Cologne headquarters. It's probably because Müller isn't back yet. There are no new ideas to interrupt the daily routine, no questions to interfere with everything. No pressure. Everyone is relaxed.

There is only one topic of conversation in the office corridors. Going public? Why now? Does the boss want to cash in? Questions and more questions. But one thing everybody is sensing is that a change is in the air. Again.

The answers come for the nervous employees on the Monday of the new year's second week, when the executive floor is fully staffed again. Going public will be good for everyone. It will give the company more security and more possibilities to shape the future.

In mid-January, the curtain goes up on the first act of a play named "Take Off". It is about the choice of the banks who are to accompany the process. The organisers have booked conference rooms in the Sheraton Hotel at Frankfurt Airport. This will be the stage for the grand "beauty contest". Over two days, 10 financial institutions will present their concepts. Over two days, Müller and his team are bombarded with presentations filled with colourful charts. Some experts have flown in from New York and London.

In financial circles, Ströer is considered one of the three largest stock market entries of 2010. The bankers take the process very seriously. Of course, they know how much Ströer is in debt. But the company's future looks good, and that alone is important.

The choice of banks turns out to be quite controversial. After hours and hours of discussions, Müller eventually makes a unilateral decision. It will be a consortium of five banks: JPMorgan and Morgan Stanley will be the leaders of a consortium, the joint global coordinators and joint bookrunners. Commerzbank, WestLB and Crédit Agricole CIB from Paris will be co-lead managers. The other five money institutions are out.

The winners applaud the decision, of course. The losers are displeased. This kind of defeat undermines money managers' self-esteem, especially those who are accustomed to success, and especially during difficult times as now.

After only a few hours, an influential board member from Deutsche Bank calls Müller and asks him, on behalf of his local colleagues, to reconsider the decision. He says it isn't possible that one of the most important stock market entries of 2010 will go ahead without any contribution from Germany's largest bank. But Müller hasn't forgotten that Deutsche Bank cancelled his credit, without explanation, all those years ago. As someone who values loyalty among business partners, this annoyed Müller tremendously. It eroded his trust in their business relationship, so he simply answers drily that, yes, it will be possible. "As you can see."

Second act, first scene: Determining the structure of the transaction and presentation of *Ströer Out-of-Home Media AG*. Before the relevant state supervisors can give their consent, the economic and organisational conditions need to be checked in detail. Result: Ströer is suitable for public flotation.

Technically Ströer, with all its subsidiaries and shares, consists of 27,708,238 single units. Each part is a share. Udo Müller and Dirk Ströer own 11,776,238 shares each. Cerberus holds 4,156,238, 15 % of the company.

The ownership situation will change when the company goes public, and they raise more capital. If everything goes well, there will be 17,317,377 new shares, representing nearly 40 % of Ströer AG. These shares can be traded on the Frankfurt exchange. Together with Dirk Ströer, Müller would hold the majority and have control over the company. That was very important for him.

But they are not there yet. The next step is the "Initial Public Offering". It documents the opportunities and risks for future shareholders, describes the business model and shows business projections. It is a delicate job. All facts and assurances have to be legally valid for a whole year.

Müller expects the prospectus to be more than just a legally confirmed guarantee for investors. The paper is to stimulate enthusiasm for out-of-home marketing and his company. The boss wants to sell a convincing and captivating story. They are in advertising, after all.

But Müller's request for more zest and sophisticated language in the prospectus meets with little understanding by the lawyers, committed to their dry phrasing. "Why is he constantly interfering?" one of the bank's lawyers complains after another long meeting. "This is not how it works!" But Müller makes more and more suggestions for improving the document, which are met with increasing annoyance, and a lack of understanding, from the committee.

In the end, a strategy paper that is usually two pages turns out to be more than 10 times as long. Müller checks every sentence two or three times. Everything must be just so, has to make sense.

It takes a while. A first date for the launch in May has to be postponed because of the financial crisis in Greece. Two of the lawyers are already threatening to quit. One will say later that he had never met a CEO like Müller, one who had actually read his shareholder prospectus in its entirety.

Another question concerns the price that investors are prepared to pay for a share. The experts believe the value should be € 17, with an upper limit of € 14. Some advisors, however, think even € 17 is too optimistic in the uncertain economic climate.

It is already the end of June when the prospectus is finally printed: 230 tightly printed A4 pages, weighing a proud 470 grams. To call such a hefty piece of work a prospectus is quite an understatement.

In financial circles, the Ströer prospectus is a much-studied piece of work.

Other people's money

At last, the day is decided. Thursday, July 15th will be the first day that Ströer shares will be traded on the Frankfurt Stock Exchange.

Curtain up, lights on: The next act is about to start. Now Müller and his finance manager take to the stage – although for the next few days, the performance will be behind closed doors. They are putting on a roadshow for a highly selective audience in Europe and the U.S.

The show is organised by the banks and the so-called bookrunners. They have worked out a complicated tour plan. It begins easily enough in London on July 1st and 2nd, with a last prep meeting with the participating banks. No potential buyers will be present. They will come only for the roadshow.

The first night of the roadshow is in Frankfurt. It's a home game. Then they're back to London, before heading to New York, Boston and back to Europe. All in all, there will be more than 80 meetings and presentations in less than 10 days.

The show for the investors has been carefully planned. The appointments are arranged hourly. The PowerPoint presentations, with questions afterwards, must not last longer than 45 minutes. It demands peak performance. Müller knows that there will be incredibly clever people in every meeting. There will be no time for small-talk. Each question will be precise and to the point. And no matter what is asked, Müller and his team need to have an immediate answer. There is no time for hesitation, lengthy research, or an insistence that "we'll send it to you later".

Then there is only 15 minutes to get to the next meeting.

Müller has worked until the final moment on the form and content of his presentation. In parts, it contains some elements of stand-up comedy, demonstrating the light-heartedness of being an entrepreneur.

But they hear some bad news in the middle of the prep phase. Another German company is cancelling its planned flotation. The Berlin property developer Chamartin Meermann considers the bad economic climate to be too damaging to its chances of floating successfully.

But Müller remains optimistic. One should not allow oneself to be shaken, he insists, and those in the know still consider the Cologne out-of-home advertising company's prospects to be good. The potential of the Cologne outdoor advertising company is still considered positively.

On July 1st, a Thursday, Müller and his team take the Lufthansa flight from Cologne to London in brilliant sunshine. Dirk Ströer, as the other major shareholder, is also with them for the first act. It is, after all, also his company that is planning to go public. But he won't participate later at the roadshow.

They land at Heathrow on time, where a driver is waiting for the three executives. The first meeting is that afternoon at JP Morgan, in London's financial district. They run through the briefs for the next two weeks: Presentations, press talks, lunch appointments. Everything is perfectly prepared. The information includes even the idiosyncrasies and preferences of some investors. They are the people who will be purchasing the Ströer shares, after all. It's vital to know the characteristics of potential buyers.

It is late when the little Ströer party ends up at their London base, in the elegant St. James Hotel. But no one is tired. Müller can feel the adrenaline running through him, until he finally drops off. All this is about a lot of money.

Friday is spent on further details and briefings. An experienced older committee member shares some advice: "Be economical with your energy, gentlemen." Late that evening they take the plane back to Cologne.

From now on, each day until July 15th has been carefully planned. Every flight, every town, every hotel, every partner to talk to. A lot of stress, lots of talking, not much sleep. But finally, the hunt for other people's money is under way. More than 80 meetings with investors in fewer than 10 days.

At weekends, Müller and Bührdel can relax. But only a bit. On Sunday a car takes them to Frankfurt to a meeting in the Liberty Room at the Hilton. There will be a press conference ahead of the stock exchange flotation.

The lead managers of Morgan Stanley have organised a trial run. Nothing will be left to chance. It is getting late. Müller and Bührdel spend a short night in the Villa Kennedy hotel, but don't get much sleep.

Monday, July 5th. It is getting serious. They are woken at 6 a.m. and have a quick breakfast. At 8 o'clock on the dot there is the first one-to-one-meeting with potential investors. A banker with the trade-union-owned investment fund Union Invest responds positively and promises to order shares. A good start.

The press conference, a common event on the first day of the roadshow, is set for 10.30 a.m. Müller introduces his project. He doesn't show the slightest sign of nerves: the master of convincing others is in his element. Müller is asked how he feels, and he smiles: "As usual." Bullish.

At noon, it's lunch with the experts of eight banks, a so-called group lunch. Eating is not an option for Müller as he gives the presentation. The bankers listen and enjoy their lovely meal.

And on it goes. Bankhaus Metzler and Allianz Global Investors, Deutsche Asset Management and Trust Investment. Four more meetings until the evening, then the first day is done. Later that evening, a plane takes him and his finance manager to the next stage of the tour in London.

On Tuesday, they have eight meetings with potential investors in the British finance capital. It's a marathon. They perform for 10 hours. That's 10 hours on full throttle.

Later that evening, the two boys from Cologne fall into their beds in the Berkeley Hotel. It had been a hard day. They understand now what the advisor had meant when he had warned them to be economical with their energy.

On Wednesday, it's the same again. This time it is 10 meetings with investors, nearly 11 hours of full concentration. They talk now as if they had learned it all by heart for a role. The questions are similar, so are the answers. They remain careful not to sound too slick.

Now the night flight to New York. At 8 o'clock, the British Airways plane is due to take off. They make it to the airport in good time and have a few relaxed hours in the first-class lounge. The time difference works in their favour and gets them to New York practically on the same day. At 10.30 p.m. on Wednesday evening local time, the plane lands at JFK airport. It already feels like it's early Thursday morning for Müller and his finance manager and they find it hard to sleep in the Ritz Carlton near Central Park. It will be a long night. The jetlag is punishing.

Here, in New York, the centre of capitalism, they will attend fourteen one-to-one meetings over the next two days, as well as one group breakfast and a video conference. They are met by an esteemed audience, the top tier of the finance world: Rothschild, Franklin Mutual Series Fund, Lone Pine Capital, Maverick Capital, Duquesne Capital and more. The German boys perform for the aristocracy of New York's finance world.

In the morning, they achieve their first breakthrough. Immediately after their performance, a young analyst orders nearly 10 % of the Ströer shares on offer "at any price". It means her company will buy, no matter how high the shares are valued at the start.

The talks last well into the evening. Sales are good. The analysts of lower Manhattan, where the New York money market is concentrated, obviously see decent potential in German out-of-home advertising.

The first reports from JPMorgan and Morgan Stanley suggest more than 20 million shares have been ordered within two days. Most offers are somewhere in the € 18-€ 11 range.

It sounds good. But the managers repeat that Ströer shares need to be at least twice, if not three times oversubscribed for considering the first day on the stock exchange a success. Many investors later buy less than they have ordered. The battle goes on. Another short night in the Ritz Carlton.

Day five. Alarm at 5.30 a.m. A car takes them to La Guardia airport for an early flight to Boston. At 8 o'clock precisely, the duo arrives on the 35th floor of the massive office tower on Huntingdon Avenue. The gentlemen of Brookside Capital Partners are expecting them. It is the first of nine meetings, plus. a video conference, in another long day.

It is July 9th, Müller's 48th birthday. No celebrations, only a quick beer in a pub.

Later that evening, they board a slightly delayed Lufthansa flight at Logan International Airport and head back to Frankfurt. They are exhausted.

In the provinces of capital

Müller spends the weekend with his family and sleeps a lot. He needs to get his strength back. It is Monday, July 12th. Only four more days until the big one on the parquet floor of the Frankfurt Stock Exchange.

But for now, the roadshow continues. Today and tomorrow, it is no longer the world financial centres. The greenest fields have been grazed. Now it is Edinburgh instead of London, Amsterdam instead of New York.

But the performance and presentations are the same everywhere. So are the arguments: Ströer is the number one in out-of-home advertising in Germany, Poland and Turkey. It has high growth rates. It is a stable business even through the financial crisis. Most of all, it has the best future projections. These remain the positive messages relayed to the provincial cities, where there is still plenty of other people's money.

Müller and his finance manager divide the load over the next few days. Otherwise, their schedule would be unmanageable only days before the stock market launch.

But the manner of their journeys is different. One of them jets to Edinburgh on a private plane to attend his appointments; the other flies with KLM to Amsterdam first and, after three or four presentations, travels by train to The Hague, Amsterdam and Brussels, then on to Paris. They meet again on Tuesday at 2 p.m. in the Paris Ritz Carlton.

During this last trip, Müller is accompanied by Stefan Hütwohl, Ströer's director for investor relations. Dirk Wiedemann, the CEO for Germany, is to assist Bührdel on his last lap. There are another 21 presentations scheduled.

It is going well for both teams. Müller and Hütwohl do seven one-to-one meetings in the Scottish capital. But they find it difficult to understand the Scottish vernacular. "I feel like a Prussian who has got lost in the Bavarian alps," Müller jokes.

The second team has problems getting through the Dutch and Belgian provinces. The timetable is very tight between the meetings, even though the trains are on time.

It is evening when the two Ströer teams finally meet up. The next day, the roadshow continues in Paris. Everything is so tightly planned that the group needs to take a private jet back to Frankfurt at the end of the day, where they have one more meeting with the banks involved in the launch. This is an extremely important step, more important than the actual notification at the stock exchange.

This is about the price for which the Ströer shares are to be offered. While Müller and his team are on the plane to Frankfurt, the advisors are on the phone again to potential investors.

The hectic commitment has paid off. By Tuesday afternoon, JPMorgan and Morgan Stanley have taken orders for more than € 10 million. The entry to the stock exchange will not be a failure. That much is now certain.

The question of all questions, however, is the price per share. If the paper is introduced at too high a price, the investors might withdraw their orders. If they go too far the other way, Ströer could miss out on a lot of money. Even a difference of 50 cents per share would mean nearly € 10 million less in capital.

The decision must be made on Tuesday evening. The price will be published on Wednesday. Thursday, July 15th, is the first trading day.

Late that evening, the pricing meeting starts inside another dark glass and steel skyscraper on Junghofstrasse, belonging to Morgan Stanley. It is empty now apart from this group of people who, over the past 10 days, have been performing night and day in their roadshow.

Udo Müller and his finance manager Alfried Bührdel, alongside banking consultants, lawyers and auditors. Ströer's supervisory board and executives are also present at this important meeting.

It is not only about money now, but also about how the financial world assesses Ströer's prospects and shares.

The consultants present the figures and their assessment. The initial share price had been estimated at between € 17 and € 14. The longer the roadshow went on, it became possible to pinpoint more precisely how much the investors were willing to pay. After a few days, they put the price between € 18 and € 11 – not quite the lower limit, but not quite the top either.

By the final day, by which point the overwhelming majority of orders had been received, the price level could be honed further. Now it is between € 10 and € 10.50. The company now tells the investors, with a warning, that they might not get any shares if they don't raise their offers to this price level.

Ströer's board of management meets at 9 p.m. Half an hour later, the supervisory board. Then the exact estimates and suggestions must be on the table. Müller of course wants to set the price as high as possible. He suggests an opening price of € 10.50. Some of the consultants agree, others advise caution. The consensus is that they shouldn't go above € 20.

Müller had hoped for more, but he listens to the more careful experts. "If it works out, we will cash in more than € 100 million. Okay, I can live with that." The supervisory board also agrees after a short discussion. € 10. That will be the opening price of the shares.

Only then will they find out whether all the shares will find a buyer.

Welcome to the system

The Frankfurt Stock Exchange. A cathedral for Capital.

On July 15th, 2010, six days after his 48th birthday, Udo Müller stands outside the venerable building of the Frankfurt Stock Exchange. In front of it are bronze statues of the bull and the bear, the saints of traders and analysts, the symbols for up and down. Inside is a columned hall in Moorish style, modelled on the mosque in

Córdoba, Spain. The air still smells of share dealing in the old trading hall, but the hectic times of triumph and desperation are in the past. Day-to-day share dealing has been done for many years now in a featureless building on the city's outskirts. Digitisation has taken over, as it has across all businesses.

The old stock exchange building opens its doors and turns on its old trading boards only for newcomers like Udo Müller. It's nostalgia alongside progress. Even the high altar of capitalism enjoys a show every now and then.

An awestruck Müller enters the old trading hall. He has been dreaming of this moment during the past few weeks. Under the large share board, a banner reads: "Deutsche Börse welcomes Ströer Out-of-Home Media". Ströer itself had put some posters up outside, with a message reading "You can see us everywhere. Now on the stock market too" in black letters on an orange background. Even the abbreviation under which the Ströer shares are to be traded sounds a little sexy: "SAX".

The famous. old hall fills up with guests, stock market pros and members of the press. Friends, colleagues, and family members arrive. The computer terminals of the dealers are all manned. They are ready to start, and everyone is keen to watch the first moves.

There he is, holding the traditional bell with the worn handle: Udo Müller, boss of the stock market's newest member. How many proud entrepreneurs have rung it before? How much capital has been raised by it? How much hope and disappointment has started here?

At 9 a.m. precisely, the clear chime echoes through the hall. Udo Müller gives the starting sign for the run to buy the shares worth exactly € 19.67 million. As agreed, Cerberus is selling its 15 %. The risky deal had been a good investment for the hedge fund. Udo Müller and Dirk Ströer hold 28 % each, the majority of the company.

The future is now. The electronic board above their heads starts to move. The first notation is exactly € 10. All Ströer shares on offer have found a buyer. There is a sigh of relief. That day exactly € 133,235,302,60 flood into the coffers of the company.

It is now irreversible. Ströer is part of rising and falling prices, of Bull and Bear. Welcome to the system. It is a world that is difficult to predict, and Udo Müller has to find his way in it now. For the novice from Cologne nothing here is controllable. It is completely different from his headquarters, where his word is law.

After only a few minutes, the value rises to € 10.60. The game has started.

On this day, the 15th of July, there are only winners. Udo and Dirk, of course, but Frank Bruno also leaves the place a winner. The Cerberus manager had bet on the right man with Müller and made the New York hedge fund € 150 million.

It is not that Udo Müller has jumped into a pool of money and can now go swimming freely. Rather, he now moves in a dangerous pool filled with hungry piranhas. He is aware of that, of course, and learns to change course again and again to avoid the bites. That too makes a good entrepreneur.

His first major private investment is a new family home. On the afternoon after the stock market launch, he is expecting a lawyer to sign on the new house. Müller is careful and a little bit superstitious. If the flotation had gone wrong, he could still have cancelled the sales contract.

Müller has never drawn capital from the company for private purposes, not at any point during its existence. He has taken a salary and a small bonus every now and then, but all profits have been reinvested. The company's growth was more important than his private wealth. And it will stay like that. Even for the purchase of his house, Müller has taken out loans. His beautiful new home is mortgaged – but banks like to lend money to private clients like Müller.

The industrialist will now have to get used to the games they play on the stock market. It's different when you have to justify yourself to the public, rather than a private creditor like Cerberus. Müller now is part of the system, dependent on the mood and expectations of fund managers and stock brokers who are only interested in profit.

The company's amount of debt is not significant anymore. Its finance strategy is different now. The banks who worked with the company for the stock market launch are the core of a credit consortium: Commerzbank, which looked after the IPO on the German side, as well as Morgan Stanley, JP Morgan and others.

They provided a so-called Facility Agreement, which describes the maximum credit limit, with respect to the EBITDA, at launch. In Ströer's case it is € 100 million. The company can call upon this sum if necessary, but it doesn't have to. These loans too are secured by a covenant, rated at 3. This means that Ströer can draw credits up to three times the EBITDA.

The company pays off its loans from Cerberus using the new Facility Agreement. The hellhound is finally banished.

Time to exhale.

But the best thing is that Udo Müller has got back his entrepreneurial freedom. No one is breathing down his neck. There are no more Oaktree bosses to irritate him.

Quite the opposite. There is now plenty of capital for

new takeovers and faster growth. The shareholders expect fast growth, after all. Müller had promised it.

Only a few days after the launch, regular life returns. There's a rumour doing the rounds that Rupert Murdoch wants to sell his Warsaw outdoor advertising subsidiary News Outdoor. That would offer a nice opportunity to underpin Ströer's top position in Poland. And so they make it happen. They negotiate. They play the game concerning the price. Sign. Integrate. Again, the Ströer empire is a bit bigger.

Perfect timing. It could go on like this. Ströer is in a strong position after the stock market launch. The hedge fund Cerberus is gone, the debts with normal banks have been refinanced on a solid basis. And there is enough breathing space to grab opportunities for further growth.

The stock exchange laws

Has Müller become addicted? Addicted to success? He finds himself looking at his iPad all the time. Even during meetings, he cannot leave it behind. He watches the Ströer share-price graph moving slightly up and down. A few cents more today, a few less the next day. The graph is like a snake, and Müller watches it like his own heartbeat. Each change has an impact on the value of his company. Sometimes it increases by a few million, then a few hundred thousands are lost. It can make you addicted.

There are rumours that he is closing in on another big deal. There are supposedly early negotiations about a takeover of the European arm of the American out-of-home advertising company Clear Channel. It would be a billion-dollar deal. The investors' imaginations are running wild.

Of course, Müller has big plans, not only including new takeovers. He expects digitisation to take place far faster than it actually is. What Hollywood already saw in the 2002 movie *Minority Report* will become a reality, in principle at least.

Müller had promised his shareholders a mixture of organic and inorganic growth, the constant expansion of existing business parts as well as big leaps into other areas. Takeovers. Buyouts. Growing turnover, rising share prices, good dividends. More and more.

This is the lure and the aim of the stock market. More and more and more.

And Müller had promised it.

Again, close to the abyss

In April 2011, only nine months after going public, the good mood seems to fall flat. National debts, insolvency in Greece and other national crises all have an impact on the German economy.

The first warning signs of the downturn appear in plain sight. The flourishing poster landscapes Müller promised his shareholders are wilting a bit. Business is flat, clients are booking less billboard space, and there doesn't seem to be an upturn on the horizon.

The Ströer subsidiaries in Poland and Turkey report problems. The consequences of the international financial crisis are now particularly noticeable in both countries.

Only a short time ago, both countries were seen as tiger states preparing to take huge leaps forward. Müller invested a lot of the capital from the stock market launch in both territories, as well as further credits. But the improvement in results they had expected didn't come to pass.

For the first time, Ströer has to revise its outlook downward.

This is about the worst thing that can happen to a public company. The stock market mantra is "under-promise, overdeliver".

Being public brings the obligation for quarterly reviews, where a company needs to project its figures for the coming quarters and report on what has happened over the previous three months. It is called guidance and expressed in bands. Between 1 % and 5 % (low-to-mid single-digit growth); between 5 % and 9 % (mid-to-high single-digit growth); or, the best, 10 % growth or higher (double-digit growth).

It's important to avoid missing these guidance figures – and only one thing is worse: being forced to revise the projections.

But Ströer now had to precisely do that, only nine months after going public. It was a fatal signal for the market.

It reacts immediately. The figures tumble downwards. On April 13th, 2011, the share price sat at a passable € 13. That is € 1 less than the highest value, but still € 1 more than at launch. However, experts recommend selling Ströer shares.

Müller still watches stock market movements constantly. And then it happens. On May 23rd, 2011, he is shocked to see the share price fall below € 10, less than its launch price. "I was so frustrated. For the first time ever, I got up from my desk in the middle of the day and went home," he remembers.

He would never have believed that his shares would fall under their emission value. After all the crises he had been through, he had been one hundred percent convinced that the company was perfectly positioned to go public. The company had weathered so many storms that it could now only go forward. Growth on all fronts. The shares as currency for further action. Digitisation as the chance of the century. A successful public company.

And now this!

At the beginning of August, the share price crashes to € 15. At the end of the month, it is € 10. After a year, Ströer shares are worth half of what they were when they launched. And that with a debt level at the upper limit of what is possible and permitted.

The situation worsens. Inquiries after the reasons behind the slump become more pressing but are answered less frequently. Only one thing is clear: It is a mixture of their own mistakes and external influences.

They had hoped that Poland and Turkey would grow faster than other countries. But the big leaps in these tiger states did not occur.

In Turkey, Müller spent several million Euros from the stock market launch on raising his stake in the subsidiary Ströer Kentzvzyon from 50 % to 90 %. One of his partners had wanted to sell, which suited Müller. He needed a majority ownership to consolidate the Turkish company on the Ströer Group's balance sheet. He relied on this business making good profits. In 2010, the EBITDA was € 15 million; for 2011 they had anticipated € 14 million. Müller committed his business partners to those figures, asking: "Can you guarantee that we make € 14 million next year?"

"No problem, we have a boom," the owners answered.

But out-of-home advertising in Turkey was crashing.

New contracts with large cities such as Ankara and

Istanbul suddenly became considerably more expensive than agreed. New sites on public land failed because of local bureaucracy. In a surprise move, private contracts with property owners were banned by the government.

By the end of 2011, Ströer will earn only about € 10 million EBITDA there – far too little to live up to the optimistic projections of the guidance.

In the years to come, the Turkish business will not bring much joy. It was a total rollercoaster. It started with great hope, shortly before the first crash when the banks asked Müller to sell the Turkish shares. During the stock market launch, it was again a sound driver for growth, only to crash again in the next Turkish economic crisis. First a growth engine, then an albatross around the neck. For 12 years, Müller had gone to Turkey once a month. And every time the investment increased.

In 2018, Ströer finally leaves Turkey behind, with considerable losses. The Ilbak brothers founded their own, separate billboard business in some parts of the city, even though their joint venture Ströer Kentvizyon had the municipal contract for billboards on public land. Furthermore, Istanbul demanded an inflation surcharge that broke the terms of the contract, while at the same time the bookings for advertising crashed because of the worsening economic crisis. A short time later the same happened in Ankara.

Müller tried to solve the problem on the political level: The then Minister for economics Peter Altmaier confirmed that he would mention the surcharges at a forthcoming visit of President Recep Tayyip Erdogan. But Erdogan changed his plans and the meeting never happened. Müller is stressed but most of all disappointed by the Ilbaks. He sells all his shares to Ilbak and his partner. He later gets confirmation that this was a wise move. Müller hears that one of Erdogan's sons was trying to muscle into the outdoor advertising business in Turkey.

The next problem is Poland, where they also invested considerably. But the outlay is not yielding the profit the company had hoped for.

The Polish economy is slowing down. Many new advertising sites had been built, but there were insufficient bookings for posters. The clients from trade and industry prefer advertising on TV, where advert prices have dropped considerably. Program costs of the private stations are the lowest in Europe.

Setting up the billboards cost a lot of money, but Müller doesn't see how they can achieve the necessary high occupancy rate to refinance the investment. Local rivals are too strong, particularly the media company Agora, publisher of the leading quality newspaper *Gazeta Wyborcza*, which has strong political connections.

There are problems in Germany too. Municipality contracts in large cities such as Munich are ending and need to be renegotiated. A bitter fight between rivals has broken out.

Until now, profitability had been the priority for all competitors. But now JCDecaux is driving up prices regardless and forces Müller to accept heavy losses. Müller had anticipated this when JCDecaux pulled out from the DSM sale before the final bidding round.

Müller foresaw that his French competitor would invest the millions it saved from not going for DSM in attacking him and Ströer during the new competition for municipal advertising sites.

If Müller wants to keep his modern billboards on public sites, he must bid too. But the contracts with the communities are getting considerably more expensive.

The city's treasurers are in high spirits about the sudden rise in income. JCDecaux can afford such a bloodbath. In contrast to the stretched Ströer empire, the French company has a lot of money.

The profitability of large investments falls considerably below the envisioned targets. The economic situation is so bad that demand is not picking up.

The narrative describing a good strategy for growth and profitability, which in 2010 had lured investors from all over the world, has gone sour. Ströer is simply not an attractive share anymore.

Shareholders panic and sell. On September 23rd, 2011, the price drops to €1.85. It's a disaster! And there is no end in sight of this downward trend. Müller, only a few months ago the much-admired star of the German media landscape, is trapped. There is no change in sight. Quite the opposite. For the last quarter alone, usually boasting the highest turnover and profit, they announce losses of several million.

One cannot say that Müller is panicking. He is shaken, yes, but his belief in his qualities as an entrepreneur, his ideas, his luck has not been shaken fundamentally.

There are moments when Müller wants some downtime. He wants to think, analyse, look for the weak points in peace and quiet. But downtime is not an option in the world of fast money. His dreams from yesterday threaten to turn into nightmares. Müller is in a trap. And he doesn't have a clue how to get out of it.

Two weeks ago, he went to New York again. It was one of those meetings for investors. Müller tried to explain the bad performance of his shares by pointing to temporary adversity: A weak advertising market in Germany, uncertainties in the financial markets and so on. It was only a sniffle, nothing more. Blow your nose and take a deep breath, then it all will be okay again. Müller has not lost his powers of persuasion.

But this time the effect is not the same. Two managers of an American pension fund who had invested millions in the Ströer flotation scold him badly. How could he dare to take such a company to the stock exchange! Müller's arguments are not heard over their angry shouts.

It is the combination of many unfortunate events that it can be likened to a "Black Swan"-event. *Black Swan* is the title of a 2010 book by the financial mathematician Nassim Nicholas Taleb. He tells of historic, economic, business and personal events that are so unbelievable that they could never have been predicted by observers, but which nevertheless had massive consequences.

This is exactly how Müller is feeling. He and his colleagues watch the markets extremely closely. The financial crisis of 2008 really seems to have been overcome. Who could have predicted that it would return so badly three years later, only this time the result of a crisis in state financing?

Ströer's shares remain under pressure – which cannot be disguised by a slight upturn at the beginning of the new year. The price on January 1st, 2012, is €12.92, with the subsequent weeks bringing alternating hope and fear.

February 15th: €13.82

March 15th: €14.29

April 16th: €12.63

In May, Müller explains the bad turnover figures in his quarterly report for the first three months of 2012. He diplomatically points to changes in the advertising business. "The tendency of large national and international clients to plan very carefully, as well as the difficult economic environment, has influenced the first quarter."

With a public company, all relevant figures are visible.

And they are not good. Ströer's turnover between January and March, the first quarter of 2012, has fallen by 3.5 % to € 118.6 million. Shareholders had expected growth. Growth and more growth. And now this!

After the publication of the results, the share price collapses again on May 16th, this time by 13 % to € 1.50. The business media focuses again on Müller, but this time on the downturn in his company.

His successes are in the past. "Ströer still in the red" shouts the *Handelsblatt*'s headline. The analysts are skeptical too. "Another disappointing quarter," the experts at DZ Bank state, and add that they expect a further slump.

And Müller? One wouldn't know that there is a crisis from looks alone. "No reason to panic."

The shareholders respond angrily at the 2012 general meeting. "You are driving the company into the ground," thunders the representative of a London investor. Müller keeps silent.

For a long time, maybe too long, he had dismissed the downturn as a simple whim of the markets and waited for a change. He was still hoping to manage the giant leap forward that he had promised investors when the company went public! Golden times, beautiful profits!

New acquisitions? Growing profit margins? Nothing has happened! Did he set the expectations too high? Maybe. The company in mid-2012 is not even worth € 150 million, factoring in the € 100 million it owes. Ströer is still suffering losses when months ago they had promised only positives. Stock market experts call this a broken IPO, a failed stock exchange launch.

And the rivals? They are cheering! Müller, the celebrated superstar of the sector, seems to have reached the end of the road. A manager at the Berlin-based rival Wall recalls the slogan of the stock market flotation as he mocks: "Ströer really can be seen everywhere ... particularly on the floor."

Observers openly speculate whether this is simply a temporary low point or the permanent end of the success story.

A shrill "Margin Call"

For the first time since he was a young man, Müller is seriously haunted by self-doubt. Back then, when he was a handball player in his 20s, an injury brutally ended his career. It came like the Big Bang without any warning. Before that, everything in his life had been centered on sports. He wanted to be a celebrated player in the national team. Everything else was unimportant. A ligament rupture in his right knee ended his dream in a second. But then a door opened to a future as an entrepreneur.

But what about now?

Now the story seems to repeat itself, albeit in a slightly different way. This time, it's not as a sharp pain that has brutally ended his dream. This time the pain has grown steadily worse before eventually becoming unbearable.

What can he do now? Where is the solution this time? Whenever things became tricky in the past, Müller had found a way out. But this time he is helpless as he watches the value of his young company plummet – and his reputation melt away.

That alone would be enough to worry about. But there is another, highly personal danger lurking – in Vaduz, the capital of the small principality of Liechtenstein in the foothills of the Alps. This is where one can find LGT bank, the largest family-owned banking and asset management group in the world. The family is that of the Prince of Liechtenstein.

Udo Müller and Dirk Ströer are among its clients with loans of up to € 10 million – some of the largest extended by the bank. But until now, the risk had only ever been theoretical for both sides. The German pair still owned nearly half of Ströer, and their shares were the security on the loans from Liechtenstein.

However, if the share price should fall below € 1, the debts will have to be paid off. Otherwise the debt goes over to the bank, meaning they can sell the pledged Ströer shares. This prospect of a so called "margin call" has so far been only theoretical. They negotiated the contract when the share price € 10. No one expected it to fall to € 1.

Müller used the millions from Liechtenstein to pay off old debts and finance risk capital. For example, he invested in a small recycling company working on technology to utilise the ashes from burned waste. The company intends to extract metal from the waste and use the remainder for road building. Only a few people knew of this project. It was a private thing. The process has cost several million so far.

The restless entrepreneur invested another few million from LGT in the building of the Humboldt Box in the centre of Berlin. Financed by ticket revenue and giant billboards, the extravagant cubic building is to serve as a viewing and event platform for the spectacular reconstruction of Berlin Castle and will be taken down afterwards.

But it doesn't go as planned. There is a lot of public attention, and the Berlin papers praise Müller's commitment to the city, even though the honeycomb structure of the blue building is somewhat controversial. But there are not enough paying customers – a contrast with a previous project at Potsdamer Platz, which Müller had not been part of. The expression "margin call" became better known in the mainstream as the title of a 2011 Hollywood movie set on Wall Street focused on the greed of unscrupulous. bankers. The world of high finance is often a good background for interesting stories, and Udo Müller himself had watched the movie recently.

So far, the Liechtenstein money had been invested in nothing more than calculated risks. Müller can hope for decent profits if his partner, a German engineer, succeeds in extracting metal from the rubbish and the slag. As for the Humboldt Box in Berlin, Müller had hoped for a decent profit, but knows that it is never guaranteed when you make courageous bets on the future.

The prospect of a margin call didn't seem quite real only a few months ago. The Liechtenstein creditors didn't expect it either. What could possibly go wrong with a share price of € 10?

But then it did happen. On May 21st, 2012, Ströer shares dropped to € 1.94. The impossible has happened. If the Liechtenstein bank now take their gloves off, this is comparable to the torn ligament. The end of a success story.

On that day, Müller is alone in his office, ruminating. He picks up the phone, dials a number in Vaduz and asks for an urgent appointment with Prince Maximilian of Liechtenstein. He then has a long conversation with his partner, friend and adoptive brother Dirk Ströer.

Two days after the phone call, Udo and Dirk enter the office of the powerful banker in Vaduz. The share price has fallen again that morning to € 1.72. It has happened. Right on time. Margin call.

Prinz Maximilian of Liechtenstein greets the Cologne duo with reserved politeness. He repeatedly glances down sternly at the papers with all the figures in front of him on the desk. Müller knows that he is dependent on the aristocratic bank manager, whether for good or bad. It is not in his nature to beg for mercy. The always slightly arrogant Müller would not be good at it.

The banker, however, only has one card up his sleeve – the margin call. If he makes it, € 10 million is due and Liechtenstein becomes Ströer's majority shareholder.

For Müller it would be the big crash, probably the end of his life's work. His previous achievements wouldn't matter anymore. It is like in sport: yesterday's triumphs don't count in a crisis. It's history.

What Udo Müller doesn't know when he greets the prince is that Liechtenstein is not interested in pushing for the margin call. LGT is not a greedy investor. Quite the opposite. Prince Max had been with JPMorgan at one time and has known about Ströer since then. Despite the low share price, he is still convinced of the company's good prospects.

Apart from that, the bank had hoped from the beginning to take over the management of their private assets. They can make money too, serious money. And that hope remains.

Liechtenstein tightens the screws in only one aspect. Loan conditions are not quite as good anymore because of the increased risk. But there won't be a crash. Not yet anyway.

The turmoil at the stock exchange continues over the next few weeks. The company continues to head toward the abyss. August 22nd: € 1.50.

At some point during these dark days, a London investor calls and announces the intention to buy a large share bundle. Is it the turning point? How did he come to think of Ströer AG, Müller wants to know. It's quite simple, the British man answers. He says he has looked across all 10 European stock markets for the companies with the worst performance. "And yours is among them, Mr. Müller."

Well, the man from London still seems to believe a recovery is possible and wants to buy. At a price of € 1, it is a small ray of hope. Very small.

The vultures are circling

Nothing works anymore. Müller only rarely shows how miserable he is feeling, and definitely not to the outside world. Previously, his face was only ever like a screen on which a viewer could see his own expectations projected back at him, rather than any genuine emotion. A poker face. But now he feels as tense as a caged lion. He values freedom but is chained.

There isn't a minute when he doesn't think of the company. And of its dire share price. He is looking for a solution continually.

The London investor who snapped up the cheap Ströer shares is not the only person interested in the stumbling poster giant from Cologne. Specialists from all over the world of finance approach Müller and make suggestions. But they don't want to buy shares. Their offers are of a different kind.

There is, for example, the German subsidiary of the New York Investment giant KKR & Co. The suggestion is that Müller should withdraw his company from the stock market, reorganise with KKR's help, and then go public again. Other large American investors, such as the Blackstone Group, also turn up in Cologne.

It is quite extraordinary how many billion-dollar finance companies from abroad are interested in Ströer during this period. Müller had, after all, gained a lot of respect over the past few years in New York money circles. The sharks admired his aggressive and successful expansion strategy. However, the Wall Street scouts also scan the market for crisis-stricken companies, looking for candidates to take over, reorganise, and then sell at a profit. Hedge funds.

A few smaller private equity companies also sense a cheap bargain in the faltering German firm, which is still number one in the sector. These allegedly charitable helpers always give the same advice: Müller should take Ströer off the stock market.

They lay out the plans: Risk-friendly investors would take over Ströer completely and pay off the smaller shareholders. At a price of €1 or thereabouts it wouldn't be a big problem. Ströer would exit the stock market, in what's known as a "take private" transaction. Both Müller and Dirk Ströer, as the major shareholders, would stay in place. Then the company would be split up into its parts and reorganised. What is left can maybe be taken back to the stock market. Müller could even remain the boss. That is how the would-be investors try to sell their ideas in Cologne.

For Müller it would be like a capitulation, an admission of total defeat as an entrepreneur. It would be a loss of face that could never be compensated for.

During such dark moments, he sees the grimacing face of failure. Your streak of luck is over, it hisses, paralysing his thoughts. Everything seems to be conspiring against him. His close friends sense the tension he is struggling to conceal. Udo reacts angrily even to trivial issues.

Müller returns to the strategy that had been so successful five years ago: The rigorous cost-saving measures he implemented in 2008. Then, too, the company had put on "too much weight", as Müller had called it. Ströer was threatened by insolvency and hardly had the money for the employees' salaries. Back then, he had checked every department for unnecessary expenses. The process had been successful. They had saved millions by cutting down on everything. They called the process "Shape" and they got themselves in shape again.

So, now they will try it again. They will start a second "Shape" process. Again Müller checks all departments and accounts. He discovers that the company hires cleaners that cost € 10,000 per year to clean the conference rooms. Cut! The employees themselves are now responsible for that. He finds out that the company spends € 12,000 on a gardener to look after the plants on the executive floor. Cut!

Müller has his biggest success in the IT department. The company is equipped with IBM technology across all its regional offices, and together with SAP has complex problem-solving software designed to reduce the workforce by at least 100.

However, Müller, with the help of some outside experts, examines the expensive program and concludes that it is far too big for the size of the company. "It's as if we've put a Ferrari engine into a Golf," one of the experts says. Even the supposed saving of 100 salaries is an illusion. Müller pulls the plug and stops the whole project. "We don't have enough money to employ salespeople, but we have installed a money-burning machine?" he thunders. The software has already cost € 15 million.

The savings measures alone are not a strategy for getting through the crisis, however, nor for setting a path for the future. Müller feels like the victim of circumstances and internal management mistakes.

The daring entrepreneur feels that the luck he had maybe taken for granted for too long has now disappeared. He feels as though he is running through a dark alleyway, filled with obstacles.

Something has to change. That much is clear. But he doesn't know how to do it. Since the stock market launch, he has focused mostly on strategic goals. The company's top managers have been dealing with the day-to-day business. Is that why the internal structure of the company has fallen apart? Because the boss was focusing on something else? Maybe. Whatever the case, costs since the stock market launch have risen much faster than profits.

But he is the boss. Even more than that, actually. He is the company. And it needs leadership, more than ever. The vultures are circling overhead.

World leader JCDecaux has been gleefully watching the decline of its Cologne-based rival. Now the French company sees its opportunity to attack. "JCDecaux wants to outdo its rival Ströer," states an article in the German business weekly *Wirtschaftswoche*. Jean-Francois Decaux uses the article to announce clearly that his company will begin attacks on Ströer's domains in the big cities where public contracts are ending and have to be renegotiated.

This is an expensive game for everyone. These kinds of negotiations with the communities have never been carried out with so much riding on them. Ströer and JCDecaux, as well as the Berlin-based outdoor advertiser Wall, offer ever higher sums to either remain in business or to push out rivals. Economic principles quickly go out of the window.

JCDecaux in particular fires up the battle. The global leader would love to become number one in Germany too and take over from Ströer. And now the French company is sensing a chance. They have enough capital for the battle. "In contrast to many of our competitors, we have no debts," the company spokesperson tells *Wirtschaftswoche*.

JCDecaux declared war on Müller believing its Cologne rival cannot last much longer. It is an assessment shared by some other competitors.

On August 3rd, 2012, a Friday, the share price is down to € 1.75, an all-time low.

Turnover and profits are also down as the bottom drops out of the share price. The company is caught in a downward spiral. Worsening business and growing debts are again pushing the company close to breaking the covenant.

There are no additional finances to be called upon, above the existing credit facility. If the company hits three times EBITDA, it's over, irrevocably over, even though the actual credit take-up has not reached its limit. Müller knows that he must act. But what can he do?

He has no money to invest. Not a penny.

His back is against the wall. Again.

Where is the exit this time? Müller is worried, worried day and night.

Cooperation with his closest colleagues Bührdel and Wiedemann is getting more difficult. No one can see a way out of this misery. All of the senior management is affected by the problems.

In short, the harmony is gone, and no one knows how to fix it. Udo Müller had managed to make Ströer number one in the out-of-home advertising sector in Germany and to expand all the way across Europe. The messages of its advertising clients can be seen everywhere, on more than 200,000 advertising sites alongside roads and in bus shelters, in public places and in railway stations. In every city between the sea and the mountains, from the Baltic to the Alps. It is market leader in Poland and Turkey, and Müller also oversaw the Europe-wide roll-out of digitally printed billboards under the blowUP branding in the UK, Spain, the Benelux and various other countries.

But at what cost? Did this aggressive growth strategy do any good? A low mood spreads down the corridors and penetrates all departments.

INTO THE NET

Searching for new opportunities

It is the mission of any enterprise to recognise when things are changing in good times, and to promote solutions that help turn visions into reality; to create and build. That is what Udo Müller had always wanted. He has risked a lot to achieve it, and often fate had smiled on him.

When he started as an entrepreneur, aged 19, outdoor advertising was a conventional business with only limited creativity. The innovations that had built the sector had become normal. In the middle of the 19th century, the Berlin printer Ernst Litfass invented the advertising column, and in Germany it is still named after him. These advertising columns, scattered throughout the country, are seen as the origin of modern poster advertising. But after their introduction, nothing exciting happened for a long time.

After the Second World War, large posters arrived. These were good business. More than 100 outdoor advertising companies could live comfortably thanks to a continuing boom in billboard advertising – until Müller came and raised the fragmented market from its deep slumber.

His role model was JCDecaux. Müller admired the creativity of the French outdoor advertiser. The global company had invented street furnishing, glass bus and tram shelters that featured space for some understated poster advertising. The posters were no longer glued in place but hung. That wasn't only faster, it also looked more elegant. It's similar to the new Citylights, backlit glass cases for advertising on public sites.

With that, JCDecaux "disrupted" the outdoor advertising market, and in a very short period completely pushed out long-established companies and methods.

JCDecaux also cleverly marketed street furnishing as a "quality segment" of the market. The poster billboards were still around but were suddenly considered old-fashioned and no longer good enough. Nevertheless, the new street furnishing still left some space for traditional large posters on buildings, and many of the smaller companies continued with posters pasted onto wooden panels.

Ströer still had many such billboards, which still brought in money. But Udo Müller would never have dreamt of relying entirely on them. To do so was to view the possibilities of advertising with blinkers on, the same way the former GDR had viewed the world.

This kind of attitude presents problems for a company; the insistence that past successes also mean future success. Müller had always considered this kind of attitude a form of vanity, and one of the worst characteristics in a manager. Good managers are always capable of discarding everything they have built as soon as they get a better idea – even if it is someone else's idea they are rejecting.

For Müller, there is no such thing as standing still. He never rested on his laurels. New things must come, new and better. This is the attitude that helped him conquer the new Federal States, then the whole of the the reunified Germany, Poland, and Turkey, to become number one.

There is no question that Udo Müller is a gifted salesman of his own plans and visions. It is due to this talent and his willpower – and a slice of luck – that he has earned the reputation for being one of the most daring and successful entrepreneurs of his generation. During the first years of his career, he rose from practically nothing to take a leading role in outdoor advertising and leave all his competitors behind.

But now something new is changing advertising again: digitisation. Most companies have recognised that they still need to do a lot of reorganisation after the chaos of the global financial crisis. They mostly try to survive through rigorous savings measures, and in most cases it works, like at Ströer.

But salvaging what they have is one thing. Much bigger and more dangerous risks are lurking around the corner for those companies that have not yet recognised the arrival of the digital age. For the newly founded digital internet companies, however, there are new and fantastic business opportunities.

The digital technology of the internet enables newcomers to disrupt one sector after another. And nearly always, the response of the established companies is the same: "It won't harm us", they whisper at their conferences and sometimes even in public.

After the music industry, it is now the advertising sector's turn. As newspapers and magazines continue to lose more and more readers and ads, and paid-for spots on TV also decrease, advertising on the Internet is rising dramatically.

Large publishers are already working with new media to bring both advertising clients and readers to their online platforms – at least in part. Meanwhile major companies and trading empires are already placing more online adverts.

At the beginning of the 2010s, online advertising was only a tiny niche of the whole advertising market, which in Germany alone was worth about €15 billion annually.

Müller could see early on that it would not stay that way. Until now, the advertising market had been split into four areas: print, radio, TV and outdoor. There was hardly any overlap between them.

But what if these areas all disintegrated because of digitalisation? How would the large brands allocate their advertising budgets then?

Ströer so far had been a pure play outdoor advertiser, in common with all its competitors. The company had a market share of more than 50 % in Germany.

But outdoor advertising in 2012 was only 5 % of the whole advertising market. And if the other segments all shrank as the Internet grew in influence, the situation would be completely different. Ströer would not be number one anymore. It would be a much smaller player in the advertising world.

What big brands would then still meet Ströer's salespeople face-to-face? How would the company have to change so Ströer could continue dealing with national clients?

Müller begins an intensive process of strategy planning and discussions. What are Ströer's strengths? The company's biggest asset is its infrastructure: the displays on the streets, at railway stations, in cities. And its relationship with clients. Only Ströer has a national sales network for local advertising, and it only has that because of its excellent relationships with local clients.

The next question follows logically: How can these existing strengths be used better for future growth. How can they produce more value? The infrastructure could be used more efficiently. But that was happening from day to day anyway. What remains is the relationship with 10,000 local clients. Only Ströer has this.

Those local clients have always been able to book different out-of-home advertising products with Ströer. They could also book adverts in local newspapers, but circulation is dwindling rapidly. It has become more and more difficult for local clients to reach their respective target groups. Local newspaper websites were still in their infancy and didn't have much coverage. Meanwhile, their rivals also had websites, which were updated daily. No one had yet bundled all these Internet opportunities to make them attractive for local advertisers.

This is what Müller planned to do.

Udo's work and Dirk's share

Müller's office is on the third floor of the Cologne headquarters. It is a large, bright room with a few historic advertising posters and modern paintings on the wall. In the corner is a plain black leather seating arrangement.

The papers on the desk are all very well organised. In perfect order. Müller was always juggling numerous balls. It makes working with him very demanding; he has a high turnover in staff. Emel Alkan is his fourth assistant since the stock market launch. Müller requires a lot of commitment from his employees. Any close associates are working pretty much 24 hours a day.

Nobody could guess how significant the decisions being made these days are. Dirk Ströer wants to speak to Udo. Dirk's office is a few hundred meters away, in the old headquarters, where everything started, where Heiner Ströer and Udo Müller formed their company together.

Shortly after the millennium, Dirk established Orange

Media, one of the first companies marketing online advertising in Germany. After a few years it became Ströer Interactive Media, and Dirk became keen to integrate the internet advertiser into the Ströer empire.

The two major shareholders have been discussing the future for quite a while now. They agree that something has to happen, that they need to turn the threat of the Internet into an opportunity for the company. They need to figure out how they can employ smart, digitally savvy new staff. Müller's favourite is Christian Schmalzl, and he has tried to get the Bavarian man to work for him for a while. Schmalzl is considered one of the best managers in the German media scene. Now Dirk, as a co-CEO, is to meet the candidate too.

When Dirk calls Udo, the latter thinks that his partner wants to talk about Schmalzl. But Dirk has something else on his mind, namely whether Udo can fly to Munich to visit a company named AdScale. Dirk thinks that this start-up is offering something new. For the Internet, of course.

AdScale is a marketplace for unsold internet advertising. Dirk likes the company. Udo doesn't know much about it. What *is* a marketplace for spare online advertising?

Udo says that he doesn't really feel like it. But the flight is already booked.

"When are you meeting Christian?" Udo asks Dirk at the end of their conversation.

"Tonight. In Stuttgart."

"Give him my regards."

As Dirk Ströer heads to Stuttgart, Müller wonders whether the short trip to Munich will be worthwhile. He sets off without much enthusiasm.

AdScale is based in an apartment block in Munich's Schwabing district. It's a small start-up. The computers are in a tiny flat: Three rooms, kitchen, hardly any furniture, a few young guys and Matthias Pantke, the managing director. The atmosphere is like it was during the rapid expansion of the postwar years.There's an air of optimism.

But this is not just a bunch of computer-obsessed nerds, as it was at the beginning of the Internet age. The AdScale boys are a new generation of web technicians. They are young and clever digital savants, who know exactly what they want. They are essential for progress, and one can only guess what the digital world will look like in a few years' time.

The AdScale people meet Müller, but he tells them he only has an hour. His taxi is still waiting downstairs. One quick appointment, then back to Cologne.

The presentation begins without any further small talk.

Matthias Pantke gets going: "AdScale works in all digital advertising spaces. For the publisher, this means that they can monetarise all their traffic. For the advertiser, it means they can present their campaigns across all end devices." He then mentions various catchwords such as display ads, mobile ads, video ads, data management, platform and programmatic buying. It's not a presentation for lay people.

It's obvious why the AdScale founders, Pantke and Stephan Kern, want to convince their visitor. They want to make money. If they only knew that Müller didn't have any, not even for a small investment!

Still, their concept and their software, already developed, sound interesting. Müller listens more carefully.

He has been looking for opportunities to market local reach online. Before the online age, this had been the domain of the regional publishers. Local papers often didn't have any competitors and reach of up to 60 to 70 %. But this is not the case online. During the early days of the Internet, the daily papers' websites were so irrelevant that their coverage was considerably less than the offline figures, often less than 10 %.

Müller wants a product that could bundle local reach from various advertisers. The target was a coverage of 70–80 %. Then, and this is the plan, his existing local sales teams could start to sell in those local markets all over Germany. Müller had described the strategy as the desire "to leverage our sales locally and develop new sources of revenue within existing structures."

It would be diversification in the best possible sense. Ströer's salespeople have so far only sold outdoor advertising.

How could they generate online reach of 70–80 %? Müller was convinced it was a new, interesting market with a good capacity for growth.

A while ago, Müller presented his thoughts to the British WPP group, the largest global advertiser. Originally, the company had produced shopping baskets, but then in 1985 a certain Martin Sorrell took over Wire and Plastic Products plc. He took less than two decades to turn what was then a three-man operation, with turnover of around £1 million, into the current giant advertiser. He made himself a legend in the process.

"WPP loved my idea," Müller remembers. "But it didn't materialise. After some discussion it turned out that commission would eat up most of the profit."

But now, maybe AdScale?

Müller asks the boys in the Schwabing apartment to explain again what they are doing. He wants to understand the state of the company and the future chances for success. At the time, start-up companies were popping up everywhere and and knocking at Müller's door practically every day. But looking at the figures makes it clear that nine out of 10 will not survive.

There is always the thought, however, that the surviving "one" could be the German Google or Facebook.

The AdScale guys show Müller the usual turnover projections, which of course include a steep upturn – the so-called hockey-stick graph – for obvious reasons. The flat bit represents the period when a lot of money still needs to be invested. But then, after an injection of cash, comes a rocket-like rise. Bingo, the market is conquered, all rivals are beaten.

All start-ups show him the hockey stick. Müller has seen it dozens of times. "Leave that out," he tells them at AdScale. "Just tell me what exactly you are doing."

Even though Müller doesn't really have the time – the hour is ticking away – the guys go into more detail.

Their marketplace for unsold online advertising worked as follows. The large advertising sites – such as focus.de, owned by Burda, or Axel Springer's bild.de – always had space the owners could not sell. Online advertising was sold, in general, according to the cost-per-thousand impressions, or CPM. It determines how much an advertising client has to pay for every 1,000 views of an advert.

Publishers are keen to keep this model stable. If there is not enough demand for online advertising, they pass on the unsold spaces to marketing organizations as "spares" instead of leaving them empty. It's better than having a website without any adverts at all.

AdScale is one of these spare space marketers. It's a marketplace for unsold online adverts. But AdScale bundles the advertising space in different packages. Instead of offering space on a certain website – say, bild.de or focus.de, for example – AdScale tells the advertisers it will present their ads to "target groups". These might be "men between 18 and 49", "pregnant women in the first two trimesters" or "migrants with a Turkish background and higher education".

This offers potential advertisers the knowledge that their advert will be seen by their desired target group. But there is a disadvantage too. The advertiser doesn't know specifically where its advert will appear. In the best-case scenario, it appears on the pages of a respected brand. But it might also be a niche website. The only thing that counts is that the targeted group sees the advert.

Müller holds his breath and tries to sound indifferent when he asks how big the local reach would be in cities like Cologne and Munich?

They tell him it would be 80–90 %.

Müller is now electrified. He remembers his own start in the advertising sector. Where once it was him in a garage in Treptow, with a camping table as a desk, now it is a bunch of ambitious young internet geeks in a Munich flat.

He tries to play down his interest, knowing already that AdScale has an EBITDA of about €1 million and a potential sale price of about 10 times as much.

After a good hour, Müller says goodbye and promises to be in touch.

"Don't wait too long," Pantke says. "There are others interested."

Oh, yes, Müller knows that.

In the taxi on the way back to the airport, Müller remains preoccupied with the AdScale presentation. Will this be his saving grace? The all-important building block for a radical overhaul of the company, propelling it towards a digital future? Is the door he had looked for for so long now opening?

With AdScale, he could offer local clients an additional new package, instead of just billboards. He could offer local online reach of more than 80 %. It is a new segment of the market, and a new concept for the leap into the digital world.

Perfect.

Perfect, because only Ströer has the necessary sales organisation on a local level in Germany. His team could now sell online advertising as well as posters, opening a completely new market for Ströer.

It was the future, and a gigantic opportunity.

But there were also risks involved.

Müller knows that everything about his company, as detailed in the stock market launch, was based on the premise that Ströer is a pure-play outdoor advertiser. Ströer does out-of-home advertising. Full stop.

That will have to change radically. Müller wants to reorganise the company completely, embracing online advertising as a new and future-oriented business. It is to be sold by the same sales team that so far had dealt with local outdoor advertising. And, in one fell swoop, that would push Müller ahead of the disrupting digital wave. He will do everything differently than his rivals. Ströer would disrupt itself. But would his employees, the market and most of all the stock exchange accept the new strategy?

Müller calls his legal and financial advisers, Anne Ossenberg and Alfried Bührdel. How can they do a deal with AdScale without any available capital? Ströer's credit volume is not exhausted, but the company is in danger of breaching its covenant and therefore cannot access any more loans.

The company paid off the Cerberus loans after the stock market launch and now gets its financing through a classic consortium of banks. Müller had negotiated a very high credit limit of € 100 million, but, as with Cerberus, the availability of the loans is directly dependent on the

EBITDA over the past 12 months. He cannot borrow more than three times the EBITDA, therefore Ströer does not have any more financial means available at this time.

Anne Ossenberg says that there are only two options available, in theory. Either Ströer buys AdScale with shares, or they must buy (with shares) another company with an EBITDA of at least € 1 million. In the second case, existing covenant rules mean that Ströer would be able to borrow three times the amount of its new company's EBITDA, i.e., about € 10 million, on the terms of the existing Facility Agreement. As AdScale is not available for shares alone, only the second option is possible. Ströer needs to buy another company with its own shares. But the share price had dropped badly, so who would be willing to sell a company for those shares?

After landing back in Cologne, Müller finds the solution. It is highly risky and very complicated. Again, he would have to bet everything on one horse. Again, he is going to have to go all in.

Udo calls Dirk and tells him about the meeting with AdScale. And then he blurts out: "We will simply buy AdScale!"

Dirk is surprised. "What? I thought we didn't have any money?"

"Well, we will do what you have wanted all along. The main company will buy Ströer Interactive. The main company pays with its own shares, and so we get the necessary EBITDA to call in the € 10 million we need from the existing credit volume."

Ströer Interactive Media belongs to Dirk Ströer. Udo Müller is a silent partner.

Dirk rolls his eyes and mumbles: "Hmmm." Initially he is against it. He has recently been negotiating the takeover of another online marketing company, freeXmedia, a

Freenet subsidiary, by Ströer Interactive Media. They are expecting to finalise the deal within days. Müller doesn't accept this as a reason. "We will find a solution. This is a unique new chance to place the Ströer empire in a completely new position. It can't fail because of problems we can overcome."

Bührdel, the CFO, is also against it, more out of principle. "We will be destroying our equity story," he says. "The investors will not like it." He adds that selling Ströer Interactive Media to the mother company, to itself, so to speak, could be considered a so-called "related party transaction". It could be legally problematic.

Müller is unconvinced. If they could buy AdScale and integrate it with Ströer Interactive Media, the company would be highly attractive for the marketing of online ads. Ströer Interactive Media was already among the top five premium marketing companies in Germany. Its subsidiary business Ad was the leading B2B marketer in online advertising. And together with AdScale, the leading marketing company for selling spare ad space, they would position Ströer perfectly in the new marketing sector. With a turnover volume of € 10 million to € 10 million, they would cover all major areas of online marketing: Premium advertising, B2B advertising and spare space advertising.

Müller takes the story to his supervisory board. Dieter Stolte, the successor to the late Wolfgang Bornheim, listens to him with interest. "It's a good idea," he says. "But it could easily turn sour."

Stolte had been in the business for a long time and was approaching retirement. "Mr. Müller, my conscience has always been clear," he says. "I don't want any problems at the end of my career because of a related-party transaction. The sale has to be transparent and legally unassailable in every respect."

He gives Müller another word of advice. He and Dirk Ströer, as the sellers, mus.t be prepared to accept significant price reductions because of the legal issues.

That decides it – but it will become an extremely complicated legal process.

The right man for the battle

Christian Schmalzl is the new man for the new times. Dirk Ströer and the new recruit get on really well from the start and talk a lot about the growing dominance of the digital world. Schmalzl, a slim and athletic Bavarian, is considered a top manager in the world of digital media. In only 10 years at Mediacom he progressed step by step from trainee to general manager for Germany.

Mediacom, a global online agency based in London, belongs to WPP, and is considered a major player in international advertising. The company organises worldwide campaigns for multinationals such as Dell, Shell, Procter & Gamble and VW. Schmalzl's former role was a job with enormous influence on the distribution of millions of dollars of advertising money. Nick Lawson, the Mediacom CEO, praised his young colleague in public as "one of the best managers" in the ad business, adding " ... and not only in Germany".

Müller met Schmalzl for the first time in 2009. That year business was not going very well. The global economy was still immersed in the financial crisis, and for the first time in a long period, the German economy and advertising budgets were shrinking.

Müller invited Schmalzl to Ströer's Cologne headquarters. He wanted to tighten the relationship with Mediacom and tried, with his usual spiel, to convince the man of the virtues of his company. Far too much money would be spent on TV spots, he declared. But out-of-home advertising ...

Schmalzl listened patiently but was not impressed. At some point he interrupted the long monologue. "Mr. Müller, please don't try to explain the business to me." He then gave his own impressions, which the poster giant didn't exactly like. But Müller was impressed. Smart guy, this Schmalzl.

Since then, Müller had tried to connect with his shrewd rival on a different level. He saw in him the right man to be by his side. It was typical Müller. He didn't want just any manager, he wanted the one he considered to be the best. They met a few times, they got to know each other and got on well. Eventually the two agreed and Müller sent him a contract that he had already signed.

Schmalz went to London to terminate his contract with Mediacom in person. Surprisingly, the WPP founder Martin Sorrell joined the conversation. "I always knew that we would have trouble with you," Sorrell told the German, even though they barely knew one another. Sorrell had just transferred a surprise bonus to Schmalzl, which would be in his bank account the next day. He said he would make him global COO of Mediacom. "You belong to us."

Global COO of Mediacom! Chief Operating Officer of a worldwide media agency, with 5,500 employees, and a client list of the world's top brands.

Schmalzl simply had to stay. He met with Müller, a man he had got to know quite well in the meantime. "Udo, I'm really embarrassed about this, because this is not my usual way. But I cannot join Ströer. I have to try out this new job." It was highly unusual for a German to get a chance at the top of such a renowned global company. And he had it offered to him by the legendary Martin Sorrell, in person.

Müller is disappointed. But the two of them agree to stay in touch. Schmalzl's new job will take him to all continents, forever on a plane, from one country to the next. Udo Müller had done that before. "Christian, in a very short time this will begin to annoy you tremendously," he tells Schmalzl as they say goodbye.

The prophesy comes true. Two years later, Schmalzl is ready for Ströer.

He had had enough of jetting around the world for more than 200 days a year, from one meeting to the next, but in the end seeing nothing of this world. Every relationship he had failed because of the jet set life in a global business. Every aspect of a private life always comes second. With Ströer he is at least hoping for a better work-life balance.

But most of all he is attracted by the challenge to reposition Ströer in the digital world together with Müller.

The first few months are rough, though. At his first board meeting, he enters the conference room alongside Müller. Alfried Bührdel, who is already there, sits at the large table and stares down at his papers without greeting them. The new man is surprised. There seems to be an iceberg between Müller and his finance manager.

Wiedemann, the head of German operations, arrives late. He didn't know of the meeting, which had been scheduled at short notice. "If you don't want me here, you have to tell me,"he complains and sits down. Schmalzl hadn't expected the atmosphere to be so hostile. But he has got the job, he reasons, and intends to make the most of it.

A few days later is the traditional Christmas party at HQ, one of the social highlights of the company. Müller introduces Schmalzl. About 500 employees stare at the brightly lit stage in the event centre in Cologne. Müller asks for silence and then announces the new man: "I proudly present …"

There he is. He is not accustomed to being in the spotlight as he peers into the semi-darkness of the hall. There is a tense silence. Instead of launching into an inspiring speech, as many had expected, Schmalzl offers only a few non-committal words. There are no grand gestures, no boastful claims of authority, no self-promotion. He offers only a very plain introduction: "I am the new man." Schmalzl feels like a manager who is out to solve problems and implement the strategic plans of the company. That was the way at Mediacom, and it will be the same at Ströer.

His two colleagues on the board, Bührdel and Wiedemann, regard him primarily as a rival who now has better access to the boss. They both know that Christian Schmalzl will be number two in the company.

Udo Müller explains that the "dark times", as he calls the last few months, finally appear to be over. They are now starting a new chapter. Optimism has returned. There will be a leap into new territory, to the Internet.

And the stock market? For weeks now Müller has been travelling from one investor to the next sharing his new plans. At the beginning of the new year the share price is at €1.75. By the end of March, shares are trading at about €1. The trend is moving upwards.

Over the next weeks and months there is one meeting and appointment after another. They talk to investors, negotiate with digital agencies. Udo Müller wants to convince investors of the new strategy and convince smaller online advertisers to sell to Ströer. All of this is supposed to steer the company back onto the road to success.

Maybe these are the moments when Müller can show off his greatest talents. To walk ahead, to convince, drive forward. To simply want something and do it. It's like when he pulled the fragmented segments of outdoor advertising together. And with the same arguments he now wants to consolidate online advertising in Germany.

Of course, giants like Google and Facebook magically attract the advertising budgets of the large brands. But on the level below, there is a hustle and bustle of dozens of German online agencies fighting for the national market. The former two are the global champions. But Müller's company wants to become the local hero in the German advertising market.

Slowly, investors gain trust in Müller's daring leap into the digital age. On July 22, 2013, the share price passes € 10 again. The trend continues upward. The EBITDA also improves from one quarter to the next, and the company can call on its existing loan capacity.

In the boardroom things have also changed. Schmalzl is now indeed second-in-command after Müller. Wiedemann, formerly head of German operations, leaves the company. Ströer was not the right place for him anymore. And Bührdel also moves on.

There are also many changes in middle management. They now need different decision makers for the online market than for the traditional poster business. In the coming two years, more than 60 % of the middle management will leave the company.

Müller and Schmalzl change Ströer radically. The former pure-play outdoor advertiser is transformed for the digital world.

The Internet – a new world

Here it is then, the world wide web. Very quickly, a gigantic panorama opens before one's eyes, bursting with possibilities. But it's far from easy to manage. Advertising has to be devised completely anew. Customers need a new approach. Everything is better, bigger, and glitzier.

The actual impact of the digital world is only just being felt. Nothing works any more without digital input. Not in people's private lives, nor in public, and not at all in the global economy. Advertising here is a weapon with an enormous explosive force. It is dangerous and must be treated sensitively for that reason alone.

Müller explains his move into virtual advertising as part of a continuous development away from the established poster business. That is logical. But he is entering unknown territory once again. Is the Cologne entrepreneur aware of the risks? Müller is convinced that he is on the right track in the online world, at least in Germany.

It has been three decades since he and Dieter Nerlich took their first steps into business, alongside his medical studies and a handball career. He has never forgotten how he revolutionized outdoor advertising in the 1990s and became the leading figure in the sector. More than 200,000 billboards and other advertising spaces now carry the striking Ströer logo. It is everywhere, on billboards in city centres, by roadsides, in railway stations and shopping malls.

Ströer's market share in Germany is over 50 %. "Digitalisation dissolves the old boundaries between the media," he tells journalists. "Before we had outdoor advertising, we had print, TV, radio. In the future you will change between screens – smartphones, tablets, PCs, and regular TV. Then there are the screens in public spaces, out of home advertising. All of that is overseen from one digital platform, the Internet."

That's his life. A short time ago Müller had desperately looked for a solution to a crisis and saw an abyss opening in front of him. But now he is busy turning his crisis-shaken poster business into a media empire.

The investors obviously see it that way too and slowly return to Ströer's shares. In January 2004, the price is around € 14, in June € 16. Müller still feels that the shares are being sold under value.

The risky deal with AdScale was only the beginning. Müller must get to grips with a whole new world. Until now, he has relied on posters you can see in the outside world, by the road, on walls, in bus shelters. Fixed, colourful pictures. But the Internet offers completely different opportunities. Do the two even fit together? It is a new and considerable risk, but there is no alternative.

Out of the blue, Müller receives a surprise offer. He is given the opportunity to take over a company called GIGA for about € 1-€ 1 million. GIGA? What was that again? Udo Müller is not quite sure what is being offered to him.

In the 1990s, when private TV began to flourish in Germany, GIGA was a real TV station. It was a subsidiary of Rupert Murdoch's media empire. At the time, experts still believed in a brilliant future for TV.

Satellite TV was booming, and GIGA broadcasted its own programs daily, at first with CBS Europe on the pay-per-view station Premiere, later renamed Sky by its new owners. Eventually GIGA landed with the cable TV network Das Vierte, where it stayed until 2006. They experimented a lot. The formats were called NBC, GIGA, GIGA green, GIGA local, GIGA "The Show" and so on. It was a promised land for creative people in the good old TV days, but that was a short and expensive phase. The end came very quickly.

But whereas other stations and program platforms disappeared a long time ago, GIGA remained on the Internet, with the web address www.giga.de.

The editorial staff is in Berlin. On its website, the digital station offers film, computer games and software for Apple and Android to a small but exclusive online community. Their motto is "passion for technology and games." Regardless, GIGA is up for sale again. Eight million tech-savvy users visit the site regularly and the asking price is € 1 million.

Müller does not immediately want to buy it, just as he wasn't instantly drawn to AdScale. He is interested in advertising space not content. Furthermore, Ströer has until now been positioned as an independent ad marketer with no assets of its own. No websites, for example.

But GIGA is a website that hosts content. So far Müller has avoided that.

But he soon becomes interested in something technical GIGA has to offer. Algorithms don't only monitor how many users visit the site and read particular articles, they can also check how much advertising money each article is raking in. This is new and offers enormous opportunities.

Müller discusses the subject with his colleagues and external experts. Is it possible to offer content without losing the neutrality of an independent ad marketer? The consensus is that this wouldn't be a problem providing the two sides of the business are clearly separated from one another. Müller makes his mind up. He'll go for it and gets ready for another paradigm shift. He buys GIGA. Now he is an online publisher as well.

Müller has now opened a new front in online business. In addition to marketing ads, he also offers content. It is a completely different market, but he aims to apply his usual rules. GIGA will be just the beginning. The first rung on a long ladder. It's a highly risky step in a competitive environment, but Ströer will now need significantly more websites if the company is to consolidate in this market too.

So, he begins to search for them. Initially he is interested in smaller sites, but he also has to get to know the market. At this early stage, he wants to avoid competition with larger content providers.

And – as usual – everything must happen quickly.

Great cinema

It is a regular Friday in the summer of 2013. Udo wants to spend the weekend with his family on the island of Sylt, but his new plan occupies all his time. On the way to the airport, he calls Dirk and asks urgently:

"Any idea what other websites we can buy?"

"Well, last week someone called me who wanted to sell kino.de."

"... and ...?"

"Nothing. I told him we aren't interested, especially as he said we had to make a quick decision. They were under pressure."

"Give me the phone number."

Approaching midday, and after several attempts, Müller finally gets through to the man who wants to sell kino.de. The story is as strange as it is interesting. The people really seem to be in a hurry.

The company belongs to the publishing house Gruner + Jahr, a subsidiary of the media giant Bertelsmann. The Hamburg publishers, home of *Stern* and other magazines, have tried for a while, with varying success, to get a foothold in the digital world. But the company apparently doesn't fit the owners' concept anymore and is to be sold off.

The man who called Dirk is a young Internet entrepreneur. He wants to take over the company but only keep some of its shares as he is mostly interested in the cinema magazines included in the package. He is not interested in the online portal kino.de, even though the website is doing well.

His chances are good. He seems to be the only one interested in buying the Gruner + Jahr subsidiary. But he is lacking capital. It's why he's looking for a buyer for kino.de.

The man tells Müller that he needs €1 million. That will give him enough capital to buy the company. The only problem is that he needs it by Monday.

"Why do you want to sell on kino.de? It's a successful platform."

"I haven't got the money to keep it all. It's urgent. I have to act quickly."

"So you're simply going to sell off the family silver?"

"Exactly. I'll be happy with what's left over. I don't want to build an empire."

It is a strange story, but it's the kind of thing Müller understands. kino.de fits perfectly with his plans. But it is Friday, and he has plans for the weekend. How can they sort out the formalities?

As a first step, he quickly calls G + J's CEO Julia Jäkel in Hamburg. He asks if the story is true. It is, and she confirms the Monday deadline.

Udo's adrenaline level rises. He has heard the starting gun. He then calls a well-known banker at Commerzbank and begins his coaxing. "Don't you still owe me a favour?" he says.

"Yes ...?"

"Well, I want €1 million of our credit volume. By Monday midday."

The man from Commerzbank explains that certain formalities must be observed and that the weekend is about to start. “We won’t be able to make it, Herr Müller.” But Müller won’t take no for an answer and eventually gets the promise he’s looking for. “Okay, I’ll do what I can.”

The next call is to Freshfields, the lawyers in Cologne. Müller’s plane has now landed on Sylt. Müller asks for Ludwig Leyendecker, one of the top lawyers. They know each other well. Udo tells him of his plan and then says: “I need a watertight contract by Monday lunchtime.”

“Udo, it’s Friday afternoon. We can’t make it. I don’t even know the details.” Müller doesn’t give in. And Leyendecker knows that any resistance is useless. “OK, we’ll do what we can.”

Udo is now relaxed enough to spend some time with his family. But only for a short while. He gets back on the phone again. He needs to fine tune everything with Commerzbank and the lawyers, give instructions to the experts led by the head of the legal department Anne Ossenberg. It’s not a normal weekend for everyone involved. Only Udo Müller seems to thoroughly enjoy the frenetic atmosphere.

It’s Monday morning, and Commerzbank transfers the €1 million. The draft contract to buy kino.de is ready and being okayed by the Ströer lawyers.

Towards lunchtime Müller meets the seller for the first time. He is a young man with a lot of entrepreneurial courage and a good knowledge of online business. The deal is done without any problems. Everyone is happy.

On the executive floor of Gruner + Jahr’s Hamburg office, people are amazed by the lightning-speed sale. Only some legal formalities remain, and they are completed by Tuesday evening.

On Wednesday afternoon, Müller gets an email from the

Freshfields lawyer Leyendecker. "Dear Udo. The deal with G + J is confirmed. Goal completed. My congratulations on your success. It was certainly your momentum that made it happen. Our office has never seen a transaction organized so quickly. Best, Ludwig."

kino.de is the second rung on the ladder to the digital content market.

The future begins anew every morning

Welcome to the new war-room for the digital world. It is wild out there. The Internet is like the Gold Rush. Virtual. Vague. Boundaries are moved, rules are broken and redefined. Repeat.

Müller is in the middle of it, this new whirlpool that is tightening its grip on the globe. It's tomorrow's media but, right now, it feels like the present and future at the same time.

It's plain that the good old days are coming to an end. Papers and magazines are fighting in vain for their future as an essential platform for advertising. They have fewer and fewer readers, plummeting sales numbers, vanishing ad space. Some German weeklies in 2013 have one third fewer advertisements than 10 years ago.

It is predominantly young people who have jumped ship to the Internet. It is broadly accepted that the future will be digital. A decade has passed since Müller recommended his employees watch the movie *Minority Report*, telling them it would give them an idea of where everything was going, including the world of out-of-home advertising.

Steven Spielberg, *Minority Report*'s director, used the film to depict a fictitious imagining of the year 2054. Giant billboards flickered from nowhere, by roads, in airports, in shopping malls. Unavoidable in size and colour. And most of all: digital.

Reality is now in the process of overtaking fiction. This is about more than posters and screens. The information society, as sociologists call the post-industrial present, is advancing, and it is irreversible.

But it is not yet certain whether Ströer's new, global strategy will manage to get the company established in the digital world. Müller needs more capital. Again. But investors are reluctant to agree to his plans.

However, the core business is running well again. More than 220,000 ad spaces in Germany and elsewhere are well booked. Money continues to flow in. Strong quarterly figures prove a clear upward trend. Christian Schmalzl's rigorous changes in the company's personnel structure and organization are paying off.

Müller and his COO have changed the structure of the parent company. All Internet activities are bundled together in the new Ströer Digital Group. It is the smallest but strategically most important part of the business, with the largest potential for growth.

In March 2014, a new finance manager joins the company. Bernd Metzner, 43, formerly with the pharma giant Bayer. His friendly smile and relentless good mood are Infectious. With Metzner, the executive board is complete again. Onwards and upwards.

Since the GIGA takeover and the weekend coup with kino.de, Ströer is busy with content providers on the Internet. It is a completely new area, strategically and operationally, and Müller is keen to power its growth through takeovers. Ströer is well on its way towards becoming a modern media empire. Success is not only dependent on catchy slogans, but also on the quality of content.

Müller, Schmalzl and Metzner present their new strategy

for the digital age to the analysts of the most important banks who are watching Ströer's shares. These include JP Morgan in London, Kepler Cheuvreux in Paris, and Goldman Sachs in New York. They present pretty revenue graphs with rising profits and a rosy outlook. But it's not only the three banks who need to believe in the company's future. The market and its investors are equally important.

Schmalzl explains the concept, which in-house they are calling Ströer 3.0. "In order to understand where we are going, we must know where we came from. Ströer began as a classic poster business, with wooden panels and glue. That was Ströer 1.0. It then introduced new and innovative ad media, such as the backlit Megalights and eventually digital advertising media. We call that Ströer phase 2.0. Now Ströer 3.0 is when the company enters the online market, with both ads and digital content."

The last two are really two different markets, but they align closely and are therefore "one logical evolutionary step." That's what Schmalzl says, anyway.

The path ahead is clear. For Müller, again, the journey itself is the goal. He doesn't seem to know any limits. With the cool Christian Schmalzl, he has found a congenial partner. The always cheerful finance manager Bernd Metzner gives new impulses and fits in beautifully with the new leadership trio.

But Müller is thinking ahead. He wants to take Ströer to the very top in this area as well.

At the top of online marketing and digital content are three companies: T-Online, bild.de and focus.de. For T-Online, owned by Telekom, the agent is Interactive Media. Publisher Axel Springer is the owner of bild.de. Focus.de belongs to Hubert Burda Media. These classic publishing houses are determined to defend their top spots during the transition from print to digital.

In the media there is nothing that cannot be measured, analysed and compressed into a statistic. Newspapers have their circulations; for TV it's viewing figures; for the Internet it's clicks.

But basically, it is all about one thing: advertising! Henry Ford, the legendary founder of the Ford car manufacturer, said in the first half of the 20th century: "I know one half of my advertising is wasted. But I'm not sure which half."

These days things are a bit more precise.

The more the advertisers can spread their alluring messages, the higher the companies' chances of luring in customers.

For decades, a couple of companies have registered, measured, and analysed circulation figures of newspapers and magazines, as well as the viewing habits for private and public TV stations

But nowhere can reach be better monitored than on the Internet. Several organisations can provide precise figures.

The growth in digital advertising is breath-taking. Ströer's figures show a revenue increase of 90.8 % between 2013 and 2014. With a turnover of €122 million, digital business in 2014 is already as big as one quarter of the classic branches of posters and billboards.

Digitalisation softens those boundaries. People watch TV on their computers and listen to the radio on their mobiles. Müller recognised much earlier than others in the media sector that advertising would also change drastically.

After the entry into online media marketing and digital content, his aim is now to consolidate those markets as quickly as possible and to become a market leader. It is why he bought AdScale and integrated it into Ströer Interactive Media. He also bought other online agencies, including Ballroom International Group in 2013, in the most important Ströer markets. Ballroom markets online advertising in Poland and Turkey. It's a perfect fit with the Ströer portfolio.

On November 13th, 2014, Ströer's share price rises above 20 Euro for the first time in three years. The market is gradually gaining trust again.

The future is becoming clearer, including on the stock exchange.

Rumours around *T-Online*

Since spring 2014, there has been a rumour in the financial world. Interactive Media, the marketing company of T-Online, may be offered for sale, maybe even T-Online itself. Deutsche Telekom AG wants to part with any subsidiaries that are not part of the core business.

Since the beginning of the year, Telekom has a new boss. Tim Höttges has replaced René Obermann. It is not an easy succession. The new man is considered a tough manager. As a first step he wants to shed all ballast in the core business. And T-Online is obviously a part of that.

Höttges, 50 years old, is focused on efficiency. There is no room for sentimentality. Necessarily, there are contradictions and victims. All decisions must be explained very well, both inside the company, to the employees, and outside to the shareholders.

Müller knows both managers. Not long ago, when Obermann was still in his post, the Telekom department then known as "Added Value Services" wanted to get into outdoor advertising. Telekom actually beat Ströer to some outdoor advertising contracts when they came up for renewal in Bremen, locking them for the next 10 years. But the responsible managers of the newcomer had little experience in the business and apparently calculated totally unrealistic revenue figures. They offered the city a lease price that was more than double the amount Ströer had achieved in annual turnover.

Müller is quite alarmed. If a large company like Telekom muscled into out-of-home advertising with such methods, it would be very risky for everyone involved. He arranges an appointment in Bonn with Telecom's "Added Value Services" manager. The meeting confirms Müller's belief that Telekom is planning to get into out-of-home advertising and is obviously accepting large initial losses. Telekom has even planned to build a factory to produce organic LED advertising media.

A short time later, Müller happens to meet the Telekom CEO Obermann in a bar of a Berlin restaurant. The two are on first name terms, so Müller mentions the contract in Bremen, which is expected to lose the company money. Müller knows the market and assumes that Telekom won't earn a single cent over its 10-year contract. Quite the opposite. It will end with a loss of at least € 10 million. But Obermann is not impressed. Initial losses are normal in any business. When Müller's then wife joins the pair and asks why the atmosphere is so frosty, Obermann answers brusquely: "Udo is annoyed because Telekom has done well in Bremen and snatched a contract from Ströer."

This sets alarm bells ringing for Müller. It will be massively dangerous if a global company like Telekom wants to use all its financial might to break into the midsize sector of outdoor advertising. Telekom is planning to be the bull in the china shop. Once the animal turns around, it destroys everything. But it then loses interest and walks away. Müller needs to find a different way to get into talks with the responsible Telekom people.

Müller hears that Telekom's CFO Höttges is planning on attending the grand opening of Freshfields' new law office in Cologne. Müller doesn't know him yet but decides to go to the party. He approaches Höttges there.

"Hello, Mr. Höttges, my name is Müller. You don't know me."

"No, but what can I do for you?" the man answers.

"You are probably well aware that the Telekom figures are wrong?"

Höttges looks Müller up and down. "What do you mean?"

The Ströer boss informs him about Telekom's deal in Bremen. "You will make a loss of at least € 10 million. It will have to be declared in the annual figures."

"I don't believe that," Höttges answers defensively.

Then Müller has an idea. Höttges is known to be competitive and focused on details. What if he suggested a bet about his predictions?

"Let's bet a case of a good Bordeaux," he says. And Höttges agrees.

A few weeks later the Telekom CFO asks for an appointment with Müller and arrives at the Cologne headquarters with the relevant manager. Höttges asks for the Bremen deal to be explained and for more details about the mechanics of outdoor advertising. Some weeks later, the company stops its expansion into out-of-home advertising altogether.

And now it looks as if Müller and Höttges will meet again about a business issue. But will Telekom really get rid of T-Online and its associated ad agency Interactive Media?

This particular story started in 1995, when T-Online became an Internet platform and independent email service. In addition to general news, T-Online streamed exclusive content, such as the first live video chat with an astronaut in space. The portal aimed to smooth users' access to the Internet, while offering latest news updates at the same time.

A year later, Deutsche Telekom outsourced its subsidiary T-Online as Online Pro Dienste GmbH & Co KG and in 2000 launched it on the stock market as T-Online International AG. The initial share price was € 17 and it triggered a boom. The share offering was oversubscribed 20 times.

But then it went downhill. At the end of 2006, Telekom bought T-Online back to fuse it with its parent company. Only after a turbulent general meeting and legal conflicts with small shareholders, which went as far as the High Court, did they manage the buy-back. But by then the share was worth only € 1.

In 2014, T-Online still has good reach, but the news platform is visibly outdated, the editorial team in Darmstadt is considered weak and too far away from where things are happening. The subsidiary doesn't have much to do with the parent company.

There are always rumours. Behind the scenes, large publishers like Springer and Burda are active. T-Online would fit in nicely with their online plans.

Who gets the golden egg?

Eventually it is official: T-Online is for sale. Interactive Media, the ad marketing company connected with it, is also on the market. But it is not clear what Telekom's priorities are for the negotiation. Does it want the best possible price? The best partner? Or maybe not to sell at all? T-Online, after all, is a kind of golden egg in the sector, something particularly precious.

In August 2014, Telekom's top manager Michael Hagspihl invites interested parties in for a talk. It is mainly large newspaper companies, where T-Online's portfolio would fit nicely. Ströer AG is also asked, which is a surprise. Telekom has obviously been watching Udo Müller's digital strategy and has taken it seriously.

In the meantime, it has become reasonably clear in what direction a possible sale might develop. Apart from the sales price, the focus will be mainly on a convincing strategy for T-Online's revitalisation. The new owners would need to give the company new impetus, stop the fall of user numbers and, even better, produce sustainable and continuous coverage growth. That would also be useful for the parent company, as T-Online is an important distribution channel for Telekom.

The rival bidders send professionals into the race, including Peter Würtenberger, Springer's Chief Marketing Officer. In the Berlin media empire, Würtenberger is the person for all things digital. Before he switched to Axel Springer in 2001, he was the German boss of Yahoo. Now this smart guy would love to get T-Online into the Springer empire.

The negotiations are lengthy. Telekom is not in a hurry. Quite the opposite. It seems that the managers responsible for the sale and the department heads are blocking one another. Their interests are too different. But they all want one thing, to keep maximum influence. Marketing, sales, general management, and of course value-added services. They don't really want to let go of T-Online.

Burda quickly withdraws from the race. But Dirk gets involved, following up a previous suggestion that he would take over the subsidiary Interactive Media from

Telekom, if it went on sale. Udo doesn't really like this option. He says that the company's customer structure is 80 % dependent on T-Online. What does that mean? "It means that it only makes sense to take over both T-Online and Interactive Media together."

There are also lively discussions with Telekom. In large organisations like Telekom, any change triggers great unrest. So many parties want to have a say: heads, regional managers, advisors. Tim Höttges, as chair of the board, has the last word. But only the last one. Up until then, a lot can happen. It is unclear whether T-Online is for sale at all. The relevant departments simply cannot agree on anything.

Höttges sees it like this: The T-Online brand has aged and needs new impetus. But who can provide that? Springer? Burda? Ströer? Or maybe United Internet? In their own words, they are "Europe's number one Internet specialist."

It is also possible that the executive board around Tim Höttges will ultimately decide against a sale and keep T-Online as part of the Telekom family.

So, everything is possible. The first meeting in Telekom's HQ in Bonn goes as expected. Some important info is exchanged. The parties check one another out. And that's about it.

The Cologne trio have grown into an efficient team. Udo is the driving force and, together with Christian, develops the strategy. At the same time, Christian sees to it that things remain calm, and Bernd tries to predict and fend off possible problems. Whether this tactic will impress the opposite party is hard to tell.

It is mainly Udo Müller who puts on the pressure. He is impressed by the logic of the deal. T-Online and the marketing company Interactive Media fit perfectly with Ströer.

Interactive Media consolidates Ströer's strong position in the online marketing business. And T-Online can become a flagship of his new strategy of growth in the online content market. Sooner or later, it will take on a leading position.

Also, Ströer has a near perfect strategy for revitalising T-Online, as required by Telekom. T-Online needs to boost its presence and reach. But Telekom is also interested in placing its Magenta "T" logo everywhere for advertising purposes.

Ströer can utilise its early and successful digitalisation strategy for this part of the process. Before, T-Online had featured on two platforms: desktop and mobile. Ströer can offer a third: digital advertising spaces outside the home. Only Ströer owns those digital advertising spaces, and T-Online can put its webpages there, alongside its Magenta T. "If we display T-Online content on all our public screens, its reach will double in one fell swoop," Müller says.

In the future, there will be more and more public digital ad spaces on more and more public screens. Megalights are gradually being replaced everywhere, and other digital screens are popping up in railway stations, on busy streets, and in numerous other places.

"Other competitors can't offer Telekom this strategic added value," Müller says. He has studied all the details by now and will use any means at his disposal to acquire T-Online.

He introduce a new medium to bring the Telekom managers on his side. Udo Müller organises a professional film to be made, calling it "Our Vision for T-Online".

The start is traditional, describing the story and relevance of the Telekom subsidiary. But threatening string music plays in the background, getting gradually louder.

Then a deep voice describes the problem at hand: T-Online as a pure online portal is facing great challenges.

And the solution is: Ströer.

"Ströer's offer takes T-Online into the real world, with Ströer Public Video. It takes it digital, with high resolution displays in the most frequented railway stations and shopping centres in Germany. With the new distribution channel Public Video, T-Online will become an omnipresent media brand and constant companion of the digital generation. This will attract particularly the young and mobile target groups, and T-Online's value will be sustainably increased." The end.

Nearly a decade later, Müller is still very happy about it the impact of the film. "It made a great impression and conveyed our concept for T-Online emotionally, in perfect visuals." But of course, only the facts count, and the strategy.

Müller uses many elaborate words to describe how T-Online could become a new member of the Ströer family. But not everyone is impressed by his enthusiasm. "The man gets on my nerves," they tell each other behind his back.

The deal is on the brink of breaking down several times – either over the price or the kind of takeover. Sometimes they argue about the valuable address list of T-Online, or about the added value that Ströer has to offer Telekom. They are often far apart. Müller frequently meets with T-Online managers in an attempt to push the deal through and realise his plans.

Müller wants T-Online. He wants it badly. The pressure is rising in-house too. The CFO Bernd Metzner, as well as specialists from his mergers and acquisitions department are as closely involved in the negotiations as the lawyers around Anne Ossenberg. The meetings are difficult. The experts get stuck in the detail.

They explore more and more variables. They examine new details. They look for compromises. Weeks turn into months. The acquisition is nerve wracking for all involved.

But Müller drives them. He doesn't hesitate. He wants the deal. The board around Tim Höttges also finds the logic of the deal interesting. For one thing, T-Online, refreshed by Ströer, would also improve Telekom's image. And the Magenta T in the T-Online logo will essentially advertise Deutsche Telekom across the whole of Germany.

The art of a perfect deal

There are clear rules to the purchase of a company – at least according to established Anglo-Saxon M&A procedures. The seller produces a so-called teaser to stimulate interest. It contains the most important information regarding the company up for sale.

Invited bidders are asked to make a first, non-binding offer. This "indicative offer" is rather vague.

Whoever is admitted to the sales process now has access to the data room where there are digital copies of all relevant documents. Initial talks begin between the management teams and their consultants.

In the following round, there are further presentations by management. Additional, more detailed information is added to the data room. A second round of offers is presented, this time a bit more precise.

What follows then is usually the final round. Often the seller limits the number of potential buyers after the second round. Some potential buyers pull out, perhaps over the price or for strategic reasons.

If it gets as far as a third round (or sometimes even more) experts from across various departments are asked to clarify specific points. Depending on how many bidders are left, the seller now opens the data room and gives access to confidential documents as well. The seller just needs to be sure that bidders don't gain knowledge that might be of benefit to a competitor, particularly if they don't manage to secure a big enough sale price.

The remaining bidders at this stage are mostly busy negotiating the sales contract. Drafts are written and commented on by both sides. This is another long-winded process. Both sides sit around a table and go through the contract line by line. They make changes as they go along.

At the end of the sales process, there is a draft contract which is accepted by both parties. Then, at the latest, the potential buyer must prove that the deal will be fully financed and presents an "unconditional financing letter".

What is left is the showdown, the day of the decision.

With the DSM deal, the bidders were in different cities, and the decision was communicated by fax. The sale of DERG went through centrally in Berlin with the DB representatives in their Bahntower on Potsdamer Platz and the buyers in their respective hotels.

In the case of the T-Online purchase, there are no other bidders in the final round. Telekom is so convinced by the strategic vision presented by Ströer that the two companies negotiate exclusively. It is not that unusual in deals of this kind. The seller can usually tell after one or two bidding rounds how the markets regard the company in question, and then concentrates – once there is a general line for the sales price – on the candidate with the best strategic vision.

Udo Müller and his team arrange to meet Telekom boss Tim Höttges and his negotiators in their Bonn headquarters.

There are, of course, emotions as well as facts and finance at play during the deal negotiations. No one wants to lose face. Any areas where there is still wiggle room have been discussed for months, until one of the parties ended the talking by drawing a red line. Twice so far, the documents were collected, and the negotiations "ended", only to restart again. And now there's one last round of negotiations. And it's still touch and go whether the sale will take place.

Some deals fail because people get obsessed with one particular issue. Müller's attitude has always been that he should "dial down his ego to zero". He tries to ensure he stays focused on the deal and does not allow his emotions to influence anything.

Most halfway decent guides for negotiating insist that you should not disclose what you consider to be the most significant aspects of the deal, i.e., the central issues of most importance to you. It's easy in theory but more difficult in practice. Often people start off with some mistruths, perhaps deliberately exaggerating some areas, or playing with emphasis. They might insist something is only accepted "over my dead body" only to abandon their resistance with a theatrical gesture later, all in service of a bigger goal. "It is important that the person you're negotiating with gets the impression that they are the winners," Müller says.

But good negotiators know these tricks, of course.

"A good deal is always one that hurts both sides," Müller says. But he adds that finding the perfect deal can be great fun. "You have to find the right pressure point. Even one tenth of a percent is important. If your demands are even a tiny fraction too high, your opposite number might walk away for good. But if you hit the sweet spot, your opposing negotiator will get visibly upset and storm out, but then cools down and comes back after 10 minutes."

Trust plays an important role. "In our fast-moving world it has even become more important," says Müller. Some people are fundamentally suspicious when meeting others – and stay that way until trust is established. But Müller takes the opposite approach. He trusts everybody immediately – but if they do something that undermines the trust, it is gone for good.

There are two sides to this. Müller always keeps his promises, today and in 20 years' time. But if people lie to him, he will never trust them again.

There are a few more ingredients that make a perfect deal – three, in particular, that inform Müller's decision-making.

Firstly, he considers it important not to be too self-centred. "I always ask everybody for their opinion," he says. "Someone always sees something that I have missed."

Secondly, the process should be refined along the way. "You have to look at every step along the path time and again. Dozens, hundreds of times. There is always something that can be bettered."

Thirdly, and maybe most importantly, is the will to win. "Whatever you want, you have to want it more than everybody else." This creates an energy that can be infectious and can get a deal over the line. "And then you have it, the 'Flow' experience. Everything suddenly comes together perfectly."

"I'm in!" – this time for real

It is the afternoon of June 16th, 2015. Müller is sitting at his desk. He is preparing for the important meeting with Tim Höttges in the Telekom HQ in Bonn, scheduled for the day after tomorrow. He and his team have already spent several months negotiating with the M&A team and the respective departments of Telekom.

Again and again, his eyes glance at the tablet on his desk that shows the live price chart of Ströer's share. A few cents up, a few cents down. It seems to be a normal trading day at the Frankfurt Exchange. € 10.20 – € 10.18 – € 10.22 …

Then, at 4.12 p.m., a low and triumphant "Yesss!" The Ströer price jumps to € 10.25. It means Ströer has a market value of € 1 billion. The feeling is incredible!

But it is only a short emotional outbreak. Müller concentrates again on his work.

The meeting with Höttges and his people must go well. They are going to meet at 6 p.m. in Bonn. Then it will be all or nothing for buying T-Online. That has been agreed with the Telekom boss.

Müller only rarely lets on how proud he is about what he has achieved. He almost immediately returns to focus on the next step, the next challenge. Onwards and upwards. It's cool strategies that count, not hot momentary emotions.

He has always been like this, whether celebrating major successes or small victories. Sometimes he displays nothing more than a small smile, sometimes a volcano of emotions as the adrenaline is released. But one way or the other, Udo Müller only enjoys his victories for a moment.

He was like this in school and when he was a handball pro. And it is the same now. He knows that there is only a narrow margin between triumph and defeat. Success is a very volatile companion. That's another lesson Müller has learned in life. He also knows that he is a lucky man, a hard-working lucky man.

And now T-Online. It's been two years since the first rumours about a possible deal. Ströer's share price at the time was € 10. Now it has quadrupled. That's another reason he can approach the Telekom deal with confidence.

Six o'clock in the evening. The meeting starts on time. Telekom boss Höttges and his manager Hagspihl are present, also the top managers Nick Jan van Damme, Hans-Cristian Schwingen and Vicente Vento. It's the Premier League.

They are greeted in a friendly but serious manner. "We will have enough time, Udo," Höttges says, "but we either get a result today, or we are out."

They then present the issues again: Ströer's new online strategy, joint infrastructure and big data alliance, local markets and the national market, sales agreements, inclusion of email accounts, use of the MagentaT, license agreements and digital content. Professional stuff.

An hour, two hours, three hours pass, and there is no end in sight. There's a short break. A few snacks. The Telekom people fight for every single cent.

The situation makes for an interesting negotiation. Both sides know that the deal makes good strategic sense for them. With Interactive Media, Ströer will become number one in the marketing of online advertising and, with T-Online, become an important actor in the digital content business. The purchase of T-Online will boost Ströer's digital out-of-home infrastructure because it will also display the new company's content. That will make the whole advertising environment more interesting.

But Telekom too has sound reasons for selling to Ströer – and that was the reason they decided to negotiate exclusively with the Cologne company after the second bidding round. Telekom is looking for a partner that can stop a loss of reach with T-Online and show perspectives for sustainable growth of the portal. It is also about advertising the "Magenta T". The more people visiting the T-Online page, the better for the brand. The same is true for all the screens in public places, which will also show the Magenta T. There was a fourth point, concerning the "small cells" – small antennae that could be built into Ströer's advertising media infrastructure. They supplement large radio masts and help prevent dead spots in the inner cities – particularly important after the roll-out of the 5G network and in the era of self-driven cars, when a signal failure would be disastrous. The "small cells" might easily be integrated into advertising columns, Citylights or street furnishings, such as bus and tram shelters.

These were the two companies' starting positions – and both parties were aware of how valuable the deal would be for the other side. Everyone knew that there was no other possible resolution. There would be a deal today. But still, they all wanted to negotiate the best conditions for their own side.

"The deal makes so much sense for Ströer that it should be worth more to you," Höttges says more than once.

"The deal makes so much sense for you that you really should drop the price," counters Müller. "We are such an ideal strategic partner."

The negotiations are underpinned by a mutual appreciation, but it doesn't make them any less demanding. More than once the parties get into such a conflict that the talks seem close to breaking down.

It wasn't only about one contract, but several, quite different ones. There is the sales contract for T-Online and Interactive Media. A licence agreement for using the brand T-Online and the Magenta T. A contract for the inclusion of email accounts on the T-Online website and of course the sales contract.

For that reason, the negotiators split up into different teams. And finally, shortly before midnight, Höttges and Müller finally shake hands. The deal is done.

"I hadn't expected us to come to a deal," Müller says.

The other man looks at him for a long time and then replies with dry humour: "Every deal dies twice."

Müller has to laugh. He realises that Telekom has deliberately accepted a series of conflicts as a means of unsettling the other side. It's an interesting strategy for negotiations.

And the price? Müller would have preferred a deal for cash, but Höttges wants Ströer shares. He wants to participate in the new Ströer SE.

It is a compliment, really. Höttges believes in Müller's digital strategy. The T-Online deal is nearly as big as the one with DSM and will make Telekom a major shareholder. They also get one or two seats on Ströer's supervisory board, which is set to grow from six to 12 members. They will have an influence.

Müller has argued against this arrangement for a long time and doesn't want to hand over a large share package to Telekom. He would have preferred to finance the deal via the capital market and to leave Telekom outside. He also fears that large shareholders – such as the Munich insurance giant Allianz, which holds 6 % of the company, as well as Telekom – could have too much influence on Ströer's strategies.

After all, Allianz and Telekom now hold a combined 20 % of available share capital. It's another reason the negotiations nearly failed. Müller is worried about his own influence on the strategic development of his company.

Finally, Müller agrees. The additional shares will be created with a capital increase against assets in kind. Telekom contributes T-Online and Interactive Media as an asset and gets new shares. The details, including some technicalities, are to be confirmed by the lawyers as soon as possible.

They prepare to make a public announcement confirming the agreement.

A good two hours later, the group says goodbye – much more relaxed than they were at the start. Apart from Höttges, most of the Telekom team has already left in exhaustion. Christian and Bernd are also ready to go. They are tired. But Udo's adrenaline level only comes down slowly. All offices in the Bonn headquarters are empty now. The Telekom tower rises dark into the night. Even the reception is empty.

The three Cologne men had left their ID cards there when they came in. It was pure routine, but they are now somewhere in a drawer. Höttges, accompanying the trio to the door, jumps over the desk and finds them after a brief search. They then head down into the garage.

But if anyone believed that everything was now done and dusted, they will soon learn otherwise. The next days are turbulent. The devil is in the detail, as everyone knows, and once again that proves to be true.

The main problems concern the final size of Telekom's share in Ströer AG. The reason is the rising share price. As Ströer stock grows more expensive, Telekom's share, in percentage terms, shrinks. They will have to agree on a deadline, a fixed date.

When the share price was €10, the Bonn company's share package represented around 20% of Ströer AG. However, the price has nearly doubled, and again the deal is on the rocks.

On a sunny afternoon, an exasperated Telekom head of negotiations leaves Ströer's Cologne headquarters. From his window, finance manager Metzner watches the man down there on the phone, gesticulating. Ten minutes later he comes back. "OK, this is our last compromise suggestion ..."

Three days later, both sides meet with Müller and Hagspihl at Freshfields' office for the final act. Their signatures will apply the seal to the tough negotiations. On the night of August 13th, 2015, the deal is made public. Telekom get 12 % of Ströer, as well as two seats on the supervisory board.

Müller is happy. Höttges and his top manager are happy too. The Bonn giant is a large shareholder of a very unusual new media star in Cologne. It's a pretty good union. "The transaction marks the beginning of a new era for our company," Udo Müller tells the press.

The stock exchange also celebrates the acquisition of T-Online. On the day after the news, Ströer's share price increases by 12.5 % to € 10.42.

But there is one fly in the ointment. Even before the Telekom deal, Udo Müller and Dirk Ströer had lost their majority ownership of Ströer AG. Müller never sold a single share after the stock market launch and is still one of the largest shareholders. The pair owns 40 % between them. If he needs to convince the managers of any large funds of some future plans, this would normally be enough to get the necessary majority in the shareholder meeting.

Each new share issue will decrease Müller and Ströer's stake in the company. But to be able to use their shares in the future as currency for an acquisition, Müller wants to change the legal form of the company into what's known in Germany as an SE & Co. KGaA – a partnership limited by shares, whose general partner is a European company, the SE, which is private. The KGaA is public. This structure will allow Müller to retain control of the company. Some other public companies, including Fresenius. or Henkel, use a similar structure.

But when Udo Müller discusses the plans with his team, most of them are skeptical. A change of the company's legal structure would for one thing reduce the influence of the shareholders. Also, with the necessary consensus limit of 75 % of the existing share capital, it would be a high hurdle to pass. Why would the current shareholders consent to it?

But Müller is optimistic that he can convince the larger shareholders. The acquisition of Telekom had again shown that his strategies create value, from which the shareholders benefit.

"I have talked to all of them in depth," he said, and eventually they agreed to the company relisting. It was the only way to undertake more buyouts. "I am asking you to trust me," he said. "In the future, we will also be able to act independently and do what is best for the company." Many signal their consent. Müller also considers it a show of appreciation for his performance, for the value he has created for shareholders.

Müller and his team ask for an extraordinary shareholder meeting, so the change in legal structure can be decided. With 51 %, Udo Müller takes over the majority of the SE part of the company, which will run Ströer's business.

Every day in the run up to the meeting, finance manager Bernd Metzner checks the number of shareholders preparing to vote in favour of the restructuring. Suddenly a large shareholder wants to vote against it. When Metzner asks why, the boss of the fund is puzzled. It turns out that an assistant ticked the wrong box on the consent form. "We'll send you a new form," Metzner says.

The decision to change the legal form of the company passes without any issues at the shareholder meeting on September 25th, 2015. Müller is happy. He considers it a great expression of trust in him and the company, and a sign of appreciation that he is on the right course strategically.

By buying T-Online and Interactive Media, Ströer's daring push into the online market takes a great stride. With

Interactive Media, Ströer becomes the leading agent for digital advertising in Germany. In addition to T-Online, Interactive Media also oversees the adverts of other well-known websites, such as *Kicker* online.

And with T-Online, one of the most prestigious online content sites in Germany, with the largest reach, becomes part of the Ströer empire. From now on, T-Online's news will be displayed on Ströer's digital advertising media, which enhances them as well. No competitor has anything similar, and it places Ströer in a singular position in the market. It is now the leading agency of online advertising and one of the leading digital publishers in Germany.

Insiders and the trade media are now full of respect for Müller's latest moves.

One trade magazine reports: "What initially looked like a crazy shopping trip is growing more and more to look like a powerful media empire. Everything seems to fit together. Without a doubt, Ströer has only needed a very short amount of time to become a modern media empire that needs to be taken seriously." *Handelsblatt* reports: "The cards are being shuffled in the German online advertising market."

All the work has been worthwhile. Buying T-Online and Interactive Media in 2015 already increased turnover by 14 % to € 124 million. The operational EBITDA even increased by 40 % to € 108 million. Müller increases the dividend per share from 30 cent to 70 cent.

Financial analysts also assess the company positively. Whether large investment banks like Morgan Stanley, Deutsche Bank and Commerzbank or smaller but respected firms like Frankfurt-based Hauck & Aufhäuser, Oddo Seydler or Düsseldorf's Lampe, all analysts recommend buying Ströer shares. The mid-term expectation is between € 10 and € 10 per share.

More pathways to the consumer

Only two months after buying T-Online, another prestigious. company appears for sale. The most important regional prestigious newspapers sell the online marketing company responsible for their websites to Ströer.

"That was a real accolade for us," said Müller. The company fitted perfectly into the rapidly growing digital firm – another important step in turning Ströer into a digital media conglomerate.

Only four days later, on September 18th, 2015, another acquisition is finalised. It adds yet another dimension to the online business. This time it concerns the digitalisation of Facebook fan pages.

The idea for this purchase stems from one of the many conversations during which Müller constantly checks his strategy and asks his partners for interesting new developments. This time it was in the Lufthansa Lounge at London Heathrow, waiting for a return flight to Cologne. He looks around. In places like this there is always a face he knows.

And there, in an armchair, reading a newspaper, is a manager he is friends with. He puts the paper down when he sees Müller. The top manager has recently left a role at the Munich media company ProSiebenSat1 to join the international Stockholm Modern Times Group.

They know each other, say hello, chat a bit. "Well, Udo, what is next on your shopping list?"

"Don't know. Do you have any ideas?"

The man did. He says that a Munich-based friend of his began a start-up four years ago, called FaceAdNet. The platform had developed into a successful player in social networking. Several large German publishers had already made offers.

That is all Müller needs to know. The catch words "social networking" and "successful" are enough. He quickly writes a mail on his mobile to his assistant to make an appointment with FaceAdNet as soon as possible.

A few days later, Björn Jopen, one of the founders of FaceAdNet, is on his way to Cologne. He is coming on his own because his partner Süleyman Acar is ill. Jopen had briefly considered postponing the meeting with the great Udo Müller to a time when he wouldn't be alone. But then got into the taxi to the airport.

About three hours later, Jopen enters Müller's office and greets him slightly sheepishly. Müller offers a relaxed "Hello, I'm Udo." They are on first name terms straightaway, but then it gets serious. Jopen explains the reasoning behind the company. "We generate traffic for all German publishers."

"Traffic" is the magic word in the digital business. It describes success with the public, expressed in the number of clicks on a website. The model of FaceAdNet is as follows: Jopen and Partners place their own websites, which can be subscribed to for free, within the large cosmos of the social media giant Facebook. They host, for example, a "Man's page", a children's platform "barco", "footballfever" and a page titled "A daily dose of useless knowledge". Jopen calls these sites his "fan pages".

FaceAdNet doesn't produce content for the pages itself. It comes from other companies, such as bild.de or kino.de. Clicking an article or image takes the user to the respective publisher's page. But each click is counted and added to the traffic stats. Traffic generates adverts. And adverts bring in money. It's that easy.

The "Man's page" alone has more than a million fans. All in all, there are millions of daily clicks. Each is registered and paid for. It is, as always on the Internet, all about attention and advertising.

Jopen and his partners came up with the idea in 2010. By the time of the meeting with Müller, FaceAdNet is the leading online social publisher in Germany.

"We bring together more than 40 million fans in online communities," Jopen explains. "We offer environments for brands and companies to communicate with others."

Müller listens carefully. It fits into his empire. Another new branch. Buy it!

But it is not that easy anymore. The time has gone when a company like kino.de could be bought over a weekend, including all the necessary contracts and formalities.

Now, in a large company, the procedure is more complicated and must go through the usual stages. It is overseen by the Mergers & Acquisitions department, followed by Controlling, then Anne Ossenberg's legal team. It's a well-oiled machine. Between 2012 and 2020, during its digital transformation, Ströer took over nearly 85 companies – more than half of the nearly 150 successful transactions in its 30-year history.

The new companies are mostly from two sectors. The first is online advertising, the fast-growing side of the business, which began with the acquisition of AdScale and Ströer Interactive in December 2012, and subsequently expanded with the takeover of Interactive Media from Telekom.

Secondly, it is websites bought for their content, including GIGA.de, Spielaffe.de, Familie.de, kino.de and of course T-Online.

There is a clear strategy. Ströer is developing from a classic outdoor advertiser – Ströer 1.0 or "Out-of-Home Pure Play" – to an integrated digital media empire. On the journey, the company passed through a phase when it developed new and innovative advertising media, such as the backlit Megalights, as well as digital media. This was Ströer 2.0. It brought the company to Ströer 3.0, which includes online marketing as well.

Ströer 3.0 is a great success. The communities are happy that news and information can also now be displayed on outdoor advertising media, while clients also benefit from additional online advertising products. Meanwhile, the company's employees are happy to see Ströer diversifying and getting ready for the future.

But what next? Udo Müller is never content and wonders what the next possible disruption could be. He thinks, for example, of Amazon, which attracts by far the largest portion of online trade. What if advertising ends up being placed only there – if trade and advertising merges? It is an extreme scenario, of course, but thinking about exaggerated possibilities sometimes makes it clearer what might happen next. Müller calls it the "Armageddon Scenario".

And that leads to Ströer 4.0: e-commerce. Müller remembers that he already owns a company in this sector. On its website, GIGA also sells repair kits for iPhones under the name GIGA Fixoo. Business was doing very well.

Why not start buying interesting e-commerce companies? For Müller those online merchants were doing a large amount of advertising already. Here, the synergies for Ströer were largest, because the company could provide them with the unsold advertising spaces on attractive terms.

After a thorough analysis, Müller begins to consider two areas of interest – or "verticals", to use the appropriate jargon: "Fashion & Beauty" and "Health & Lifestyle". This is where he sees the largest reach in the relevant target groups, both online and offline. Advertising plays a major part in both verticals and therefore fits well into the Ströer realm.

As usual, Müller has a clear strategy when he enters e-commerce. Instead of taking over 100 percent of any company, he now insists that the founders themselves stay financially involved and continue to run the business as CEOs. Further, Ströer provides unsold online and offline advertising space at "technical cost", for a fraction of the list price. If it works, the e-commerce company can increase its turnover and, hopefully, its profit as well. Ströer can also monetise the unsold ad spaces.

A fourth point of the strategy was known in business as "drag along, tag along". It means that if the founders should want to sell, Ströer would have the right to shed its shares as well.

"With these four points, we were quite well placed for a test run," Müller said.

As if *Ströer* had wings ...

All relevant parties share the same feeling towards the end of the year 2015: Success. Projections for the coming year are also very positive. All graphs trend upwards.

It is as if Ströer has grown giant wings. The company is flying higher and higher. Over the past few months, the company has become an absolute shooting star on the German stock market. After a record high in November – €13.36 – the shares consolidate at a very high level.

Even fierce rivals concede that Müller is moving in the right direction. His competitors are no longer outdoor advertisers. His new integrated digital media empire has left them behind. Müller is now competing with the classic media empires such as ProSiebenSat1, Springer, Burda and others.

The battles over the display of news are being fought simultaneously on large screens and small smartphones. Müller's new strategy encompasses both.

Müller is also aiming at something else. He wants to move up on the stock market from the S-DAX to the M-DAX. In that league – the second most important share index after the main DAX – 50 large companies, including Airbus and Wacker Chemie, plus media empires such as Axel Springer SE and Osram Light AG, compete for investors.

Shortly before Christmas, the board of the German stock market announces that, as from December 21st, 2015, Ströer will be registered on the M-DAX. Is this the highlight of Müller's career as an entrepreneur? In the past decades, only a handful of companies have managed to move up that far. But Müller has always considered success only as another step, and it hasn't changed. The rising share price is only the visible sign of his success. Here too, the dynamic entrepreneur sees more chances for growth.

ALL HELL BREAKS LOOSE

Pirates of the stock market

The stock market is the combat zone of capital. Success attracts a completely different kind of opportunist. In the U.S., the large playground of money, financial sharks and hedge funds notice the successful company in Germany that does everything differently from its rivals. Without its managers knowing it, Ströer has become a prime target. That is not good for Müller, not good at all.

There are highly controversial speculators on the stock exchanges: the short sellers. Those figures operate mainly in the dark and from a safe place of hiding. They may be controversial, but they're legal.

Reputable short sellers position themselves as guardians of the stock exchange. They look for companies whose share price they consider exaggerated. But there are also less reputable short sellers who look for companies about whom they can tell a credible but false story. This may persuade others to sell holdings. There are also out-and-out criminal short sellers who fabricate an entire story while trying to finish off the company under attack.

Even large hedge funds take part in short selling. One company's loss can be another's gain. Short sellers are the pirates of the financial oceans. These self-styled controllers are busy around the globe. In Germany, for example, at this point in time the payment company Wirecard, the industry service tycoon Bilfinger and the K + S company are the targets.

Short sellers pay a small fee to borrow shares from banks or other actors in the financial market. They think the shares are overvalued and expect them to fall. But disreputable and criminal short sellers are not interested in the correct valuation. They are interested only in money.

They sell the shares they have borrowed and speculate on the rapidly falling share price. As soon as the price has fallen far enough, they buy them back and give them back to the original seller.

Some short sellers do draw attention to overvalued or even criminal companies. But others are dubious if not downright criminal themselves. They arrange things beforehand with other short sellers or hedge funds. This "acting in concert" is illegal but extremely difficult to prove. The larger the number of borrowed shares, the bigger the impact of the (combined) attack on the stock market and the higher the chances of extremely high profit. These kinds of short sellers sell their borrowed shares all together at an agreed date. They thus flood the stock exchange and trigger an avalanche.

These days, most share dealing is automatic. It's computers rather than people who deal at the stock exchange. At the same time, most shares are secured with so called stop-loss orders. As soon as a share price falls below a pre-determined threshold, it will be sold automatically. This usually makes sense to limit losses.

But with a short seller attack, the stop-loss orders can speed up the crash. And like all avalanches, once it has started, it cannot be stopped. The more a share price falls, the more stop-loss positions are triggered, and more shares appear for sale.

There are no buyers, and so the crash goes on. And on. And on. Often it can only take a few minutes – all because an automated process that takes place within fractions of seconds, and without any human input.

Ströer SE & Co KGaA is a perfect target for disreputable short sellers. In only three years, the share price rose from about € 1 to close to € 10, a nearly tenfold increase. Anyone riding this share price rally will have made a decent profit. But there is now the question of how long the upward trend can continue. Shareholders will be asking themselves whether they should stay invested or cash in.

These kinds of positions cause people to get nervous and receptive to the negative and damaging stories peddled by short sellers. With Ströer, there is also the fact that the company does nearly everything differently from other outdoor advertisers, particularly because Udo Müller realised much earlier than others how much digitalisation would disrupt the business. "To be ahead of the curve," he calls it – but the result is that outsiders often don't understand the reasoning behind his strategies. This provides the short sellers with the basis of a story. They can claim that the majority of companies is right, and that any company doing everything differently must be a fraud.

Five of Ströer's developments in particular serve as a kind of "invitation" to disreputable short sellers. The first two are obvious: the nearly tenfold increase in share price, coupled with the company's position ahead of the curve. Thirdly, Ströer continues its strategy of near-weekly company takeovers as a way of building a strong digital force. This is a way of mitigating against the potential disruption caused by digitalisation to Ströer's traditional outdoor advertising business. The fourth point: As a family company, Ströer has, in the form of Udo Müller, a strong anchor shareholder who – point five – runs the business too!

Studies suggest that companies where the main owner and board share the same interests generally develop better than their competitors. But disreputable short sellers flip these positive characteristics on their head. They claim that when you are a strong owner/shareholder as well as CEO, you are able to manipulate everything.

Back in the autumn of 2005, finance manager Metzner first noticed the rising short positions of Ströer shares. A report in the financial magazine *The Analyst* expressed doubts about Ströer's top management. It said that the company's success was dubious, and its shares overvalued. The magazine is not well known, but its recommendation is very clear: Ströer shares should be sold.

But shareholders evidently don't take the report too seriously. The share price drops temporarily but soon recovers.

Board members discuss so-called empty sales for the first time in November 2015. Metzner said: "We know of 8 million Ströer shares being controlled by short sellers, with the value of € 100 million."

That is around 40 % of so-called free floats, meaning shares that are on the open market.

Also, outsiders ask ex-employees more and more often about possible irregularities during takeovers. Or how the atmosphere in the company was and how Udo Müller behaves during transactions.

As soon as Müller hears about the questions, he encourages everyone to be open. Neither he nor anybody else in the company has anything to hide. But when the ex-employees try to call back the people asking the questions, the numbers no longer exist.

"Do you know what's behind this?" Müller asks. Metzner

shrugs his shoulders. In Germany, according to Metzner, the short sellers must report their borrowed shares to the German financial regulator BaFin if the packet of borrowed shares is more than 1 % of the free shares of a company. If it's more than 0.5 %, any bet on falling prices must be published on the official federal stock market.

The BaFin agency for financial control wanted to make increased short attacks on German companies more transparent, Metzner says. But this obligation to report was not sufficient protection. "There are several bets by hedge funds on our share price falling," he says. "They include Third Point and Mainstone."

"Third Point?" Müller raises his head from his tablet in surprise. He has just checked the share price: €12.34. "Isn't that the hedge fund that once owned a lot of our shares?"

Five years have passed since the deal with Third Point. The price then was €1. The hedge fund had asked Müller whether he wanted to sell shares. They wanted a million of them. Müller rejected the proposal. But the company found a different way to get hold of a share packet. The price rose shortly after, and the hedge fund sold the shares at a considerable profit.

"Maybe they are hoping to make another nice profit," Metzner says.

Müller asks: "What can happen?"

Metzner: "Nothing - as long as the short sellers are playing by the rules. But if several short sellers gang up and create a few negative rumours, they would be acting in concert against us, which would be illegal. And if they then sell at the same time, it would trigger a dangerous downward spiral and crash the price. But that too would be illegal."

Müller: "Is it possible?"

Metzner: "Difficult to say. We have the evidence. But, as I said, it is all illegal."

"Okay. What else?"

Metzner proceeds to the next point on the agenda. A bond loan of more than € 100 million is to be issued for financing future takeovers.

The finance manager doesn't see a problem getting the necessary capital. Even a large Chinese bank says it will provide € 10 million. To make sure, Metzner asks at the end: "So, is it business as usual?"

"Why not?" is Müller's laconic answer.

Robbery in broad daylight

It is shortly after 6am in New York, on Thursday April 21st, 2016. Carson Block is in a good mood as he leaves the Mayflower Hotel on the Upper West Side, talking on his phone. He gets into a waiting limousine.

Carson Block is not unknown in American financial circles. He is sometimes described as the man who "dances with share prices". Very few people like him, most people fear him or even despise him. Block is the co-founder and boss of the San Francisco hedge fund Muddy Waters Capital. He has a reputation as a short seller who is keen on publicity and, if necessary, he plays on it.

Muddy Waters attacks between three and five companies per year, somewhere in the world. The attacks are not always successful, but Block has his tricks to remain on the sunny side.

This morning Block is on his way to Bloomberg Tower on Lexington Avenue, not far from Wall Street. The media giant is housed in a 250-metre-high building with 54 floors.

The name Bloomberg sounds good, and not only in the

financial world. The company was founded at the beginning of the 1970s by the financial professional and eventual New York mayor Michael Bloomberg, who grew it into a worldwide leader. It publishes the internationally renowned magazine *Business Week* from here, and Bloomberg TV also sends its news across the world from this site.

By April 2016, Bloomberg TV's *Bloomberg GO* has been broadcasting at 7a.m. for a little while. It's a unique kind of breakfast show. According to its own promotions, the program intends to "show viewers worldwide what they need to know about the economy and finances – with facts and perspectives that they would not get anywhere else".

The anchor of the program is the star journalist David Westin. For many years, Westin had been considered among the most reliable journalists in the U.S. – a moral authority. Between 1997 and 2010 he was president of the U.S. TV giant ABC News, responsible for all its news output. Then he was made to retire. Obviously too old for primetime TV.

Five years later, at 62, he returns to the screens. Bloomberg Tower was the right address for him to find a lucrative senior job and Westin is a good fit for the new morning show.

But Westin doesn't follow the strict rules of journalism anymore. A certain amount of showbiz and entertainment is necessary to entice the viewers. People don't want to see just dry figures at this early hour. For the editorial team of the program, this means that a company's spectacular crash is a much better story than a slow ascent.

So it is that on this sunny spring morning, Muddy Waters boss Block is David Westin's star guest. It's showtime for the investor who likes to play in the grey areas of the financial markets. He is good at telling his stories convincingly, even though they might be at best dubious and at worst simply wrong.

It is shortly after 7a.m. when Westin announces his guest and gets straight to the point: "What kind of a story are you presenting to us today?"

Block: "There is a media conglomerate in Germany, called Ströer or so. On analysis we have noticed several irregularities."

At the same time as the interview, Block publishes online a 62-page report on Ströer. It is entirely negative. It mentions the tenfold increase of the share price in less than three years, the ascent from stock market basement to bestseller. It mentions the buyout of numerous small start-ups and other companies. Block's verdict is that this suggests dubious practice.

At Bloomberg, they presumably guess that today's star guest is playing his own game and is betting on a crash of Ströer's shares. They offer him the stage so the coup can properly get going.

They don't consider it necessary to do their own research or ask anybody at Ströer itself. Block is permitted to present his story without anybody checking its veracity. In proper journalism, both sides are approached and given a hearing. But in this case, Ströer is neither contacted nor even informed.

Carson Black promised a bit of juicy news. And he delivered.

The share price crashes – live on TV

In Cologne, it is 2.21p.m.. Dorothee Beu-Rudat, assistant to the financial board, tries to put a call from London through to her boss. Bernd Metzner doesn't really want to be disturbed, but the caller is a friend and insists on being put through.

Her voice on the phone sounds agitated. "Are you watching Bloomberg?"

"No, should I?"

"Of course. Switch it on, quickly."

Instinctively Metzner expects something nasty. Only seconds later he is watching Bloomberg's morning show – and some white capital letters, on a blue background, at the bottom of the screen: CARSON BLOCK SHORTS GERMAN AD FIRM STRÖER.

It then changes to a full-size graph showing the company's share price movement – and its steep decline.

Block is now describing what he dislikes so much about Ströer. He says that in the past two years, the company has grown so precipitously because of aggressive buyouts and because it has broken serious economic rules.

In his view there would be no credible entrepreneurial strategy, Block drones on. In an attempt to get a foothold in the online space by taking over companies, Ströer now would have an obscure collection, a confused patchwork with the most varied digital platforms.

Block continues. He assumes illegal insider deals, opaque financing and much too optimistically interpreted figures. The company would not have the liquidity accounted for. He doubted that the story would have a good ending. The share price was far too high, and this would eventually be very bad for the shareholders.

Carson Block seems made for such a performance. He is not one of those ice-cold hedge fund managers who turn up in Hollywood blockbusters like *Wall Street* or *Margin Call*. Block is pretty much the opposite. He is inelegant, slightly overweight, with short hair and a melancholic expression in a round face. He could be just a regular guy-next-door. But it is often these types who turn out to be the nastiest.

Strictly speaking, by broadcasting this on its morning show, Bloomberg is a co-conspirator in the attack. Westin, who is mainly feeding Block buzzwords to bolster his accusations, asks whether he is implying that Ströer was a fraudulent company.

Block says: "It is not my task to judge."

He doesn't have to say more. And Westin, the journalist, doesn't follow up with a request for evidence. This is definitely not old-school journalism, but it doesn't matter. At this point Block has got what he was aiming for.

The screen now shows a live chart from the Frankfurt Stock Exchange. The graph points steeply downwards as an expert explains what is happening.

They would be witnessing something extraordinary, as in the last half hour alone the price of Ströer's shares had crashed by more than 20 %. Such a steep fall in such a short time was very unusual.

Carson Block now can hardly suppress his smirk.

"How could that happen? Did you foresee this crash?"

Block replies innocently that they had presented the results of their research in a report and published it online. It could be looked at by everyone and was obviously very convincing.

The graph appears on the screen again, showing the share price dropping more and more. Metzner realises what is happening. "It is a disaster," he mumbles. He gives his assistant a few orders and rushes upstairs to his boss's office.

Müller is sitting at his desk, staring at his tablet in disbelief. As usual he has been watching the livestream of Ströer's share price from the Frankfurt exchange. Usually, the figures go down a bit, but mostly upwards. There are constant movements as the shares are bought and sold. At midday, the price was around € 14.

But then it happens. More and more investors are obviously selling their Ströer shares. The price drops further and further. As Metzner bursts in, the price is at € 12 – and the downward trend goes on. It is hell. Müller feels as though by looking at the tablet he is staring into the abyss.

Metzner briefly outlines what is happening in New York. Müller, behind his desk, has turned to stone. The price has already crashed by 25 %.

By now, several copies of Muddy Waters' ominous 70-page study have been downloaded and printed. Müller, Metzner, Christian Schmalzl and communications director Marc Sausen go through the pages.

Metzner recognises a pattern in the analysis. Block has followed in large parts one of his own papers on the development of the company. But there's a vital difference: all Metzner's positive analyses have become negative. It's a copy and paste job, but with contradictory conclusions.

The Muddy Waters report from April 2016 claimed that Ströer's annual cash flow statement violated International Financial Reporting Standards and organic growth in digital and overall appeared to be greatly overstated.

As it turned out later, Muddy Waters had put up for sale all its borrowed Ströer shares during Carson Block's interview. Presumably – although not provably – some other short sellers had done the same. Weeks later, an analyst tells Udo Müller that on the morning before the opening of the stock market, he received an email from a Scandinavian short seller with whom he had previously discussed Ströer.

The email was extremely short.

It was only one word.

"Boing."

In contrast to the previous negative stock market report in *The Analyst*, Carson Block's performance and his substantial report were enough to trigger the avalanche. The share price plummets downward and hits one stop-loss after the other. Within seconds, the computers offer more Ströer shares for sale. And again, it passes one stop-loss after another. On and on and on.

Once an avalanche like that is triggered, it cannot be stopped. Safeguards to stop this kind of situation are only introduced years later – particularly if there's a suspicion of market manipulation.

Müller and his team can only sit motionless as they watch the scenes on Bloomberg.

"This man was allowed on live TV to claim that I was the biggest fraud ever, and that he would have to protect the world from me," Udo Müller remembers. "It felt like being in a bank robbery in broad daylight, with the police standing idly by."

The phones start ringing in Ströer HQ. Questions from investors, banks and the media come flooding in. Gradually the shock turns to anger. Christian Schmalzl remains mostly calm. "We need to stay rational," he says. "We need to publish our point of view, as absurd as the accusations may be. We have to put that online, point by point."

The share price keeps on dropping. It's slower than it was a few minutes ago, but it still continues. Müller decides to act. "We can't accept this," he says. "We have to refute this nonsense before the stock exchange opens tomorrow morning."

They release a statement immediately, saying that the company will analyse the study and then publish the results.

A short time later, experts from all departments gather

in the large conference room. As the minutes pass, Müller's anger becomes a concentrated urge to fight back. They have a long night ahead of them.

Point by point, they use facts to counter Carson Block's manipulative assessments. Müller, Metzner, Schmalzl and the experts dictate. A secretary types it on a laptop. They edit it together. Then Anne Ossenberg, the lawyer, checks it. Müller demands precision and objectivity. "Otherwise, we don't have a chance against these vicious accusations." To work, then.

It is nearly morning by the time the "Executive Summary" is complete, a preface to a 16-page document. It states: "The report published yesterday by Muddy Waters Capital primarily consists of a manipulation of facts known and already published by Ströer, which have been presented intentionally in a misleading fashion and with false claims, presumptions and assertions to deliberately distort the situation in order to cause damage for the shareholders of Ströer in its own economic interest (short position)."

Under Point 4, Müller's anger shows through: "Muddy Waters Capital has overstepped ethical and legal lines. We hope that this case will form the basis for such business practices constituting unfair trading being made more difficult in the future ... Business development in the current year to date and the outlook stand in stark contrast to the assertions made by Muddy Waters Capital."

The statement's final line is almost ironic. "With the incorrect conclusions in its report published yesterday, driven by its own interests, Muddy Waters Capital is contradicting the assessments published by all 14 analysts on the Bloomberg finance portal.

. All analysts are giving a 'buy' recommendation for Ströer stock across the board, with an average target price of just under EUR 72."

Even before the Frankfurt Stock exchange opens, the "Detailed statement by Ströer SE & Co KGaA on the short attack by Muddy Waters Capital and outlook on current business development" appears as a press release. The text is translated into English and posted online in time for the opening of analysts' and fund managers' offices in New York.

It is only a few hours since the share price crashed from €54 to €37. Will the herculean work they put in through the night pay off? The Ströer team is exhausted. But now is not the time to rest. The fight goes on into the next round. One thing they all agree on: it will be a long battle, through several rounds.

Udo Müller is sure that the attack, combined with Carson Block's performance on the Bloomberg show, is only one of several planned raids from other hedge funds. Others share this opinion. "It all looks like acting in concert," Metzner believes.

On a normal trading day, about 100,000 Ströer shares are bought and sold. On the day of the attack, the volume was 80 times as high: 8 million shares were traded. It's more than on the day of the IPO.

Ströer sends out invitations for a midday call, a kind of conference with investors and the media. Normally about 50 people ask for accreditation for this kind of conference, but this time it is about 500. Nearly half of them are journalists.

Carson Block wants to participate as well. Müller blocks him. He is still too angry at the American. Block doesn't give in. He wants to carry on making trouble. During the conference, he continues to make comments on Twitter, having somehow gained access to the meeting. His fresh claims are utterly absurd: he says he asked an FBI language expert to analyse Müller's voice – and the result was that Müller was lying.

It is typical in these kinds of situations to simply claim that the other side is lying. Time and time again. Every word is flipped on its head. Time and time again. Unfortunately, the strategy is as successful as it is perfidious. The more mud you throw, the greater the chances that some sticks. It doesn't matter how inaccurate the accusations may be.

On Friday afternoon, the news leak from well-informed sources that Muddy Waters closed its position in the first hours of the attack. It shows that Block himself did not believe the rumours he was spreading about Ströer. "Nil conviction," it is called. The whole thing was just about making a quick and high profit.

Muddy Waters probably made an extraordinary amount from the raid on Ströer. They initially sold the borrowed Ströer shares at around €18, then triggered the avalanche. After two hours, when the price was half the initial price, they bought back the Ströer shares and returned them to the lender. It earned a €11 profit per share.

Eight million shares were traded during the attack. If Block was responsible for maybe 20 %, his profit would have been around €10 million. Within two hours.

That Muddy Waters pulled out so quickly is for Müller another piece of evidence that the whole attack was constructed to manipulate the share price illegally.

"Short sellers who are convinced that the company was overvalued would stay longer," he says. "It is obvious. If someone really knows that a company is worthless, they wouldn't cash in only two hours after an attack."

Still, even as the attack on Ströer is still ongoing, Carson Block is preparing for his next coup. His victim this time is the company St. Jude Medical in Minnesota. Block suggests that the company's pacemakers and other products are vulnerable to hackers. Again, the short seller is hoping for a quick plunge in share price and a decent profit.

Another victim has still not recovered from Block's attack. Nearly a year ago, he targeted Groupe Casino in Saint- Etienne, France. The trading company did business with supermarkets such as Monoprix, Giant Casino and Spar, mostly in Asia and South America. It had an annual worldwide turnover of around € 15 million.

Then, unexpectedly, Muddy Waters turned up with an explosive report, saying that Casino was overvalued, that its most recent figures were practically meaningless. There are charts, figures, graphs, and tables, as well as speculative comments such as: "Casino increasingly resembles the structure of a leveraged hedge fund." It's a horror scenario.

After another Carson Block performance on Bloomberg, Casino's shares crashed. Shareholders panicked and dropped them like hot potatoes. The share price halved.

Now the story seems to repeat itself. The stock market is the shark pool where hunters and prey eye each other nervously. No textbook ever mentions how quickly you can get gobbled up. Even those who seem to know everything never know what the next day might bring.

The investors are on board

On the day after the near disaster, normality returns to the Cologne headquarters. But on this Friday of all days a new credit facility is due, worth € 100 million, for further acquisitions. The anxious question is how the financiers will respond to the attempted robbery at the stock market.

They can breathe out. Nobody has even winced. Quite

the opposite: Ströer's managers are encouraged to continue with their forward-looking strategy. And how do the large shareholders outside the familiar circle respond? Since the T-Online sale six months ago, Telekom has owned nearly 12 % of Müller's company. An investment subsidiary of the Munich insurance company Allianz has been on board since the stock market launch with 10 %. It wants to stay that way. The Swiss bank Credit Suisse wants to keep its 5 %. They all trust Ströer and Müller.

A more delicate matter concerns two imminent meetings in London. Regular meetings with analysts and investors are part of the business. Since the beginning of the year there have already been 11 events of this kind in Munich, Milan, Boston, Chicago, and San Francisco, among other places. Then came the attack by the short sellers.

On Thursday, a week after the share price crash, there is a meeting with investors in the London branch of the international Frankfurt private bank Hauck & Aufhäuser. The following day is "Ströer Capital Markets Day", which was planned a while ago. Müller considers it a chance to detail his strategy again and to criticise the disgraceful act of the short sellers.

Müller, Schmalzl and Metzner continue to show their united front. The presentation at Hauck & Aufhäuser goes well, with colourful graphs focused on facts. Organic growth. Operating profit. Integration of takeovers. Expectations for the next quarter and the whole of 2016.

Then there is a Q&A. The trio is well prepared to deal with the explosive topic of short selling. It goes better than expected considering the attack is still in some ways going on.

However, the mood has shifted by Friday's "Ströer Capital Markets Day", held at the luxury Andaz Hotel in Liverpool Street. Müller and his team decide to arrange security for the event to protect themselves. Who knows what the other side has planned.

Udo Müller does the introductions. More than a hundred analysts and investors have turned up, significantly more than usual. A company under fire is much more interesting than the routine of normal presentations.

After Müller's brief presentation of the history of his company, they take a short break. Schmalzl takes over, shows charts and explains the cornerstones of the actual business and its strategy. And Metzner introduces the audience to the world of figures.

Then the questions. They are aggressive. They get repeated. The answers prompt more questions. It seems as if the rivals have planted a few provocateurs. That would not be unusual for short sellers.

Udo Müller finds it difficult not to rise to the bait. Good job that Christian Schmalzl is around. He remains cool and answers each question calmly and expertly. Bernd Metzner's normal equilibrium is not shaken either. Finally, after five hours, the torture is over. "I have never been questioned so hard," Bernd confesses, exhausted.

But the fight is not over. Block's performance on Bloomberg TV still lingers in the memory. The shares climb again through May and June, but then go down.

Business magazines such as *Bilanz* and *Wirtschaftswoche* are not exactly helpful. *Bilanz* balances a mixture of admiration and disgust for Carson Block: "It was a virtual blitzkrieg." This kind of crash is a story too interesting to ignore and is seasoned with gleeful commentaries. Schadenfreude is wonderful when you are not the victim.

On the weekend of the attack, Müller immediately issued an order not to communicate with the media. He wants to get the issue out of the headlines as soon as possible. But he still talks frequently to investors and analysts instead.

After a thorough investigation, the Frankfurt prosecutor opens a case against Block, citing "market manipulation through Muddy Waters against Ströer". But it won't have any impact. The law in cases such as this is always dreadfully slow to prove illicit activities. Why should this case be any different?

Whatever happens, the damage is done.

After the attack

The attack left its mark on Udo Müller.

More than two and a half decades have passed since he founded Ströer City Marketing, together with Heiner Ströer, in a garage in Berlin. The partnership started with the expansion into East Germany after the fall of the Berlin Wall.

Müller took only two years to make Ströer City Marketing number one in outdoor advertising. In addition to billboards on private sites, he also managed to enter the "street furnishing" market. He further added important communal marketing contracts in East Germany. In the West, he began his expansion with the takeover of a Cologne outdoor advertising company – in Ströer's own city.

Without this backstory, it would have been inconceivable that Ströer could take over the much bigger, market-leading DSM. Without a doubt, that takeover was a risky and daring act, and very few people would have even dreamt of it. Everything was stacked against it. It wasn't just that Ströer didn't have any money. It also needed the consent of 26 communities. Practically unthinkable.

But Udo Müller did it. He jumped all the hurdles, found a solution, and eventually did the deal with the help of the hedge fund Cerberus.

Before the integration of DSM was even halfway complete, he followed the coup with the acquisition of the railway advertising company DERG. That helped to consolidate the outdoor advertising market in the whole of Germany. Furthermore, the company could build up strong positions in Poland and Turkey, at the time the most promising of all emerging markets in Europe.

The next step came in 2006, when Ströer expanded from Europe into the rest of the world, financed by Oaktree. The move towards global leadership was disrupted by the international financial crisis of 2008-09.

The subsequent recession in Germany pushed Ströer towards the abyss again. At the beginning of 2009, the company's then CFO warned of an imminent breach of credit arrangements, the covenant. Müller responded with a radical cost-cutting program. People still tell the anecdote of how Müller unscrewed two lightbulbs in the HQ lift, in front of employees, to save electricity. Every cent counted.

With the financial crisis hardly over, problems with state debts started. Advertising markets were crashing again – not just in Germany, but especially in Poland and Turkey. The expectation of growth in those three countries was the foundation of Ströer's successful stock market launch.

But then the share price began to fall.

Müller again did some soul-searching, while also discussing the situation with everyone who might contribute to a solution. What could a new strategy for the company look like?

At this point, it was already clear that in addition to the

considerable problems in the world of out-of-home advertising, digitalisation would present new challenges. According to all predictions, the separation between print, TV, radio, and outdoor advertising would disappear. The flickering ad displays in Steven Spielberg's 2002 blockbuster *Minority Report* slowly became reality.

Ströer was still number one in outdoor advertising. But what if the different areas of advertising grew together in the digital world? Where would the Cologne outdoor advertiser be then?

"At Ströer, we are in a continual process of checking our strategy," Müller said. Together with his colleagues, he looked for ways to embrace digitalisation and diversify the company beyond its existing areas of business. He wanted to make it fit for the future.

The most important building block was the expansion into online marketing and, as a second step, into digital content. As the only agency for out-of-home advertising, the company has a strong national customer list as well as the only nationwide sales organisation for local advertising.

With Ströer Interactive as a premium provider, AdScale as a marketer for unsold ad spaces, and the business-to-business marketer BusinessAd and T-Online as an anchor company for online content, the company had a dynamically growing arm for the marketing of online advertising and digital content. To achieve a critical size and make the branch profitable, Müller also quickly acquired numerous suitable companies.

Thanks to this kind of strategic thinking, Udo Müller and his colleagues started the second decade of the 21st century on the front foot.

In hindsight, and with the experience of nearly another decade, it became clear that all the above contributed to the Muddy Waters' attack.

"Our strategy was clearly always ahead of the curve, and that made it difficult for outsiders to copy us and assess us correctly," Müller says.

With his manipulative interpretations, Carson Block found it easy. He based his claims on the assertion that Ströer was a patchwork of unmatched companies bought to streamline the figures. Years after the attack, there were still journalists who used the same arguments, stating that Müller randomly bought companies and start-ups without a coherent strategy.

But the opposite is true. All the acquisitions were part of a clear strategy. With every new acquisition between 2012 and 2020, Müller followed the same path. He wanted to change Ströer from an "pure-play-out-of-home" business to an integrated digital media group with a profitable footprint in e-commerce.

Müller could only go on these shopping trips because the Ströer business was doing so well during these years. It was especially true in 2016, the year of the Muddy Waters attack, when each quarter was better than the last.

Analysts who regularly scrutinised Ströer's strategy and had known the company for a while didn't see any reason to doubt the further success of the company, despite the previous slump at the stock market.

Christoph Schlienkamp, chief analyst of the Düsseldorf private bank Lampe, didn't share the short sellers' skepticism. "In the end there is no right or wrong – it's all a question of perspective," he said. He added that he considered Müller's strategy to be "operatively on a good path" and still advised buying Ströer shares.

Most analysts shared the positive assessment. The recommendations were a repeated "buy, buy, buy". Only Oddo Bank was more skeptical, downgrading its rating of Ströer to "neutral". No analyst advised selling the shares.

"The company's response to the negative accusations was detailed and credible," said Deutsche Bank. It too advised keeping or buying the shares.

That was the situation in the summer of 2016. Business okay, shares ... not so much ...

"All in" – a deal a week

There is intense interest now in Udo Müller's hectic strategy for digital advancement. "For Udo, each week in which he doesn't make a deal is a lost week," jokes Christian Schmalzl, now Müller's co-CEO and an indispensable alter ego.

In the five years since Müller started to find his footing on the Internet, he had bought nearly 85 companies, with more being added each year. Ströer will have spent about a € 1 billion in its radical makeover to embrace its digital future.

In addition to the core digital investments, such as T-Online, Interactive Media, AdScale and Statista, the food delivery Foodist, the portal for healthy eating BodyChange and the mail order pharmacy Vitalsana have also been integrated into the Ströer empire.

These e-commerce companies are all part of the strategically defined verticals of "Fashion & Beauty" and "Health & Lifestyle". After a while, though, Müller develops some doubts about whether the last step in the digital transformation strategy was right. The Ströer 3.0 phase meant a radical move towards online marketing and online content. It was extraordinarily successful and made Ströer a role model for how to transform a company in the digital era.

But the "Armageddon scenario" – namely, the merging of online trade and online advertising under the management of dominant players like Amazon – has so far not materialised. And that was the basis for Ströer 4.0 and the purchase of various e-commerce companies.

Do they now have to revise the 4.0 strategy? Müller's doubts grow with each further transaction. The complexity increases with every step. However, Ströer is in the so-called B2C category, business to consumer, selling to consumers directly for the first time rather than just B2B, business to business.

He goes to a conference with Thomas Ebeling, the then chairman of the TV station ProSiebenSat1. Digitalisation had placed private stations under a great deal of pressure. There were new streaming services, such as Netflix. And large advertising agencies now had the online platforms to offer many new opportunities for targeted ads, rather than large "general interest" private stations.

Ebeling started to buy e-commerce platforms about the same time as Müller. His strategy was called "Media for Equity". He offered e-commerce providers free advertising time on ProSiebenSat1 (media) for shares (equity) with the online dealers.

At the conference, he proudly presented a strategy that he thought was a perfect all-encompassing cure for the disruption caused by digitalisation. He presented it in one sentence, which Müller will remember forever: "You cannot digitalise chocolate – and that is why we became a product company."

You cannot digitalise chocolate. In other words: chocolate is analogue. You buy it. You eat it. Done. There is no such thing as digital chocolate. If the web shops of ProSiebenSat1 offer chocolate, digitalisation cannot affect them.

When Udo Müller hears that sentence from Ebeling, he knows immediately that he is on the wrong path with his Ströer 4.0 strategy. TV stations see their future as sellers of chocolate? Outdoor advertisers like Ströer believe they can muscle in on the market with mail order pharmaceuticals?

"I realised two things straightaway," Müller says, explaining how he came to a new insight. "Thomas Ebeling will not be chairman of the board of ProSiebenSat1 for much longer. And we have to rework our e-commerce strategy."

Indeed, Thomas Ebeling resigns from his position as chair of the TV group on February 22nd, 2018.

Müller, however, begins to change his strategy the very next day. "Sometimes you have to start something to realise that it wasn't a good idea," he says looking back. "Selling goods directly to consumers was completely different to selling advertising to businesses."

E-commerce and marketing of adverts don't go together in the same company. They don't fit. The businesses are too different.

So, get rid of it! This is also part of being a good entrepreneur. "Whenever you walk into a wood, only go so far that you remember the way back." Again, it's about analysing a strategy repeatedly, questioning everything and, if necessary, abandoning something, even if it has been successful in the past.

He therefore either sells the trading companies, dissolves them, or transfers them elsewhere.

He keeps only one, and it's a special case: The cosmetic producer Asambeauty, where Ströer holds 51 % of the shares.

The company was founded in 1963 by Ingrid and Erich Asam. In their own laboratories, they successfully produced a cosmetic range based on grapeseed oil. As early as 2003, their son Marcus and his wife Mirjam successfully advertised the products on the teleshopping station HSE24, which at the time was extraordinarily innovative.

Two years later they managed to get into the difficult U.S. market and then expanded worldwide.

When Marcus and Mirjam Asam met Udo Müller, they planned to develop a comprehensive "Beauty Experience". The three met for dinner in the Michelin-starred restaurant Nagaya in Düsseldorf, Udo Müller's favourite Japanese restaurant in Germany. "We got on really well straightaway and had a lovely evening," Müller remembers. What the Asams were planning made sense to him. The same evening, he suggested that Ströer should take a stake in the company. They shook hands on it that same night.

Ströer would hold most of the shares, Marcus and Mirjam would run the company. It developed fantastically. In only five years, turnover and profit increased fivefold.

THE FUTURE

The red button

It has been two years since T-Online joined the Ströer family. Two turbulent years. T-Online, the flagship of the Ströer content department, is completely reorganised under the new boss Marc Schmitz and chief editor Florian Harms. The old editorial team in Darmstadt is closed. As with DSM before, all employees are referred to an employment agency.

This agency's task is to get everyone a new job as soon as possible, but redundancies always create a bad atmosphere. The employees organise a demonstration and carry a coffin labelled T-Online through Darmstadt city centre.

But T-Online is not dead. Quite the opposite. Its new staff occupy a state-of-the-art newsroom in Berlin, equipped with all the new technology for its website operation. The official opening day is June 27th, 2017 – and it's a special day for Udo Müller. In the cathedral-like lobby of the tall office block in the centre of Berlin, Müller finds his way to the podium through a crowd of more than 300 invited guests. Next to him is the mayor of Berlin, Michael Müller of the SPD.

Chancellor Angela Merkel was supposed to join them on stage, but she declined as she had too much to do. But the chancellery sends its congratulations. The mayor is grateful that Ströer has brought the news centre, with more than 100 journalists and other employees, to the capital.

In front of the two Müllers stands a plain table with a bright red buzzer on top of it. This button recalls a historic event from August 25th, 1967. At a prestigious electronics fair in West Berlin, the then chancellor Willy Brandt, a social democrat and former mayor, pressed a similar button to begin the era of colour TV. With this button, Müller and Müller now begin another new media era in the Ströer company.

The loudspeakers blare a countdown from ten to one. Then both Müllers press the button together and open Germany's most modern digital newsroom. From now on, more than 100 people will publish world news online around the clock.

A new era in the battle over page-views and clicks has begun. It is not only about the presentation of journalism and information. Müller is mostly after the advertising budgets of the whole economy. It is a fast moving and constantly growing billion-dollar business.

This was Müller's precise vision when he started to battle his rivals for T-Online and bought the Telekom portal. It was a master stroke. Some memories of his own past might have been part of it as well.

The day reminds Udo Müller of a previous business experience. A long time ago, he started a career in publishing but had to deal with painful defeat. He published the *Berliner Sportmagazin* three decades ago, on March 25th, 1986, with a print run of 4,000. By the third edition, it had practically zero sales – and the capital of about 45.000 dollars, was gone. Müller was practically bankrupt. The magazine's life ended.

But now there is another news medium in Udo Müller's empire, and it is one of the biggest German-language news portals in Europe. Before it was taken over by Ströer, the former Telekom subsidiary T-Online had wide coverage, but the editorial part of the news platform was small. The online offshoots of *Der Spiegel*, *Stern*, *Bild*, *Focus* and other print titles were all well ahead.

Müller wants to change this. Today they are opening an ultra-modern, digitalised editing suite, a newsroom from which dozens of journalists will cover all news: politics and the economy, culture, and sport plus some entertainment stories. They'll send it under the label T-Online.de to millions of screens, tablets, and smartphones in Germany and the rest of the world.

June 27th, 2017, is the beginning of one of the most ambitious media projects of the past few years. There are speeches and interviews. Cameras are buzzing. To borrow a phrase: It is a small step in the history of media, but a giant leap for Ströer's new media empire.

Müller talks about the rapid development of digital opportunities and the chances his company is going to take. He also mentions his special relationship with Berlin. The German capital always had its finger on the pulse, and that is why Ströer has established its new newsroom here. The need for good journalism is particularly strong in Berlin.

The new editor-in-chief of T-Online is Florian Harms. He is considered one of the most talented and ambitious journalists in the sector. Previously online editor of the news magazine *Der Spiegel*, he is Müller's man to guarantee good journalism.

Harms is excited by his new role and the possibilities that T-Online already offers as the platform with the largest coverage in Germany. He lays down a marker for Müller's ambitious project, stating: "We want to become Germany's new leading digital medium."

Wow. It's an ambitions target. Harms' former employer, *Der Spiegel*, still considers itself the market leader. But the new editor-in-chief wants to change that, at least in the online sector. When he is asked later whether the target might be a bit too ambitious, and whether it has been agreed with Müller, the company's spokesperson answers with a smile: "No idea, but I'm sure Udo won't mind."

That Müller didn't mind soon becomes obvious. A few months later, in November 2018, T-Online.de is ranked third on an influential list of German news sites. It is above focus.de and Springer's welt.de. Only *Der Spiegel* and *Bild* are ahead.

Statista: The diamond you only find once in your life

Things work out at least just as well, if not even better, when Müller makes a second major digital investment – this time in the world of data, not news. Shortly after buying T-Online in September 2015, Müller goes to Hamburg. He had been tipped off about Statista and wanted to take a look for himself. Founded in 2007, it is not really a start-up anymore. In 2012 its two founders Dr. Friedrich Schwandt and Tim Kröger received a prestigious German media award for newcomers in the industry.

Schwandt is an economist, Kröger a media scientist. They met as business consultants. While working on a shared project, they became annoyed by how difficult it was to get hold of reliable and solid data. Both knew about statistics, but there was no platform to find the figures. So, they built one themselves: Statista.

Two and a half years later, the company now makes a profit. It has 60 employees. There are pages in English,

Spanish, and French. Every second DAX company uses Statista's statistics.

When Udo Müller arrives at the Statista offices in Hamburg, all the big German media companies have been already. Many of them use the easy and well-prepared Statista graphs in their content, but even those who don't use them yet want to buy the company.

Schwandt and Kröger are in anenviable position. They are looking for investors to help finance international expansion and are even prepared to sell the majority of their company.

The two make a presentation. Udo Müller listens.

He is thrilled. At first glance, it is not obvious how Statista would fit in with Ströer. But Müller is fascinated by the uniqueness of the company Schwandt and Kröger have created.

It is not one of those Internet clones transferring a Silicon Valley idea to Germany. It has an original, unique business model, invented in Germany and now ready to roll out worldwide.

He wants to be part of it.

"I think what you are doing is amazing," he tells the owners. "I'd love to be on board. How much is it?"

Schwandt and Kröger look at each other. They then leave the room.

When they return, Müller has figured out a sum himself. He has seen the presentation and done hundreds of M&A processes. But the figures are not that important at this juncture.

He knows that any price the three of them will agree on will probably be too high compared with the actual value of the company. But Statista is clearly a bet on the future. It's a rough diamond.

When Schwandt and Kröger quote a figure, Müller

agrees immediately, even though it is the most expensive Ströer takeover ever, relatively speaking (taking current turnover into account). It is another handshake deal, again at the first meeting.

Statista indeed grows very rapidly. The business model is unique. Whoever wants comprehensive and reliable statistics goes to Statista. And users are prepared to pay for it. "Paid content" is the magic word in online content marketing.

Like Netflix, Statista has a subscription model. Individual users book a premium deal for a year and can then call up most statistics in all current data formats. Companies and organisations pay according to the number of users and their content needs, in addition to an annual subscription fee.

On the website of the awards organisation, Statista was described as follows:

> *"We want to be the first port of call for obtaining statistical information for all relevant economic topics." That's how economist Dr. Friedrich Schwandt and media expert Tim Kröger explain Statista's aim ... Statista sifts through a flood of data and prepares it in a way that the required information can be found at the click of a button and is also understandable for lay people. Type in a search word, and the statistics, studies and topic packets are ready to download.*

At the awards ceremony, the speakers coined a laudatory phrase about the website: "Statistics? Statista!" It quickly becomes very appropriate.

With the money from Ströer, Statista expands to the most important markets worldwide, and builds up other content while consolidating its technical infrastructure.

In addition to its general statistics packages, it now adds regional, national, and international rankings, like "best employer", "best garage" or "best lawyer", for example. These rankings are then marketed internationally with partners like Burda in Germany or Forbes and Bloomberg in the U.S.

Statista also gets involved in the lucrative business of industry reports – "market outlooks" – as well as a global consumer survey, producing results based on more than 700,000 interviews in 55 countries with 6,500 brands in more than 50 market sectors.

Soon, founder Friedrich Schwandt talks of Germany's "largest team of economics journalists". In addition to processing data from official sources, the team also begins to research its own data, which it checks and processes. Half the data is now based on Statista's own research, which means the company has the largest data editing team in the country. Müller calls the business model "Data as a Service" (DaaS).

There are also synergies with Ströer. Statista can raise its profile by promoting selected statistics via the digital displays of Ströer and the T-Online website.

Schwandt is surprised by how well it all works. Statista puts together city-specific content for places where Ströer has digital displays: a "number of the day" or a quiz about the city's bridges, for example.

The company name appears on the displays – "Powered by Statista" – alongside the Magenta T. It has a tremendous advertising effect for everyone involved. "It works perfectly," Schwandt says in July 2018.

Statista has a long client list. "We have them all, from football clubs to churches, political parties to dentists. Everyone now has to prove everything with data." The list includes companies such as Google, Samsung, PayPal,

Adobe, Volkswagen, Huawei, and Mercedes, plus 45 universities worldwide.

By 2020, 70 % of the turnover is earned outside Germany. It is in all the largest markets – Europe, the U.S. and Canada – as well as numerous Asian countries. But the customers themselves drive the worldwide expansion. As soon as Statista notices an increase in traffic from a certain country, the company can begin to tailor its product to that market.

By mid-2022, Statista has more than 2 million registered users who have access to more than a million statistics for 170 industries on 80,000 topics. There are 31 million visitors to the website per month.

"Statista is unique in the world," Udo Müller says happily. He gets calls near enough on a weekly basis asking whether he wants to sell Statista. But Müller has other plans. He believes that in the medium term, he can make Statista even more valuable than Ströer itself.

A little while after Ströer bought its share in Statista, Müller asked the two founders why he was able to beat the other candidates attempting to buy the company.

"Why did you sell to me?" he asks.

"That's simple," Schwandt and Kröger answer. "All the others turned up with great fanfare, with lawyers, consultants, you name it. You came by yourself, and so we thought, Ströer, they don't have so many departments and people to get on our nerves later. It was important to us that we would be allowed to carry on as before. You were nice, and that's why we sold to you."

A few years later Schwandt goes further: "No one can resist Udo Müller's charm."

Business principles

The Statista founders had wanted an investor who would mainly leave them alone. That fitted well with Udo Müller's "business principles". He never told someone to do something they didn't agree with.

"Always take the time to persuade people," Müller says. "If someone does something they're not convinced of, there is a greater than 50 % chance that you lose them. Once you lose trust, they won't give the required hundred percent anymore, and without that, you won't achieve anything."

This is the reason he always attempts to engage employees in all strategic decisions, every step of the way. It is important to go through all the small steps of any process repeatedly.

"As a company, you only achieve the power to succeed when at least 80 % of the people move in the same direction – and it's even better when it's 90 %. It's the hive mind, which you only achieve with clear goals, transparency, authenticity, and by questioning yourself time and again and involving everybody."

Ten people can then have the power of 20. "It is your task, as a leader of a company, to create this hive mind. Leadership can only be achieved through competency, not hierarchy."

For that reason, all employees at Ströer have the right to talk to their boss's boss.

"If you don't have an honest interest in your colleagues, you would be unsuitable as a leader."

"Everyone notices that quickly. When do your colleagues go the extra mile for you? It's about transparency and honesty."

And respect.

"As a leader it is your task to get the very best from your team."

He learned this lesson from his handball trainer early on in life. He had a strange but memorable comparison: "Why would I drain the sink if I didn't have fresh water?"

What he meant was: "I have to work with the resources I've got. So, I don't only treat them well, but I do everything I can to encourage them all."

The process also means accepting one's deficiencies and looking for people "who can do better what you believe you do well. Then you can put together a top team."

There is also, of course, the classic rule: "Top people employ top people, even when they are even better at something. That's how you create something even better. Second class people employ third class people, because they fear that better people could threaten their own position."

He also thinks that the greatest danger for any manager is vanity. Or if people become too accustomed to success. The biggest threat to success is success itself. It breeds complacency. People believe it will go on for ever.

For this reason, it is essential that any business strategy is reviewed time and again. "You have to question everything, including your own decision-making. Nothing is for ever. There is nothing that cannot be improved." Even if you go through every step 100 times, you will still find something that can be optimised.

It is also fundamentally important to keep an eye on the goal. It's not enough just to manage the process. "A process manager is at point A and moves to the first obstacle, preparing to deal with one issue after the other. At best they will make it to the second problem but will have already lost their way. They will have lost sight of where they are going."

A results-focused manager is different. "If they want to get from A to B, they focus on B and think about how to get there. Obstacles are only steps in between; they are not important. They take notice of them, but they don't stop. They will eventually reach the target." Good managers in leadership positions must be able to switch constantly between the strategic and the operational level.

One of Müller's favourite examples is the case of the sandwich guy. A consultant told him about it. The man was in the kitchen all day making sandwiches. They were delicious, but his company didn't do well. Business was lousy.

The consultant looked at the business. He agreed that the sandwiches were delicious, but he also saw the problem. Instead of working strategically to push his company forward, the owner got bogged down in operational tasks.

The consultant's advice was clear. Instead of spending his time in the kitchen, it would be better to employ somebody to make the sandwiches while the owner went out and looked for new customers – or the other way around.

It is about an "intuitive recognition of when you need to change from the general to the specific, or the other way around. If you always concentrate on the particulars, you become like the sandwich man and become forever chained to the kitchen. Instead, it is necessary to develop a strategy and let others do the rest."

"Changing from strategic thinking to be operative is vitally important," Müller says. "You have to look at the steps in the process over and over again. There is always something that can be improved."

Soon Müller gets another opportunity to optimise Ströer even more.

A plus for "out-of-home"

Ströer's motto has always been: "Connecting brands to consumers". The traditional approach is for Ströer's salespeople to visit local advertising clients and to present various methods of outdoor and online advertising. But it is time-consuming and expensive. For a while, Udo Müller has been hoping to change the sales process from personal visits to telephone contacts – at least for local businesses. One option was call-centres for local sales groups.

Müller begins to check with his contacts in the M&A scene whether anyone has a call centre for sale. Someone knows an entrepreneur who is looking for a partner. In 2017, Müller meets up with the Leipzig entrepreneur Thorsten Krause. He is a specialist in dialogue marketing and runs the Avedo GmbH sales call centres in seven regions. The company has an annual turnover of € 10 million.

Krause is looking for a strong partner to expand his company further. He offers Müller a majority holding in his company.

Müller doesn't have to think about it for long. Out-of-Home advertising, online marketing, websites, and dialogue marketing – they are all geared towards connecting brands with consumers. The Avedo call centres can support the local Ströer sales departments. Christian Schmalzl likes the idea as well.

Deal!

After the contracts have been signed, the press release states: "With this value-added acquisition, we complete a logical and necessary expansion of our sales department. We emphasise the relevance of Ströer with our customers and focus on performance-oriented sales models. We also expect significant synergies regarding the consequent development of our sales units in all relevant product groups."

It's all marketing speak, but it's clear for experts. It's all about getting the consumer's attention. Müller's strategy remains focused on that even after buying Avedo.

"We have a very clear strategy for our company," Müller says. The new Ströer concept also gets a catchy name: "Out of Home Plus." (OoH+) In short it is about something familiar: Connecting brands and consumers.

The company is now built on three main pillars:

1: OoH media. Outdoor advertising, once the star category, is still the foundation on which the company rests.

2: Digital media, encompassing the flagship T-Online platform, plus online marketing. This is the rapidly growing online part of the group.

3: Dialog media. The dialogue marketing arm includes the sales-supporting call centres and the direct sales business.

The companies Statista and Asambeauty are also part of the group.

Müller's highly competent friend and co-CEO Christian Schmalzl is also a key part of the group's success. Müller is the passionate visionary, Schmalzl the experienced senior manager.

Their roles are very different, something it is important to remember as the company develops.

"What are you? Founder? Entrepreneur? Manager?" Müller asks himself. "Are you still the right person for the stage the company is in now?"

He likes to compare the company with a football team. It helps to identify the roles. The entrepreneur is like a striker, with a clear task of scoring goals. The manager is more like a midfielder, with a better overview, directing the game.

The images of a rowing boat, speedboat and tanker are also helpful. The founder is the one with the crazy ideas – many of the best ones still in the pipeline, faced with numerous obstacles. At this stage, they are still in the rowing boat. You need a hell of a lot of energy to move it.

But if the idea is good, the rowing boat can become a speedboat. The company grows extremely quickly, with two- or sometimes three-figure growth rates.

At some point it might become a tanker: much bigger, but less mobile. Decisions must be made differently, perhaps by other people. With the speedboat you can still change direction quickly and even go in the wrong direction for a while. That is no longer possible with a tanker. It must be steered calmly, and it takes longer to turn around.

Christian Schmalzl is the perfect foil. He says: "Udo knows what he is capable of. But also, what he is not capable of. He is confident enough to let things go." Schmalzl and Müller complement each other perfectly and can lead Ströer together to the digital future.

Shares are doing well too. The group now has a market value of more than €1 billion. At the end of 2019, a share costs €72, €30 Euro higher than a year ago. The turnover is at a record high of €1.6 billion. The EBITDA is €570 million.

Müller is happy, the shareholders too. At the traditional Christmas party Müller again praises the spirit of the company and thanks his 12,000 employees.

In 2010, the year of the stock market launch, turnover was €130 million. Now, not even a decade later, it has trebled.

Long may it continue!

Coronavirus: the ultimate stress test

It's 2020. New plans, new goals. In January, Müller and Schmalzl have the usual conversations with the group's senior managers. The mood is excellent.

But then it arrives, this new danger from China. A few weeks ago, the media first talked about a new virus apparently emerging from a market in Wuhan, a large city in China. But not many people take notice of it. Wuhan? In China? Coronavirus? It's just another one of those strange viruses. Far away.

In February, images from the Italian town of Bergamo shock the world. They show coffins on military transport vehicles carrying coronavirus victims to crematoriums. What is eventually called Covid-19 has shown its deadly face.

Horror news from all over the world comes to dominate the headlines. The U.S.A., India, Australia, Russia. The deadly Virus spreads everywhere. Virologists talk of a pandemic as the illness spreads globally in waves. People begin to panic, and governments soon announce measures to keep it at bay.

Business at Ströer is still going extremely well. Udo Müller recalls the good figures he announced on Friday during a conference call with investors. So far, the company hasn't suffered any ill effects from the coronavirus. The first three months are set to be the 30th consecutive successful quarter.

But by the following Monday, it is all over. "Not a single order," Müller reports. It stayed like that for a full ten weeks.

Müller still sounds shocked when he talks about those days. Practically from one minute to the next, orders for outdoor advertising drop to zero. Because of the strict lockdowns people can't leave their houses. Hardly anybody passes a billboard in railway stations and shopping malls. Traffic is drastically reduced. It is a situation like never before, and advertising clients react accordingly. They cancel all orders for adverts on columns, billboards, and large screens.

At the same time Müller is certain that Ströer will somehow benefit from having always been ahead of the digital curve. Müller recognised the opportunities and significance of digitalisation much sooner than the others. He knew early on that digitalisation not only meant the need to get your own products somehow "onto the Internet", but that the whole business would have to be redeveloped and restructured, with a focus on exploiting the opportunities offered in the digital world. Coronavirus would now be the ultimate stress test for this strategy.

Digitalisation is such a fundamental change that it can only be compared with the industrial revolution. But if you only sit and watch while the curve grows steeper, you can only react rather than act. "Then it is too late," Müller says.

To stay ahead of the curve, you must anticipate how things will develop. Sometimes you make mistakes, but you'll gather the necessary experience to make a company future proof. This might trigger a negative reaction on the stock market before the strategy is understood later. Müller concedes in hindsight that he had underestimated these stumbling blocks.

But now, faced with the challenges of Covid, he prepares to make the most of his position. Ströer is not a global monster like Google, but a specialist in innovative and large coverage communication products, mostly in Germany. It is a "local hero". Germany is the largest market in Europe. With the Ströer 3.0 strategy, the company moved into online marketing. The "Out-of-Home-Plus" strategy added dialogue media to digital media. This in turn led to the three business departments: OoH media, digital media, and direct media. Müller is sure that he now has the most resilient business model for the digital world, especially compared with the "OoH pure play" model. It's also true even when faced with the new crisis.

The way Ströer is structured is also an advantage. It's a family company with three decades of continuity under Müller's leadership. What other CEO of a public company has this experience? The Ströer team responds immediately. "After 72 hours, we had switched to crisis mode," Müller reports. Christian Schmalzl takes over the crisis team and encourages the employees. "We all have to stick together. We are driving into thick fog."

One of the first measures is to send the complete workforce to work from home. This is not a problem. The company had created the technical conditions for it long before Covid arrived. The HQ and regional offices are now empty. The phone, video conference facilities and the Internet are now the most important tools. The company's internal intranet keeps the staff informed. Schmalzl sends regular video messages with the latest news. But will it be enough?

The top team around Müller wonders whether the banks can remain stable in such an unprecedented crisis. They want to make sure that Ströer has sufficient financial backing to see it through the pandemic.

The group has a credit line with the banks of half a million Euro. Müller and his colleagues consider calling up the whole sum, a "full drawdown request", to test how the banks will react. They arrange a call.

The banks agree immediately. No problem. There is enough money. There are no signs of a banking crisis, even though many companies like Ströer now start to make use of their credit facilities.

Nearly half a billion Euros goes into Ströer's account. Never has there been so much cash. In April the group applies to move its employees to short-time working, and it makes up almost all of the resulting shortfall in wages.

Board members and the bosses of the various arms of the group waive parts of their salaries for three months.

During the summer, as Covid cases decrease, orders pick up again. The staff has got used to the new arrangements. Schmalzl tries to foster a good atmosphere through new activities.

The beginning of the pandemic hit outdoor advertising particularly hard. It is still a major part of the Ströer empire. But the digital business improves during the pandemic. People are at home more often and use more digital media. T-Online reports excellent figures. Asambeauty sells more through its online shop. Statista too has more clicks than usual.

The pandemic changes society, but the group proves resilient. A press agency reports on August 17th, 2021: The ad marketer Ströer has recovered well thanks to a significantly improved outdoor advertising business and growth in its media and data areas. In the third quarter of 2020, turnover and operational results are expected to be higher than in 2019."

In November, Christian Schmalzl confirms the projections for 2021: they expect a group turnover of € 1.6 billion.

"The increased expansion of our digital infrastructure gives us reason to face the future optimistically. We are perfectly positioned to grow the business sustainably and profitably."

Müller is very proud of how his co-CEO Schmalzl and

the rest of the team have managed this "ultimate stress test".

"It has shown me that the company is in a great position, 30 years after it was founded," he says. "We have a strategic portfolio that makes us significantly more crisis-resistant than our competitors. And we have a team that has performed sensationally well during the crisis."

It makes him feel great to have achieved as an entrepreneur everything that could possibly be achieved.

Indeed, Ströer has mastered the crisis much better than its competitors and without any losses. There was not a single cent of loss, and the shareholders continued to receive their dividends.

It is clearer than ever that Udo Müller has created with Ströer the media group of the future. It is a company that can continue to create more and more value, for its clients, employees, and shareholders. It has a structure and strategy that can continue to prosper.

At the beginning of the digital revolution, Müller explored all possible paths for adding value. Ströer reaches people along the whole customer spectrum up to the point of sale. Whether in the street, on the underground or at home, whether on public screens, their mobile device or via dialogue marketing – whoever wants to reach people with advertising and information, Ströer can provide it.

"It is the perfect position for the digital age," says Udo Müller.

As the group's founder, he feels especially proud. "I am grateful – and always have been – that I was lucky enough to find something I have always considered a vocation. Working has never been a burden for me. Nothing was more satisfying for me than to put my ideas into practice and as an entrepreneur to build an eco-system in which I myself can operate."

He had his fair share of luck, he thinks. "To be in the right place at the right time to make the right decisions."

Müller is an entrepreneur who always works without any buffers, who is prepared to risk everything. All or nothing. It happened when he convinced Frank Bruno, the Cerberus man, to finance the whole of the DSM deal. He then secured a record order of E-Plus to prevent breaching the covenants of the credit arrangement with Cerberus. When Ströer's shares dropped to € 1, he staked everything on the takeover of AdScale and prepared to enter the world of online advertising. And there are countless other examples.

"You are standing at the bottom of a cliff and don't know how you're going to get up it," is how Udo Müller describes the feeling. "You have to think and think again, ask every question, think about every answer. And somehow there is always a way out. Always."

Many people give up, exhausted, a few metres from the goal. Only a few more questions, only a few more steps, and they would have found the right path.

Müller admits, however, that this strategy has its contradictions. You must stay on a straight path, with eyes on the target, yet also question everything and be prepared to dismiss everything one has learned before.

"It is difficult to explain and has a lot to do with instinct," he says. "Where is the limit? You always have to go so far until your gut feeling tells you: no further."

Sometimes one also has to listen to reason and make rational decisions. It happened above the clouds on the plane to Shanghai when he stopped Ströer's international expansion. A short time before, he had invested € 10 million of his own money, when no one – not the financier Oaktree, nor his management at home – still believed in the plan. But he did it, based on his gut feelings alone. But faced with the global financial crisis, there was nothing he could do. In hindsight, he doesn't see the international expansion as a failure. He learned a lot from it.

Here, too, fate had a hand. Because the supervisory board then insisted on a strict separation of the outdoor advertising business in Germany and the international expansion, the core company was never threatened.

The expansion into e-commerce also ended with him pulling out of the sector. Again, he managed to do it in the nick of time, and it made money in the end. But he had learned from the failed international expansion and had acted more carefully.

He spent around €1 billion on 85 company takeovers during the digital transformation. But only Statista and Asambeauty increased their respective values, so that both companies together are worth two to three times the whole of the digital investment. "The decisions that have proved as not so productive were not so relevant that they would have presented a problem," is how Müller describes the Ströer M&A track record.

The underlying strategic logic is that new business areas must support the core business either directly or indirectly. They must also earn money. If it turns out that they don't support the core business or that they do not make money, they are sold on again.

"The fascinating thing is to have an idea and to be able to develop it into something individual," says Müller. "For me, that is the ultimate satisfaction, when you see your ideas realised and, ultimately, watch them grow independently from you."

Maybe only a handful of company founders over the past 30 years have managed to develop their firms to be among the 90 largest listed companies in Germany. In the media business during this time, Udo Müller is by far the most successful of his generation

Ströer today is one of the largest outdoor advertisers in the world, across the broadest spectrum. What began as a traditional business gluing posters to wood, grew into an integrated media group, working in partnership with its clients and best positioned for the digital future.

EPILOGUE

Signposts

In their book *The Triple Package*, the American writers Amy Chua and Jed Ruben identified three common characteristics of successful people: 1) They feel superior to others, 2) They have an underlying insecurity, and 3) They are self-disciplined.

Add "vision" to the list, and it all applies to Udo Müller.

Müller is in his office in his Berlin flat and takes stock. As strange as it may sound, success is not primarily about money for him. The financial advantages are a pleasant by-product of success. Very pleasant.

The pandemic was not only the ultimate stress test for him, but also the last and defining challenge in the three decades as an entrepreneur. A situation that no one could have foreseen. No orders from one day to the next. Hardly anybody outside. No need for outdoor advertising. And still, his top team and staff handled it. Ströer emerged even stronger from the crisis because the company had been perfectly positioned for the digital future.

"The pandemic was a horror trip," Müller says. But on the other hand, it was also "a kind of final test for an entrepreneur". And it demonstrated that his group was now in such good shape that Ströer could grow and flourish without him, if necessary.

He has asked himself, particularly in the past few years, how life as an entrepreneur would end – at least in respect to the company. Selling it would never have been an option. Therefore, he had wanted position Ströer so that it could function without him. He had succeeded – and in the year of his 60th birthday, things would conclude.

Everything is set. In September 2021, Udo Müller and Dirk Ströer transferred the majority of their shares into two respective family foundations.

"It means that the company will be safe and stable at a generational changeover," Müller says. "The shareholders will benefit and Ströer can carry on being successful."

It was a difficult decision, Müller admits, and many people advised against it. It would restrict him too much. But Müller is now convinced that the foundation is the right step in the interests of the company.

The Ströer founder remembers a management meeting on Schloss Lerbach many years ago. The company had hired a psychologist to moderate the meetings. And out of the blue she had asked Müller: "Have you thought about your succession yet?"

"Succession? Are you joking?" he had retorted. "I am only 47 and have only just started." In fact, he had been building Ströer for more than 20 years already. "But for me it felt as if it only had been yesterday."

Müller has never forgotten the episode, because he realised quickly what the psychologist was driving at: the danger that the founder becomes inseparable from the company. Müller had started thinking about it then.

"In the end you must decide: Is the company there to satisfy your desire for money, power or appreciation? Or is the company an entity of its own?"

Müller knows that being an entrepreneur has an addictive power. "You are completely externally driven, have always more to do than is good for you and you don't think about yourself at all."

The business consultancy Kinsey calls this personality type an "insecure overachiever", someone who is always fully engaged. Someone who never gives up and keeps looking until the door opens, and the way out becomes clear.

Like Udo Müller.

"Mr. Müller, you are the perfect fit for business," another psychologist confirmed. "But I'm not sure whether it will make you happy."

It had taken him a long time to understand what the man had meant by that. Maybe it's that one must be content with what one has. To live in the here and now. Not question everything. Not always work towards a goal.

"That is a real challenge for managers and entrepreneurs," Müller thinks. "In the end, we can't get more out of life than other people – namely happiness."

"Of course, as an entrepreneur, you have this intense but quickly vanishing happiness when you have pulled off a good deal, taken over a rival company or have achieved something extraordinary thanks to a smart idea," Müller says. "But it vanishes within seconds. Then comes the next goal. It simply goes on and on."

A Ströer investor once asked him whether he had a dynastic or a capitalist approach.

"Dynastic? Not at all. I don't believe in that," Müller says. "Each person has different capabilities. And the pressure I would put on my children would be extremely high."

He adds: "It would also be unfair for everybody else working at Ströer, who always give more than just their best. They all give one hundred percent."

Capitalist? "What I do is not primarily about money,"

says Müller. Time and again through the years he received offers to sell or take Ströer from the stock market. "It would have made much more money, but that was not my driving force."

Not dynastic, not capitalist. What then?

"Work for me is a passion and is about having fun," says Müller. "It is tremendous fun for me to analyse things, to have ideas and put them into practice, to build something up."

To have a company. Ströer.

Photo credit

© Benjamin Pritzkuleit/Ströer: fig. 16, 17, 18
© Gerhard Blank: fig. 6
© Guido Schiefer: fig. 15
© Martin Joppen: fig. 14
© Ströer: fig. 8
© blowUP media/Jan Willem Steenmeijer: fig. 25
© blowUP media: fig. 20, 21, 22
© picture-alliance/dpa/Jörg Carstensen: fig. 10, 11
© private archive Udo Müller: fig. 1, 2, 3, 4, 5, 7, 9, 12, 13, 23, 24
Screenshot Video turi2tv/: fig. 19

We have tried to find the rights holders. This has not been successful in all cases. We are grateful for information to the publisher.